THE MAKING OF THE MODERN LAW OF DEFAMATION

The modern law of defamation is frequently criticised for being outdated, obscure and even incomprehensible. *The Making of the Modern Law of Defamation* explains how and why the law has come to be as it is by offering an historical analysis of its development from the seventeenth century to the present day. Whilst the primary focus of the book is the law of England, it also makes extensive use of comparative common law materials from jurisdictions such as Australia, South Africa, the United States and Scotland. This book will be essential reading for anyone interested in the law of defamation, in media law and in the relationship between free speech and the law.

The Making of the Modern Law of Defamation

Paul Mitchell
School of Law, King's College London

·HART·
PUBLISHING

OXFORD AND PORTLAND, OREGON
2005

Hart Publishing
Oxford and Portland, Oregon

Published in North America (US and Canada) by
Hart Publishing c/o
International Specialized Book Services
5804 NE Hassalo Street
Portland, Oregon
97213-3644
USA

Hart Publishing is a specialist legal publisher based in Oxford, England.
To order further copies of this book or to request a list of other
publications please write to:

Hart Publishing, Salter's Boatyard, Folly Bridge,
Abingdon Road, Oxford OX1 4LB
Telephone: +44 (0)1865 245533 or Fax: +44 (0)1865 794882
e-mail: mail@hartpub.co.uk
WEBSITE: http//www.hartpub.co.uk

British Library Cataloguing in Publication Data
Data Available
ISBN 1–84113–304–3 (hardback)

Typeset by Hope Services (Abingdon) Ltd.
Printed and bound in Great Britain on by
MPG Books, Bodmin, Cornwall

For Susan, Ben and Amelia

Acknowledgements

I would like to thank the following people for their help at various stages in this project: Eric Barendt, Lionel Bently, Robert Burrell, John Davies, Alan Dignam, Richard Hart, David Ibbetson, Mark Lunney and John Phillips. Their support and encouragement have been much appreciated. I am also grateful to two institutions for their assistance: King's College London (for a grant of sabbatical leave) and the Law Faculty Library, University of Cambridge (for allowing access to Baron Parke's commonplace book).

Paul Mitchell
London
September 2004

Contents

Table of Cases

Table of Legislation

Note that national legislation relates to the United Kingdom unless otherwise stated

Statutory Instruments

Conventions and Instruments

Introduction

This is a study of the emergence of the modern English law of defamation. Only a superficial acquaintance with the modern law is needed to realise that there is a lot of explaining to do. For, unlike negligence with its reasonable man test[1], defamation seems to lack any coherent unifying principles, and to consist of a series of arbitrary, unrelated technical rules. As this book shows, the appearance of chaos is a result of divergent legal development: individual rules developed independently of the general principles that traditionally supported them, and could not then be reintegrated into a coherent structure. It is this historical drift that has made the modern law of defamation what it is today.

Individual chapters of the book trace the historical changes that have given particular facets of defamation their current form. Comparative historical analyses of the law in Australia, New Zealand, Scotland, South Africa and the United States are also included, where they shed particular light on the English developments. There is one deliberate omission: the defence of truth has been the one constant landmark in several hundred years of legal change. It was there right at the start, when the ecclesiastical courts dealt with defamation[2], and today it shows no sign of weakening. It is, therefore, the one aspect of the tort that did not call for historical analysis.

Every other aspect, by stark contrast, has undergone major changes in the years that followed the common law courts' assumption of jurisdiction in the sixteenth century. Seventeenth and eighteenth century developments are examined fully in the chapters that follow, but the focus is often on the nineteenth century, because it was during this period that some of the most crucial, and little analysed, changes occurred. In particular, at the start of the nineteenth century it was possible to perceive an overall coherence in the structure of the tort[3] by dividing its rules into those relating to the claimant's loss, and those relating to the defendant's wrong. The latter were essentially elaborations of the requirement of malice. That same structure has been deliberately borrowed here for two reasons. First, it avoids imposing anachronistic categories on historical materials. Second, it serves to underline that, once upon a time, the now disparate parts of defamation did fit together coherently. A deeper understanding of what has changed, and why, should make it easier to identify what still needs changing if we are to have a coherent law of defamation again today.

[1] *Donoghue v Stevenson* [1932] AC 562.
[2] Helmholz (ed), 'Select Cases on Defamation to 1600' (1985) 101 *Selden Society* at xxx–xxxii.
[3] Starkie, *Law of Slander, Libel, Scandalum Magnatum and False Rumours* (London, 1812).

Part I

The Claimant's Loss

1

Libel and Slander

WHERE A PUBLISHED writing exposes the claimant to hatred, ridicule or contempt (libel) it is actionable without the claimant having to show that he has suffered damage. Spoken words exposing the claimant to hatred, ridicule or contempt (slander) are not actionable automatically: unless the words come within one of four exceptions a claimant has to prove damage to succeed in his claim.

Over fifty years ago Richard Donnelly began a major article on defamation by attacking the basis for the distinction: 'The anomalous and haphazard history of the law of defamation has led to the survival until the present day of two torts—libel and slander—dealing with what is essentially an invasion of the same interest, namely, the interest in reputation and good name'[1]. Another writer described the distinction as 'entirely modern, accidental and insular'[2]. Donnelly's view still holds true today, and the sub-title of his article—'Proposals for Reform'—summarises the modern attitude to the distinction. Today it remains difficult to see why there should be two legal categories—defamation by writing and defamation by speech—when writing and speech merely seem to be two different ways of committing the same wrong.

This chapter investigates both the historical origins of the distinction and the varying ways in which it has been adapted and criticised.

1. THE DISTINCTION

In *Thorley v Lord Kerry*[3] the Court of Common Pleas looked back in search of the origin of the distinction between libel and slander. It did so with reluctance, as Mansfield CJ made clear:

> If the matter were for the first time to be decided at this day, I should have no hesitation in saying, that no action could be maintained for written scandal which could not be maintained for the words had they been spoken.[4]

[1] Donnelly, 'The Law of Defamation: Proposals for Reform' (1949) 33 *Minnesota Law Review* 609.
[2] Fisher, 'A Chapter in the History of the Law of Libel' (1894) 10 *LQR* 158.
[3] (1812) 4 Taunt 355.
[4] *Ibid* at 366.

Despite this misgiving the Court felt unable to ignore the established line of cases dating from the time of Charles II.

Before the 1670s there seems to be no indication that different rules applied to written as compared with spoken words[5]. A person defamed sought his remedy by bringing an action on the case for words. The dominant idea in this action was that damages were given for actual (or 'temporal') loss—indeed, the ability to award monetary damages for loss was the factor that marked off the common law's jurisdiction over defamation from that of the ecclesiastical law. However, a claimant did not always need to demonstrate that he had suffered loss; sometimes the courts felt able to presume loss from the nature of the words[6]. The two major situations where this presumption was made were when a secular crime was imputed and when the words affected the claimant in his trade or profession[7].

In *King v Lake*[8], however, a distinction seemed to be made between spoken and written words. The claimant complained of the following language used by the defendant in a written reply to a petition presented by the claimant:

> The prosecutor is Mr King whose violence both formerly and lately is very notorious, to say nothing before his Majesty's happy restoration, of which might be said too horrid to be related . . . and also said in the consistory court in Lincolnshire with a loud voice, in the presence of many people, that he would strike at the root; whereas this respondent conceives (always referring himself to the judgment of this honourable House) that there is no root under God of ecclesiastical government, but the King himself: . . . and that the petition is stuffed with illegal assertions, ineptitudes, imperfections, clogged with gross ignorances, absurdities and solecisms.

A verdict was found for the claimant and counsel for the defendant argued, in arrest of judgement 'that the words, as recited, were too general to ground an action upon'[9]. Hale CB, whose view the Court shared, rejected the argument: 'although such general words spoken once, without writing or published them, would not be actionable; yet here they being writ and published, which contains more malice, than if they had but once been spoken, they are actionable'[10].

There was nothing either in the claimant's declaration or in the argument (as reported) to suggest that Hale CB was drawing on established

[5] Kaye, 'Libel and Slander—Two Torts or One?' (1975) 91 *LQR* 524 at 526.

[6] Ibbetson, *A Historical Introduction to the Law of Obligations* (Oxford, 1999) at 118–22.

[7] For the origin of this latter category see Helmholz, 'Select Cases on Defamation to 1600' (1985) 101 *Selden Society* at lxxix and Rose, 'Early Occupational Defamation and Disloyal Lawyers: "He is Ambodexter. There Cannot be a Greater Slander"' [2001] *Cambrian Law Review* 53.

[8] (1670) Hardres 470.

[9] *Ibid.*

[10] *Ibid.*

doctrine. However, the brevity of the report makes it difficult to ascertain the analytical basis of this innovative decision. Kaye has argued that the key issue is malice[11]. In his view the reason why the words would not have been actionable if merely spoken once was that speaking once suggested no malice. He continued:

> We take the reasoning behind *King* v *Lake* to be, that although words falling outside the recognised categories would not normally be actionable *per se*, because those categories could not be extended, any publication of them in a malicious form would be actionable because damage to the person defamed might be presumed in such cases.[12]

Kaye's view, however, is not without its difficulties. It is difficult to see why malice should be the key analytical concept here. It was well established that proof of speaking the words raised a presumption of malice against the defendant. Such a presumption could be rebutted[13] but it is incorrect to say that speaking defamatory words once 'suggested no malice'; the opposite was true. Indeed, the reference to writing having 'more malice' suggested that Hale CB regarded spoken words as having some malice already. Furthermore, Kaye's construction of the reasoning behind the decision interprets the phrase 'general words' as meaning words falling outside the recognised categories of words actionable without proof of damage. This seems to be inconsistent with the use of the phrase by Hale CB. He described the words used by the defendant as 'such general words'[14] and they clearly fell within a recognised category by touching the claimant in his profession as a barrister, as the claimant had pointed out in his declaration.

A simpler explanation for *King v Lake*[15] can be found by focussing on the argument to which Hale CB was responding. The rule that words were not actionable if they were too general can be traced back to the early Elizabethan period[16]. For instance, in *Stanhope v Blith*[17] it was held that the words 'M. Stanhope hath but one manor, and that he hath gotten by swearing and forswearing' were not actionable as they were too general. As Coke put it, 'words which shall charge any one with an action, in which damages shall be recovered, ought to have convenient certainty.' This requirement of certainty made sense where a claimant was complaining that a crime had been imputed to him. The reason such an imputation was actionable was that it put the claimant at risk of criminal punishment; if the imputation was vague there was little risk that it would be acted on by

[11] 'Libel and Slander—Two Torts or One?' (1975) 91 *LQR* 524.
[12] *Ibid* at 532.
[13] Eg *Crawford v Middleton* (1662) 1 Lev 82; *Peacock v Reynal* (1612) 2 Brownl & Golds 151.
[14] (1670) Hardres 470.
[15] *Ibid.*
[16] Helmholz, 'Select Cases on Defamation to 1600' (1985) 101 *Selden Society* (1985) at xcix.
[17] (1585) 4 Co Rep 15a.

a prosecutor. The objection of lack of certainty was also available where the words appeared to touch the claimant in his business or profession[18]. However, the courts did not lose sight of the underlying basis of the words being actionable—their tendency to cause loss: the rule against general words was not absolute. Thus, for example, where the defendant called the claimant a 'cozening knave' the court held that the words were actionable, although they would ordinarily be too general, because of their tendency to injure the claimant in his profession as a surveyor[19].

So the argument in *King v Lake* was that the words were too vague and uncertain to cause loss. The response of Hale CB was that this argument was unavailable where the words were written. Such a response was not surprising given the historical context. In the late seventeenth century the courts emphatically discarded many of the limitations that had been placed on slander actions in the Elizabethan period[20]. Chief among these limitations was the doctrine of construing the words in the sense most favourable to the defendant. The rule against general words could be seen as similarly objectionable since it gave the courts the power to deny recovery by invoking an unpredictable rule of construction[21]. Indeed, the rule against general words could even be seen as facet of the wider rule that defamatory words must be construed in the sense most favourable to the defendant[22]. Furthermore the significance of the words being written *and printed*[23] should not be underestimated. At the time a vigorous system of press censorship was in operation under the Licensing Act 1662[24]. Judicial sympathy with press censorship can be seen from the fact that after the expiry of the Licensing Act in 1679 common law judges were quick to recognise the criminal offence of seditious libel[25]. It was even said to be a criminal offence to print 'any newspaper of pamphlet of news whatsoever'[26]. In this context it is hardly surprising that a publisher of printed defamation was denied some of the anachronistic benefits conferred by precedent on a mere speaker.

[18] *Redman v Pyne* (1669) 1 Mod 19.

[19] *Blunden v Eustace* (1618) Cro Jac 504.

[20] Kaye, 'Libel and Slander: Two Torts or One?' (1975) 91 *LQR* 524 at 525. For an examination of some of the limitations see Holdsworth, 'Defamation in the Sixteenth and Seventeenth Centuries' (1924) 40 *LQR* 302, 397, 404–12.

[21] Ibbetson, *A Historical Introduction to the Law of Obligations* (Oxford, 1999) at 124.

[22] Baker and Milsom, *Sources of English Legal History; Private Law to 1750* (London, 1986) at 640 classify the leading case on general words, *Stanhope v Blith* (1585) 4 Co Rep 15a, under the wider rule.

[23] (1670) Hardres 470.

[24] Lovell, 'The "Reception" of Defamation By the Common Law' (1962) 15 *Vanderbilt Law Review* 1051 at 1068.

[25] *R v Harris* (1680) 7 How St Tr 927; Donnelly, 'History of Defamation' [1949] *Wisconsin Law Review* 99 at 120.

[26] *R v Carr* (1680) 7 How St Tr 1114; Donnelly, *ibid.*

The subsequent citation of *King v Lake*[27] in *Austin v Culpeper*[28] confirmed the focus on whether the words were too general or vague to be actionable. In *Austin's case* the defendant had made a picture of a pillory and written beneath it 'For Sir John Austin and his suborned, forsworn witnesses'. After a verdict for the claimant the defendant's counsel moved in arrest of judgment that the allegation was not actionable 'for there is nothing certain forsworn'[29]. In another report he is said to have argued that the words would not have been actionable if spoken[30]. Counsel for the claimant cited *King v Lake* and judgment was given in the claimant's favour. In Shower's report the Court is reported as saying that 'an action lies for scandalizing a man by writing those words, which will not, being spoken, bear an action'[31]. This was an obviously correct application of *King v Lake*. The version of the judgment in Skinner's report is rather different: "twas said, that to say of anybody that he is a dishonest man is not actionable, but to publish so, or put it up upon posts is actionable'[32]. This fell a long way short of being a general statement that all scandalous words were actionable when written. Given its context perhaps the best interpretation is that he objection of want of certainty would not be available even against the most general written allegation of criminality.

The first case to set out clearly the modern distinction between libel and slander was not decided until 1769. In *Villers v Monsley*[33] the court held that it was actionable to write and publish that the claimant had the itch and stank of brimstone. Wilmot LCJ asserted that 'if any man deliberately or maliciously publishes anything in writing concerning another which renders him ridiculous, or tends to hinder mankind from associating or having intercourse with him, an action well lies against such publisher'[34]. Bathurst J agreed, and added:

> I wish there were some more solemn determination, that the writing and publishing anything which tends to make a man ridiculous or infamous ought to be punished; for saying a man has the itch, without more, perhaps an action would not lie without other malevolent circumstances.[35]

Gould J also agreed. He emphasised the distinction between writing and words: 'a libel is punishable both criminally and by action, when speaking the words would not be actionable in either way'[36].

27 (1670) Hardres 470.
28 (1683) 2 Show 313; Skinner 123.
29 Skinner 124.
30 2 Show 313.
31 2 Show 314.
32 Skinner 124.
33 (1769) 2 Wils KB 403.
34 *Ibid.*
35 *Ibid* at 404.
36 *Ibid.*

The reference to punishment by both Bathurst and Gould JJ suggested that both had drawn inspiration from the law of criminal libel. The emphasis on the claimant being made 'ridiculous' also seemed to have been borrowed from criminal libel[37]. None of the judges mentioned any civil action where the distinction between libel and slander had been previously laid down.

There was little to suggest that the courts enthusiastically adopted the distinction propounded in *Villers'* case[38]. Following a passing reference to the point in one report of *Harman v Delany*[39] and a brief remark in *Bell v Stone*[40] the question was still regarded as unsettled in 1809, when Campbell reported that the Court of Common Pleas was waiting for the decision in *Kaye v Bailey*, a case 'depending in the Exchequer Chamber'[41], which would resolve matters. That case seems never to have been decided—at least there is no report of it—but it must have focussed attention on the fact that the question was still regarded as open. It may even have prompted Starkie's contribution to the debate[42], in which he argued that the weight of authority—including, but not limited to, *King v Lake*—required the different treatment of written defamation to be recognised, even though it could not be supported as a matter of principle.

Finally, in 1812, the Court of Common Pleas decided *Thorley v Lord Kerry*[43] and embedded the distinction firmly into English law. The defendant had written a letter to the claimant accusing him of hypocrisy. The letter was opened and read by the servant instructed to carry it. Hypocrisy was not within the categories of words actionable in themselves and the claimant did not allege special damage, so the outcome turned on whether the wide approach to written defamation set out in *Villers v Monsley* was correct. The Court reluctantly held that it was correct. In an analysis that closely followed Starkie's treatise (published earlier that year)[44], Mansfield CJ rejected all principled bases for the distinction. Writing might show greater malice, but the basis of the action was damage. Writing might be more widely diffused, but then again it might not be. However, there was an established line of cases setting out the distinction 'as far back as Charles the Second's time'[45] and the Court was not pre-

[37] Kaye, above n 20 at 530.

[38] (1769) 2 Wils KB 403.

[39] (1731) Fitz-Gibbon 121, 253, 254. The other report of the case (2 Str 898) does not assert the distinction (see Kaye, above n 5 at 536).

[40] (1798) 1 Bos & Pul 331.

[41] (1809) 2 Camp 251 at 255 (note to *Earl of Leicester v Walter*).

[42] Starkie, *Law of Slander, Libel Scandalum Magnatum and False Rumours* (London, 1812) at 126–44.

[43] (1812) 4 Taunt 355.

[44] Starkie, *Law of Slander, Libel Scandalum Magnatum and False Rumours* (London, 1812) at 126.

[45] (1812) 4 Taunt 355 at 364.

pared to go against them. The judgment was a demonstration of the power of legal history to shape the course of the law. Perhaps if the Court had been aware that the line of cases did not extend to Charles II's reign, and that it really consisted of one firm decision and a couple of passing references, it might have felt free to take a more critical, principled line.

2. RESPONSES AND VARIATIONS

The immediate response to the decision in *Thorley v Lord Kerry*[46] was to accept its result if not its reasoning. In *Clement v Chivis*[47] for example, the Court referred to the different treatment of written and oral defamation and explained that written defamation was premeditated and more permanent than the spoken variety. The judgment in *Thorley's case* had rejected both reasons. The situation in the United States was similar. Before the judgment in *Thorley's case* was reported the Supreme Court of Pennsylvania had acknowledged that the distinction between written and oral defamation was 'clearly settled'[48] and justified by the permanency of writing. Once a report of *Thorley's case* was available it was cited and followed. The Supreme Court of Vermont was unusual in both accepting the decision and echoing the regret expressed in *Thorley* that it had to be made at all[49]. More often states adopted the distinction and supported it with the traditional arguments of permanency and widespread diffusion[50]. The Supreme Court of New York took a radical approach. In *Cooper v Greeley*[51], where the defamation had appeared in a newspaper, counsel for the defendant invited the Court to reject the distinction, arguing that it 'deserves less countenance when we find that it was commenced in the Court of Star Chamber during the arbitrary reign of Elizabeth'. The Court's rejection of the argument was emphatic but, unlike in *Thorley*, it was not based on reluctance to go against a venerable line of case law. In the Court's view a distinction between spoken and written words was essential 'in more modern times, when the tendency of the public press is so strong to licentiousness'. 'Public policy' demanded that the distinction be made.

The grudging acceptance of special rules for libel in *Thorley's case* was transformed during the course of the nineteenth century into a widespread

[46] (1812) 4 Taunt 355.

[47] (1829) 9 B & C 172.

[48] *M'Corkle v Binns* (1812) 5 Binn 340.

[49] *Colby v Reynolds* (1834) 6 Vt 489.

[50] Eg *Stow v Converse* 3 Conn 325 (Supreme Court of Errors of Connecticut, 1820); *White v Nicholls* 44 US 266 (Supreme Court of the United States, 1845); *Iron Age Publishing Co v Crudup* 5 So 332 (Supreme Court of Alabama, 1889).

[51] (1845) 1 Denio 347.

enthusiasm. Slander came to be seen as the oddity explicable only by historical factors. One catalyst for this change of view was the report of a Select Committee of the House of Lords chaired by Lord Campbell[52]. The report asserted that the distinction between libel and slander did not have any solid foundation and recommended that 'wherever an injury is done to character by defamation there ought to be redress by action'[53]. In essence, slander was to be assimilated to libel. The Committee was concerned, however, that there might be frivolous actions. To discourage such actions the report recommended that, except where an indictable offence was imputed, the jury should consider whether the words spoken were likely to have injured the claimant's reputation; if the jury concluded that injury was unlikely, they should find for the defendant.

The Committee's proposal was not implemented in England. Ironically, the last case that Lord Campbell heard[54] was one in which he had to deny the claimant a right of action which, had the report's proposal been adopted, she would have received. Abroad, however, the proposal of Lord Campbell's committee faired better: it was enacted in 1847 in New South Wales[55]. The report's proposal also continued to receive powerful academic support, both in England[56] and the United States[57].

Academic commentators favouring the assimilation of slander to libel invoked the position in other countries to support their claim. One of the earliest commentators[58] pointed to the position in Scotland, where all defamatory words (whether spoken or written) gave rise to an action[59]. American commentators could also point to Louisiana[60], where an attempt to introduce the English taxonomy of actionable defamatory words had been emphatically rejected[61]. In Sri Lanka, another jurisdiction that made selective use of English law, the courts consistently held that all defamatory publications were actionable without proof of special damage[62].

52 The report is set out in full at 1 *Law Times* 341.

53 *Ibid.*

54 *Lynch v Knight* (1861) 9 HLC 577.

55 See Barry, 'Radio, Television and the Law of Defamation' (1949) 23 *Australian Law Journal* 203 at 206.

56 Eg Holdsworth, 'Defamation in the Sixteenth and Seventeenth Centuries' (1924) 40 *LQR* 302, 397 (1925) 41 *LQR* 13 at 19.

57 Veeder, 'The History and Theory of the Law of Defamation' (1903) 3 *Columbia Law Review* 546 (1904) 4 *Columbia Law Review* 33 at 55–56.

58 Anon, 'The Law of Libel—V' (1867) 11 *Solicitors' Journal and Reporter* 1052.

59 *Brownlie v Thomson* (1859) 21 D 480; Normand, 'The Law of Defamation in Scotland' [1938] 6 *CLJ* 327 at 332.

60 Veeder, 'The History and Theory of the Law of Defamation' [1904] 4 *Columbia Law Review* 33 at 54; Donnelly, 'The Law of Defamation: Proposals for Reform' (1949) *Minnesota Law Review* 609 at 611.

61 *Miller v Holstein* 16 La 389 (Supreme Court of Louisiana, 1840).

62 *Appuhami v Kirihami* (1895) 1 NLR 83 at 85; *Wickremanayake v The Times of Ceylon, Limited* (1937) 39 NLR 547 at 550; Athulathmudali, 'The Law of Defamation in Ceylon—A Study in the Inter-Action of English and Roman-Dutch Law' (1964) 13 *International and Comparative Law Quarterly* 1368 at 1380.

The proposal of the Select Committee and the enthusiastic response to it in some quarters showed that there was a case for expanding the scope of liability. The traditional categories of slander actionable *per se* had developed because the courts were prepared to assume that words in those categories would cause temporal loss. The basis of the law of libel was very different: words were actionable if they tended to expose the claimant to hatred, ridicule or contempt. The push to assimilate libel to slander showed the attractiveness, to some, of a tort protecting the claimant's reputation rather than his finances.

Whilst powerful ideological reasons underpinned the proposal to assimilate slander to libel, aesthetic reasons—'the importance of system and symmetry'[63]—justified assimilation either way. In Virginia the assimilation was of libel to slander, a change not without academic support[64]. Although the first Virginian case on the point may have accomplished assimilation by accident[65], a line of later cases has emphatically asserted that assimilation has taken place[66]. In one of the more recent decisions the Supreme Court of Virginia refused counsel's invitation to overrule the earlier cases, saying that there was 'no logical reason'[67] to do so. It is hard to disagree. As a matter of logic applying the same rules to all cases of defamation, whether written or spoken, cannot be challenged.

Assimilation was the most radical response to the distinction between libel and slander. There were also more subtle responses, such as the compromise advanced in the Empire Press Union Bill of 1938[68]. The Bill proposed that defamatory words should not be actionable without proof of financial loss unless they imputed sexual immorality, drunkenness, cruelty, a criminal offence punishable by imprisonment, an 'obnoxious contagious disease' or related to the claimant's office, trade or profession. This was a more sophisticated proposal than a straightforward assimilation of libel to slander[69] because it added as actionable words those imputing immorality to men (the Slander of Women Act 1891 only applied to women), drunkenness and cruelty. The Bill was withdrawn on the Government's promise to set up a Committee to report on the reform of the

63 Anon, 'The Law of Libel—V' (1867) 11 *Solicitors' Journal and Reporter* 1052 at 1053.

64 Courtney, 'Absurdities of the Law of Libel and Slander' 36 *American Law Review* 552 (1902).

65 *M Rosenberg & Sons Inc v Craft* 29 SE 2d 375 (Supreme Court of Appeals of Virginia, 1954); GMM, 'Defamation in Virginia—A Merger of Libel and Slander' (1961) 47 *Virginia Law Review* 1116 at 1125.

66 *Carwile v Richmond Newspapers, Inc* 82 SE 2d 588 (Supreme Court of Appeals of Virginia, 1954); *O'Neil v Edmonds* (United States District Court ED Virginia, Norfolk Division, 1958); *Weaver v Beneficial Finance Company, Inc* 106 SE 2d 620 (Supreme Court of Appeals of Virginia, 1959); *Shupe v Rose's Stores, Inc* 192 SE 2d 766 (Supreme Court of Virginia, 1972); *Fleming v Moore* 275 SE 2d 632 (Supreme Court of Virginia, 1981).

67 *Shupe v Rose's Stores Inc* 192 SE 2d 766 (Supreme Court of Virginia, 1972) at 767.

68 For the full text of the Bill and a commentary see O'Sullivan, 'The Bill to Amend the Law of Libel' (1938) 85 *LJ* 440.

69 Cf O'Sullivan, *ibid* at 441.

law of defamation[70]. The Committee, however, made no proposal for either assimilation[71], or for one set of rules to cover all defamatory utterances.

Perhaps the most complex variation on the distinction between libel and slander was the American sub-division of libel into libel *per se* and libel *per quod*. Libel *per se* denoted that the defamatory meaning was clear on the face of the language used; in such a case the claimant did not need to prove that he had suffered damage. A libel *per quod* was one where the defamatory meaning was 'covert—not apparent on the face of the language used'[72]; here a claimant had to aver and prove damage. The division appeared to be simple enough, but the divergent applications of it in different state courts made it a doctrine of unpredictable complexity.

The requirement that the language be clearly defamatory on its face gave courts a wide discretion. Two contrasting extreme examples may be taken. In *Tennessee Coal, Iron & Railroad Co v Kelly*[73] the Supreme Court of Alabama held that a letter demanding the claimant's dismissal on the ground that he 'had run some of the [defendant's] non-union laborers out of their houses' was not a libel *per se*. In the Court's view there was not 'necessarily'[74] a defamatory meaning: the claimant's acts might have been justified, or done as a joke. By contrast in *Sauerhoff v Hearst Corporation (Baltimore News American Division)*[75] the United States Court of Appeals held that it was a libel *per se* where a newspaper report had described the claimant's dispute with his 'girlfriend' over a winning lottery ticket they had bought whilst working in the same office. The Court held that: 'Not a moment's reflection is needed; the message comes through immediately . . . it all ties in to suggest a covert office "extra-marital affair"'[76].

Similar unpredictability surrounded the courts' approach to cases where the defamatory meaning was clear but the reference to the claimant was not. The Supreme Court of Montana held that to be a libel *per se* the language 'must on its face show that the derogatory statements, taken as a whole, refer to the plaintiff, and not to him or some other person'[77]. The Court of Appeals of Kentucky, on the other hand, held that a libel *per quod* was one that required an innuendo (an allegation of some extrinsic fact) to make clear its defamatory meaning. Who the words referred to was a matter dealt with in the *colloquium* (the introductory part of the statement of claim). A publication not making clear reference to the claimant was, therefore, held to be a libel *per se* as it did not require an innuendo[78].

[70] Todd, 'The Defamation Act, 1952' (1953) 16 *MLR* 198.
[71] See *Report of the Committee on the Law of Defamation*, Cmd 7536 (London, 1948) at para 60.
[72] *Tonini v Cevasco* 46 P 103 at 104 (Supreme Court of California, 1896).
[73] 50 So 1008 (Supreme Court of Alabama, 1909).
[74] *Ibid* at 1011.
[75] 538 F 2d 588 (United States Court of Appeals, 4th Circuit, 1976).
[76] *Ibid at* 591.
[77] *Rowan v Gazette Printing Co* 239 P 1035 at 1037 (Supreme Court of Montana, 1925).
[78] *EW Scripps Company v Cholmondelay* 569 SW 2d 700 (Court of Appeals of Kentucky, 1978).

A more difficult theoretical question was what happened if the libel imputed an indictable criminal offence, or touched the claimant in his profession or business. Such imputations, if spoken, were actionable without proof of special damage whether or not the language was defamatory on its face. If the libel *per se* rules applied, oblique imputations of criminality or professional unfitness would be actionable if spoken, but not if written. The earlier cases were equivocal. Some authorities suggested that the libel *per se* requirements did not apply to imputations affecting a person in his trade[79]. A similar inference in respect of criminal imputations could be drawn from *Tennessee Coal, Iron & Railroad Co v Kelly*[80], where the Court ruled that the words did not impute a criminal offence before going on to apply the libel *per se* criteria. On the other hand, the Supreme Court of North Dakota applied the libel *per se* test to allegedly defamatory matter concerning a lawyer printed in a law directory[81]. Some measure of certainty may have been introduced by the later consideration of the point in *Gibson v Kincaid*[82], where it was held that imputations of crime, loathsome disease, unfitness in trade or unchastity whether *per se* or *per quod*, without proof of damage.

Not all states adopted the distinction[83]. Kansas, for instance, appeared to adopt it, but then failed to require claimants in libel *per quod* cases to prove special damage[84]. New York flirted. In *O'Connell v Press Publishing Company*[85] the Court of Appeals held that it was not a libel *per se* to state that the claimant had invented a device that others had put to criminal use. This was an orthodox application of the libel *per se* criteria. Eleven years later, in *Sydney v MacFadden Newspaper Pub Corporation*[86] the same court appeared to repudiate the distinction. There the words complained of were that the actress Doris Keane was Fatty Arbuckle's 'latest ladylove'. Doris Keane was in fact married; she sued in her married name of Sydney. The Court held that the words were actionable in the absence of special damage, and said that the courts should interpret the defamatory publication in the same way that the public 'acquainted with the parties and the subject would take it'[87]. This approach to interpretation allowed the Court

[79] *Fry v McCord* 33 SW 568 (Supreme Court of Tennessee, 1895); *NS Sherman Mach Co v Dun* (Supreme Court of Oklahoma, 1911).

[80] 50 So 1008 (Supreme Court of Alabama, 1909).

[81] *Ellsworth v Martindale-Hubbard Law Directory Inc* 268 NW 400 (Supreme Court of North Dakota, 1936).

[82] 221 NE 2d 834 (Appellate Court of Indiana, Division No 1, 1966).

[83] Precisely how many did became a point of bitter contention between Prosser and Eldredge. See Prosser, 'Libel Per Quod' 46 (1960) *Virginia Law Review* 839; Eldredge, 'The Spurious Rule of Libel Per Quod' (1966) 79 *Harvard Law Review* 733; Prosser, 'More Libel Per Quod' (1966) 79 *Harvard Law Review* 1629.

[84] *Jerald v Huston* 242 P 472 (Supreme Court of Kansas, 1926).

[85] 108 NE 556 (Court of Appeals of New York, 1915).

[86] 151 NE 209 (Court of Appeals of New York, 1926).

[87] *Ibid* at 211.

to consider extrinsic facts. Ten years later the Supreme Court in *Kuhn v Veloz*[88] applied *Sydney's case* where the words were defamatory only by reason of extrinsic facts; the decision was reversed by the Appellate Division[89], citing *O'Connell's case*. The matter seemed to be settled by *Remington v Bentley*[90], which applied the orthodox criteria. But there was a final twist: it applied them to slander as well as to libel[91]! New York had occupied every possible position on the issue.

The uncertainty surrounding the division into libel *per se* and libel *per quod* and the lack of a clear doctrinal basis provoked academic criticism. Carpenter, whose hostility bordered on hysteria, called the division 'a new creature . . . that . . . is ugly and illegitimate and ought promptly to be strangled'[92]. Eldredge[93], whilst more moderate in tone, was vehemently opposed to Prosser's proposal[94] to incorporate the division into the *Restatement*. Perhaps the most elegant academic explanation of the doctrine was that of Wade who, in a statement at a meeting of the American Law Institute, suggested that the real concern of the courts was with fault. There was no overt recognition of this in the cases, as Eldredge pointed out[95], but the division was clearly concerned to target the more deliberate and blatant examples of defamation. English judges had accepted that written defamation tended to be more malevolent than spoken words; American judges seemed to be saying that blatantly defamatory writings tended to be more malevolent than covert ones. Neither assumption was necessarily true all of the time, but enough judges seem to have thought that these assumptions were true enough of the time to merit making them into legal rules.

3. SLANDER

The growing acceptance of the rules governing libel during the first half of the nineteenth century was paralleled by a decline in the scope and importance of slander. Imputations of having committed an indictable offence continued to be actionable without proof of special damage, and even experienced a slight expansion. In *Fowler v Dowdney*[96] it was held to be

[88] 296 NYS 39 (Supreme Court, New York County, New York, 1937).

[89] 299 NYS 924 (Supreme Court, Appellate Division, 1st Department, New York, 1937).

[90] 88 F Supp 166 (United States District Court, SD New York, 1949).

[91] See also *Korry v International Telephone & Telegraph Corporation* 444 F Supp 193 (United States District Court, SD New York, 1978).

[92] Carpenter, 'Libel *Per Se* in California and Some Other States' (1943–44) 17 *Southern California Law Review* 347.

[93] 'The Spurious Rule of Libel Per Quod' (1966) 79 *Harvard Law Review* 733.

[94] Prosser, 'Libel Per Quod' (1960) 46 *Virginia Law Review* 839.

[95] 'Variation on Libel per Quod' (1972) 25 *Vanderbilt University Law Review* 79.

[96] (1838) 2 M & Rob 119.

actionable to say that the claimant was a 'returned convict'. Counsel for the defendant had pointed out that there was no risk of damage as the sentence had been served, but the Court held that 'the obloquy remains'[97]. Judged by the traditional criteria the decision in *Fowler's case* seemed to be mistaken: what had made words actionable was their tendency to cause damage and these words had no such tendency. However, as we have seen, there was at the time a powerful sense, derived from the law of libel, that what made words actionable was their tendency to expose the claimant to hatred, ridicule or contempt. It was this sense that had inspired Lord Campbell's Select Committee to recommend assimilating slander to libel. Judged by this new criterion the decision in *Fowler* was correct. The same approach could be seen over a century later, when it was held that a company could sue for the imputation of an indictable offence: clearly the company could not be imprisoned, but its reputation would be harmed[98]. In the United States the category of words imputing a criminal offence maintained a similar stability despite some initial uncertainty over its scope[99].

The second category, words imputing an obnoxious disease such as leprosy or syphilis[100], also remained stable[101], although it was of marginal importance. It was in the third category—where words touched the claimant in his trade, business or profession—that the decline in the scope and importance of slander took place.

In the seventeenth century it was clear that the courts took a broad approach. The fundamental question was whether the words had a tendency to cause loss[102], and the courts seem to have been very receptive to the idea that words not otherwise tending to cause loss might do so if they affected the claimant's livelihood. Thus, for instance, in *Cawdry v Highley*[103] it was held actionable to say of a physician that he was 'never a scholar . . . and not worthy to speak to a scholar'. Similarly, in *Dod v Robinson*[104] the defendant had said that the claimant, a clergyman, was 'a drunkard, a whoremaster, a common swearer, and a common lyar, and hath preached false doctrine, and deserves to be degraded'. After a verdict for the claimant the defendant argued in arrest of judgment that the words were not actionable 'because the crimes charged impute no civil

[97] *Ibid* at 120.

[98] *D and L Caterers Limited v D'Ajou* [1945] KB 210.

[99] *Brooker v Coffin* 5 Johns 188 (Supreme Court of New York, 1809); *Miller v Parish* 25 Mass 384 (Supreme Judicial Court of Massachusetts, 1829); *Widrig v Oyer* 13 Johns 124 (Supreme Court of New York, 1816).

[100] For suggestions as to why these two diseases were associated see Green, 'Slander and Libel' (1872) 6 *American Law Review* 593 at 606; Helmholz, 'Select Cases on Defamation to 1600' (1985) 101 *Selden Society* xcvi—xcvii; Ibbetson, *A Historical Introduction to the Law of Obligations* (Oxford, 1999) at 120–21.

[101] *Bloodwork v Gray* (1844) 7 M & G 334.

[102] Ibbetson, *A Historical Introduction to the Law of Obligations* (Oxford, 1999) at 120.

[103] (1633) Cro Car 270.

[104] (1647) Aleyn 63.

or temporal damage'[105]. The court disagreed, saying that the matters charged would justify degrading the claimant, 'whereby he should lose his freehold [as a clergyman], which is temporal damage to him[106]'. The only limitation seems to have been that some trades were seen as lacking status, and the courts therefore refused to presume damage to their members[107].

The identical approach continued into the eighteenth century. In *Stanton v Smith*[108], for example, the defendant had said that the claimant, a brewer, was 'a sorry pitiful fellow, and a rogue, he compounded his debts at five shillings in the pound'. The court held that the words were actionable because they 'must greatly lessen the credit of a tradesman, and be very prejudicial to him'[109]. In *Onslow v Horne*[110] the fundamental basis of the courts' approach was made explicit—'There must be some certain or probable temporal loss, or damage, to make the words actionable'[111]. The court also set out a 'general rule':

> . . . words are actionable when spoken of one in an office of profit, which may probably occasion the loss of his office, or when spoken of persons touching their respective professions, trades and business, and do or may probably tend to their damage.[112]

This general rule was clarified in *Lumby v Allday*[113]. The claimant was a clerk, employed by the Birmingham and Staffordshire Gas Light Company, of whom it had been said, 'You are unfit to hold your situation . . . for your conduct with whores'. At the trial Alexander LCB appeared to draw on the 'general rule' from *Onslow v Horne* when he directed the jury that they should find for the claimant 'if they thought that the words might probably have occasioned the loss of the plaintiff's situation'[114]. The jury found for the claimant. Bayley B, delivering the judgment of the Exchequer of Pleas, held that the direction was incorrect and criticised the general rule in *Onslow v Horne* on two grounds. First, the word 'probably' was 'too indefinite and loose'[115]; a better expression would be 'having a natural tendency to'. This might at first glance appear to be a cosmetic change, but it was a subtle change of substance. 'Probable' consequences might include foreseeable but unreasonable acts by a third party—such as the dismissal of the claimant from his employment. 'Natural tendency'

105 *Ibid.*
106 *Ibid.*
107 *Bell v Thatcher* (1675) Vent 275.
108 (1726) 2 Ld Raym 1480.
109 *Ibid.*
110 (1771) 3 Wils KB 177.
111 *Ibid* at 187.
112 *Ibid* at 186.
113 (1831) 1 C & J 301.
114 *Ibid* at 302.
115 *Ibid* at 305.

excluded such unreasonable acts[116]. Second, Bayley B held that the rule in *Onslow v Horne* went further than the authorities permitted. He asserted that:

> Every authority which I have been able to find, either shews the want of some general requisite, as honesty, capacity, fidelity, &c, or connects the imputation with the plaintiff's office, trade or business.[117]

Again the concern seemed to be to make it clear that the risk of an unreasonable reaction to the words by third parties was not enough to make words actionable. Applying these criteria to the facts of the case, he concluded that there was no allegation of a lack of those qualities that a clerk ought to have, nor was there any reference to the claimant's conduct as a clerk. Therefore the words were not actionable.

So, in 1831 a stable position had been established for slander affecting the claimant's business. Words imputing either the lack of some general requisite, or some kind of professional misconduct were actionable because their natural tendency was to cause a loss of employment. Unlike in libel, the emphasis was on losing work, not losing reputation, with the result that an actionable allegation of professional incapacity need not expose the claimant to ridicule. In *Miller v David*[118] the Court of Appeal attempted to bring imputations affecting employment into line with the general requirement of hatred, ridicule or contempt, but five years later an imputation of inexperience against an architect was held actionable[119]. When the Court of Appeal later widened the test for defamatory words in order to include language that would tend to make reasonable people 'shun and avoid' the claimant[120], it effectively overruled its own earlier decision in *Miller's* case. Now situations where an accusation might affect the claimant's employment could be seen in terms of inducing customers or employers to 'shun and avoid' the claimant. Thus, it was actionable to say that a boxer was drawing his old-age pension[121], that a beautician looked like an old boot[122], and that an actor looked like Frankenstein's monster[123].

In 1834, however, the rule that an imputation of a lack of general requisite was actionable seemed to be discarded: *Ayre v Craven*[124] has been seen as a turning point, introducing the restriction that, to be actionable in

[116] See *Vicars v Wilcocks* (1806) 8 East 1, where the 'legal and natural consequence' test was applied so as to exclude the unreasonable dismissal by the claimant's employer.

[117] *Ibid* at 305–6.

[118] (1874) LR 9 CP 118.

[119] *Botterill v Whytehead* (1879) 41 LTNS 588.

[120] *Youssoupoff v Metro-Goldwyn-Mayer Pictures, Limited* (1934) 50 TLR 581.

[121] *Bergman v Macadam, The Times*, 9 October 1940.

[122] *Winyard v Tatler Publishing Co Ltd, The Independent*, 16 August 1991.

[123] *Berkoff v Burchill* [1996] 4 All ER 1008.

[124] (1834) 2 Ad & E 2.

themselves, words must impute professional misconduct[125]. The claimant was a physician who, it was said, had been one of the parties 'in a crim con affair'[126]; the words were held not actionable. Lord Denman CJ began his judgment by alluding to the 'obvious and very good reasons for the jealousy with which the Courts have always regarded actions of slander'[127]. As illustrations of this jealousy he referred to two cases which had:

> proceeded to a length which can hardly fail to excite surprise; a clergyman having failed to obtain redress for the imputation of adultery; and a school mistress having been declared incompetent to maintain an action for a charge of prostitution. Such words were undeniably calculated to injure the success of the plaintiffs in their several professions; but not being applicable to their conduct therein, no action lay.[128]

A requirement that the words imputed misconduct in one's profession seemed to exclude those allegations that imputed the lack of a general requisite. However, Lord Denman CJ went on to approve the principle set out in *Lumby v Allday*, which allowed words imputing a 'want of general requisite'[129] to be actionable. He then proceeded to consider the facts of the case. He saw the crucial point as being the form of the declaration. It simply alleged that the words were spoken of the claimant 'as a physician'. As Lord Denman CJ admitted, the words might have been understood to mean that the claimant had abused his position as a physician in order to carry on the affair. However, 'in actions of this nature, the declaration ought not merely to state that such scandalous conduct was imputed to the plaintiff in his profession, but also to set forth in what manner it was connected by the speaker with that profession'[130].

The main point of the case, therefore, related to pleading: where the connection between the words and the claimant's profession was unclear the claimant had to allege in his declaration exactly what connection the speaker had made. It was more difficult to identify the effect on substantive law. The initial reference to cases limiting actionable words to imputations of professional misconduct seemed to contradict the unqualified approval of *Lumby v Allday* in the next paragraph. Furthermore, on closer inspection the two cases cited in support of the proposition that an allegation of professional misconduct was required did not in fact support it. In *Parrat v Carpenter*[131] a clergyman was denied an action for an imputation of adultery on the ground that such slander was only actionable in the Spiritual Court. In *Wharton v Brook*[132], where an imputation of ignorance

[125] See *Jones v Jones* [1916] 2 AC 481 at 505 (per Lord Parmoor).
[126] Criminal conversation, ie, adultery.
[127] (1834) 2 Ad & E 2 at 7.
[128] *Ibid* at 7–8.
[129] (1831) 1 C & J 301 at 305–6.
[130] (1834) 2 Ad & E 2 at 8–9.
[131] (1597) Cro Eliz 502.
[132] (1675) 1 Ventris 21.

against a midwife was held actionable, Twisden J, dissenting, referred to a case where a school mistress was called a whore and the action failed because 'to slander one in such a profession was not maintainable without special damage'[133]. The objection to the action was not the failure to allege professional misconduct; it was the perceived low status of the claimant's profession[134]. It is also difficult to maintain that, given the facts and the result, the Court must be taken to have rejected the proposition that an imputation of lack of general requisite was actionable. An examination of the submissions of counsel for the claimant reveals that no attempt was made to argue that moral respectability was an essential quality in a physician. The decision was later criticised for its failure to recognise the need for a physician to be morally respectable[135], but it seems harsh to upbraid a court for failing to deal with a point that, in hindsight, could have been put to it.

Although a close reading of *Ayre v Craven*[136] showed that its remarks on substantive law were equivocal and unconvincing, it served as a catalyst in narrowing the range of imputations actionable in themselves. For instance, in *Wilby v Elston*[137] counsel for the claimant conceded that, after the approving reference to *Wharton v Brook*[138] in *Ayre v Craven*, it was unarguable that a charge of prostitution against a school mistress was actionable. The courts went on to apply the perceived rule from *Ayre's case* to other professions. In *Doyley v Roberts*[139], for instance, the defendant had said that the claimant, an attorney, had defrauded his creditors. The jury found that although the words did not refer to the claimant in his business as an attorney, they had 'a tendency to injure him morally and professionally'[140]. The Court held that no action lay, because the words were not spoken of the claimant 'in his character of attorney'[141]. Tindal CJ observed that 'the authority of *Ayre v Craven* is conclusive'[142]. *Pemberton v Colls*[143], where the rule was applied to the clergy, demonstrated the new narrow limits of actionable words. There were two separate utterances. In the first the defendant accused the claimant of having tricked him into signing a bill for 2500l for a reading in church; in the second the defendant said that he had signed the bill for 2500l because he was 'completely pigeoned'[144] by the claimant. The Court held that only the words in the first count were

133 *Ibid.*
134 See similarly *Bell v Thatcher* (1675) 1 Ventris 275.
135 Eg *Gallwey v Marshall* (1853) 9 Ex 294 at 297 (per Alderson B).
136 (1834) 2 Ad & E 2.
137 (1849) 8 CB 142.
138 (1675) 1 Ventris 21.
139 (1837) 3 Bing NC 835.
140 *Ibid* at 836.
141 *Ibid* at 840 (per Vaughan J).
142 *Ibid.*
143 (1847) 10 QB 461.
144 'Make a dupe of; trick; swindle' (*New Shorter Oxford English Dictionary*).

actionable as reflecting on the claimant in his professional character. The same rule was also applied to the minister of a dissenting sect[145].

However, the courts did not apply *Ayre v Craven*[146] across the board. Where, in *Jones v Littler*[147], a brewer was accused of insolvency it was held that, even assuming that the words only referred to him in his private capacity, an action lay. The Court cited *Stanton v Smith*[148] and explained that any imputation of insolvency must be injurious to a tradesman because his credit depended 'upon his general solvency'[149]. Similarly, it was assumed in *Rumsey v Webb*[150] that an allegation of unchastity against a maidservant was actionable, although there was no connection between the unchastity alleged and the maidservant's duties. There was even a retreat from the position taken in *Pemberton v Colls*[151] relating to clergymen. In *Gallwey v Marshall*[152] it was held that an allegation of an affair with a married woman made against a clergyman would have been actionable if the claimant had alleged that he was beneficed (ie held a post). The Court drew support from *Dod v Robinson*[153] in concluding that the words would endanger the claimant in his office. A further layer of refinement was added when the courts endorsed the distinction between offices of profit and offices of honour; allegations relating to the latter were not actionable if they only imputed want of ability[154].

When the appellate courts came to consider the whole matter in *Jones v Jones*[155] they were, therefore, faced with a picture of some complexity. The claimant was the headmaster of a council school; the defendant had said that the claimant had committed adultery, but had made no reference to the claimant's profession. The claimant relied on the cases about tradesmen such as *Jones v Littler*[156], arguing that imputing a lack of solvency to a trader was like imputing a lack of morals to a teacher. The Court of Appeal, however, rejected the argument, stating that it was bound by the cases. It made clear that it found against the claimant with reluctance:

> the law of slander is an artificial law, resting on very artificial distinctions and refinements, and all that the Court can do is to apply the law to those cases in which heretofore it has been held applicable.[157]

145 *Hopwood v Thorn* (1849) 8 CB 293.
146 (1834) 2 Ad & E 2.
147 (1841) 7 M & W 423.
148 (1726) 2 Ld Raym 1480. See above n 108.
149 (1841) 7 M & W 423 at 426.
150 (1842) 11 LJ (CP) 129.
151 (1847) 10 QB 461.
152 (1853) 9 Ex 294.
153 (1647) Aleyn 63. See above n 104.
154 *How v Prinn* 2 (1702) Salk 695; *Alexander v Jenkins* [1892] 1 QB 797; *Wood v Barney, The Times*, 5 May 1913.
155 [1916] 1 KB 351; [1916] 2 AC 481.
156 (1841) 7 M & W 423.
157 [1916] 1 KB 351 at 358.

The general rule, it explained, was as set out in *Ayre v Craven* and required the imputation to 'relate to his conduct in the office, profession or business, or [be] connected with his professional duties'[158]. The cases on tradesmen were 'exceptional', the law having 'always been very tender of the reputation of tradesmen'[159].

The House of Lords similarly felt that its hands were tied by the authorities, and that the trader cases were exceptions. It also adjusted the general principle set out in *Lumby v Allday*: Viscount Haldane thought that Bayley B could only have been referring to the trader cases when he said that a lack of general requisite was actionable[160]; Lord Sumner interpreted the principle as requiring a reference to the claimant's trade even where the allegation was of a lack of general requisite[161]. The unqualified approval of this principle in *Ayre v Craven*[162], however, was not mentioned. Overall their Lordships' position was that the general rule set out in *Ayre v Craven* could only be altered by legislation. As with the distinction between libel and slander, the conclusive judicial recognition of a fundamental point came from a court that felt that it had no choice in the matter.

Legislative intervention came eventually. But before it arrived a later Court of Appeal demonstrated how, with a little ingenuity, the principle in *Ayre v Craven* could be circumvented. The claimant in *De Stempel v Dunkels*[163] was a diamond broker of whom it was said: 'Victor is a Jew-hater'. Most of the customers of the firm that employed the claimant were Jewish. The Court unanimously held that these words were actionable as touching the claimant in his profession. Greer LJ emphasised that the words were spoken to the claimant's employer in an attempt to get him dismissed—they must therefore have related to his profession. In his view *Ayre v Craven* would have been decided differently if the words had been spoken to the President of the Medical Association in an attempt to have the claimant removed from its lists[164]. Slesser LJ felt able to create an addition to the exceptional categories where professional misconduct need not be alleged: just as imputing insolvency to a tradesman was actionable, so was imputing 'Jew-hating' to a diamond broker[165]. Perhaps the nineteenth- century authorities were not as restrictive as the House of Lords had previously thought.

Legislative reform eventually came in the shape of the Defamation Act 1952 s 2, which made actionable *per se* defamatory words 'calculated' to

[158] *Ibid* at 360.
[159] *Ibid* at 361.
[160] [1916] 2 AC 481 at 491.
[161] *Ibid* at 499.
[162] (1834) 2 Ad & E 2.
[163] (1937) 158 LT 85.
[164] *Ibid* at 88.
[165] *Ibid* at 90–91.

injure the claimant in his trade, business or profession. One perplexed commentator on the Act wrote that:

> The effect of the change is perhaps intended to be difficult to characterize; it seems, in essence, an admonition to the courts to be more ready than in the past to protect professional reputation without making merely generally defamatory remarks actionable without proof of special damages.[166]

Help could be found in the case law predating *Ayre v Craven*, where the test for actionable defamatory words had been whether they had a natural tendency to injure the claimant in his profession. 'Calculated' was synonymous with 'having a natural tendency to'[167]. In effect this legislative reform returned the law to the position it had occupied immediately after the decision in *Lumby v Allday*. To a lawyer of the 1830s, s 2 would have made perfect sense.

Slander not imputing an indictable offence, an obnoxious disease, or professional incompetence might still be actionable if the claimant could prove that the words had caused him special damage. This requirement of special damage was thought to be particularly harsh by the 1841 Select Committee:

> falsely and maliciously to impute, in the coarsest terms and on the most public occasion, want of chastity to a woman of high station and unspotted character, or want of veracity or courage to a gentleman of undoubted honesty and honour cannot be made the foundation of any proceeding civil or criminal; whereas an action may be maintained for saying that a cobbler is not skilful in mending shoes . . . The committee conceive that these distinctions, which are quite peculiar to the law of England, do not rest on any solid foundation . . .[168]

Reform, however, took only the limited shape of granting an action to a woman for an imputation against her chastity[169].

Proving special damage was a difficult hurdle to overcome. First there was the question of causation, as to which one authority suggested that proof by the defendant of any other concurrent cause would defeat the claim[170]. The loss had to be the 'natural consequence' of the words, a test which excluded any unreasonable response. Thus, for instance, in *Lynch v Knight*[171] it was held that a wife had suffered no special damage when her husband refused to live with her and sent her away because the husband's reaction to the slander was unreasonable; a reasonable response would have been to watch his wife carefully. The same conclusion was reached

[166] Anon, 'Reform in the Law of Defamation: The English Defamation Act of 1952' (1953) 66 *Harvard Law Review* 476 at 478.
[167] See eg *Haire v Wilson* (1829) 9 B & C 643.
[168] *Report from the Select Committee on the Law of Defamation and Libel* (1843) 1 *Law Times* 341.
[169] Slander of Women Act 1891 s 1.
[170] *Vicars v Wilcocks* (1806) 8 East 1 at 4.
[171] (1861) 9 HLC 577.

where an employer dismissed the claimant after being told that the claimant owed money to his landlord[172]. Furthermore, the courts had a wide discretion over what they recognised as being a natural consequence in law. Where a claimant became seriously ill as a result of the words it was held that no special damage had been suffered because the illness was not a natural consequence[173]. Martin B formulated the test in a way that could perhaps never be satisfied: 'Special damage must be the natural, general and, I may say, the universal result upon all mankind placed in the same circumstances'[174]. Bramwell B's analysis hinted at the policy basis behind the decision, describing the illness as 'not an immediate result in law, however natural in point of fact'[175].

Secondly there was the nature of the special damage itself. At the very least it had to be a loss of 'some substantial or material advantage'[176]. For instance, where the claimant was excluded from membership of a religious congregation in consequence of the slander it was held that she had suffered no special damage as she could still attend services at the chapel if she wished[177]. Courts tended to focus on financial loss. For example, a claimant who lost the society of her husband, the company of her friends and their hospitality only suffered special damage because she lost free food and drink[178].

This focus on substantial, ideally financial, loss reflected the origins of the tort of defamation in the action on the case for words. The basis of that action was that it aimed to give monetary damages for temporal loss; the ecclesiastical courts dealt with other hurtful allegations. However once the dominant idea behind defamation became compensating those exposed to hatred, ridicule or contempt, the narrow definition of special damage was bound to attract criticism. Glanville Williams argued that 'actual damage' should be redefined so as to take account of the claimant's mental suffering[179]. It was a powerful argument, but was not acted upon. Perhaps the reason was, as an earlier commentator had put it, that 'To say that mental distress . . . should be sufficient damage to support an action, would be in effect to say that all slanders are actionable'[180]. Although on the surface it was a modest proposal, Williams' suggestion would in effect have gone

[172] *Speake v Hughes* [1904] 1 KB 138.
[173] *Allsop v Allsop* (1860) 29 LJ (Ex) 315.
[174] *Ibid* at 317.
[175] *Ibid.*
[176] *Roberts v Roberts* (1864) 5 B & S 384 at 389 (per Cockburn CJ).
[177] *Ibid.*
[178] *Davies v Solomon* (1871) LR 7 QB 112.
[179] Williams, 'Dominion Legislation Relating to Libel and Slander' (1939) 21 *Journal of Comparative Legislation* 161 at 163.
[180] Anon, 'The Law of Libel—V' (1867) 11 *Solicitors' Journal & Reporter* 1052 at 1053. See, to identical effect, *Allsop v Allsop* (1860) 29 LJ (Ex) 315 at 317 (per Bramwell B).

further than either the Porter Committee[181] or Parliament itself[182] was prepared to go.

4. LIBEL OR SLANDER?

Written words were libel, spoken words were slander; but writing and speech did not exhaust the possibilities of communication. Disputes over defamatory matter conveyed using different means forced the courts to formulate criteria for what counted as libel. Initially it seemed that the key factor was permanency. As Lopes LJ said in a case holding that a waxwork in Madame Tussaud's was a libel,

> Libels are generally in writing or printing, but this is not necessary; the defamatory matter may be conveyed in some other permanent form. For instance, a statue, a caricature, an effigy, chalk marks on a wall, signs, or pictures may constitute a libel.[183]

Permanency only needed to be relative—burning someone in effigy was 'libellous' not 'slanderous'[184]. In fact it seemed that permanency had been reduced to almost nothing when the Court of Appeal held that defamation in a film constituted 'permanent matter'[185]. As one commentator observed, the communication looked transient[186]. Another possible ground of distinction that the Court of Appeal used in holding that a film was libel was that libel appealed to the eye and slander to the ear. However, this basis for the distinction seemed to be supported neither by law[187] nor by principle.

Even where the means of communication was not new, defamatory imputations conveyed by a combination of orthodox means caused doubt. For instance, where an employer dictated a letter to a secretary there was English authority that the employer published a libel[188]. The Court of Appeal of New Zealand asserted that this conclusion was analytically flawed. Communication of a defamatory writing required that the writing

[181] *Report of the Committee on the Law of Defamation*, Cmd 7536 (1948) at paras 38–40.

[182] 178 *House of Lords Debates* col 304 (5th series, 1952).

[183] *Monson v Tussauds Ltd* [1894] 1 QB 671 at 692.

[184] *Eyre v Garlick* (1878) 42 JP 68.

[185] *Youssoupoff v MGM Pictures Ltd* (1934) 50 TLR 581 at 587 (per Slesser LJ). In New York it had been assumed that film amounted to libel: *Merle v Sociological Research Film Corporation* 152 NYS 829 (Supreme Court of New York, 1915); *Brown v Paramount Publix Corporation* 270 NYS 544 (Supreme Court of New York, 1934).

[186] Shatwell commenting on Barry, 'Radio, Television and the Law of Defamation' (1949) 23 *Australian Law Journal* 203 at 218. See also Hall Williams, 'Committee on the Law of Defamation: The Porter Report' (1949) 12 *MLR* 217 at 221.

[187] It was settled that a person reading out a defamatory document published a libel: *Forrester v Tyrrell* (1893) 9 TLR 257. This case is discussed further below.

[188] *Pullman v Hill & Co* [1891] 1 QB 524 at 527.

be in existence before the communication; it was therefore impossible to say that 'the creation of such defamatory writing can be a communication of it to the person who is creating it'[189]. The American position on this general question was less confident. Where a message was transmitted by one telegraph operator to another, who transcribed it in the ordinary course of business, it had been argued that the publication was a libel because the sending operator intended the recipient to write it down[190]. The point does not seem to have been resolved by a court. When an opportunity arose to decide the issue in relation to the dictation of a letter to a secretary, the Court of Appeals of New York avoided it, holding that a libel was published because the employer instructed his secretary to read and transcribe her shorthand notes. Telling the secretary to read her notes was a communication of defamatory writing[191].

The reverse situation—where a person read out a defamatory writing—also caused some uncertainty. The point seemed to have been settled in *Forrester v Tyrrell*[192] where the Court of Appeal relied on two seventeenth-century Star Chamber criminal libel cases[193] in holding that the publication was a libel. It was seen as the obvious conclusion—'It would be strange if it were not so'[194]—and the Court did not elaborate. As one commentator tartly observed, 'The judgment contains no reasoning'[195].

The Court of Appeal was not alone, however, in feeling that these two criminal libel cases from Coke's Reports needed no explanation—nineteenth-century American courts had been happy to apply them without comment[196]. Similarly, twentieth-century courts in a range of jurisdictions either cited the seventeenth-century cases directly[197] or simply applied *Forrester v Tyrrell*[198]. There was, however, a little English judicial disquiet when, in *Osborn v Thomas Boulter and Son*[199], Scrutton LJ expressed his dissent from the conclusions in the seventeenth-century cases[200].

[189] *Angelini v Antico* (1912) 31 NZLR 841.

[190] Smith, 'Liability of a Telegraph Company for Transmitting a Defamatory Message' (1920) 20 *Columbia Law Review* 30 at 42–45.

[191] *Ostrowe v Lee* 175 NE 505 (Court of Appeals of New York, 1931).

[192] (1893) 9 TLR 257.

[193] Anon, 'The Case De Libellis Famosis, or of Scandalous Libels' (1609) 5 Co Rep 125a; *John Lamb's Case* (1610) 9 Co Rep 59b.

[194] (1893) 9 TLR 257.

[195] Barry, 'Radio, Television and the Law of Defamation' (1949) 23 *Australian Law Journal* 203 at 209.

[196] *Adams v Lawson* 17 Gratt 250 (Supreme Court of Appeals of Virginia, 1867); *Snyder v Andrews* 6 Barb NY 43 (Supreme Court, New York County, New York, 1849).

[197] *Ohio Public Service Co v Myers* 6 NE 2d 29 at 32 (Court of Appeals of Ohio, 9th District, Lorain County, 1934); *Bander v Metropolitan Life Insurance Co* 47 NE 2d 595 at 602 (Supreme Judicial Court of Massachusetts, Suffolk, 1943); *Patching v Howarth* [1930] 4 DLR 489 at 490 (British Columbia Court of Appeal).

[198] *Robinson v Chambers (No 2)* [1946] NILR 148 at 150.

[199] [1930] 2 KB 226.

[200] *Ibid* at 231.

Widespread disquiet surfaced in the United States and Australia when the courts were faced with cases of defamation by radio broadcast. Where the defamatory words had been read from a script *Forrester v Tyrrell*[201] suggested that the publication was a libel and therefore actionable without proof of special damage[202]. This analysis, however, did not have universal appeal. In *Meldrum v Australian Broadcasting Co Ltd*[203], both at first instance and on appeal, *Forrester v Tyrrell* and the seventeenth century cases on which it was based were closely analysed and rejected. At first instance Cussen ACJ pointed out that the criminal libel cases required careful handling and distinguished *Forrester* from defamation by radio. In *Forrester* the defendant had read out a defamatory letter to a group of people present, whereas listeners to a defamatory radio broadcast had no reason to know they were hearing a document being read out. Defamation by radio was, therefore, slander only.

On appeal the Full Court went further. Mann J denied that the criminal cases offered any authority at all on the scope of the civil action and criticised Coke's system of reporting cases. McArthur J, with whom Mann J agreed, took a more direct approach to *Forrester v Tyrrell*: he said it was wrongly decided. In his view, 'so long as the communication is by word of mouth it is . . . slander and not libel'[204]. Lowe J took a view that was closer to that of Cussen ACJ. For him libel required that that the recipient be aware of the permanent form of the communication. The hearers in *Forrester* were aware of the permanent form (they could see the letter); radio listeners were not aware of any writing.

The decision in *Meldrum's case* attracted criticism for its failure to recognise the policy factors—especially the potential for widespread harm—that favoured treating a radio broadcast from a script as libel[205]. However, from the point of view of policy the rule asserted in *Forrester v Tyrrell* was not an ideal solution either, for it made classification as libel or slander turn on whether the words had been read from a script.

There was some attempt to defend the idea that the words being in a script made their utterance worse[206], and in New York it was held that an interpolated defamatory remark was slander[207]. The Court invoked the principle that 'What gives the sting to the writing is its permanence of form'[208], and

201 (1893) 9 TLR 257.

202 *Sorenson v Wood* 243 NW 82 (Supreme Court of Nebraska, 1932).

203 [1932] VLR 425.

204 *Ibid* at 439.

205 Hamson, 'Moot Case on Defamation' (1948) 10 *CLJ* 46 at 51–52; Barry, 'Radio, Television and the Law of Defamation' (1949) 23 *Australian Law Journal* 203 at 208–211.

206 *The Charles Parker Company v The Silver City Crystal Company* 116 A 2d 440 at 443 (Supreme Court of Errors of Connecticut, 1955).

207 *Locke v Gibbons 164 Misc 877* (Supreme Court, New York, 1937) affirmed by Supreme Court, Appellate Division, First Department 2 NYS 2d 1015 (1938).

208 *Ibid* at 880 (quoting from *Ostrowe v Lee* 175 NE 505 (Court of Appeals of New York, 1931)).

acknowledged that the result might be different where the defamation was read from a script[209]. Other courts[210] and other judges however, were not convinced. In *Hartmann v Winchell*[211] the Court of Appeals of New York considered a defamatory radio broadcast read from a script. The majority applied *Forrester v Tyrrell* and concluded that the broadcast was a libel. Fuld J, however, seized the opportunity to analyse the overall position in depth. To him it was 'unreal'[212] that liability turned on the existence of a script. On the other hand he admitted that the application of the 'classic criteria of libel'[213], particularly the requirement of permanency, would point to radio broadcasts being slander. The solution, he felt, was frankly to recognise that the potential for widespread damage required radio defamation to be classed as libel[214].

What Fuld J had in mind was judicial legislation. Some courts might be reluctant to take such a step. After the decision in *Meldrum's case*, for example, Sir Charles Lowe had expressed his regret at a result which, he explained, was compelled because the court lacked 'the power of legislation'[215]. When commentators called for legislation, their appeals were not directed to the judiciary[216]. Even the Court that subsequently approved the analysis of Fuld J, calling it 'compelling logic'[217], reached the conclusion that an unscripted broadcast was libel without overtly legislating. It preferred to take a line suggested by several academic commentators: permanence was not an absolute prerequisite for libel, it was merely a way of identifying particularly damaging forms of defamation; the vast potential audience of broadcasts showed that they could also be particularly damaging[218].

Non-judicial legislators did not need to worry about apparent consistency with common law doctrines. Legislators on opposite sides of the Atlantic took opposite views. In the United States calls for federal regulation of defamation by radio[219] were ignored. However, this did not result

209 *Ibid.*

210 Eg *Irwin v Ashurst* 74 P 2d 1127 at 1129–30 (Supreme Court of Oregon, 1938).

211 73 NE 2d 30 (Court of Appeals of New York, 1947).

212 *Ibid* at 32.

213 *Ibid.*

214 Fuld J's reasoning had been anticipated a decade earlier by a student's entry to an essay prize competition—see Newhouse, 'Defamation by Radio: A New Tort' (1938) 17 *Oregon Law Review* 314. The essay was awarded second prize!

215 Comment on Barry, 'Radio, Television and the Law of Defamation' (1949) 23 *Australian Law Journal* 203 at 220.

216 Newhouse, 'Defamation by Radio: A New Tort' (1938) 17 *Oregon Law Review* 314; Keller, 'Federal Control of Defamation by Radio' (1936–37) 12 *Notre Dame Lawyer* 15.

217 *Shor v Billingsley* 158 NYS 2d 476 at 480 (Supreme Court, New York, 1956).

218 Finlay, 'Defamation by Radio' (1941) 19 *Canadian Bar Review* 353 at 353–61; Donnelly, 'Defamation by Radio: A Reconsideration' (1948) 34 *Iowa Law Review* 12 at 14–17; Shatwell, comment on Barry, 'Radio, Television and the Law of Defamation' (1949) 23 *Australian Law Journal* 203 at 218–219.

219 Eg, Keller, 'Federal Control of Defamation by Radio' (1936–37) 12 *Notre Dame Lawyer* 15.

in the 'crazy-quilt'[220] pattern of state regulation predicted by one commentator: state legislation was remarkably consistent. Essentially broadcast defamation was only actionable if damage was proved. The impetus behind this legislation was the National Association of Radio and Television Broadcasters (NARTB), which had responded to court decisions classifying radio defamation as libel—and therefore actionable without proof of damage—by drafting and tirelessly promoting a model statute achieving the opposite result. Several states obligingly passed the statute; others did so after making minor amendments[221].

English legislators passed the Defamation Act 1952, which stated in s 1 that all broadcast defamation was deemed to be 'publication in permanent form', or, in other words, libel. In passing s 1 Parliament was implementing a recommendation of the Porter Committee, but it was rather strange that the Committee had taken an interest in the point at all. Unlike in America, there had been no controversy in the courts over the classification of broadcasting. There had only been two cases. In the first, *Williams & Norgate Ltd v British Broadcasting Corporation*[222], the action for slander had settled; in the second, *Bergman v Macadam*[223], it was not even argued that the publication might be libel. The only sign of doubt on the point was expressed in *Topp v Lire*, a moot case[224]!

One reason for the Committee's interest in the point may have been that it was aware of the developments in America and Australia[225]. But if the Committee really was responding to developments abroad, its brief, almost perfunctory treatment of the point was surprising. It reported that the 'generally accepted view' was that a broadcast from a script was a libel, and a broadcast spoken *extempore* was a slander[226]. The distinction was artificial, so all broadcasts should be treated as libel[227]. This hardly did justice to the range, depth and complexity of common law analyses available in America and Australia.

A more convincing explanation for the content and style of the Committee's recommendation emerges when closer attention is paid to its membership and perspective. The Committee's recommendations were thought to be very favourable to the Press[228]. This was hardly surprising given the strong Press representation on the Committee: there were nearly

[220] *Ibid* at 37.
[221] For more detail see Leflar, 'Radio and TV Defamation: "Fault" or Strict Liability?' (1954) 15 *Ohio State Law Journal* 252 at 267–69.
[222] *The Times*, 24 April 1926; noted (1926) 70 *Solicitors' Journal* 613.
[223] *The Times*, 9 October 1940.
[224] Hamson, 'Moot Case on Defamation' (1948) 10 *CLJ* 46.
[225] The Committee commissioned reports on the law of defamation in British Dominions and the United States from Glanville Williams and Winfield respectively. See *Report of the Committee on the Law of Defamation*, Cmd 7536 (1948) at para 3.
[226] *Report*, para 42.
[227] *Ibid*, para 43.
[228] Eg, Lloyd, 'Reform of the Law of Libel' (1952) 5 *Current Legal Problems* 168 at 169–70.

as many laymen as lawyers; all of the laymen were from the Press or publishing[229]. One lawyer Committee member even admitted that it had been difficult to 'hold the scales evenly'[230] between claimants and defendants. Relations between newspapers and the British Broadcasting Corporation (Britain's only broadcaster at the time) were both changeable and delicate. In the early years of the Corporation the newspapers' concerns about competition from the broadcaster were alleviated by a series of voluntary arrangements entered into between the Corporation, newspapers and press agencies[231]. These arrangements limited both the times and content of news broadcasts. By the late 1930s, however, the balance of power was starting to shift in the Corporation's favour[232], and in 1939, with the outbreak of war, the Corporation's attitude to newspapers changed abruptly[233]. Now it was a direct competitor. It was not entirely surprising, then, that the Press did not want its new competitor to enjoy a more generous legal regime. Indeed, a concern with unfair competition could be read into the first, apparently banal, sentence of the Report's paragraph on broadcasting:

> A defamatory statement transmitted over the radio in a broadcast, reaching, as it may, an audience of many millions, is calculated to cause as much, if not more, damage than a written report in a newspaper however large its circulation.[234]

The legal distinction between libel and slander, whatever its general justifications, was clearly inappropriate as a tool to regulate competition between media.

5. CONCLUSION

The history of the distinction between libel and slander is dominated by contrasting judicial attitudes to change. The court that decided to borrow the criminal law formulation of libel and grant a civil remedy for it was clearly not inhibited by the absence of precedent. The court that formally ratified the distinction, by contrast, only did so because it felt that the authorities left it no choice. Similarly, the rules about slander affecting the claimant's business had to be reformed by statute because the courts felt that they could not escape from their own precedents.

On the other hand, there are also examples of courts using broad, working assumptions, and not worrying about the marginal cases: the

229 Wade, 'Defamation' (1950) 66 *LQR* 348.
230 *Ibid.*
231 Briggs, *The Golden Age of Wireless* (London, 1965) at 153.
232 *Ibid* at 159.
233 Briggs, *The War of Words* (London, 1970) at 47.
234 *Report*, para 42.

distinction between libel and slander itself is an example, as it the American doctrine of libel *per se*. Here the concern with doing justice most of the time could be seen to prevail over the fine detail of precedent or the distraction of hypothetical hard cases.

Finally, in the use made of the distinction there is an illustration of the varying judicial attitudes to expanding categories. These ranged from frank calls for judicial legislation at one extreme, to an apologetic refusal to innovate at the other. How the law developed was entirely controlled by the unpredictable interplay between these judicial attitudes.

2

Interpretation

A CRUCIAL PART OF any defamation claim is proving that the words were defamatory and referred to the claimant. Ascertaining the meaning of those words is therefore a fundamental matter. Furthermore, a defendant might well seek to justify the words in a sense different to the sense that the claimant alleges they bear. Again, ascertaining the correct meaning of the words is the key question. This chapter examines the techniques used by the courts to interpret language that allegedly defames the claimant. The first part of the chapter deals with the general principles; the second with specific rules of interpretation relating to defamation of goods and groups.

1. GENERAL PRINCIPLES

The most important development in construing defamatory words took place around the start of the eighteenth century, when the Court of King's Bench laid down that defamatory words had to be given their ordinary natural meaning. The courts themselves[1] and subsequent historians[2] emphasised that this was a change of direction: previously words had been given the least offensive meaning possible, an approach that had led to artificial, arguably absurd, interpretations.

According to the traditional explanation, the seventeenth-century courts had committed themselves to this artificial, unrealistic approach on grounds of policy[3]. They were concerned at the increase in the number of defamation actions in the early years of the seventeenth century, and adopted the rather crude method of construing the language against the claimant if at all possible (*in mitiori sensu*) in order to keep the numbers down. However, a closer examination of the cases from the period shows a more complex picture.

[1] Eg *Baker v Pierce* (1704) 6 Mod 23.
[2] Eg Baker, *An Introduction to English Legal History*, 4th edn (London, 2002) at 443.
[3] Holdsworth, 'Defamation in the Sixteenth and Seventeenth Centuries' (1924) 40 *LQR* 302, 397, 404–7.

The *in mitiori sensu* approach is supposed to have been a concerted effort by the courts but there are frequent assertions of general principle against it and court decisions inconsistent with it. For instance, in 1585 Wray CJ, speaking for the Court of King's Bench, declared that 'actions for scandals should not be maintained by any strained construction or argument'[4]. Similarly, in *The Lord Cromwell's Case*[5], an action for *scandalum magnatum*, the Court said:

> God forbid that a man's words should be by such strict and grammatical construction taken by parcels against the manifest intent of the party upon consideration of all the words, which import the true cause and occasion which manifest the true sense of them.[6]

Both of these statements called for a natural construction to be given to the defamatory words. Other courts reiterated the same theme less floridly, requiring words to be taken 'according to the usual and common sense of them'[7] or as understood 'in common speech'[8].

Perhaps even more striking were decisions where courts did the opposite of *in mitiori sensu* and deliberately took the words in their worst sense. In *Sir Thomas Beamond v Sir Henry Hastings*[9], *Lewes v Walter*[10] and *Kellan v Manesby*[11], for instance, the King's Bench acknowledged that it was interpreting the words 'in the worst sense'. In *Levet's Case*[12] it construed an allegation that an innkeeper's house was 'infected with the pox' as meaning the great pox, not the small pox, the latter being the less serious allegation, as the Court acknowledged.

So the approach to interpretation seems to have been more varied than the traditional account would allow. Nevertheless, some strangely lenient constructions could be found in the reports, and the reasons for this need explaining. The courts' overriding concern seems to have been with certainty. As the King's Bench put it in *Stanhope v Blith*[13], 'words which shall charge any one with an action, in which damages shall be recovered, ought to have convenient certainty'[14]. On the facts of that case it was held that the statement 'Stanhope hath but one manor, and that he hath gotten by swearing and forswearing' was too general to be actionable. First, it might have been someone other than Stanhope who did the swearing and forswearing. Second, it was not generally actionable to accuse a person of

[4] *Stanhope v Blith* (1585) 4 Co Rep 15a at 15b.
[5] (1578) 4 Co Rep 12b.
[6] *Ibid* at 14a.
[7] *Dame Morison v Cade* (1607) Cro Jac 162.
[8] *Powell v Plunket* (1626) Cro Car 52.
[9] (1609) Cro Jac 240.
[10] (1616) Cro Jac 406; Roll Rep 444.
[11] (1604) Cro Jac 40.
[12] (1592) Cro Eliz 289.
[13] (1585) 4 Co Rep 15a.
[14] *Ibid*.

forswearing: a person might be forsworn in casual conversation, and 'forswearing' was a word of passion or anger, like saying someone was a 'rogue'.

The requirement of certainty for imputations of crime was the source of some delicate reasoning. Thus, in *Brown v Michel*[15] the allegation was that the claimant 'had delivered untruths upon his oath, in his answer to the bill of JS in the Chancery'. The words were held not actionable, because a person might honestly swear things to be true to his knowledge which were later shown to be false. A particular source of difficulty arose where the defendant accused the claimant of theft, then gave as an example removal of a thing that could not be stolen, such as a tree. The courts decided that the crucial point was how the general allegation of theft and the example were linked. If the defendant said 'thou art a thief, *for* thou hast stolen a tree' no action lay[16], because the second half of the statement showed that there was no imputation of felony. If, however, the words were 'thou are a thief, *and* thou hast stolen a tree' an action lay. As the King's Bench explained:

> the action lies for calling him thief generally: and the addition "and thou hast stolen" is another distinct sentence by itself, and is not the reason of the former speech, nor any diminution thereof, but an addition thereto.[17]

This emphasis on certainty was not purely for its own sake or in order arbitrarily to exclude claims. It was consistent with the courts' general approach to actions for defamation in the early seventeenth century, namely, to give damages for words tending to cause loss[18]. If an allegation of crime was vague or ambiguous it was unlikely to trigger a prosecution and conviction. In short, the certainty requirement filtered out those allegations unlikely to cause loss. However, the tendency of the words to cause loss remained the fundamental issue. In *Blunden v Eustace*[19], for instance, it was held that the claimant, a surveyor, could sue for the allegation that he was a 'cozening and a shifting knave, and a cheating knave'. Such an allegation, said Montague CJ, would not normally be actionable, 'yet for such a particular person, this touching him in his means of living, the action well lies'[20].

It should also be noted that some courts were prepared to take into account the degree of malice when assessing whether words should be actionable. The reasoning in *Stanhope v Blith*[21], for instance, acknowledged

[15] (1595) Cro Eliz 500.
[16] *Gyer v Ormsted* (1609) Cro Jac 231.
[17] *Minors v Leeford* (1606) Cro Jac 114.
[18] Helmholz, 'Damages in Actions for Slander at Common Law' (1987) 103 *LQR* 624 at 636.
[19] (1618) Cro Jac 504.
[20] *Ibid.*
[21] (1585) 4 Co Rep 15a.

that an accusation of forswearing could easily be made in the heat of the moment, and that was a factor against allowing an action. On the other hand, in *King v Lake*[22] it was held that putting the defamation in writing 'contains more malice'[23] than merely speaking it; the objection of lack of certainty was, therefore, not open to the defendant. What emerged from the case law read as a whole was a nuanced, sophisticated range of techniques.

The objection of lack of certainty was not only available in respect of the defamatory allegation, it also applied to reference to the claimant. For instance, in *William Wiseman v Wiseman*[24] it was held that if one of several brothers had said 'my brother is perjured' no action would lie. In 1675 the point was described as 'a doubt long controverted for the uncertainty'[25].

The *Wiseman* case was also important because it laid down an important distinction between two types of uncertainty. The first was where 'the words themselves import in themselves apparent uncertainty'; the second, 'when they may be ascertained by averment'[26]. In other words, nothing could cure the uncertainty of the first type, but the second type would become actionable if the claimant explained their precise meaning and reference in his pleading. Thus, for example, where one of several brothers said 'my brother is perjured' the words would import uncertainty that could not be dispelled by pleading. If, however, there were only two brothers, one of whom said 'my brother is perjured' the second brother could dispel any uncertainty by pleading that he was the speaker's only brother, and the words therefore referred to him. A statement might well contain both types of uncertainty. For example, in *Foster v Browning*[27] the words were 'Thou art as arrant a thief as any is in England; for thou hast broken up JS chest, and taken away forty pounds'. The first part of the sentence was held not to be actionable because the claimant should have pleaded that there were thieves in England; this was an example of uncertainty being ascertainable by an averment. The second half of the sentence was also held to be not actionable, because a person might openly break open a chest to claim what was rightfully due to him; this was an example of the words being uncertain in themselves.

This distinction between words uncertain in themselves and words ascertainable by pleading is a crucial factor to bear in mind when assessing the seventeenth century approach to interpretation. In many instances what at first glance appeared to be a technical or absurd rejection of a claim was, in effect, an objection to the way the claimant had pleaded his case.

22 (1670) Hardres 470.
23 *Ibid.*
24 (1606) Cro Jac 107.
25 *Henacre and Bets v* _ [sic] (1675) 1 Keb 525.
26 (1606) Cro Jac 107.
27 (1625) Cro Jac 688.

For instance, in *Holt v Astgrigg*[28] the statement was that 'Sir Thomas Holt struck his cook on the head with a cleaver, and cleaved his head; the one part lay on the one shoulder, and another part on the other'. After a verdict for the claimant the defendant moved in arrest of judgment that the words were not actionable as the claimant had not pleaded that the imputation was that the cook had died. The King's Bench agreed, saying that 'notwithstanding such wounding, the party may yet be living; and it is then but trespass'[29]. The decision has been described as 'the most absurd of all these cases'[30], but it should be emphasised that the King's Bench was not saying that the words spoken could never be sued on. Rather, it was making the claimant pay the price for a defective pleading. The gist of the imputation might have been clear, but there was a formal requirement to state the obvious in the pleadings.

The contrast between the early seventeenth and early eighteenth-century approaches to interpretation was, therefore, less sharp than the traditional view would allow. The early seventeenth-century courts took a range of approaches, some of which were identical to the early eighteenth-century technique of construing the words in the sense that an ordinary bystander would give to them. In fact, it may be more accurate to describe the late seventeenth- and early eighteenth-century cases as clarifying what the dominant test was, rather than as imposing a new technique.

The late seventeenth-century insistence on taking words 'in a common sense sounding to the vulgar intendment of the by-standers'[31] was expounded most emphatically by Holt CJ. He was clearly impatient with some of the earlier caution about certainty, particularly in relation to the distinction between alleging 'You are a thief *for* . . .' and 'You are a thief *and* . . .'[32]. However, he did make clear that there was still a role for *in mitiori sensu*: that rule could be used 'where the words in their natural import are doubtful, and equally to be understood in the one sense as in the other'[33]. It should also be noted that Holt CJ's application of the ordinary bystander test was cautious: for instance, he doubted whether an allegation of 'stealing' conveyed felony[34]; and he agreed that saying a person 'stole my Lord's deer' should be understood as referring to wild deer—it therefore only imputed a trespass[35].

Holt CJ also hinted at the reasons behind his insistence that the words be construed as an ordinary bystander would understand them. In *Somers*

[28] (1607) Cro Jac 184.

[29] *Ibid*. An imputation of trespass was not actionable without proof of special damage.

[30] Holdsworth, 'Defamation in the Sixteenth and Seventeenth Centuries' (1924) 40 *LQR* 302, 397, 412.

[31] *Somers v House* (1694) Holt 39.

[32] *Baker v Pierce* (1704) 6 Mod 23 at 23–24.

[33] *Somers v House* (1694) Holt 39.

[34] *Baker v Pierce* (1704) 6 Mod 23 at 24. Powell J took a wider view.

[35] *Ogden v Turner* (1704) 6 Mod 104.

v House[36] he remarked that the court 'would give no favours to words, and should give satisfaction to them whose reputation is hurt'[37]. He elaborated in *Baker v Pierce*[38]: 'wherever words tended to take away a man's reputation he would encourage actions for them, because so doing would contribute much to the preservation of the peace'[39]. In other words, if the courts did not give claimants 'satisfaction' they might seek it elsewhere, by duel.

Duelling[40] had been on the increase since the Restoration, and was a matter of great public controversy and concern. Most duels seem to have been fought between courtiers, but they attracted widespread fascination and interest. The royal attitude was ambivalent: Charles II issued proclamations against duelling, but was also quick to pardon duellists.

The last third of the seventeenth century saw a concerted campaign against duelling. Parliament led the way. In the 1660s there were three attempts to pass bills against duelling, one in the House of Lords and two in the Commons. The bills failed because a majority felt that the proposed penalty—forfeiture of all land and goods to the Crown—was too severe. In the 1690s a further Parliamentary momentum developed, and two bills against duelling were put forward in the Commons. Again, both failed.

These attempts to make duelling a serious criminal offence were accompanied by a debate about the extent to which duellists' demands should be met by legal remedies. Whilst there was a view that duellists should be left to invoke whatever common law remedy available, there was a powerful argument that the common law was inadequate. As Sir Richard Temple put it in 1675, 'the great occasion of duels is, that the law gives not remedy proportionable to injuries received'[41]. Temple went on to draw a contrast with France, where courts of honour had been set up to provide remedies for potential duellists. The contrast with France was to become a major theme in the debates about duelling in the late seventeenth and early eighteenth centuries. A treatise published in 1685, for example, gave an account of the suppression of duelling in France, and by the early eighteenth century references to the French courts of honour were frequent.

The views expressed by Holt CJ about interpreting defamatory words can therefore be seen as a contribution to an intense contemporary debate. It was also a distinctive contribution. Opponents of duelling had tended to one of two polarised views: either they believed that duellists should be left to their common law remedies, or they believed that a new court was

36 (1694) Holt 39.

37 *Ibid.*

38 (1704) 6 Mod 23.

39 *Ibid* at 24.

40 Peltonen, *The Duel in Early Modern England: Civility Politeness and Honour* (Cambridge, 2003) at 201–22 gives a fascinating account of anti-duelling campaigns between 1660 and 1720.

41 *Ibid* at 219.

required to deal with affronts to honour. Holt CJ was somewhere in between: he favoured common law remedies, but sought to adapt them in order to give 'satisfaction'. Perhaps his main concern was to show that there was no need for a new (rival) court to give potential duellists what they sought.

The approach to interpretation propounded by Holt CJ had become the orthodoxy in England by the middle of the eighteenth century[42] and was quickly adopted in America[43]. It remains the orthodoxy today, with some additional variations and refinements discussed below.

Before those variations and refinements are discussed, however, it is important to highlight one major procedural development, which altered the form in which the courts considered the question of interpretation. This was the determination by Parliament in 1792 that whether a writing was a libel was a question for the jury.

The controversy over who decided a writing was libellous had arisen in relation to seditious libel. Judges had directed juries that as a matter of law the particular publication was a libel, and left to the jury only the (often admitted) question of publication. Fox's Libel Act 1792 reversed this position, making clear that libel or no libel was a question for the jury. Initially the Act was assumed to have no application to civil libel cases[44], but in about 1840 that view changed: in *Parmiter v Coupland*[45] Fox's Act was applied directly to a civil libel claim. The Act was now seen as a declaration of the common law[46] relating to both criminal and civil cases; on this basis its provisions were even given effect by the Supreme Court of New York[47].

Since libel or no libel was a question for the jury the courts had to work out what their role was, if any. Some judges took a minimalist approach. For instance, Lord Abinger CB once validly directed a jury that 'I own I find a difficulty in saying whether it is a libel or not. Gentlemen, can you assist me?'[48] Certainly there was no obligation on the judge to give his opinion[49]. It seems to have become settled quite quickly that, as with other factual issues, a judge was required to withdraw a case from the jury if there was no evidence on which they could find for the claimant. In civil defamation cases this test was expressed in terms of whether reasonable

[42] *Harrison v Thornborough* (1714) 10 Mod 196, *Button v Heyward* (1722) 8 Mod 24, *Gardiner v Atwater* (1756) Say 265.

[43] Eg, *Hoyle v Young* 1 Wash (Va) 150 (Supreme Court of Appeals of Virginia, 1793); *Goodrich v Davis* 11 Metcalf 473 (Supreme Judicial Court of Massachusetts, 1846).

[44] *Snyder v Andrews* 6 Barb NY 43 at 49 (Supreme Court, New York, 1849).

[45] (1840) 6 M & W 105.

[46] *Baylis v Lawrence* (1841) 11 Ad & E 920. See also Campbell, *Lives of the Lord Chancellors*, 4th edn (London, 1857) vol VII, ch CXLVIII, at 47.

[47] *Snyder v Andrews* 6 Barb NY 43 (Supreme Court, New York, 1849).

[48] *Baylis v Lawrence* (1841) 11 Ad & E 920 at 922.

[49] *Ibid*.

men would be likely to give the words a defamatory meaning[50]. If the words are left to the jury it is for them to decide how a reasonable person would understand the allegation.

The fundamental approach to interpreting defamatory words remains today to ask how an ordinary bystander would understand them. Within this fundamental principle, however, a number of sub-rules and refinements have emerged. For instance, written material might be given a 'proper and natural meaning, according to the ordinary rules for the interpretation of written instruments'[51], whilst for slander 'canons of construction properly applicable to contracts and statutes are a very unreliable guide to the reasonable interpretation of angry and ill-chosen words'[52].

The main focus of development has been on the attributes of the reasonable person. Interpretation should not be strictly limited to logical meanings, for instance, because ordinary people sometimes draw illogical conclusions[53]. To put the same point slightly differently, one should not assume that a tabloid newspaper article will be read with the perceptive analysis of an Oxford don[54]. On the other hand, the courts have been concerned to emphasise that they are seeking the 'reasonable'[55] meaning of the language. Thus, one cannot seize upon any bad interpretation of the words if there are several non-defamatory ones[56]. In other words, one should not assume that the reasonable reader is 'avid for scandal'[57]. Similarly, the claimant cannot rely on an interpretation based on the assumption that some readers might glance through a newspaper and see only the pictures and the headlines[58].

Despite these attempts to make the test of construction as realistic as possible, it is, ultimately, impossible to avoid some artificiality. Doubtless some people read more into statements than they ought to; many readers might only glance through a newspaper. Furthermore, there is no requirement to produce evidence to show how readers or hearers understood the words: the test focuses on how the hypothetical reasonable reader ought to have understood the words. It is therefore possible that the legal interpretation of any given defamatory words might not correspond with the interpretation of any actual reader.

[50] *Capital and Counties Bank v George Henty & Sons* (1882) 7 App Cas 741 at 745 (per Lord Selborne LC); *Lewis V Daily Telegraph* [1964] AC 234 at 259 (per Lord Reid).

[51] *Capital and Counties Bank v George Henty & Sons* (1882) 7 App Cas 741 at 744 (per Lord Selborne LC).

[52] *Hopwood v Muirson* [1945] KB 313 at 320.

[53] *Capital and Counties Bank v George Henty & Sons* (1882) 7 App Cas 741 at 763 (per Lord Penzance).

[54] *Morgan v Odhams Press Ltd* [1971] 2 All ER 1156 at 1180 (per Lord Donovan).

[55] *Capital and Counties Bank v George Henty & Sons* (1880) 5 CPD 514 at 540.

[56] *Ibid* at 541 (per Brett LJ); (1882) 7 App Cas 741 at 792 (per Lord Bramwell); *Nevill v The Fine Art and General Insurance Company Ltd* [1897] AC 68 at 73 (per Lord Halsbury LC).

[57] *Lewis v Daily Telegraph Ltd* [1964] AC 234 at 260 (per Lord Reid).

[58] *Charleston v News Group Newspapers* [1995] 2 All ER 313.

The fact that the test relies on the interpretation of a hypothetical reasonable person has been the source of criticism. One commentator, for example, has contrasted the legal approach unfavourably with the academic linguistic approach[59]. The latter emphasises that what imputations are understood by a hearer turns on that person's individual association of images, values and other criteria[60]. As the commentator put it, 'For the linguist, it would not be an exaggeration to state that the imposition of a right-thinking person is nothing short of heresy in natural language interpretation . . . the right-thinking person effectively stifles the subjectivity dynamic . . .'[61]. Thus, whilst a linguistic analysis recognises the potential for the same words to carry multiple meanings to different hearers, the law fixes on a single meaning that it declares is how 'reasonable people' would understand the words. As Diplock LJ once pointed out,

> . . . the argument between lawyers as to the meaning of words starts with the unexpressed major premise that any particular combination of words has one meaning which is not necessarily the same as that intended by him who published them or understood by any of those who read them but is capable of ascertainment as being the 'right' meaning by the adjudicator to whom the law confides the responsibility of determining it.[62]

There remains the question why the law has chosen to adopt an apparently unrealistic attitude to interpreting defamatory words. Diplock LJ in *Slim v Daily Telegraph Ltd*[63] gave as the reason (quoted above) that the law assumed that words had one correct meaning. This was, however, slightly inaccurate: it is open to a claimant to prove additional facts known to some readers or listeners which led them to give otherwise innocent words a defamatory meaning[64]. The law of defamation does, therefore, acknowledge that the possibility that different meanings may be conveyed by the same words. However, Diplock LJ surely was right to emphasise the difference between a lawyer's approach to interpretation and a layman's. The layman normally seeks to ascertain meaning for its own sake; the lawyer, however, is seeking to attribute liability and damages[65]. The legal rule of construction ought, therefore, to contain an element of fairness to the speaker. The current rule of interpretation does this by limiting the defendant's responsibility to those meanings which a reasonable person would give to the words. In essence the defendant is being made liable

59 Harkess, 'A Linguistic Inspection of the Law of Defamation' (1998) 8 *Auckland University Law Review* 653.

60 *Ibid* at 661.

61 *Ibid* at 667.

62 *Slim v Daily Telegraph Ltd* [1968] 2 QB 157 at 172.

63 *Ibid.*

64 *Eg, Cassidy v Daily Mirror Newspapers Ltd* [1929] 2 KB 331.

65 For a similar distinction in relation to causation see Hart and Honoré, *Causation in the* Law, 2nd edn (Oxford, 1985) at 1–25.

only for those damaging interpretations that he ought to have anticipated. The ordinary linguistic approach, by contrast, needs to pay no attention to the interests of the speaker. The differing purposes of the rules justify their differing contents.

The development of the principles for construing defamatory words can thus be seen as a gradual evolution rather than an abrupt change. The natural meaning test was one of several approaches used in the seventeenth century, but it came to dominate as a result of Holt CJ's exposition of it. Whilst the courts subsequently invested it with as much realistic detail as possible, it remained fundamentally a legal test, and could produce results at odds with actual hearers' understanding of the words used. Far from being a defect in the test, this discrepancy between the results of the legal test and a linguistic analysis was an inevitable product of the fact that the legal and linguistic rules served different purposes.

2. SPECIAL CASES

There are two important special cases where the general principles of interpretation have been modified. The first is where the claimant asserts that he is so clearly associated with a particular thing that criticism of the thing amounts to a defamation of him personally. The second is where the defamation is directed against a group.

(a) Defamation by association

An actionable defamation did not need to refer to the claimant by name: even asterisks might give a sufficient indication of who was meant[66]. In the course of the nineteenth century some claimants sought to go even further, arguing that they were defamed personally as a result of their close connection with a thing.

In *Archbold v Sweet*[67], for example, it was found that publishing the third edition of Archbold's *Summary of the Law relative to Pleading and Evidence in Criminal Cases* defamed Archbold. The construction of a defamatory meaning drew on the background to the publication. Archbold had assigned the copyright to Sweet after the second edition; the third edition, not edited by Archbold was packed with errors. There was, however, nothing on the title page, or elsewhere, to indicate that the third edition was not Archbold's work.

[66] *Bourke v Warren* (1826) 2 Car & P 307.
[67] (1832) 5 Car & P 219.

A similar readiness to derive a defamatory meaning from the association between the claimant and an object could be seen in *Ingram v Lawson*[68]. There a letter imputed that a ship that had advertised for passengers had been unseaworthy on its previous voyage and had been sold for transporting convicts. The court held that this was a libel on the master of the ship personally. Coltman J took a particularly broad view of the association between people and things:

> To say of a shipowner, that he has sold his ship to carry convicts when she was in a condition in which she must be expected to go to the bottom, is as bad as saying of a wine merchant, that his wine is poisoned, or of a tea dealer, that his tea is made green by drying it on copper.[69]

Four years later, however, there seemed to be a change of approach. The defendant in *Evans v Harlow*[70] had published a newspaper advertisement stating that the claimant had sold siphons that did not work properly. The claim for defamation failed: the imputation was 'only on the goods'[71], not against the claimant as a tradesman. If there had been a suggestion that the claimant knew his goods were bad, the result would have been different[72]. This reasoning seemed to be merely an application of the general principles of interpretation. Viewed purely in such terms it was not particularly convincing. As Coltman J had pointed out in *Ingram v Lawson*[73] allegations about a merchant's wares might well injure his reputation. Here the words were surely capable of being read as imputing lack of skill or judgment by the claimant, and should therefore have been allowed to go to a jury.

However, there were also allusions to reasons of policy. Lord Denman CJ expressed concern that allowing an action here would 'open a very wide door to litigation'[74]. The main reason for the door being so wide was that the claimant was not alleging that he had suffered special damage: if the allegation reflected on him in his trade, it was actionable *per se*[75]. A further, related policy reason could be seen in the judgment of Patteson J. He pointed out that a caution against goods was actionable, but only if the claimant proved special damage. Essentially this was a point about classification: the claimant should have sued for slander of goods, not defamation.

Although the policy reasons enunciated in *Evans v Harlow*[76] were important, they enjoyed little prominence in the later case law. Indeed the

68 (1840) 6 Bing NC 212.
69 *Ibid* at 216.
70 (1844) 5 QB 624.
71 *Ibid* at 632 (per Lord Denman CJ).
72 *Ibid* at 633 (per Patteson J).
73 (1840) 6 Bing NC 212 at 216.
74 (1844) 5 QB 624 at 631.
75 For analysis of this category see ch 1, above.
76 (1844) 5 QB 624.

next case dealing with the association between a person and a thing was the high-water mark of the courts' liberality in allowing a claimant to sue for an imputation on his goods. In *Jenner v A'Beckett*[77] the Queen's Bench allowed the statement that an item's name was 'very silly, very slangy and very vulgar' and had been 'forced on the public ad nauseam' to go to a jury as a libel. The words were held to be capable of casting an imputation of 'untradesmanlike'[78] behaviour against the maker of the item. Later courts refused to endorse the decision[79].

Jenner v A'Beckett might have gone too far, but subsequent cases shared its fundamental approach by simply applying the general rules of interpretation without regard to policy. Thus, for instance, in *The Empire Typesetting Machine Company of New York v The Linotype Company Limited*[80], where the defendant made allegations about the claimant's customers rejecting machines, Smith LJ stated that the publication was capable of being defamatory if 'a person of ordinary intelligence reading it might naturally come to the conclusion that [it] imputed to a trader either misconduct or want of care, or of qualification, or of skill in his business'[81]. Smith LJ went on to give a striking example: 'To falsely write of a trader that he sells or sets up worthless or unworkable wares is a libel upon the trader, for it imputes either carelessness or incapacity therein'[82]. If this was right, *Evans v Harlow*[83] was wrong. A majority of the Court of Appeal found that the publication was capable of being defamatory.

The House of Lords[84] confirmed that the question was merely one of interpretation. Lord Halsbury LC emphasised that the court must be astute in identifying a criticism of goods that also reflected on the seller. For instance:

> Could it be gravely argued that to say of a fishmonger that he was in the habit of selling decomposed fish would not be a libel upon him in the way of his trade? And, if so, would it not be a mere juggle with language to alter the form of that allegation and to say that all the fish in A's shop is decomposed?[85]

The most recent authority on the point reflects the tensions between a purely interpretive approach and one more concerned with policy. In *Drummond-Jackson v British Medical Association*[86] the claimant had devel-

[77] (1871) LR 7QB 11.
[78] *Ibid* at 13 (per Mellor J).
[79] *The Empire Typesetting Machine Company of New York v The Linotype Company Ltd* (1898) 79 LT 8 at 10; *Griffiths v Benn* (1911) 27 TLR 346 at 348.
[80] (1898) 79 LT 8; (1899) 81 LT 331.
[81] (1898) 79 LT 8 at 9.
[82] *Ibid.*
[83] (1844) 5 QB 624.
[84] (1899) 81 LT 331.
[85] *Ibid* at 333.
[86] [1970] 1 WLR 688.

oped a dental technique which was severely criticised in a scientific paper published by the defendant. The majority of the Court of Appeal adopted the interpretive approach, and considered that the words should be left to the jury since technique 'may be considered to be an essential part of [a claimant's] professional activity and of him as a professional man'[87]. Lord Denning MR dissented. At the forefront of his analysis he placed the issue of classification: was this case defamation or malicious falsehood? In his view it was the latter, because the publication was 'impersonal and objective'[88]. He also went on to make clear that the issue should not be controlled by interpretation:

> It may be that, in criticising the plaintiff's technique, they are casting some reflection on him. That cannot be helped. Every criticism of a technique tends to cast some reflection on those who practise it. But that does not give cause for a libel action.[89]

Today establishing defamation by association remains a matter of applying the general rules of interpretation: the general principles have been allowed to obscure more fundamental questions about policy and classification.

(b) Group defamation

Defamation directed against a group has been subject to distinct rules that modify the general principles of interpretation. Those rules can be divided conveniently into two categories: the first, where the group is incorporated, the second where it is not.

The right of a company to sue for defamation was first asserted unambiguously in *Metropolitan Saloon Omnibus Company (Limited) v Hawkins*[90]. There the claimant had asserted in his declaration that the libel had caused the company to be 'greatly damaged, injured and brought into public disgrace and contempt, and the value of the property of the Company and of the shares therein was depreciated'[91]. The defendant pleaded that he could not be sued as he was a shareholder. The claimant demurred to the plea.

The court agreed that the defendant's plea failed, but unfortunately the judgments did not give a consistent account of what was required for a successful claim by a company. Pollock CB analysed the position as follows:

[87] *Ibid* at 698 (per Lord Pearson).
[88] *Ibid* at 694.
[89] *Ibid* at 695.
[90] (1859) 4 H & N 87.
[91] *Ibid*.

> That a corporation at common law can sue in respect of a libel there is no doubt. It would be monstrous if a corporation could maintain no action for slander of title through which they lost a great deal of money. It could not sue in respect of an imputation of murder, or incest, or adultery, because it could not commit those crimes. Nor could it sue in respect of a charge of corruption, for a corporation cannot be guilty of corruption, although the individuals composing it may. But it would be very odd if a corporation had no means of protecting itself against wrong; and if its property is injured by slander it has no means of redress except by action. Therefore it appears to me clear that a corporation at common law may maintain an action for a libel by which its property is injured.[92]

This was a complex piece of reasoning in which several ideas were interacting. One idea was that a company could not sue for the allegation that it had committed an offence of which it was incapable in law. This was to prove a point of contention in the future. A further idea was that a company must be able to sue for slander of title which caused loss. Why this was relevant was not entirely clear: the defendant on the facts had not slandered the company's title, he had accused it of insolvency and mismanagement. Furthermore, the company had made no allegation of special damage; it had made only a very generalised claim of depreciation of property value. Yet another idea was that a company ought to be able to protect itself against wrongs. Out of these three ideas came the conclusion that 'a corporation may maintain an action for libel by which its property is injured'.

What exactly was meant by 'injury to property' was, therefore, left obscure. 'Injury' seems to have meant nothing more than loss—Pollock CB held that the claim as expressed in the declaration was valid, and the declaration had made no mention of property damage. 'Property' was more difficult. The reference to slander of goods, and the allusion in the declaration to a depreciation of property value seemed to suggest that some physical property owned by the company must be affected. On the other hand, it has been suggested that Pollock CB used 'the notion of property injury in order to embrace all actions other than those traditionally associated with natural persons only'[93]. Perhaps the most likely explanation is that Pollock CB had in mind a wide concept of corporate property, including intangible interests such as goodwill, that could be affected by slanders.

The other two members of the court took a less complex approach. Martin B expressed the view that a company could sue where a libel caused 'injury done to its trade'[94]. Watson B asserted that a partnership

[92] *Ibid* at 90.

[93] Patfield, 'The Origins of a Company's Right to Sue for Defamation' (1994) 45 *Northern Ireland Legal Quarterly* 233 at 238.

[94] (1859) 4 H & N 87 at 91.

could sue for 'all wrongs'[95] done to it, and that a corporation was in no worse position.

Although Pollock CB was the only member of the court to set out restrictions in relation to corporate capacity and injury to property, his judgment was very influential. For instance, in *The Mayor, Aldermen and Citizens of Manchester v Williams*[96] the Divisional Court invoked his requirement of injury to property when dismissing the claim[97]. However, the Divisional Court offered no explanation of what 'property' meant. The point was rendered irrelevant by the decision in *South Hetton Coal Company Ltd v North-Eastern News Association Ltd*[98], where the Court of Appeal held that a corporation could sue for libel reflecting on its business or causing it proven special damage. Despite this clarification, a sense seems to have remained that property damage was necessary. In *National Union of General and Municipal Workers v Gillian*[99], for instance, Birkett J considered it necessary to make a finding about injury to property (broadly construed) to found a claim by a trade union. When the case reached the Court of Appeal the point about property was firmly extinguished: 'The claim in the action is not a claim to property'[100]. Nevertheless, even as late as 1979 counsel sought to raise the question whether proof of injury to property was not a requirement for a successful libel claim by a trade union[101].

The other restriction set out by Pollock CB, relating to corporate capacity, was not so easily dealt with. The judgments in *South Hetton Coal Company Ltd v North-Eastern News Association Ltd*[102] revealed a variety of views. The strictest approach seems to have been taken by Lopes LJ, who insisted that:

> A corporation or company could not sue in respect of a charge of murder, or incest, or adultery, because it could not commit these crimes . . . The words complained of must attack the corporation or company in the method of conducting its affairs, must accuse it of fraud or mismanagement, or must attack its financial position.[103]

This strict approach was unconvincing. It implicitly assumed that what made an imputation of crime actionable was the fact that it exposed the claimant to the risk of prosecution and conviction. Whilst this may have been a correct assumption in the early seventeenth century, when the

[95] *Ibid* at 93.
[96] [1891] 1 QB 94.
[97] *Ibid* at 96.
[98] [1894] 1 QB 133.
[99] [1945] 2 All ER 593.
[100] [1946] KB 81 at 88 (per Uthwatt J).
[101] *Electrical, Electronic, Telecommunication and Plumbing Union v Times Newspapers Ltd* [1980] QB 585 at 594.
[102] [1894] 1 QB 133.
[103] *Ibid* at 141.

focus of the action for defamation was on the tendency of the words to cause loss[104], by 1893 it was false. By then it was settled that the tendency of the words to injure the claimant's reputation was the basis of the claim. Thus, for instance, it was actionable to say that a person had committed and been punished for a crime: there was no risk of prosecution, but the claimant's reputation was still affected[105].

Lord Esher MR took a different approach. Rather than imposing a restriction based on corporate capacity, he explained that the basic test was same, whether the claimant was a company or an individual, namely, 'did the publication tend in the minds of people of ordinary sense to bring the plaintiff into contempt, hatred or ridicule or to injure his character'[106]. Some imputations, he continued, might affect an individual's reputation but have no effect on a company's, such as an allegation of having no manners. On the other hand, an allegation about the conduct of business would affect both individual and corporate reputations. Kay LJ seemed to agree with Lord Esher MR, saying that a corporation could sue to protect its trading reputation[107].

As one commentator has cogently pointed out, the approach taken by Lord Esher MR resulted in far more allegations being actionable than under the strict approach of Lopes LJ. As she put it, 'it does not matter whether the company was capable of the act, but whether the ordinary person would believe it to be so'[108]. Thus allegations of corruption, whilst not actionable under the approach of Lopes LJ, could be sued on if Lord Esher's view prevailed. Even saying a company had no manners might be actionable: reasonable people might easily understand it to mean that the company breached business etiquette. Perhaps the true limit of actionable imputations was when the allegation could only be understood to relate to an individual—for instance, drunkenness, or infidelity to a spouse. Such allegations would not tend to lower the company's reputation because they would be incomprehensible.

Today a company's ability to sue is governed by the *South Hetton Coal* decision[109]. As with defamation by association, the courts essentially apply the general rules of interpretation. In contrast to the cases on defamation by association, however, the disappearance of special policy reasons from the company cases is not a cause for regret. 'Injury to property' was hopelessly vague; corporate capacity was inconsistent with

104 Helmholz, 'Damages in Actions for Slander at Common Law' (1987) 103 *LQR* 624 at 636.

105 *Fowler v Dowdney* (1838) 2 M & Rob 119.

106 [1894] 1 QB 133 at 137.

107 *Ibid* at 145.

108 Patfield, 'The Origins of a Company's Right to Sue for Defamation' (1994) 45 *Northern Ireland Legal Quarterly* 233 at 244.

109 *D & L Caterers Limited v D'Ajou* [1945] KB 364.

the basis for liability in defamation. Of course that is not to say that other policy restrictions might not be appropriate. It has been powerfully argued, for instance, that the degree of power and control that some companies exercise is equal to that of the state over its citizens; such corporations should therefore be subject to restrictions on its ability to sue for defamation similar to those imposed on government[110]. That, however, is a matter of future reform, not history.

(c) Unincorporated groups

Defamation of an unincorporated group is treated entirely differently from defamation of a company. No action lies at the suit of the group[111], so the only possible civil[112] remedy is by individual members' actions.

The seventeenth-century courts showed the same concern about certainty that had characterised their approach to general questions of interpretation. In *Foxcroft v Lacy*[113], for instance, where the defendant had said 'These defendants . . . helped to murther Henry Farrer', the court held that the action was properly brought. The claimant had explained in his declaration that he was one of sixteen defendants who were being sued for conspiracy by the defendant. In the court's view, every one of the sixteen could have sued for defamation 'as if they had been specially named'[114]. The allegation might, however, be such that no individual member was identified with certainty. Thus, it was said in *William Wiseman v Wiseman*[115] that the allegation 'my brother is perjured' would not be actionable if the defendant had several brothers, and there was no indication who was meant.

This focus on certainty seems to have relaxed in the eighteenth century. In *Harrison v Thornborough*[116], for example, the defendant was held liable for saying that either the claimant or another person had bribed a witness to give false evidence. Counsel for the defendant had argued that the words were too uncertain in their reference to the claimant, but the Court disagreed: for the words 'A or D . . .' 'either A or D might bring an action'[117]. In a slightly different context it was held that a libel on 'an East India director', of whom there were a total of twenty-four, could be

[110] Patfield, 'Defamation, Freedom of Speech and Corporations' [1993] *Juridical Review* 294.

[111] *Electrical, Electronic, Telecommunications and Plumbing Union v Times Newspapers Ltd* [1980] QB 585 at 595.

[112] Criminal remedies may be available if the requirements of the offence are satisfied. For libels against racial groups see Public Order Act 1986 ss 17–28.

[113] (1613) Hob 89.

[114] *Ibid.*

[115] (1605) Cro Jac 107.

[116] (1714) 10 Mod 196.

[117] *Ibid* at 198.

prosecuted as a libel on the East India Company[118]. The Court emphasised that the crucial issue was how readers would understand the words[119], and allowed that those readers might use sophisticated methods. As Probyn J put it, 'By the common rules of construction it is a libel upon the whole company, for by the figure metonymy the part stands for the whole'[120].

Restrictions on the ability of members of a group to sue for defamation seem to have emerged earlier more clearly in America than in England. In New York, for example, it was laid down as early as 1815 that 'A writing which inveighs against mankind in general, or against a particular order of men, is no libel, not is it even indictable'[121]. A similar declaration of principle was not to be found in England until 1857[122]. The dominant explanation for the restriction was that he words could not be taken to refer to the individual claimant. Thus, it was said that 'If a man wrote that all lawyers were thieves, no particular lawyer could sue him unless there is something to point to the particular individual'[123]. One American court offered a more elaborate analysis using the same basis:

> Where slanderous or libellous matter is published against a class or aggregate body of persons, an individual member, not specially included or designated, cannot maintain an action, for this, among other reasons, that the body may act very corruptly or disgracefully, yet the individual may have been in the minority, or may have been opposed to the measures alluded to.[124]

This was strikingly similar to the kind of reasoning that had been used by the seventeenth-century courts when they were on the lookout for uncertainty. Fundamentally the point seemed to be that reasonable people did not take generalisations literally.

This explanation based on interpretation was not, however, the only one advanced. It was also suggested that, unlike with a libel on an individual, malice against the claimant could not be presumed from publishing a libel on a group of which the claimant happened to be a member[125]. The Supreme Court of New York put forward another very different explanation[126]. Its starting point was that damage to the individual could not be presumed from a group libel, but it then went on to emphasise policy

118 *R v Jenour* (1740) 7 Mod 400.

119 *Ibid* at 401 (per Lee CJ) and 402 (per Probyn J).

120 *Ibid* at 402.

121 *Sumner v Buel* 12 Johns 475 at 2 (Supreme Court of New York, 1815) (Westlaw transcript).

122 *Eastwood v Holmes* (1857) 1 F & F 347 at 349.

123 *Ibid* at 349.

124 *Ellis v Kimball* 16 Pick 132 at 135 (Supreme Judicial Court of Massachusetts, 1834).

125 *Ryckman v Delavan* 25 Wend 186 at 7 (Court for the Correction of Errors of New York, 1840) (Westlaw transcript). See also *Eastwood v Holmes* (1857) 1 F & F 347 at 350, where Willes J gave as a reason for disallowing an action by a member of a defamed group that 'It does not appear that the defendant knew of [the claimant's] existence.'

126 *Sumner v Buel* 12 Johns 475 (Supreme Court of New York, 1815).

reasons. A group libel, in its view, was more appropriately dealt with by indictment as a criminal matter, and should only be actionable by individuals on proof of special damage. The Court drew an analogy with public nuisance, where only those individuals suffering special damage could sue, and concluded that justice to the defendant called for the same rule in libel: otherwise the 'multiplicity of suits' might bankrupt the defendant 'by the payment of costs'[127]. This was no longer a matter of interpretation, but one of classification.

The analogy with public nuisance seems not have been developed further, and the explanation based on malice became untenable once the presumption of malice was made irrebuttable[128]. That left the approach based on interpretation, which the courts continue to use today[129]. Inherent in this approach was the assumption that the court is merely asking whether a reasonable person would understand that the claimant was being referred to. It followed that an apparently general class might be understood as referring to a particular individual[130], and also that each and every member of a class might be referred to. The latter point was often seen as turning on the size of the group. As one American court put it, 'if the language employed is directed towards a comparatively small or restricted group of persons, then any member thereof may sue'[131]. The court went on to give the example of defamation of a jury, where each of the twelve members could sue. Recent English case law has confirmed that defamation of a group of twelve would entitle each member of the group to sue[132].

However, in the leading House of Lords case on the point[133], Lord Porter (with whom Lord Atkin and Lord Thankerton agreed) asserted that the size of the class defamed was not the sole determining factor: other relevant matters were 'the generality of the charge and the extravagance of the accusation'[134]. He even envisaged a situation where the size of the defamed class would be irrelevant: 'I can imagine it being said that each member of a body, however, large, was defamed where the libel consisted in the assertion that no one of the members of a community was elected as a member unless he had committed a murder'[135]. In the range of potential

[127] *Ibid* at 3. Contrast the current English approach to public nuisance, which focuses on whether it is reasonable to expect an individual to take proceedings on his own responsibility: *Attorney-General v PYA Quarries Ltd* [1957] 2 QB 169 at 191 (per Denning LJ).

[128] *Knuppfer v London Express Newspapers Ltd* [1943] KB 80 at 89 (per Goddard LJ). The presumption of malice is analysed in ch 5, below.

[129] *Knuppfer v London Express Newspapers Ltd* [1944] AC 116.

[130] *Le Fanu v Malcolmson* (1848) 1 HLC 637.

[131] *Ewell v Boutwell* 121 SE 912 at 914 (Supreme Court of Appeals of Virginia, 1924).

[132] *Riches v News Group Newspapers Ltd* [1986] QB 256.

[133] *Knuppfer v London Express Newspapers Ltd* [1944] AC 116.

[134] *Ibid* at 124.

[135] *Ibid.*

factors to be considered, this approach was strongly reminiscent of the seventeenth century cases.

Whilst the House of Lords insisted that the issue was regulated solely by application of the general rules of interpretation[136], what the courts actually do appears more complex. According to the Lords' own criteria the gravity of the accusation was relevant, yet on the strict application of the rules of interpretation that would cast no light on who was referred to. Furthermore, the cases showed a policy against actions for generalisations on the basis that generalisations are not taken seriously. Lord Atkin, for instance, referred to 'unfounded generalisations' being 'occasionally intended to be a facetious exaggeration'[137]. A Scottish court dealing with the same point[138] dismissed a series of generalisations about publicans as 'silly'[139]. On the other hand, Lord Porter's analysis seemed to acknowledge that some generalisations might well cause harm. As one earlier American commentator had observed: 'The unflinching adherence to an iron-clad presumption that there is no possibility of accrual of private damages in cases of class defamation is to argue from a premise from which there is no warrant in fact'[140].

The House of Lords' position, however, was not simply based on whether the words could be presumed to cause damage. It was even more complex than that, as their application of the principles to the facts showed. The claimant was the representative of the Young Russia Party, which the defendant had accused in 1941 of assisting Hitler. There were twenty-four Party members in Britain. It is difficult to think of a more serious accusation than assisting the enemy in wartime, the class was small, and the claimant called witnesses to show that they thought of him when they read the libel. On the face of it, he satisfied all the requirements for a successful claim, but he lost. Some further factor was in play. Perhaps the court sensed that the claimant had sued for political purposes, in order to draw publicity to his Party, rather than to redress any injury to his personal reputation. The action might have been seen as an inappropriate use of the legal process[141]. Or perhaps it was thought that criticisms of political parties should be uninhibited for policy reasons[142].

[136] *Ibid* at 121 (per Lord Atkin).

[137] *Ibid* at 122.

[138] *Wardlaw v Drysdale* (1898) 25 R 879.

[139] *Ibid* at 882.

[140] Wilner, 'The Civil Liability Aspects of Defamation Directed Against a Collectivity' (1941–42) 90 *University of Pennsylvania Law Review* 414 at 425.

[141] The Nazis' rise to power in Germany had been helped by a clever manipulation of the law of defamation, both as claimant and defendant: see Riesman, 'Democracy and Defamation: Fair Game and Fair Comment I' (1942) 42 *Columbia Law Review* 1085, particularly at 1092–1100.

[142] Such policy reasons were recently made explicit in *Goldsmith v Bhoyrul* [1997] 4 All ER 268.

Whatever the real reasons for the decision, the key point is that asserting that it is all a matter of interpretation is unhelpful. Important and relevant policy factors are obscured, and one can only guess at what weight they had. A more satisfactory and informative approach would be to make explicit what policy factors are at work and why. In the present state of the law of group defamation the emphasis on the general principles of interpretation is misplaced and misleading.

3. CONCLUSION

Interpreting defamatory language is more difficult than it looks. The seventeenth-century courts acknowledged the complexity, and brought a range of techniques to bear on the question, articulating concerns about certainty, the tendency of words to cause loss, and the degree of malice involved. Their decisions on lack of certainty in pleadings may now appear over-zealous, although not out of line with contemporary strictness in matters of form; but on matters of substance their reasoning was sophisticated and clear.

The reasonable reader test, by contrast, was deceptively simple, and the kind of criterion that no one could criticise. In essence, it said that the words meant in law what ordinary people would take them to mean. That was superficially attractive, but ultimately vacuous. For there may well have been no consensus as to meaning, and even if there was, the courts made no attempt to find reasonable readers and ask them what they thought.

The truth is that interpretation and policy cannot be neatly separated, in the way that the reasonable reader test implies. In determining the meaning of a particular statement the courts should be mindful that the question is not merely 'What does this mean?', but 'Ought the defendant to be responsible for this meaning?'. In cases concerning imputations against inanimate objects the policy reasons are even clearer: should the claimant be able to take advantage of the presumptions of malice and damage in defamation, or be forced to prove both in an action for malicious falsehood? Group defamation cases raise similar policy questions about classification as between the criminal law and the civil law. They may also raise further questions about the political manipulation of the courts, as happened in the leading House of Lords case. These are all difficult questions of policy that call for direct analysis. It is no answer to say that we must leave it all to our imaginary friend, the reasonable reader.

3

Damages

DAMAGES, THE PRIMARY remedy for defamation, are generally[1] presumed from proof that the defamatory language was published. They have been the focus of much modern case law, but their history is less complicated than any of the other aspects of defamation because damage was traditionally a question of fact, and was left to the jury. The jury gave no reasons for its decision, so there was little scope for the development of legal ideas surrounding damages. The history of the law of damages for defamation is, therefore, a history of what a jury could be told and how its verdict could be overturned on appeal. This chapter considers these questions in relation to basic compensation, factors increasing damages, and factors reducing them.

1. BASIC COMPENSATION

When the common law courts first started to hear actions for defamation in the 1520s[2], they offered claimants one major attraction: money. The ecclesiastical courts, which had dealt with defamation since the thirteenth century, could not award damages to the claimant. The common law option became increasingly popular until, by the end of the sixteenth century, the judges started to worry that too many cases were being brought[3]. Perhaps one of the most powerful reasons for the success of the action on the case for defamation was that the claimant did not generally have to prove the loss he had suffered. Certain categories of words were seen as having a 'tendency' to cause loss: proof that such words had been spoken raised a presumption that loss had been suffered, and the case was then left to the jury for them to ascertain the amount of that loss. The action on the case for words, therefore, contained very little law on the assessment of damages.

Leaving the question to the jury in this way may initially appear unstructured and unsatisfactory, especially to a modern lawyer. However,

[1] For details of when slander is not actionable without proof of damage, see ch 1, above.
[2] See generally Helmholz (ed), 'Select Cases on Defamation to 1600' (1985) 101 *Selden Society*.
[3] *Stanhope v Blith* (1585) 4 Co Rep 15a.

the system was in fact very well suited to the needs of the parties, because the jury was not presumed to be ignorant of everything that had taken place outside the court-room. The opposite was true: it was presumed to know. Since trials at first instance (*nisi prius*) would usually take place where the claimant lived it was in fact perfectly sensible to assume that twelve jurors from that place would know what effect the words spoken had had on the claimant's reputation.

So juries provided a good method of assessing damages. But they were not infallible. When they awarded spectacularly too much the common law courts intervened[4]. They would hear a motion in arrest of judgment on the ground of excessive damages, and refuse to enter judgment for the claimant until he agreed to accept a more reasonable sum. Given the judges' concern that there were too many actions for defamation, it was not surprising to find them reducing damages awards that suggested that slander actions were a way to make money. Significantly, there was no interference with excessively small awards.

After 1622 the courts seem to have abandoned the technique of refusing to enter judgment until a more reasonable sum was agreed. Helmholz[5] suggests that the explanation for this lay in the way that the action for slander was developing. Actions were no longer confined to the standard imputations of criminal offences, but were starting to include matters not otherwise actionable which had caused proven actual damage. Whilst judges might consider themselves as capable of assessing the 'tendency' of words as a jury, they were at a disadvantage when it came to actual damage, for that required some local knowledge. Whatever the true explanation, the effect of the courts' change of policy was clear: the jury's unfettered assessment was final.

Once the courts had abandoned interfering with the jury's award on the ground that it was excessive, a different approach to overturning jury awards was needed. From the start of the eighteenth century the courts started to order new trials in defamation on the ground of excessive damages, but the basis for doing so was very different to the previous technique. Now the rationale was not that the jury were wrong; rather, it was said that the amount showed that the jury could not have performed its role properly. In the language of one mid-seventeenth century case, the appellate court generally granted new trials for 'miscarriages of juries'[6]. When applied to defamation damages, this kind of test acknowledged that damages were for the jury alone. The court's interference was justified only 'to protect the party against the hardly possible existence of violence or corruption'[7].

[4] Helmholz, 'Damages in Actions for Slander at Common Law' (1987) 103 *LQR* 624.
[5] *Ibid* at 636–37.
[6] *Wood v Gunston* (1655) Style 466.
[7] *Clark v Binney* 19 Mass 113 at 114 (Supreme Judicial Court of Massachusetts, 1824).

Various forms of words were used in the course of the eighteenth and nineteenth centuries to describe the situation where a jury's award of damages demonstrated that it had not performed its task correctly. In *Praed v Graham*[8] two tests were given particular prominence. The first was that 'if . . . the Court thinks that, having regard to all the circumstances of the case, the damages are so excessive that no twelve men could reasonably have given them, then they ought to interfere with the verdict'[9]. The second, regarded by Lord Esher MR as 'equivalent'[10], was that a new trial should be awarded on the ground of excessive damages where the amount was 'such that no reasonable proportion exists between it and the circumstances of the case'[11].

These principles for overturning jury awards were, as one court put it, 'easy of enunciation, but most difficult of application'[12]. Two related factors contributed to the difficulty. First, damages were presumed to flow from the publication of the defamatory words; there was no need for a claimant to produce any evidence of loss. The jury were therefore required to guess what sum would compensate the claimant for injured feelings and harm to reputation using their own common sense. It was hard to say that they had guessed wrong. As Lord Atkin colourfully put it, 'It is impossible to track the scandal, to know what quarters the poison may reach: it is impossible to weigh at all closely the compensation which will recompense a man or a woman for the insult offered or the pain of a false accusation'[13]. Perhaps the most striking example of the Court of Appeal's reluctance to say that the jury had gone wrong can be seen in *Youssoupoff v Metro-Goldwyn-Mayer Pictures, Limited*[14]. There the claimant had been portrayed in a film as having been either ravished or raped by Rasputin. The jury awarded £25,000, the equivalent of over £1 million today[15]. Later courts have been shocked by the amount[16], but the Court of Appeal did not feel that it could intervene. As Greer LJ put it,

> the damages are very large for a lady who lives in Paris, and who has not lost, so far as we know, a single friend and who has not been able to show that her reputation has in any way suffered . . . [but] It is very difficult to put a money value upon the mental pain and suffering that were undergone.[17]

[8] (1889) 24 QBD 53.
[9] *Ibid* at 55.
[10] *Ibid.*
[11] *M'Grath v Bourne* 10 Ir Rep CL (Ex) 160.
[12] *Harris v Arnott* (1890) 26 LR (Ir) 55 at 65.
[13] *Ley v Hamilton* (1935) 153 LT 384 at 386.
[14] (1934) 50 TLR 581.
[15] Kenyon, 'Problems with Defamation Damages?' (1998) 24 *Monash University Law Review* 70 at 71.
[16] Eg, *Broome v Cassell & Co Ltd* [1971] 2 QB 354 at 394, commenting that the award exceeded £100,000 at 1971 values; *Sutcliffe v Pressdram Ltd* [1991] 1 QB 153 at 186—£900,000 at 1989 values.
[17] (1934) 50 TLR 581 at 586.

The second, related difficulty in applying the excessive damages test was that each court was on its own. The assessment of damages took into account all the circumstances of the case—the gravity of the defamation, its range of publication, the claimant's position, the defendant's conduct, etc—so awards in other cases were of no assistance. As one judge put it, 'cases are of little or no value in reference to the question of amount, as distinguished from that of principle. Each case must depend emphatically upon its own peculiar circumstances'[18].

The Court of Appeal's decision in *Youssoupoff v Metro-Goldwyn-Mayer Pictures, Limited*[19] was the high-water mark of judicial deference to jury damages awards in defamation. Later developments, culminating in a flurry of activity around 1990, were to erode the jury's freedom and power to award whatever sum it thought fit. The courts in those later cases put forward reasons specific to the law of defamation to justify their change of policy. Those reasons are dealt with further below. First, however, it is useful to consider the general background developments in relation to awards of damages by juries. These developments can be seen as clearing the way for a more sceptical attitude to defamation jury awards, and also as suggesting what limiting techniques could be employed.

Defamation was not unusual in leaving questions of fact (including damages) to a jury. In the common law courts until 1854 trial by jury was the rule. Quite simply, there was no other procedure available. In 1854 the Common Law Procedure Act introduced provisions for trial by judge if the parties consented, but the fundamental principle of trial by jury remained. The Judicature Acts 1873–1875 and Rules made under them altered the presumption—the default position came to be trial by judge—but gave either party the option to have a trial by jury. In effect they made no change of substance. The major change of substance came with the Juries Act 1918 where, in order to relieve the strain on the jury system during wartime, the right to jury trial was limited to certain causes of action (including defamation). For all other causes of action there could be trial by jury only if a judge ruled that it was more convenient for the case to be tried by jury than by judge alone.

The Juries Act 1918 was only a temporary measure. But it was evidently a success, because in 1920 the legislature effectively re-enacted it[20], causing some judicial consternation[21]. In 1933, the year before the decision in *Youssoupoff*, Parliament enacted the Administration of Justice (Miscellaneous Provisions) Act. Section 6 provided that:

[18] *Harris v Arnott* (1890) 26 LR (Ir) 55 at 67–68 (per Palles CB).
[19] (1934) 50 TLR 581.
[20] Administration of Justice Act 1920 s 2.
[21] *Blurton v Ford* (1922) 38 TLR 801.

(1) . . . if, on the application of any party to an action to be tried in the [Queen's] Bench Division of the High Court . . . the court or a judge is satisfied that—(a) a charge of fraud against that party; or (b) a claim in respect of libel, slander, malicious prosecution, false imprisonment, seduction or breach of promise of marriage, is in issue, the action shall be ordered to be tried with a jury unless the court or judge is of opinion that the trial thereof requires any prolonged examination of documents or accounts or any scientific or local investment which cannot conveniently be made with a jury; but, save as aforesaid, any action to be tried in that Division may, in the discretion of the court or a judge, be ordered to be tried either with or without a jury;

The juxtaposition of *Youssoupoff v Metro-Goldwyn-Mayer Pictures, Limited*[22] and this statutory provision is striking. Clearly defamation, along with a small number of other claims, was a special case. For all other causes of action, however, the benefits of trial by jury were not persuasive enough to call for a general rule. On the advantages of trial by jury, the jury was still out.

As a result of the legislation from 1918 onwards, similar cases could be tried by different methods. Differences in result became particularly noticeable in assessments of general damages for personal injury. These awards had not previously been reported, but in 1947 reports started to appear in *Current Law*. In 1954 the first edition of Kemp and Kemp's *The Quantum of Damages in Personal Injury Claims* was published, responding to the Court of Appeal's earlier indication that similar cases of personal injury damages could be cited to it[23]. As a reviewer of Kemp and Kemp put it, in assessing general damages,

Assistance can only be derived from the amounts awarded in similar cases. The difficulty hitherto has been to discover such cases; and the authors have earned the gratitude of the profession by their labours in compiling a body of cases—many of them unreported (or like *Paris v Stepney London Borough Council* [1951] AC 367, reported only on the question of liability)—which deal with the assessment of damages for personal injuries.[24]

Initially the Court of Appeal was not disturbed by the evidence that judges and juries awarded different amounts for similar injuries. Thus, in *Bocock v Enfield Rolling Mills Ld*[25] Singleton LJ, with whom Morris and Denning LJJ agreed, said:

it has been said more than once that a judge sitting by himself is not in as good a position to assess damages as are twelve members of a jury. They have an opportunity of discussing the matter among themselves, and though they may not have great experience in the matter, twelve heads should be better than one.[26]

22 (1934) 50 TLR 581.
23 *Bird v Cocking & Son Ltd* [1951] 2 TLR 1260.
24 Ellenbogen (1955) 18 *MLR* 642.
25 [1954] 1 WLR 1303.
26 *Ibid* at 1305.

His view seemed to be that the choice whether to have trial by jury was simply another hazard of litigation: 'if a party chooses to have a jury, he ought to be bound by the assessment of the jury of the damages'[27].

In *Scott v Musial*[28] Morris LJ developed a slightly different approach, that also seemed to favour jury awards over those of judges. He acknowledged that awards of general damages made by judges often conformed to a pattern, but 'if . . . an award of a jury does not seem to conform to such pattern, that is not to prove that the jury is necessarily wrong. The views of juries may form a valuable corrective to the views of judges.'[29]

The third member of the Court of Appeal in *Bocock*'s case[30], Lord Denning MR, went on to reverse its policy entirely. In *Ward v James*[31] the full Court of Appeal held that personal injury cases should not normally be tried by jury. Jury awards were too random and unpredictable to be suitable. As Lord Denning MR put it, a continuing lack of uniformity in awards would cause 'great dissatisfaction in the community, and much criticism of the administration of justice'[32]. Judicial awards, on the other hand, were uniform and predictable, because standard amounts were awarded for each type of injury. Lord Denning MR explained the judicial approach as follows:

> No money can compensate for the loss. Yet compensation has to be given in money. The problem is insoluble. To meet it, the judges have evolved a conventional measure. They go by their experience in comparable cases.[33]

Central to this judicial approach was the ability to find out what the conventional measure was. It would have been impossible without reports of quantum decisions. Counsel, in the course of argument, put it succinctly:

> Criticism has developed since the publication of awards of damages by Current Law since 1947 and Kemp and Kemp on Damages since 1954. It would be startling to think that those publications were to have the effect of abolishing trial by jury in personal injuries actions.[34]

It may have startled counsel, but it did not worry the Court of Appeal.

Of course the availability of quantum reports did not necessarily mean that the decision had to be made by a judge. In theory a jury could be referred to such reports and thereby ascertain the appropriate figure. However, the Court of Appeal made it clear that in practice this was a bad idea. Counsel for each party would refer the jury to various authorities,

27 *Ibid* at 1306.
28 [1959] 2 QB 429.
29 *Ibid* at 438.
30 [1954] 1 WLR 1303.
31 [1966] 1 QB 273.
32 *Ibid* at 300.
33 *Ibid* at 296.
34 *Ibid* at 287.

and make analogies to the facts of the case before them; counsel would also attack and criticise each other's analogies. 'The inevitable result would be that the minds of the jury would be distracted from the instant case and left in confusion'[35].

What is particularly striking about the Court of Appeal's approach in *Ward v James*[36] is the method it identifies for assessing general damages. It is no longer a question of picking a figure that seems appropriate to the immediate case. Instead there is a concern with consistency in awards—a dimension of distributive justice. Perhaps most importantly the method of assessment required an exercise of legal reasoning in making analogies with, and distinctions from, earlier case law. Damages might still technically be a question of fact[37], but in practice they had taken on the techniques associated with a question of law.

The ambivalence to jury awards encapsulated by the decisions in *Youssoupoff*[38] and *Ward*[39] set the tone for further judicial exploration of the jury's role in defamation awards. The key points of contention were, first, what was required for an appellate court to overturn a jury's verdict and, second, how much guidance the jury could be given at the trial.

The test for setting aside a jury's award changed in the late twentieth century. In place of asking whether twelve reasonable people could have come to the amount awarded, the test is now 'Could a reasonable jury have thought that this award was necessary to compensate the plaintiff and re-establish his reputation?'[40]. The change was prompted by the European Convention on Human Rights (ECHR), Article 10, which requires restrictions on freedom of speech to be necessary in a democratic society and proportionate. The Court of Appeal noted that this new test 'lowered' the 'barrier against intervention'[41].

In relation to guidance, the tendency has been to give the jury ever more instructions. Some of that guidance is difficult to criticise. For instance, a jury may be told to consider how much income their award would yield if invested as a lump sum[42]. They may also be told to think of what their award would buy in general terms, such as a car or a house[43]. Perhaps more controversially, a jury may be referred to other damages awards[44]. However, not all damages awards are relevant. Under the Courts and

35 *Ibid* at 302.
36 [1966] 1 QB 273.
37 *Bocock v Enfield Rolling Mills Ld* [1954] 1 WLR 1303 at 1305.
38 (1934) 50 TLR 581.
39 [1966] 1 QB 273.
40 *Rantzen v Mirror Group Newspapers (1986) Ltd* [1994] QB 670 at 692.
41 *Ibid*.
42 *McCarey v Associated Newspapers Ltd* [1965] 2 QB 86; *Sutcliffe v Pressdram Ltd* [1991] 1 QB 153.
43 *Gorman v Mudd*, Court of Appeal (Civil Division) 15 October 1992.
44 *Rantzen v Mirror Group Newspapers (1986) Ltd* [1994] QB 670.

Legal Services Act 1990 s 8(1) the Court of Appeal was given power to set aside excessive awards of jury damages, and by s 8(2) to substitute its own figure. Only awards substituted or approved by the Court of Appeal can be referred to.

The explanation for referring the jury to these awards was twofold. First, it was deduced from the wording of the statute: 'it must have been the intention of the framers of the Act of 1990 that over a period of time the awards made by the Court of Appeal would provide a corpus to which reference could be made in subsequent cases'[45]. As the phrase 'must have been' suggested, there was no explicit reference in the Act to a corpus of awards. Second, it was thought that preventing reference to such awards might contravene the ECHR, Article 10, which requires any restriction on freedom of expression to be, inter alia, 'prescribed by law'. This phrase has been interpreted as meaning that legal rules must be laid down with sufficient certainty to allow a citizen to regulate his own conduct with a reasonable foresight of the legal consequences[46]. In any event, the decision to refer a jury to other awards introduces those elements of legal reasoning by analogy and distinction that the Court of Appeal in *Ward v James*[47] had thought were so unsuitable for juries. Indeed, it may even be harder to draw appropriate analogies and distinctions in defamation than it is in personal injury[48]. Certainly it is difficult to imagine a jury engaging in the mathematical comparisons of awards undertaken in one recent Court of Appeal case[49].

The most controversial development has been the decision to refer juries to awards of general damages in personal injury cases. The idea had first been floated by Diplock LJ in *McCarey v Associated Newspapers Ltd*[50] when, partly anticipating what was to be said a year later in *Ward v James*[51], he said:

> justice is not justice if it is arbitrary or whimsical, if what is awarded to one plaintiff for an injury bears no relation at all to what is awarded to another plaintiff for an injury of the same kind, or, I would add, if what is awarded for one kind of injury shows a wrong scale of values when compared with what is awarded for injuries of a different kind which are also incommensurable with pounds, shillings and pence.[52]

He could not believe that the law 'was more jealous of a man's reputation than of his life or limb. That is the scale of values of the duel'[53].

45 *Rantzen v Mirror Group Newspapers (1986) Ltd* [1994] QB 670 at 694.
46 *The Sunday Times v United Kingdom (No 2)* (1991) 14 EHRR 229.
47 [1966] 1 QB 273.
48 *Kiam v Neil (No 2)* [1996] EMLR 493 at 516 (per Pill LJ).
49 *Jones v Pollard* [1997] EMLR 233.
50 [1965] 2 QB 86.
51 [1966] 1 QB 273.
52 [1965] 2 QB 86 at 108.
53 *Ibid* at 109.

This suggestion of Diplock LJ was not well received. In *Cassell & Co Ltd v Broome*[54] the House of Lords seemed to reject it when Lord Hailsham LC said that because defamation damages should contain an element of vindication it was 'not necessarily fair'[55] to compare them with personal injury awards. The Court of Appeal in *Sutcliffe v Pressdram Ltd*[56] was more direct, identifying two reasons to reject reference to personal injury awards. First, whilst personal injury damages were for pain and suffering, libel damages were for pain, suffering, aggravation and vindication[57]. The Court might also have added that defamation damages contained an element of presumed actual damage lacking in personal injury awards[58]. Second, conventional awards for personal injury reflected the views of judges. A jury might think those awards were inadequate, and should be free to give their 'gut reaction'[59]. This second reason bore a close resemblance to the analysis of the Court of Appeal in *Bocock v Enfield Rolling Mills Ld*[60] and Morris LJ in *Scott v Musial*[61].

Ultimately, however, the arguments for consistency across the whole range of tort awards succeeded. In *John v MGN Ltd*[62] the Court of Appeal went back on its earlier pronouncement, and held that reference could be made to personal injury awards. As in *Ward v James*[63] there was a concern about public perceptions:

> It is in our view offensive to public opinion, and rightly so, that a defamation plaintiff should recover damages for injury to reputation greater, perhaps by a significant factor, than if that same plaintiff had been rendered a helpless cripple or an insensate vegetable.[64]

The Court of Appeal was, however, careful to limit the use that could be made of personal injury figures. It acknowledged that the precise basis of libel and personal injury awards were different, saying 'it is one thing to say (and we agree) that there can be no precise equiparation between a serious libel and (say) serious brain damage'. 'But', it continued, 'it is another to point out to a jury considering the award of damages for a serious libel that the maximum conventional award for pain and suffering and loss of amenity to a plaintiff suffering from very severe brain damage

54 [1972] AC 1027.
55 *Ibid* at 1071.
56 [1991] 1 QB 153.
57 *Ibid* at 175.
58 Kenyon, 'Problems with Defamation Damages?' (1998) 24 *Monash University Law Review* 70 at 72.
59 [1991] 1 QB 153 at 175.
60 [1954] 1 WLR 1303.
61 [1959] 2 QB 429.
62 [1997] QB 586.
63 [1966] 1 QB 273.
64 [1997] QB 586 at 614.

is about £125,000 and that this is something of which the jury may take account'[65].

Later cases have been cautious about tying personal injury awards to defamation cases. Thus, for instance, in *Jones v Pollard*[66] the Court of Appeal rejected the submission that it followed from *John v MGN Ltd*[67] that the most serious libels should receive the same amount of damages as the most serious personal injuries. The Court made clear that, 'save possibly in the most exceptional case'[68] the most severe damage to reputation was not comparable with injuries like quadriplegia and total blindness. Personal injury damages were there simply to 'to maintain a sense of proportion'[69].

The same arguments that had been used in personal injury cases to justify reference to other awards were now being used to justify reference to personal injury awards in defamation. Only the final step in the analysis—that juries were unfit to carry out the legal reasoning required—remains to be taken.

2. FACTORS INCREASING DAMAGES

Damages are generally presumed from the publication of defamatory words, but that presumed damage does not limit the extent of recovery. A claimant may prove that he has also suffered some specific loss as a result of the defamatory publication, and recover for that loss. This is known as recovering 'special damage'.

The law on recovery of special damage has developed very little, and there still remains considerable uncertainty over fundamental points. For instance, what actually counts as special damage has never been definitively clarified. In *Roberts v Roberts*[70] Cockburn CJ appeared to give a broad test, saying that 'anything substantial'[71] counted as special damage. But that apparent generosity has to be seen against the decision on the facts, where the court held that loss of membership of a religious society did not amount to special damage. The focus on 'substantial' damage also led to a distinction being drawn between loss of friends, which was not recoverable, and loss of hospitality, which was, since other people's hospitality provided a saving on food and drink[72]. One of the most intriguing,

65 *Ibid*.
66 [1997] EMLR 233.
67 [1997] QB 586.
68 [1997] EMLR 233 at 257.
69 *Ibid*.
70 (1864) 5 B & S 384.
71 *Ibid* at 389.
72 *Davies v Solomon* (1871) LR 7 QB 112.

and unresolved, questions about special damage is whether the availability of an alternative legal claim to remedy the loss prevents it being claimed as special damage in defamation. The point was raised in *Vicars v Wilcocks*[73], where the claimant proved that his employer had discharged him as a consequence of hearing the defamatory words. At the trial Lawrence J nonsuited the claimant, saying that:

> the supposed special damage was the loss of those advantages which the plaintiff was entitled to under his contract with his master; which he could not in law be considered as having lost, as he still had a right to claim them of his master.[74]

The nonsuit was upheld on different grounds by the Court of King's Bench.

The analysis used by Lawrence J raised very difficult questions. On the one hand it seemed unfair to allow the defendant to force the claimant into bringing further proceedings against someone else. On the other hand, definitions of detriment often included some legal element—in contract, for instance, the doctrine of consideration was subject to the requirement that the benefit or detriment be recognised by law.

The Court of King's Bench in *Vicars v Wilcocks*[75] focused on causation rather than on the definition of special damage. In its view special damage had to be the 'legal and natural consequence'[76] of the words; the employer's decision to dismiss the claimant was 'an illegal consequence'[77]. It was, said Lord Ellenborough CJ, the same as if after the words had been spoken a crowd had gathered, and thrown the claimant 'into a horsepond by way of punishment'[78].

Later cases suggested that the test for causation set out in *Vicars v Wilcocks*[79] was too stringent. In *Knight v Gibbs*[80], for instance, Lord Denman CJ said that 'the proper question' was, simply 'whether the injury was sustained in consequence of the slanderous words having been used by the defendant'[81]. In *Lynch v Knight*[82] Lord Wensleydale went further, expressing the view that the rules set out in *Vicars v Wilcocks*[83] were 'too restricted'[84]; in his opinion there would have been liability in Lord Ellenborough's example about the horsepond. The House of Lords agreed

73 (1806) 8 East 1.
74 *Ibid* at 2–3.
75 (1806) 8 East 1.
76 *Ibid*, at 3.
77 *Ibid*.
78 *Ibid*.
79 (1806) 8 East 1.
80 (1834) 1 Ad & E 43.
81 *Ibid* at 45.
82 (1861) 9 HLC 577.
83 (1806) 8 East 1.
84 (1861) 9 HLC 577 at 600.

that the test was simply whether the loss was a natural consequence of the defamation[85].

Other factors, not so precisely quantified as special damage, could also be taken into account to increase damages. To put it broadly, the entire circumstances of publication and conduct of the defendant could be considered. This was not a rule unique to defamation. Thus, for instance, in *Huckle v Money*[86] the Court held that 'in cases of criminal conversation, battery, imprisonment, slander, malicious prosecutions, &c. the state, degree, quality, trade or profession of the party injured, as well as of the person who did the injury, must be, and generally are, considered by a jury in giving damages'[87]. As Lord Esher MR later put it, the jury was 'entitled to look at the whole conduct of the defendant from the time the libel was published down to the time they give their verdict'[88]. This test embraced the way that the litigation was conducted. For instance, persisting in a plea of justification but then offering no evidence was a ground for increasing damages[89]; so was aggressively cross-examining the claimant, then offering no evidence[90]. Presumably a bona fide attempt by the defendant to exercise his right of defence was not a ground for increasing damages, although the authority to support that proposition had to be sought in Australia[91].

Also relevant was the defendant's motive. Malice made it worse. Thus in *Pearson v Lemaitre*[92] it was said that:

> this appears to us to be the correct rule, viz that either party may, with a view to the damages, give evidence to prove or disprove the existence of a malicious in the mind of the publisher of defamatory matter.[93]

In other words, 'we think that the spirit and intention of the party publishing a libel, are fit to be considered by a jury, in estimating the injury done to the plaintiff'[94].

Given later developments, when the award of increased damages for a defendant's malicious motive were eliminated[95], two points should be made about the nineteenth-century case law. First, there is never any attempt to limit the increase in damages to reflect the extent to which the claimant was upset by the defendant's conduct. Second, when the courts

85 (1861) 9 HLC 577, at 591 (Lord Campbell LC and Lord Brougham), 595 (Lord Cranworth) and 600 (Lord Wensleydale).
86 (1763) 2 Wils 205.
87 *Ibid* at 206.
88 *Praed v Graham* (1889) 24 QBD 53 at 55.
89 *Simpson v Robinson* (1848) 18 LJQB(ns) 73.
90 *Sutcliffe v Pressdram Ltd* [1991] 1 QB 153.
91 Samuels, 'Problems of Assessing Damages for Defamation' (1963) 79 *LQR* 63 at 74–75.
92 (1843) 5 M & G 700.
93 *Ibid* at 719–20.
94 *Ibid* at 720.
95 *Rookes v Barnard* [1964] AC 1129.

say that the defendant's conduct, including his motive, was relevant to damages there is no suggestion that this was controversial, or a special rule for defamation. Examples of the defendant's motive increasing damages could be found in cases of trespass[96], false imprisonment[97] and negligence[98], to name but three. Thus Winfield, in the first edition of his textbook could write the following in his general chapter on remedies:

> In contemptuous damages we have seen that the Court can take into account the plaintiff's moral conduct. In exemplary damages it can punish the defendant for misbehaviour. These represent the jury's indignation at an especially outrageous attack on the plaintiff's security, or at wanton misconduct on the defendant's part.[99]

Nevertheless, to a modern lawyer the relevance of malice to damages may not be obvious. Clearly if the claimant knows of the malice his feelings may be more hurt than if he does not know of it, but the nineteenth-century case law imposed no such restriction. Furthermore, it is difficult to see how damage to the claimant's reputation would be affected by the motive of the defendant. Surely the damage was the same whatever the reasons for publishing.

The explanation lies in an approach to compensation different to the one we are familiar with today. The current approach is, broadly, to focus on correcting loss; the approach that can be seen in the late eighteenth and early nineteenth centuries, by contrast, awarded damages for loss *and* to mark the fact that the claimant had suffered a wrong. 'Injury', to use the word employed in *Pearson v Lemaitre*[100], was not a synonym for loss. It was both the wrong and its consequences.

Two early nineteenth-century cases can be used to illustrate this point. In the first[101] the defendant deliberately scattered poisoned barley on the claimant's land in order to kill the claimant's poultry. Abbott J is reported to have directed the jury in the following terms:

> It had always been, that for trespass and entry into the house or lands of the plaintiff, a jury might consider not only the mere pecuniary damage sustained by the plaintiff, but also the intention with which the fact had been done, whether for insult or injury, and he said, that they were not confined in this case, to the mere damage resulting from throwing poisoned barley on the land of the plaintiff, but might also consider the object with which it was thrown[102].

96 *Williams v Currie* (1845) 1 CB 841.
97 *Clark v Newsam* (1847) 1 Ex 131.
98 *Emblen v Myers* (1860) 6 H & N 54.
99 Winfield, *A Text-Book of the Law of Tort* (London, 1937) at 153.
100 (1843) 5 M & G 700.
101 *Sears v Lyons* (1818) 2 Stark 317.
102 *Ibid* at 318.

The second case[103] underlines that there was no restriction limiting damages to injured feelings. The claimant was shooting on his own estate when the defendant, 'a banker, a magistrate and a member of parliament, who had dined and drank freely'[104] drove past in his carriage and insisted on joining in. When the claimant refused, the defendant 'used very intemperate language, threatening, in his capacity of a magistrate, to commit the Plaintiff, and defying him to bring an action'[105]. The claimant remained calm throughout. The jury made an enormous award of damages (500l), but the Court of King's Bench refused to set it aside as excessive, and at the same time praised the claimant for his 'laudable and dignified coolness'[106]. Clearly the high damages were not to reflect the claimant's injured feelings.

Why the eighteenth- and nineteenth-century courts took into account the method of inflicting the damage as an ingredient of liability is not clear. It may have been, as one judge suggested, that 'It goes to prevent the practice of duelling, if juries are permitted to punish insult by exemplary damages'[107]. By the mid-nineteenth century, however, such an explanation was no longer compelling, since duelling had died out[108].

Another explanation is that the judges were inspired by Roman law. Under Roman law there was a separate delict of *iniuria*, which rendered actionable contemptuous (or contumelious) behaviour towards others[109]. Examples of such behaviour included assault and libel, but the delict was deliberately formulated so as not to be limited to particular acts or conduct. The study and knowledge of Roman law was widespread, and the similarity of the Roman and English concepts is enough to make this explanation plausible. However, there is also detailed evidence of influence. In *Merest v Harvey*[110], for instance, Gibbs CJ gave an example of how, if the recovery for trespass were limited to pecuniary damage, a man might repeatedly commit a trespass in a most invasive and offensive manner, but only have to give the claimant a halfpenny damages to settle his legal liability. This example is suspiciously similar to a problem discussed in the Roman texts of a man, knowing that the damages for *iniuria* were fixed, going around slapping people's faces and then instructing his slave to hand over the fixed payment. More explicit borrowing could be seen in

[103] *Merest v Harvey* (1814) 5 Taunt 442.

[104] *Ibid.*

[105] *Ibid* at 442–43.

[106] *Ibid* at 444.

[107] *Merest v Harvey* (1814) 5 Taunt 442 at 443 (per Heath J).

[108] Peltonen, *The Duel in Early Modern England; Civility, Politeness and Honour* (Cambridge, 2003) at 309.

[109] Gaius, *The Institutes of Gaius* (de Zulueta, Oxford, 1991) 3.220ff; Justinian, *The Institutes of Justinian* (ed Thomas, Amsterdam, 1975) 4.4; Thomas, *Textbook of Roman Law* (Amsterdam, 1976) at 369–71.

[110] (1814) 5 Taunt 442.

Tullidge v Wade[111], where the action was for loss of a daughter's services. Bathurst J said: 'In actions of this nature, and of assaults, the circumstances of time and place, when and where the insult is given, require different damages; as it is a greater insult to be beaten upon the Royal Exchange, than in a private room'[112]. This should be compared with Justinian's *Institutes*, 4.4.9, where one of the factors said to make an affront more serious is 'the place where it is committed, eg, if the affront were perpetrated in the theatre or in the market place'[113].

On this evidence calls for the courts to take inspiration from Roman law[114] are misplaced; they had already done so in the eighteenth century. It is also interesting to note that in Australia the exemplary damages requirement had explicitly Roman roots. In *Whitfield v De Lauret & Co Ltd*[115] the High Court of Australia approved the test that there must be a case of 'conscious wrongdoing in contumelious disregard of another's rights'[116]. This phrase was taken from a passage in Salmond's *Treatise on the Law of Torts*[117], where the author discussed the Roman approach to compensation for insult. 'Contumelia', the Latin for contempt, was the word used in the Roman texts to describe the kind of conduct that was actionable.

Until 1964 it was settled law that a defendant's malice increased the appropriate amount of damages for defamation. In 1964, however, the House of Lords recast the law of exemplary damages with its decision in *Rookes v Barnard*[118]. Lord Devlin, with whom the other Law Lords agreed, began his analysis by stating that exemplary damages punished the defendant, and this 'confuses the civil and criminal functions of law'[119]. The civil law's role was only to compensate. However, his Lordship continued, that was not to say that the civil law was confined to compensating pecuniary loss. A court or jury could take the motives of the defendant into account

> where they aggravate the injury done to the plaintiff. There may be malevolence or spite or the manner of committing the wrong may be such as to injure the plaintiff's proper feelings of dignity and pride.[120]

Lord Devlin acknowledged that there were cases where the punitive element had been recognised, so for it to be abolished entirely would

[111] (1769) 3 Wils 18.
[112] *Ibid* at 19.
[113] Translated in Justinian, *The Institutes of Justinian* (ed Thomas, Amsterdam, 1975) at 276.
[114] Birks, 'Harassment and Hubris: The Right to an Equality of Respect' (1997) 32 *Irish Jurist* 1.
[115] (1920) 29 CLR 71.
[116] *Ibid* at 77.
[117] Fifth edition (London, 1920) at 129.
[118] [1964] AC 1129.
[119] *Ibid* at 1121.
[120] *Ibid.*

require 'a complete disregard of precedent'[121]. His Lordship therefore proposed that exemplary damages should be retained, but that they should be confined to certain categories. So far as defamation was concerned, only one category was relevant—where 'the defendant's conduct has been calculated by him to make a profit for himself which may well exceed the compensation payable to the plaintiff'[122].

The response to Lord Devlin's analysis was scornful. The High Court of Australia rejected it immediately, and reasserted the Australian test of 'conscious wrongdoing in contumelious disregard of another's rights'[123]. The Privy Council found it impossible to say that, as a matter of Australian law, they were wrong[124]. The most devastating attack, however, was to come from the English Court of Appeal. In *Broome v Cassell & Co Ltd*[125] it was held that there was so much to object to about *Rookes v Barnard*[126] that it should not be followed. Some of the problems that the Court of Appeal identified were relatively minor. For instance, one of the counsel who had appeared in *Rookes v Barnard*[127] also appeared in *Broome v Cassell & Co Ltd*[128]; he told a sympathetic Court of Appeal that there had been no opportunity to make submissions about the categories before the House of Lords. But some of the Court of Appeal's objections went to the root of the principles set out by Lord Devlin.

One powerful point related to precedent. As Salmon LJ put it in relation to the second category, 'Lord Devlin was unable to cite any authority for such a proposition. There was none'[129]. The categories had been 'conjured up out of the air, no doubt with artistry but also with the most strange and unfortunate results'[130]. This emphatic criticism highlighted a strange inconsistency in Lord Devlin's reasoning. As described above, Lord Devlin had said that he would not go as far as the abolition of exemplary damages, because that would involve a complete disregard of precedent. But in formulating his second category (as in his first) he derived propositions from cases for which they were not strictly authority. The reference to profits in *Crouch v The Great Northern Railway Company*[131] was an *obiter dictum*; in *Williams v Currie*[132] it was part of the reasoning of one out of the three judges. In *Bell v Midland Railway Company*[133] profit-making was only

[121] [1964] AC 1129 at 1226.
[122] *Ibid*.
[123] *Uren v John Fairfax & Sons Pty Limited* (1966) 117 CLR 118.
[124] *Australian Consolidated Press Limited v Uren* [1969] 1 AC 590.
[125] [1971] 2 QB 354.
[126] [1964] AC 1129.
[127] *Ibid*.
[128] [1971] 2 QB 354.
[129] *Ibid* at 387.
[130] *Ibid* at 391.
[131] (1856) 11 Ex 742.
[132] (1845) 1 CB 841.
[133] (1861) 10 CB (NS) 287.

a part of the conduct justifying exemplary damages. Other relevant factors mentioned by the Court of Common Pleas (and excluded from Lord Devlin's category) were that the defendant had committed 'a grievous wrong, with a high hand and in plain violation of an act of parliament'[134]. Lord Devlin was not prepared to disregard precedent, but he was not prepared to follow it either.

The Court of Appeal's second powerful objection to *Rookes v Barnard*[135] was directed to the principled basis of Lord Devlin's second category. Salmon LJ asked, rhetorically,

> Why should the man who commits a tort calculating that he will make more money out of it than any damages and costs which he will have to pay be less favourably regarded by the law than the man who, out of venomous malice, commits a tort in order to break an innocent neighbour regardless of the cost?[136]

Phillimore LJ looked forward to hearing more defendants giving evidence that they were 'solely actuated by hatred and a desire to do the maximum injury to the plaintiff'[137].

The House of Lords[138] felt that the Court of Appeal had gone too far. Viscount Dilhorne thought that the suggestion that *Rookes v Barnard*[139] was decided *per incuriam* 'could be taken, though I cannot believe it was so intended, as of a somewhat offensive character'[140]. Lord Hailsham LC had to remind himself to use 'studied moderation'[141] when dealing with the Court of Appeal's instruction to judges of first instance not to apply *Rookes v Barnard*[142]. In essence their Lordships reasserted emphatically and at length that *Rookes v Barnard* was good law, and it remains the leading case today.

Given the fierce debates and discussion that *Rookes v Barnard* produced, it is surprising that Lord Devlin himself thought that he had, in effect, changed very little. He commented that his judgment would

> remove from the law a source of confusion between aggravated and exemplary damages which has troubled the learned commentators on the subject. Otherwise, it will not, I think, make much difference to the substance of the law or rob the law of the strength which it ought to have.[143]

The reason was that 'aggravated damages in this type of case can do most, if not all, of the work that could be done by exemplary damages'[144].

134 *Ibid* at 307.
135 [1964] AC 1129.
136 [1971] 2 QB 354 at 387.
137 *Ibid* at 398.
138 *Cassell & Co Ltd v Broome* [1972] AC 1027.
139 [1964] AC 1129.
140 [1972] AC 1027 at 1107.
141 *Ibid* at 1053.
142 [1964] AC 1129.
143 *Ibid* at 1230.
144 *Ibid*.

This may have been true to some extent, but the important change that Lord Devlin had effected was that the focus of the assessment had shifted from the defendant's motive to the plaintiff's 'proper feelings of dignity and pride'[145]. Damages were not being increased because the wrong was more serious, but because the harm was greater. In practice victims of more serious wrongs might be correspondingly more upset, but the correlation was not inevitable. A person who showed the 'laudable and dignified coolness' of the claimant in *Merest v Harvey*[146], for instance, would seem to be disadvantaged under Lord Devlin's new approach. Ultimately it came down to a very difficult question of policy: what were defamation damages for? The answer that *Rookes v Barnard*[147] imposed was that they were not to reflect the gravity of the wrong, but were, henceforth, purely to correct the losses flowing from it.

3. FACTORS REDUCING DAMAGES

As with factors increasing the damages, a very wide range of circumstances were relevant to reducing damages. For example, just as the defendant's conduct of the litigation could increase the award, the claimant's tactics could reduce it. As one judge remarked, 'a jury would seldom be disposed to give more than a farthing damages in an action for libel when the plaintiff did not appear as a witness'[148]. Similarly, just as the claimant could increase the damages by proving the defendant's malicious motive, so the defendant could prevent an increase by showing his good motive[149]. In the same vein, evidence that the defendant had been provoked by the claimant moderated the damages[150].

The most controversial factor reducing damages was evidence that rumours were already circulating about the claimant at the time that the tort was committed. The debate over whether such rumours were admissible continued throughout the nineteenth century, as different courts and individual judges adopted their own positions and dug in.

At the outset of the discussion it is important to emphasise that admissibility of evidence is not an abstract question. The issue is—admissible to prove what? Evidence may be admissible to prove one matter, but inadmissible to prove another, and should be disregarded when that second matter is being determined[151].

145 *Ibid* at 1221.
146 (1814) 5 Taunt 442.
147 [1964] AC 1129.
148 *Maclaren and Sons v Davis* (1890) 6 TLR 372 at 373 (per Cave J).
149 *Bryce v Rusden* (1886) 2 TLR 435.
150 *Tarpley v Blaby* (1835) 7 Car & P 395; *Watts v Fraser* (1837) 7 Ad & E 223.
151 *Eg, Associated Newspapers Ltd v Dingle* [1964] AC 371 (newspaper reports admitted to disprove malice could not be considered in relation to the claimant's already damaged reputation).

One strand of the authorities dealt with the admissibility of rumour in relation to proof of motive. Thus, in one case it was successfully argued that evidence showing the claimant's alleged misconduct had been the subject of frequent conversation and rumour was admissible, because it showed that the defendant had not invented the slander[152]. Where the evidence was that the defendant had heard the imputation from one other person the question was more difficult. The cause of the difficulty was that until 1829 the common law recognised a complete defence to an action where the defendant had named his source at the time of speaking[153]. The defence had to be pleaded specially. The difficult question was whether the defence defined exhaustively the legal relevance of having heard the allegation from another person. In *Mills v Spencer*[154] Gibbs CJ thought that it did, and refused to admit the evidence in mitigation of damages. Even after the special defence based on naming the source had been eliminated, there was still a sense that in order to prove absence of malice in mitigation, the requirements of the former defence had to be met[155].

The second, and more controversial, way in which defendants sought to rely on evidence of prior rumours was to prove that the claimant already had a bad character. The leading case was *Earl of Leicester v Walter*[156], where the defendant sought to introduce in mitigation of damages that there were rumours that the claimant had been accused of committing the offence imputed by the publication. Counsel for the defendant sought to persuade the court that the evidence should be admitted as a matter of fairness. He asked rhetorically whether the claimant should 'receive more than nominal damages if before the publication of the libel he was an outcast from society and had no character to lose?'[157]. As a matter of fairness, however, Mansfield CJ agreed with the trenchant arguments for the claimant, that a person's character could be ruined by bringing an action if rumours were admissible. Two different reasons ultimately persuaded the court to admit the evidence. First, there was some authority. Second, the claimant's declaration had stated that he had had a good character until the time the libel was published; this statement was open to challenge by evidence.

Despite the narrow reasoning in *Earl of Leicester v Walter*[158], the case was quickly expanded and seen as representing a general principle. Thus, in — *v Moor*[159] the Court of King's Bench held that evidence of rumour that

[152] *Richards v Richards* (1844) 2 Mood & Rob 557.
[153] For more details see ch 6, below.
[154] (1817) Holt 533.
[155] *Bennett v Bennett* (1834) 6 Car & P 588.
[156] (1809) 2 Camp 251.
[157] *Ibid* at 253.
[158] (1809) 2 Camp 251.
[159] (1813) 1 M & S 284.

the claimant was guilty of similar unnatural practices to those the defendant had imputed was rightly admitted. Lord Ellenborough CJ referred to the *Leicester* case, and continued, 'a person of disparaged fame is not entitled to the same measure of damages with one whose character is unblemished: and it is competent to shew that by evidence'[160]. A general principle of admissibility had emerged[161].

That was not to say that the principle was uncontroversial. In *Waithman v Weaver*[162] Abbott CJ, who, as counsel for the defendant in *Earl of Leicester v Walter*[163] had persuaded the court to admit the evidence, said that he 'had always had doubts'[164] about the case. Clearly the doubts had not inhibited his advocacy. Two months later, in *Jones v Stevens*[165], those doubts had crystallised into emphatic dissent. The Court of Exchequer acknowledged the earlier cases, but its attitude to them was encapsulated by Richards LCB when he said 'I cannot . . . hold them to be declaratory of the Law of England . . . and I sincerely hope they never will'[166]. The objections were based on fairness, both substantive and procedural. As a matter of substance it was inappropriate to allow defendants 'to impeach all the transactions of a man's life who may seek redress in Courts of Justice'[167]. The threat of rumour evidence might well inhibit claimants from suing at all, and thereby encourage libellers to act with impunity[168]. As a matter of procedure, since rumour evidence would be admissible under a general plea of not guilty, the claimant could have no means of anticipating it; he would be unfairly taken by surprise.

The decision in *Jones v Stevens*[169] was not taken up by the Court of King's Bench[170]. But nor was it specifically disapproved. The result was uncertainty and hesitancy. For instance, in *Thompson v Nye*[171] the Court of Queen's Bench was tentative and reluctant to express a view; in *Bracegirdle v Bailey*[172] Byles J felt that he had to consult Willes J before ruling that no evidence of bad character was admissible. Clarification was badly needed.

It was provided in *Scott v Sampson*[173]. Cave J approached the question by classifying the kind of evidence that might be relied upon. There were three categories:

160 *Ibid* at 286.
161 *Wyatt v Gore* (1816) Holt 299; *Newsam v Carr* (1817) 2 Stark 69.
162 (1822) 11 Price 257.
163 (1809) 2 Camp 251.
164 (1822) 11 Price 257.
165 (1822) 11 Price 235.
166 *Ibid* at 265.
167 *Ibid*.
168 *Ibid* at 282.
169 (1822) 11 Price 235.
170 Starkie, *Evidence*, 3rd edn (London, 1842) vol 2 at 641–42.
171 (1850) 16 QB 175.
172 (1859) 1 F & F 536.
173 (1882) 8 QBD 491.

> 1. . . evidence of reputation; 2, evidence of rumours of and suspicions to the same effect as the defamatory matter complained of, and, 3, evidence of particular facts tending to show the character and disposition of the plaintiff.[174]

Evidence in the first category was admissible, whilst evidence in the second and third was not.

Cave J justified the admissibility of evidence in the first category as a matter of principle: how much damage had been caused to the claimant's reputation depended on the estimation in which he had previously been held. He quoted the following passage from Starkie's textbook with approval: 'To enable the jury to estimate the probable quantum of injury sustained a knowledge of the party's previous character is not only material but seems to be absolutely essential'[175]. In modern terms, and borrowing an expression from personal injury law, one could say that the defendant was entitled to benefit from taking the victim as he found him[176]. Cave J also pointed out that the problem of procedural fairness, that had troubled the Court of Exchequer in *Jones v Stevens*[177], had been solved. Under the current system of pleading all material facts had to be pleaded in advance: there could be no unfair surprise.

Evidence of rumours was inadmissible 'as only indirectly tending to affect the plaintiff's reputation'[178]. However, the apparently clear line between evidence of bad reputation and evidence of rumours was blurred by the next sentence: 'If these rumours and suspicions have, in fact, affected the plaintiff's reputation, that may be proved by general evidence of reputation'[179]. Evidence of actual misconduct was inadmissible for a similar reason: it did not go to prove the claimant's reputation, but only to show what reputation he deserved to have.

It can be seen immediately that Cave J was classifying the types of evidence in a way that had not been previously done. In fact he was using a scheme developed in the United States cases, and set out in Townshend's textbook on libel[180], which had been cited by counsel[181]. Whatever the intrinsic merits of the new categories, it took some inventiveness to make the English authorities fit into them. For instance, in *Earl of Leicester v Walter*[182] evidence of rumours that the claimant had committed the acts alleged was admissible. Cave J reinterpreted the decision, saying that, 'in that case it was proposed to prove that the plaintiff's relations and former

[174] *Ibid* at 498.
[175] *Ibid* at 503.
[176] For a parallel in personal injury law see *Baker v Willoughby* [1970] AC 467.
[177] (1822) 11 Price 235.
[178] (1882) 8 QBD 491 at 504.
[179] *Ibid.*
[180] Townshend, *A Treatise on the Wrongs Called Slander and Libel*, 3rd edn (New York, 1877) at 677–82.
[181] (1882) 8 QBD 491 at 493.
[182] (1809) 2 Camp 251.

acquaintances had ceased to visit him on account of these rumours and suspicions, so that the evidence would seem really to have amounted to evidence of general reputation'[183].

A more fundamental problem lay in the distinction between evidence of bad reputation and evidence of rumours of guilt. The former was admissible, whilst the latter was not, unless, as Cave J had explained, the rumours had affected the claimant's reputation. Applying this rule to the facts of the case it was held that evidence that a witness had heard the allegation against the claimant previously, in a club, was inadmissible. Cave J emphasised that it was not shown that the claimant's reputation was affected by such gossip[184]. But this seems to contradict the fundamental basis of defamation, that most spoken and all written defamatory language does cause harm to reputation—the tendency of the words leads inevitably, as a matter of law, to the damage. It seems to follow from *Scott v Sampson* that defamatory words automatically cause harm to reputation when the defendant utters them, but not when he hears them. That is not an obviously coherent position.

Later cases have developed and refined the position set out in *Scott v Sampson*[185]. Two important points have emerged. First, evidence of general reputation has been narrowed to general reputation in the sector of the claimant's life about which the allegation was made. Thus, for instance, a claimant's reputation as a Nazi sympathiser was irrelevant to mitigate an allegation that he had been a party to murder[186]. At the same time, however, a minute dissection of the claimant's reputation in similar areas is not necessary, particularly if he is alleging that his general reputation has suffered[187]. The second important point is that evidence of prior bad reputation cannot include evidence of the damage done by earlier instances of the same allegation[188]. As Lord Morris put it, 'It ought not . . . to avail a defendant to prove that a plaintiff has been under a temporary cloud of suspicion when the success of the plaintiff in libel proceedings demonstrates that there need never have been any such suspicion'[189]. This rule was, strictly, inconsistent with the emphasis in *Scott v Sampson*[190] on what reputation the claimant actually had at the time of publication, as opposed to the one he deserved to have. It was justified, though, by powerful reasons of fairness.

183 (1882) 8 QBD 491 at 504.
184 *Ibid* at 507.
185 (1882) 8 QBD 491.
186 *Plato Films Ltd v Speidel* [1961] AC 1090 at 1102 (per Devlin LJ), 1140 (per Lord Denning).
187 *Jones v Pollard* [1997] EMLR 233 at 251.
188 *Associated Newspapers Ltd v Dingle* [1964] AC 371.
189 *Ibid* at 417.
190 (1882) 8 QBD 491.

The most recent developments have tended to be liberal in allowing evidence to be given in mitigation of damages. For instance, in *Pamplin v Express Newspapers Ltd*[191] Neill LJ expressed the view that 'a defendant is also entitled to rely in mitigation of damages on any other evidence which is properly before the court and Jury'[192]. This must, presumably, include evidence showing lack of malice in the defendant, and it prompts a question that may need further consideration. Since malice in the defendant cannot, of itself, increase damages[193], does it not follow that absence of malice, in itself, cannot reduce them either? In other words, is good motive only relevant to the extent that it causes a correspondingly smaller injury to feelings?

A similar liberality in admitting evidence can also be seen in the most recent case, *Burstein v Times Newspapers Ltd*[194]. There the Court of Appeal ruled that evidence of specific activities by the claimant should have been admitted, since it was directly relevant to the context of publication. The Court of Appeal was partly inspired by the Civil Procedure Rules, particularly the overriding imperative to deal with the case justly and speedily. Indeed, it may be that the Court intended to signal that rules about evidence in defamation should be viewed less rigidly in future, and seen as part of the Court's overall discretion. It remains to be seen, however, how far defence counsel will exploit the Court of Appeal's observation that 'every publication has a contextual background, even if the publication is substantially untrue'[195]. The Court of Appeal was concerned that excluding such evidence of context would put a jury 'in blinkers'[196]; but blinkers, it should be remembered, are a useful way of making sure the horse does not get distracted. An excessively liberal approach risks making trials longer and less fair, by allowing in material that discredits the claimant in the eyes of the jury, without being strictly relevant to his prior reputation.

4. CONCLUSION

The law of damages for defamation has followed a trajectory of ever-increasing complexity. Starting as a pure question of informed guesswork for the jury, it later took on the subtleties associated with questions of law, and, in relation to exemplary damages, became embroiled in tort theory. For matters mitigating damages the key moment was the change of direction signalled by *Scott v Sampson*, when an American scheme of

191 [1988] 1 WLR 116 n.
192 *Ibid* at 120.
193 *Rookes v Barnard* [1964] AC 1129.
194 [2001] 1 WLR 579.
195 *Ibid* at 598.
196 *Ibid*.

classification was imported in order to give a clearer structure. However, the increasingly elaborate rules of damages were at odds with the fact that they were still being applied by juries. So the judges had a dilemma: on the one hand they wanted to tell the jury everything, but, on the other, they did not want to cause confusion. It has proved a difficult balance to maintain.

4

Injunctions

THE HISTORY OF the injunction for defamation has been dominated by three successive factors. The first was that only courts of equity had jurisdiction to award injunctions, and that the basis of the award was an unlawful interference with property. Reputation was not obviously a property interest, so the courts were reluctant to grant an injunction restraining defamatory words. The second factor was the statutory attempts in 1854 and 1873 to integrate the courts of equity and common law more coherently, so as to create a more rational system for litigants. These statutes were eventually seen as conferring a jurisdiction to grant an injunction for defamation. The final dominant factor was the emergence of strict rules controlling the exercise of the jurisdiction. These rules were unique to defamation, and ensured that it was not enough for the grant of an injunction to prove that 'the balance of convenience' favoured it. This chapter examines these factors in turn.

1. THE PROTECTION OF PROPERTY RIGHTS

At the very start of the nineteenth century there is some evidence to suggest that the courts were prepared to consider the injunction as a remedy for defamation. In *Du Bost v Beresford*[1] the owner of a provocative picture, entitled 'La Belle et la Bête', sued for damages caused to it by the defendant. In the course of analysing how the damages should be assessed, Lord Ellenborough asserted that if the picture was a libel the law could not consider it as being of value, since 'Upon an application to the Lord Chancellor, he would have granted an injunction against its exhibition'[2]. Also, in *Lord Byron v Johnston*[3] the defendant had advertised poems for sale representing that they were the work of the claimant. The court granted an injunction against the defendant, preventing him from publishing the poems as advertised. Unfortunately the only report contains no reasoning—an omission

[1] (1810) 2 Camp 511.
[2] *Ibid* at 512.
[3] (1816) 2 Mer 29.

which weakened the case's subsequent authority[4]. However, two points can be made about it. First, it looks like a defamation case, and was so interpreted[5]. Second, it is interesting that the court apparently found it such a simple case to deal with: there seems to have been no difficulty in identifying an interest that could be protected by an injunction.

Two years later, in *Gee v Pritchard*[6], a very different approach could be seen. The case concerned an attempt by the defendant to publish letters sent to him by the claimant; the claimant was seeking an injunction to prevent such publication. Counsel for the defendant argued that the only instance of interference with publication of letters was when the Star Chamber had restrained libels. Lord Eldon LC interjected that counsel need not develop that argument further. In his view, 'The publication of a libel is a crime; and I have not jurisdiction to prevent the commission of crimes'[7]. 'The question', he continued, 'will be, whether the bill has stated facts of which the Court can take notice, as a case of civil property, which it is bound to protect'[8]. He concluded that there was such property, because when a letter was sent, it was not a gift to the receiver. The receiver acquired only 'a special property' which entitled him to read and retain physical possession of the letter, but did not entitle him to publicise it.

This was a subtle and important piece of legal analysis. The point that libel was a crime, and equity could not restrain a crime, was hardly conclusive. As Pound pointed out, libel was also a tort, and 'equity is not precluded from preventing irreparable injury through a civil wrong because that act, in another aspect, may be the subject of a criminal prosecution'[9]. Rather, the key point seemed to be the requirement of a property right before an injunction could be granted. However, there was also a certain ambiguity about the requirement of property. As an abstract proposition it seemed to lay down a restrictive test. But its practical application to the facts revealed that there was scope for creativity in the identification of property rights. Pound even suggested that the insistence on a property right should be seen as 'a mere formal peg on which to hang the substantive relief'[10].

The tension between the formal insistence on interference with a property right and the liberal approach to identifying such interference was to shape the later case law. In *Routh v Webster*[11], for instance, an injunction was granted to restrain the defendant from continuing to represent that

[4] See, for example, *Clark v Freeman* (1848) 11 Beav 112 at 119.

[5] *Day v Brownrigg* (1878) 10 ChD 294 at 300.

[6] (1818) 2 Swans 402.

[7] *Ibid* at 413.

[8] *Ibid*.

[9] Pound, 'Equitable Relief Against Defamation and Injuries to Personality' (1915–16) 29 *Harvard Law Review* 640 at 643.

[10] *Ibid* at 644.

[11] (1847) 10 Beav 561.

the claimant was the trustee of a company. What the property right was, was not made clear. Similarly, in *Clark v Freeman*[12] the defendant advertised pills for sale as if they had been manufactured by the claimant, an eminent physician. The court denied an injunction, but the Court of Appeal later said that the case had been wrongly decided[13], and lower courts were quick to agree[14]. As Cairns LJ put it, the claimant in *Clark*'s case 'had a property in his own name'[15].

Perhaps the most striking example was provided by *The Emperor of Austria v Day*[16]. There the Emperor of Austria sought to restrain the defendant from printing new currency for Hungary, which the defendant's customer intended to introduce into Hungary once the Emperor had been deposed from the Hungarian throne. The Court of Appeal made it clear that the injunction could be granted only on the basis of interference with a property right[17], but proceeded to find such a right in either the public revenue of the Hungarian state[18] or the value of existing currency held by Hungarian citizens, whom the Emperor represented[19].

This liberal approach did not extend, however, to the recognition of reputation as property. In *Clark v Freeman*[20], for instance, Lord Langdale MR asserted that 'granting the injunction in this case would imply that the Court has jurisdiction of a libel, and I cannot think that it has'[21]. Similarly, in *The Emperor of Austria v Day*[22] the Court of Appeal showed great creativity in finding a property right infringed, but Lord Campbell LC added that he had 'no hesitation in saying that Lord Ellenborough was wrong when he laid down in *Du Bost v Beresford* that the Lord Chancellor would grant an injunction against the exhibition of a libellous picture'[23].

In addition to the problem of property, injunctions for libel also faced a further legal objection relating to procedure. Defamation cases were tried by juries, as the fierce struggle culminating in Fox's Libel Act 1792[24], had established. As one early House of Lords case pointed out, it was difficult to see how the fundamental principle of trial by jury could be reconciled with the pre-emptive judicial remedy of injunction[25]. Thus, by the early

12 (1848) 11 Beav 112.
13 *Maxwell v Hogg* (1867) LR 2 Ch App 307 at 310 (per Cairns LJ).
14 *Springhead Spinning Company v Riley* (1868) LR 6 Eq 551 at 561; *Lee v Gibbings* (1892) 67 LT 263 at 265.
15 *Maxwell v Hogg* (1867) LR 2 Ch App 307 at 310.
16 (1861) 3 De G F & J 217.
17 *Ibid* at 232 (per Lord Campbell LC).
18 *Ibid* at 247 (per Knight Bruce LJ).
19 *Ibid* at 253 (per Turner LJ).
20 (1848) 11 Beav 112.
21 *Ibid* at 119.
22 (1861) 3 De G F & J 217.
23 *Ibid* at 238–39.
24 See above, p 37.
25 *Fleming v Newton* (1848) 1 HLC 363.

1860s it seemed to be settled that no injunction could be granted for defamation.

Such certainty was, however, short-lived. In 1869, in *Dixon v Holden*[26], Malins VC granted an injunction against the repetition of a libel. He made it plain that 'property' should be understood broadly:

> What is property? One man has property in lands, another in goods, another in a business, another in skill, another in reputation; and whatever may have the effect of destroying property in any one of these things (even in a man's good name), is, in my opinion, destroying property of a most valuable description.[27]

On the facts of the case the libel had imputed bankruptcy to a businessman. It could, therefore, have been said that the threatened injury to property was the claimant's financial loss as a result of other businessmen avoiding him. Malins VC, however, rejected such a narrow approach:

> I go further, and say if it had only injured his reputation, it is within the jurisdiction of this Court to stop a libel of this description which goes to destroy his property or his reputation, which is his property, if possible, more valuable than other property.[28]

This was not the first time that Malins VC had invoked a very broad concept of property in order to justify granting an injunction. Less than a year earlier, in *Springhead Spinning Company v Riley*[29], he had held that a trade union could be restrained from putting up notices asking people not to work for the claimants until a pay dispute had been settled. The notices were destroying the value of the claimant's mill. Nor was it to be his last time. In *Day v Brownrigg*[30] he held that the claimant's property right had been infringed when his neighbour decided to give his house the same name as the claimant's.

These decisions of Malins VC were radical in their results and proved controversial. The Court of Appeal immediately reversed the decision in *Day v Brownrigg*[31], and the decision in *Dixon v Holden*[32] fared little better. In *Prudential Assurance Company v Knott*[33] the Court of Appeal was scathing in its criticism. Lord Cairns LC stated that the general propositions in *Dixon v Holden* were wrong[34], and James LJ commented that Malins VC was 'by his desire to do what was right, led to exaggerate the

[26] (1869) LR 7 Eq 488.
[27] *Ibid* at 492.
[28] *Ibid*.
[29] (1868) LR 6 Eq 551.
[30] (1878) 10 ChD 294.
[31] *Ibid*.
[32] (1869) LR 7 Eq 488.
[33] (1875) LR 10 Ch App 142.
[34] *Ibid* at 147.

jurisdiction of this Court'[35]. One American commentator went further, describing the decision in *Dixon v Holden* as 'judicial legislation'[36].

However, it is submitted that these harsh criticisms were unfair, because in their fundamental technique these decisions of Malins VC were orthodox. He had asked the classic, traditional question for the grant of an injunction: had the claimant's proprietary legal right been infringed?[37] Like many earlier judges he had used some ingenuity in identifying such rights. He may, perhaps, have been a little too ingenious, but, given the context, his innovations look more like careful judicial incrementalism than the invention of new rules.

2. THE STATUTORY BASIS FOR JURISDICTION

The emphatic assertions by the Court of Appeal in *Prudential Assurance Company v Knott*[38] seemed to make it clear that there could be no injunction for libel. Such certainty was, however, to be short-lived. Two years later, in *Thorley's Cattle Food Company v Massam*[39], the question of an injunction for libel arose again, when the claimant sought to restrain the defendant from publishing advertisements stating that the defendant alone knew the secret for compounding Thorley's Food for Cattle. The motion for an injunction was refused by Malins VC, but he thought that the question was still open. Naturally, this position required a narrow view of *Prudential Assurance*. There, he said, Lord Cairns LC had not said that *Dixon v Holden*[40] was wrongly decided; rather, he had merely expressed 'dissent from the general doctrine that this Court can issue an injunction to prevent a libel'[41]. Malins VC went on to assert his own 'individual opinion' that he had 'not the slightest doubt whatever that it is, and it ought to be, as much the principle of this Court to stop publications which go to destroy property as to prevent the darkening of ancient lights . . .'[42]. He then invoked Judicature Act 1873 s 25(8) in support of his position. This subsection stated (so far as was relevant) that:

> A mandamus or an injunction may be granted or a receiver appointed by an interlocutory order of the Court in all cases in which it shall appear to the Court to be just or convenient that such order should be made, and any such order may be made either unconditionally or upon such terms or conditions as the Court shall think just;

[35] *Ibid.*

[36] Clapp, 'Commentary on *Hermann Loog v Bean*' (1884) 32 *American Law Register* 701 at 709.

[37] Meagher, Gummow and Lehane, *Equity—Doctrines and Remedies* (Sydney, 1975) at para 2107.

[38] (1875) LR 10 Ch App 142.

[39] (1877) 6 ChD 582.

[40] (1869) LR 7 Eq 488.

[41] (1877) 6 ChD 582 at 588.

[42] *Ibid.*

Malins VC believed that this subsection superseded the decision in *Prudential Assurance Company v Knott*[43], although, since this was an interlocutory hearing, he preferred not to express a concluded view.

It was to be almost three years before *Thorley's Cattle Food Company v Massam* came to trial[44]. Meanwhile, the significance of s 25(8) for defamation cases remained ambiguous. In one briefly reported decision[45] the Master of the Rolls seemed to suggest that the Judicature Act made an injunction possible. However, in *Saxby v Easterbrook*[46] the Divisional Court made the position less clear. Here the parties were rival firms of engineers and the defendant had falsely asserted that the claimant's application for a patent had been cancelled on the grounds of piracy and dishonesty. An injunction against repetition of the libel was granted, but the Divisional Court rejected any statutory basis for it, with Lord Coleridge CJ saying that he did 'not appreciate'[47] the reference to s 25(8). The basis for the jurisdiction was said to be that the libel was calculated to injure the claimant's property, but this was somewhat problematic. In *Prudential Assurance Company v Knott*[48] the Court of Appeal had made it quite clear that reputation could not be regarded as a form of property for the purposes of equitable remedies. Furthermore, it had also been made clear in the same case that loss of business caused by a libel could not be regarded as property damage. As Lord Cairns LC had trenchantly pointed out, 'with regard to nine out of ten libels, the same thing might be said'[49]. As a matter of authority, it was not clear that *Saxby v Easterbrook*[50] could be good law.

When *Thorley's Cattle Food Company v Massam* finally came on for trial[51] the legal landscape looked rather different from when the interlocutory hearing had taken place. Malins VC granted the injunction permanently, saying that it was now 'not necessary'[52] to go into the general question of whether an injunction was available for defamation. The question before him was narrower—'whether one man is entitled to . . . make a statement injurious to the business of another'[53]—and *Saxby v Easterbrook*[54] showed that an injunction could be granted. In the Court of Appeal, the brief judgments affirmed the decision, Bramwell LJ commenting that there was clearly a libel on the claimant's trade[55].

[43] (1875) LR 10 Ch App 142.
[44] (1880) 14 ChD 763.
[45] *Hinrichs v Berndes* 1878 Weekly Notes 11.
[46] (1878) 3 CPD 339.
[47] *Ibid* at 343.
[48] (1875) LR 10 Ch App 142.
[49] *Ibid* at 145.
[50] (1878) 3 CPD 339.
[51] (1880) 14 ChD 763.
[52] *Ibid* at 773.
[53] *Ibid.*
[54] (1878) 3 CPD 339.
[55] (1880) 14 ChD 763 at 784.

The reasoning in *Thorley*'s case did not, therefore, rely on s 25(8). Rather, it used the traditional test of property damage applied in a way that an earlier Court of Appeal had pronounced illegitimate. However, s 25(8) did not go away. The conflict with *Prudential Assurance Company v Knott*[56] was so direct that one commentator was driven to say that *Thorley*'s case could only be explained using the statute[57]. Furthermore, there was still a sense in judicial circles that s 25(8) had a role to play: in a case heard less than a fortnight after *Thorley*'s case Fry J granted an injunction for libel in trade, invoking 'the evident intention of the Legislature, as indicated by the 25th section of the Judicature Act of 1873, to enlarge rather than to diminish the power of the Court in respect of injunctions'[58].

Two years later, in *Quartz Hill Consolidated Gold Mining Company v Beall*[59], the Court of Appeal put forward what was to become the dominant account of the statutory foundations of the jurisdiction to grant an injunction for libel. According to this account, the jurisdiction to grant an injunction for libel had emerged first in the common law courts as a result of Common Law Procedure Act 1854 ss 79 and 82. Section 79 stated:

> In all cases of breach of contract or other injury, where the party injured is entitled to maintain and has brought an action, he may, in like case and manner as hereinbefore provided with respect to mandamus claim a writ of injunction against the repetition or continuance of such breach of contract, or other injury, or the committal of any breach of contract or injury of a like kind, arising out of the same contract or relating to the same property or right.

Section 82 authorised the common law courts to grant interlocutory injunctions as well as final injunctions at the conclusion of the trial. This jurisdiction was transferred to all of the Divisions of the High Court by the Judicature Act 1873. Section 25(8) of the 1873 Act had, according to the Court of Appeal, a supplementary role, conferring 'a larger jurisdiction to grant injunctions than existed before'[60].

This new account of the foundations of the jurisdiction to grant an injunction for defamation was strikingly new, particularly in its use of the 1854 Act. Surprisingly, the 1854 Act seemed to indicate that a jurisdiction to grant injunctions for defamation had existed at common law for nearly thirty years. In other words, until 1873 the common law courts had had greater powers to grant injunctions than the courts of chancery. Baggallay LJ confirmed that this understanding was correct:

[56] (1875) LR 10 Ch App 142.
[57] Clapp, 'Commentary on *Hermann Loog v Bean*' (1884) 32 *American Law Register* 701 at 710.
[58] *Thomas v Williams* (1880) 14 ChD 864 at 873.
[59] (1882) 20 ChD 501.
[60] *Ibid* at 507.

> The cases in which the Court of Chancery could grant injunctions were of certain limited though well ascertained classes, but the language of the Common Law Procedure Act authorized the granting of an injunction in all cases of breach of contract or other injury, where the party injured is entitled to maintain and has brought an action.[61]

Although this use of the 1854 Act was strikingly new in defamation, it was not the first time that the Act had been used to claim wide powers. In *Beddow v Beddow*[62], for instance, Jessel MR had granted an injunction to restrain a person from acting as a referee after he had become indebted to one of the parties to the dispute. The basis for the jurisdiction was said to be s 79 of the 1854 Act, which had given common law courts the power to grant injunctions 'in the largest terms'[63]. Similarly, the same judge invoked s 79 to justify appointing a receiver where none could have been appointed before[64].

If the Court of Appeal's use of s 79 in *Quartz Hill Consolidated Gold Mining Company v Beall*[65] was correct, the consequences were far-reaching. For one thing, all of the attempts to have reputation recognised as a type of property, and thereby obtain an injunction for defamation, had been completely pointless. Similarly, claimants who had been denied an injunction for defamation since 1854 had failed merely because they had (understandably) gone to the wrong court.

But was the Court of Appeal correct? One factor that immediately raises doubts is the timescale. A modern treatise has described the *Quartz Hill* case as an 'early'[66] recognition of the broad powers conferred by the 1854 Act, but nearly thirty years is scarcely a rapid response. There was also the fact that, in those intervening thirty years, ingenious counsel had attempted to obtain injunctions for libel, but they had never used the 1854 Act. In the *Quartz Hill* case Baggallay LJ admitted as much when he said, with something of an understatement, that 'It is quite true that that power was very seldom exercised in the shape of granting an interlocutory injunction'[67]. Finally, there is the difficulty that such a radical reform was supposedly accomplished so quietly. The 1869 edition of Starkie's textbook on defamation, for example, makes no allusion to the possibility that the courts of common law could grant injunctions for libel[68]. As Pound later put it, rather cuttingly,

61 (1882) 20 ChD at 509–10.
62 (1878) 9 ChD 89.
63 *Ibid* at 92.
64 *Anglo-Italian Bank v Davies* (1878) 9 ChD 275 at 287.
65 (1882) 20 ChD 501.
66 Meagher, Gummow and Lehane, *Equity—Doctrines and Remedies* (Sydney, 1975) at para 2111.
67 (1882) 20 ChD 501 at 510.
68 Folkard, *Starkie's Treatise on the Law of Slander and Libel*, 3rd edn (London, 1869) at 547–48.

> we are to believe, the Act of 1854 put liberty of the press and all the common-law rights of Englishmen into the hands of judges, so far as injunctions may affect them, subject to no restraint beyond the judicial sense of what justice may demand.[69]

A closer examination of the 1854 Act confirms these doubts. The Act was the result of proposals made by the Second Report of the Common Law Commissioners (1852–1853)[70]. In the section of their Report dealing with injunctions, the Commissioners quoted and endorsed the principle advanced by an earlier panel of Commissioners in 1831:

> There seems to be no reason why a Court of Law should not exercise the same jurisdiction, and restrain violations of *legal* rights in the cases in which an injunction now issues for that purpose from the Courts of Equity . . . it would obviously be attended with great advantage and convenience, that where common law rights are concerned, the whole litigation relating to them should fall within the cognisance of a Common Law Court; not only because the expense and delay of a suit in equity may be thus avoided, but because the common law judges are more competent than those in equity to decide any question of law which the application for an injunction may involve.[71]

The Commissioners were pleased to note that this principle had already been acted upon in the Patent Law Amendment Act 1852 s 42, but pressed for its more general adoption. The identical proposal was also made for specific performance. In other words, the proposed reform was aimed at ending the inconvenience and expense of claimants having to initiate two sets of proceedings, one in the common law courts to vindicate their legal rights, and one in equity to claim any equitable remedies. It was meant to be a reform of procedure, not substance.

Commentators on the 1854 Act acknowledged its origins. One edition of the Act even reprinted the entire Commissioners' Report, the editor asserting its importance in the highest terms:

> Convinced, from repeated perusal, that the Second Report of the Common Law Commissioners, would be found advantageous for reference in court, and deeming it no disparagement to any of the numerous editions of this Act to say, that the Report, considering its source, is likely to prove the best commentary upon the Act, the Editor has preferred printing the Report entire . . .[72]

Naturally, the new provisions relating to the new powers to award injunctions and specific performance attracted comment, and two editions

[69] Pound, 'Equitable Relief Against Defamation and Injuries to Personality' (1915–16) 29 *Harvard Law Review* 640 at 665–66.

[70] See generally Cornish and Clark, *Law and Society in England 1750–1950* (London, 1989) at 41.

[71] Second Report of the Common Law Commissioners, reprinted in Thompson, *The Common Law Procedure Act 1854* (London, 1854) at 44.

[72] Thompson, *The Common Law Procedure Act 1854* (London, 1854) at iii.

of the Act contained short treatises on those subjects[73]. The dominant view was that the Act could only give the same jurisdiction to common law courts that equity had previously had, such as the power to issue injunctions restraining waste, breach of copyright, or breach of contract. However, there was an awareness that the words of the section were very broad, and two authors speculated that they might be read more widely. They observed that:

> . . . in one point of view, the jurisdiction of the Courts of Law under this act may, perhaps, be held to be more extensive than that of Courts of Equity; inasmuch as the latter Courts have, except in the case of infants, lunatics, &c, no jurisdiction over persons, but only in respect of property. They would not interfere in respect of merely personal wrongs, such as to restrain the repetition of a libel, or the continuance of any other act merely affecting personal character. It may be a question, whether the power of the Common Law Courts will not be more extensive; but we apprehend that such question must be answered in the negative, as it would seem, from the use of the words 'property or right' in the latter part of sect. 79, that such extension was not contemplated; and, further, in most cases where personal character is affected by libel, it would probably be considered that damages would be a sufficient compensation, and that, therefore, the Courts of Common Law, acting upon the principle laid down in Equity, would not interfere by injunction.[74]

This was a subtle reading of the general phrase 'property or right'. In a similar vein, one might add that the prominent allusions to breach of contract suggested that something narrower than the full range of wrongs was intended to be covered by the section.

One commentator went further. In his discussion of s 68, which conferred the power to grant specific performance in similar terms to the power to grant injunctions (and was indirectly referred to when s 79 mentioned the power to grant mandamus), Philips considered whether extensions should be made to the specific performance jurisdiction[75]. He acknowledged that the Act derived from the Commissioners' proposals, and that their aim had simply been to confer the same jurisdiction as that exercised in equity. He also agreed that applying the equitable rules would give greater certainty, 'but', he concluded, 'it is to be observed that there is nothing in the language of the act to lead to the inference that the legislature intended that the exercise of this jurisdiction should be thus limited, or that the writ should be refused in any case where it can be granted consistently with justice'[76]. The same could have been said (though Philips did not repeat it) of s 79.

[73] Thompson, *The Common Law Procedure Act 1854* (London, 1854); Holland and Chandless, *The Common Law Procedure Act, MDCCCLIV* (London, 1854).

[74] Holland and Chandless, *The Common Law Procedure Act, MDCCCLIV* (London, 1854) at 87–88.

[75] Philips, *The Common Law Procedure Act, 1854* (London, 1854) at 48.

[76] *Ibid.*

Thus the use made of s 79 to justify injunctions for defamation was controversial, to say the least. It is also surprising that defendants advanced none of the arguments about the source and aims of the 1854 Act, which were so widely understood at the time of its enactment. The explanation for both of these oddities is, perhaps, one of judicial personality. Sir George Jessel MR was the judge who consistently relied on s 79 as transforming the jurisdiction to award injunctions, and his judicial techniques were highly distinctive. He was noted for studying the case in advance[77]; when the case was heard it was said that 'He did not often need counsel to inform him of the law; he informed counsel.'[78] He also made a point of construing Acts of Parliament in a plain manner, simply giving the words 'their ordinary grammatical meaning'[79]. As he himself put it, 'I read the Act for myself. If I think it clear I express my opinion about its meaning'[80]. A further distinguishing characteristic was his speed of working: he made up his mind and gave judgment immediately. Indeed, he once remarked that 'I do not understand that a judgment is any better for being held over for a long time'.[81] Except for two occasions, he never wrote down a judgment[82].

These qualities made Jessel MR highly respected and popular with litigants. Apparently members of the public visited his court 'to witness his despatch, and listen to his terse, racy observations'[83]. However, his technique would not have been well suited to dealing with the 1854 Act. If counsel were not forewarned that the Act was to be discussed they could not have had the Commissioners' Report in mind (or to hand), and construing the Act surely called for some appreciation of its source and aims. It is difficult to avoid the conclusion that here Sir George Jessel's speed and directness came at a price.

The other statutory provision used to justify granting an injunction for defamation was Judicature Act 1873 s 25(8)[84]. Jessel MR consistently asserted that the subsection transformed the power to award injunctions. In *Beddow v Beddow*[85], for instance, he stated that the effect of s 25(8) was that 'I have unlimited power to grant an injunction in any case where it would

[77] Finestein, 'Sir George Jessel 1824–1883' (1958) 18 *Transactions of the Jewish Historical Society of England* 243 at 271.

[78] Willis, *Sir George Jessel: A Lecture* (London, 1893) at 20.

[79] *Ibid* at 24.

[80] *Ibid* at 25.

[81] *Ibid* at 27.

[82] Finestein, Sir George Jessel 1824–1883' (1958) 18 *Transactions of the Jewish Historical Society of England* 243, at 272.

[83] Willis, *Sir George Jessel: A Lecture* (London, 1893), at 20.

[84] 'A mandamus or an injunction may be granted or a receiver appointed by an interlocutory order of the Court in all cases in which it shall appear to the Court to be just or convenient that such order should be made, and any such order may be made either unconditionally or upon such terms or conditions as the Court shall think just'.

[85] (1878) 9 ChD 89.

be right or just to do so'[86]. In *Anglo-Italian Bank v Davies*[87] he took a similar approach, asserting that s 25(8) had 'enlarged very much the powers which Courts of Equity formerly possessed of granting injunctions or receivers'[88].

The logical consequence of the position taken by Jessel MR could be seen in his decision in *Aslatt v Corporation of Southampton*[89]. There he granted an injunction restraining the corporation from holding a meeting to disqualify the claimant from holding the position of alderman. The claimant had shown that the statutory conditions for disqualification were not met, but, as Jessel MR pointed out, there would previously have been no injunction: common law courts could not grant injunctions, and courts of equity did not interfere to protect all legal rights. Jessel MR continued that:

> Such a state of things loudly called for a remedy; and, in my opinion, there was a remedy given by the 25th section (sub-sect. 8) of the Judicature Act of 1873 . . . Of course the words 'just or convenient' did not mean that the Court was to grant an injunction simply because the Court thought it convenient: it meant that the Court should grant an injunction for the protection of rights or for the prevention of injury according to legal principles; but the moment you find there is a legal principle, that a man is about to suffer a serious injury, and that there is no pretence for inflicting that injury upon him, it appears to me that the Court ought to interfere.[90]

Here, as with his approach to the Common Law Procedure Act 1854, Jessel MR was using his distinctive pace and directness in construing a statute. His involvement with the Judicature Acts[91] may have made him even less prepared than normal to go into the statutory background.

However the construction of s 25(8) was not as straightforward as it might have appeared. In *Anglo-Italian Bank v Davies*[92], for instance, whilst Jessel MR confidently expounded the effect of the subsection, Brett LJ refrained from expressing an opinion. In *The North London Railway Company v The Great Northern Railway Company*[93] Brett LJ finally put forward his view, as did Cotton LJ. Both judges differed from Jessel MR, and from each other.

The facts of the case involved a defendant who was determined to pursue a hopeless arbitration claim against the claimant. The claimant was refusing to take part, and was seeking an injunction to restrain the defendant from taking further steps. This was, therefore, removed from the question of an injunction for defamation, particularly because the claimant seemed to be asking for an injunction where no wrong had been

[86] *Ibid* at 93.
[87] (1878) 9 ChD 275.
[88] *Ibid* at 286.
[89] (1880) 16 ChD 143.
[90] *Ibid* at 148.
[91] Peter, *Analysis and Digest of the Decisions of Sir George Jessel* (London, 1883) at iii.
[92] (1878) 9 ChD 275.
[93] (1883) 11 QBD 30.

committed, but the defendant was behaving in an unreasonable, vexatious manner.

Both judges agreed that no action could lie for mere unreasonable or vexatious behaviour, and the claimant's claim therefore failed. However, both of them went on to give a detailed exposition of the meaning of s 25(8).

Brett LJ expressed 'a very strong opinion'[94] that the Judicature Act had 'not dealt with jurisdiction at all, but only with procedure'. His view was that the Act had conferred the jurisdiction of the previously distinct courts of common law and equity on each Division of the new High Court, 'but . . . it has not given to any Court jurisdiction which no Court had before'[95]. In other words, 'if no Court had the power of issuing an injunction before the Judicature Act, no part of the High Court has power to issue such an injunction now'[96]. Brett LJ doubted whether *Aslatt v Corporation of Southampton*[97] had been correctly decided[98].

Cotton LJ adopted a construction of the subsection wider than Brett LJ and narrower than Jessel MR. He could not accept that there was an intention to give 'the enormously increased power'[99] that the claimant was asking the Court to exercise. However, it seemed to him that the subsection did widen the jurisdiction of the High Court, to the extent that it could now protect any legal right by an injunction. Cotton LJ thought that this construction of the subsection also enabled *Aslatt*'s case to remain good law, since one could interpret the judgment as saying 'that the plaintiff had independently of the Judicature Act a legal right of action'[100].

This interpretation of *Aslatt v Corporation of Southampton*[101] was, perhaps, reading into the judgment a restriction that was not there, but it enabled the case to be used as authority subsequently[102]. The wider debate about s 25(8), however, remained unresolved. As Meagher, Gummow and Lehane put it, over a century after the statute was enacted, 'What, then, is the importance or meaning of the provisions of s 25(8) . . .? Nobody knows.'[103]

In relation to injunctions for defamation the role of s 25(8) seems to have been settled by *Monson v Tussauds Ltd*[104], where Lord Halsbury LC, sitting in the Court of Appeal, applied the subsection and commented on the

94 *Ibid* at 36.
95 *Ibid*.
96 *Ibid* at 36–37.
97 (1880) 16 ChD 143.
98 (1883) 11 QBD 30 at 37.
99 *Ibid* at 39.
100 *Ibid* at 40.
101 (1880) 16 ChD 143.
102 *Richardson v Methley School Board* (1893) 3 Ch 510.
103 *Equity—Doctrines and Remedies* (Sydney, 1975) at para 2114.
104 [1894] 1 QB 671.

'unqualified language'[105] of the statute, that permitted the Court to do what was 'just and convenient'. Lopes LJ also referred to s 25(8), saying that it conferred 'a larger jurisdiction to grant injunctions than existed before'[106]. As with the earlier decisions of Jessel MR, it was unfortunate that no attempt was made to draw on the purposes of the Act.

The position had been reached, therefore, where there was clearly a jurisdiction to grant an injunction for defamation. But whilst the existence of the jurisdiction was clear, its basis was not: there were three competing strands. First, that libels on a person's trade could be seen as damage to property, and could therefore be brought within the traditional equitable jurisdiction to grant injunctions protecting property. This strand enjoyed early popularity: it was relied on in *Saxby v Easterbrook*[107]and *Thorley's Cattle Food Company v Massam*[108], then reasserted by Lindley LJ (who had been a member of the Court in *Saxby*) in *William Coulson and Sons v James Coulson and Co*[109]. However, it came to be seen as overtaken by the statutory reasoning[110]. Indeed, Coleridge CJ, who had given the leading judgment in *Saxby v Easterbrook*[111], reinterpreted that judgment, saying that it was the first example of the jurisdiction being exercised under the Common Law Procedure Act 1854[112]. This left two, not particularly compelling, statutory strands: the Common Law Procedure Act 1854 and the Judicature Act 1873. Sometimes the strands could be intertwined, as when it was said that 'Since the Judicature Acts, the Chancery Division has on motion granted injunctions restraining the further publication of statements calculated to injure a man's trade'[113]. But the general perception was, that the jurisdiction was the creation of statute. As one American judge put it, when invited to follow the English authorities, those cases 'depend on certain peculiar acts of Parliament of Great Britain, and not on the general principles of equity jurisprudence'[114].

3. THE EXERCISE OF THE JURISDICTION

Various restrictions surrounded, and continue to surround, the exercise of the jurisdiction to award an injunction for defamation. One limitation concerns the type of injunction issued. In essence three types of injunction are available in equity: permanent, interlocutory and *quia timet*. Permanent

105 *Ibid* at 688.
106 *Ibid* at 693.
107 (1878) 3 CPD 339.
108 (1880) 14 ChD 763.
109 (1887) 3 TLR 846.
110 See eg *Monson v Tussauds Ltd* [1894] 1 QB 671 at 690 (per Lord Halsbury LC).
111 (1878) 3 CPD 339.
112 *Bonnard v Perryman* [1891] 2 Ch 269 at 283.
113 *Collard v Marshall* [1892] 1 Ch 571 at 578.
114 *Kidd v Horry* 28 F 773 at 774 (Circuit Court, ED Pennsylvania, 1886).

injunctions are granted at the conclusion of the trial, once the parties' rights have been finally determined. Interlocutory injunctions are granted to restrain repetition of acts or conduct that the claimant alleges infringe his rights, and is suing for, but on which the court has not yet made a decision. *Quia timet* injunctions restrain a defendant in advance from doing an act which might well infringe the claimant's rights. Only permanent or interlocutory injunctions seem to be granted for defamation. One reason given for this is that under Common Law Procedure Act 1854 s 79, a wrong must have been committed before an injunction can be issued[115]. On the other hand the language of Judicature Act 1873 s 25(8) and its successor, the Supreme Court Act 1980 s 37(1) is very general and unqualified[116]. The absence of *quia timet* injunctions for defamation is, therefore, perhaps best explained on grounds of policy, as a reflection of the courts' concern with protecting freedom of speech[117]. In any event the point is likely to be of little practical importance, since a *quia timet* injunction requires evidence that the wrong is likely to occur. However, giving a third an indication of what one is going to publish also amounts to committing the tort of defamation: it is therefore difficult to imagine an application for an injunction to restrain defamation that could not be formulated in terms of repeating a wrong already committed[118].

Some of the restrictions on injunctions for defamation are inherent in the nature of the remedy: an injunction is a court order, breach of which exposes the defendant to criminal proceedings for contempt. It is, therefore, not to be awarded lightly. For instance, it was established in the early 1890s that there must be evidence of an intention to publish the defamatory words[119], which mirrored the approach in other areas, such as patent infringement[120]. The requirement of an intention to repeat the defamatory words has been described relatively recently as 'sensibly a pre-requisite'[121].

Two other factors flowing from the nature of the remedy are that the court is reluctant to grant an injunction in wide terms[122] and is particularly cautious about granting an injunction against the repetition of slander[123].

[115] Meagher, Gummow and Lehane, *Equity—Doctrines and Remedies* (Sydney, 1975) at para 2113.

[116] *Holley v Smyth* [1998] QB 726 at 734 (per Staughton LJ).

[117] See further below at 94–95.

[118] One possible example is where the defendant tells only the claimant what he is intending to publish. Cf *Holley v Smyth* [1998] QB 726, where the threat to the claimant was made via the claimant's solicitors.

[119] *Pink v The Federation of Trades and Labour Unions* (1892) 67 LT 258.

[120] *Proctor v Bayley* (1889) 42 ChD 390. Cf *Millington v Fox* (1838) 3 My & Cr 338, where an injunction was granted despite the absence of a threat to repeat the wrong, but the lack of threat was reflected in the award of costs.

[121] *Al Fayed v The Observer Ltd*, HC, 11 July 1986.

[122] *Liverpool Household Stores Association v Smith* (1887) 37 ChD 170.

[123] *Hermann Loog v Bean* (1884) 26 ChD 306.

Ideally the courts seem to prefer to grant injunctions against republishing a particular document[124]. The reason for this is that the criminal consequences of breach of injunction require that it should be clear to the defendant what he can do, and that there should be clear evidence of breach. A widely framed injunction may make it difficult for the defendant to know where he stands; evidence of repeated slander may well be unreliable.

Restrictions have also developed as a result of the nature of the action for defamation, which have resulted in a distinctive approach to injunctions for defamation. In particular, the courts have consistently asserted that the usual 'balance of convenience' requirement for granting an injunction is not sufficient in defamation cases[125].

One important theme has been the role of the jury. The jury's role in a defamation action was to construe the defamatory words and, by its general verdict, also to determine the success of any defences. Of course, once the verdict had been given, granting a final injunction did not interfere with the jury's role[126]. However, if an interlocutory injunction were granted, that seemed to pre-empt the jury's decision. Indeed, in 1848 the House of Lords expressed that this marginalisation of the jury meant that no injunction was available for defamation at all.

Once the jurisdiction to grant an injunction for defamation had been established, the Court of Appeal quickly established a rule that reconciled the availability of interlocutory injunctions with the role of the jury. In *William Coulson and Sons v James Coulson and Co*[127] Lord Esher MR, after explaining that it was for the jury to construe the libel, continued:

> Therefore the jurisdiction was of a delicate nature. It ought only to be exercised in the clearest cases, where any jury would say that the matter complained of was libellous, and where if the jury did not so find the Court would set aside the verdict as unreasonable.[128]

Here was an explicit recognition of the importance of the jury's role: the court would only grant an injunction where it was beyond the limits of rationality to hold that the words were not defamatory.

The rule was applied by the Court of Appeal subsequently[129], but was also subject to criticism. In *Monson v Tussauds Ltd*[130] Lord Halsbury LC expressed a reluctance to acknowledge that any 'rule' limited the court's equitable jurisdiction[131]. Lopes LJ strongly disagreed, asserting that

124 *Liverpool Household Stores Association v Smith* (1887) 37 ChD 170 at 179, 181.

125 *Bestobell Paints Limited v Bigg* [1975] FSR 421 at 430; *Herbage v Pressdram Ltd* [1984] 1 WLR 1160 at 1162.

126 *Saxby v Easterbrook* (1878) 3 CPD 339.

127 (1887) 3 TLR 846.

128 *Ibid.*

129 *Liverpool Household Stores Association v Smith* (1887) 37 ChD 170.

130 [1894] 1 QB 671.

131 *Ibid* at 690.

William Coulson and Sons v James Coulson and Co[132] had established a fixed rule[133]. Davey LJ adopted a midway position, characterising the rule as one of 'practice'[134]. Despite these criticisms, the rule continued to be applied in England, although not always with the rigour appropriate to a decision to grant an injunction[135]. A recent Court of Appeal decision strongly reasserted the rule, with Staughton LJ paraphrasing it as follows:

> When there is a dispute as to the meaning of what has been published in the past, it seems to me that a plaintiff must show that he will inevitably succeed on that issue at the trial.[136]

It is interesting to note that in Australia the law has developed differently. There the test that the words be clearly defamatory is only a 'prima facie'[137] requirement. The key authority is *Chappell v TCN Channel Nine Pty Ltd*[138], where Hunt J insisted that the general equitable approach of awarding an injunction on the balance of convenience could not be displaced by the rule in *William Coulson and Sons v James Coulson and Co*[139]. Hunt J emphasised the characterisation of the rule as one 'of practice', and went on to say that 'the time has now come in New South Wales to reject *as rigid rules of practice* those rules laid down . . . in [*Coulson*'s case]'[140]. Instead, a more flexible approach was called for. He gave the following illustration:

> It is not difficult to imagine a situation where the prospect of a verdict of no libel is so slight, where the prospect of injury to the defendant if publication is delayed (or prevented) is also so slight, and where the prospect of enormous or overwhelming injury to the plaintiff if publication is permitted is so great, that it would be both unjust and unreasonable to deny interlocutory relief merely because Lord Esher's rule has not been wholly satisfied.[141]

The English courts took the same approach to the defendant's potential defences as they took to defamatory meaning. Thus, in *William Coulson and Sons v James Coulson and Co*[142] Lord Esher MR, having set out the rule for defamatory meaning quoted above, continued:

> The Court must also be satisfied that in all probability the alleged libel was untrue, and if written on a privileged occasion that there was no malice on the

132 (1887) 3 TLR 846.
133 [1894] 1 QB at 694.
134 *Ibid* at 697.
135 *Jarrahdale Timber Company (Limited) v Temperley and Co* (1894) 11 TLR 119.
136 *Maxwell Communication Corporation plc v Newspaper Publishing plc*, CA (Civil Division), 1 August 1991.
137 Balkin and Davis, *Law of Torts*, 2nd edn (Sydney, 1996) at 586.
138 (1988) 14 NSWLR 153.
139 (1887) 3 TLR 846.
140 (1988) 14 NSWLR 153 at 163.
141 *Ibid.*
142 (1887) 3 TLR 846.

> part of the defendant. It followed from these three rules that the Court could only on the rarest occasions exercise their jurisdiction.[143]

The form of words attributed to Lord Esher MR was interesting, for he made no mention of a requirement that the defendant had pleaded justification. This was highly significant. In defamation the words used are presumed to be false, unless the defendant shows them to be true by successfully pleading justification. But here Lord Esher MR seemed to be departing from that general rule, and saying that the burden of proof of falsity was on the claimant. Perhaps a defence of justification had been pleaded—a later Court of Appeal speculated that it had[144]—but nevertheless it is striking that Lord Esher MR did not mention that such a defence was important.

Furthermore, additional support could be found for the idea that the burden of proof of falsity automatically moved to the claimant seeking an interlocutory injunction. Five years earlier, in *Quartz Hill Consolidated Gold Mining Company v Beall*[145] Jessel MR, in refusing an injunction, had said, 'As a general rule the Plaintiff who applies for an interlocutory injunction must shew the statement to be untrue'[146]. The other members of the Court of Appeal in that case did not discuss the point. Certainly one leading American commentator understood that the burden of proof was reversed: writing in 1890, Townshend summarised the English law position as being that 'the court will not in general interfere unless satisfied that the statements complained of in the document are untrue'[147].

The Court of Appeal's decision in *Bonnard v Perryman*[148], the following year, subtly altered the position and gave prominence to a new principle. There the defendant had pleaded justification to words that were clearly defamatory. The Court of Appeal held that no interlocutory injunction could be granted, because it was not convinced that the defence would fail. Lord Coleridge CJ, delivering the judgment of an impressive majority[149] now put the theoretical emphasis on freedom of speech. He said:

> . . . the subject-matter of an action for defamation is so special as to require exceptional caution in exercising the jurisdiction to interfere by injunction before the trial of an action to prevent an anticipated wrong. The right of free speech is one which it is for the public interest that individuals should possess, and, indeed, that they should exercise without impediment, so long as no wrongful act is done; and, unless an alleged libel is untrue, there is no wrong

[143] *Ibid.*
[144] *Holley v Smyth* [1998] QB 726 at 738.
[145] (1882) 20 ChD 501.
[146] *Ibid* at 508.
[147] Townshend, *A Treatise on the Wrongs Called Slander and Libel*, 4th edn (New York, 1890) at 692.
[148] [1891] 2 Ch 269.
[149] Lord Coleridge CJ, Lord Esher MR, Lindley, Bowen and Lopes LJJ.

committed; but, on the contrary, often a very wholesome act is performed in the publication and repetition of an alleged libel.[150]

This emphasis on freedom of speech was to be echoed in many later judgments[151] and, indeed, was seen as displacing the previous emphasis on the jury[152]. However, there is some irony in the fact that by holding that there should be no injunction 'until the trial and determination of the plea of justification'[153] the Court of Appeal effectively made it easier to obtain an injunction. This came about because the ruling in *Bonnard v Perryman*[154] was taken as defining when an injunction could be granted, and, therefore, obscured the earlier cases where the Court of Appeal had suggested that the burden of proof of falsity was reversed whenever a claimant sought an interlocutory injunction. Now the defendant had to plead justification, and the burden of proof was on him, not the claimant.

Admittedly the burden of proof on the defendant under *Bonnard v Perryman*[155] was not heavy, especially since the defendant's supporting affidavits did not need to make any assertion other than that he believed the truth of what he had alleged[156]. Indeed, in one Australian case it was said that the normal requirement that an affidavit must set out the grounds for the belief expressed by the deponent was deliberately waived because of the public policy in protecting freedom of speech[157]. On the other hand, there are good reasons why a defendant might be inhibited from pleading justification for allegations that he believed were true. For instance, the evidence he had of truth might be inadmissible; or he might be a journalist concerned to protect his sources, and would not therefore want to call those sources as witnesses. Tactically it might also be unwise to advance a plea of justification: there is always the risk that a jury (or judge) will find opposing evidence more plausible, and a failed plea of justification could not only aggravate the damages[158], but could also be seen as evidence of malice[159], thus destroying other defences such as fair comment or qualified privilege. In short, convincing policy reasons supported the previous position, that there was no need for a defendant to enter a formal plea of justification. Ultimately, therefore, the decision in

150 [1891] 2 Ch 269 at 284.

151 Eg, *Fraser v Evans* [1969] 1 QB 349 at 360; *Holley v Smyth* [1998] QB 726 at 739.

152 Eg, *Moran v Heathcote*, HC, 15 February 2001.

153 [1891] 2 Ch 269 at 285.

154 [1891] 2 Ch 269.

155 *Ibid.*

156 See the affidavits relied on in *Bonnard's* case. Cf the dissenting judgment of Kay LJ, which centred on the failure of those affidavits to satisfy the requirement that an affidavit must state the grounds on which the belief is based.

157 *National Mutual Life Association of Australasia Ltd v GTV Corporation Pty Ltd* [1989] VR 747 at 753.

158 *Sutcliffe v Pressdram Ltd* [1991] 1 QB 153 at 193 (per Russell LJ).

159 *Simpson v Robinson* (1848) 18 LJQB (ns) 73.

Bonnard v Perryman[160] should be seen as ambivalent: its attractive rhetoric was at odds with its effect.

Bonnard v Perryman was applied by the English courts[161], and continues to be the major leading case today. In particular, the courts have consistently held that the defendant's malicious motive is irrelevant if he has pleaded justification[162], although there may be an exception where the criminal offence of blackmail is established[163].

In Australia, the development has again been different. As with the rule requiring the defamatory meaning to be unquestionable, the Australian courts have preferred a less rigid approach. The more flexible, nuanced analysis can be seen clearly in *National Mutual Life Association of Australasia Ltd v GTV Corporation Pty Ltd*[164], where a current affairs programme contained allegations of misselling against a pension company. At first instance Ormiston J noted the rule in *Bonnard v Perryman*[165], but insisted that 'the real question on any application such as this, where the defamatory nature of the evidence is not disputed, is whether it is 'just and convenient' to grant relief, and this is to be determined in particular by what is the balance of convenience and hardship'[166]. He therefore refused to accept that a genuine plea of justification would always prevent an injunction being granted. In his view, a more subtle evaluation was needed:

> The nature of the material which will be sufficient to deny a plaintiff interlocutory relief must vary according to the sources of the defendant's information and according to the form of discussion which the publication of the defamatory material will take and the extent to which it may be seen to be genuine, serious and in the public interest.[167]

On appeal, the Full Court expressly approved this approach[168].

As with the approach taken to defamatory meaning in Australia, there is a certain attraction in this more flexible and nuanced approach. However, it should be noted that the consequence of adopting this approach is to make injunctions more easily available than under the more rigid English rules, and also to introduce an element of uncertainty in the sense that the weight given to each factor by individual judges will vary[169]. It is not obvious that these consequences are outweighed by the benefits of flexibility.

160 [1891] 2 Ch 269.

161 Eg *London and Northern Bank (Limited) v George Newnes (Limited)* (1899) 16 TLR 76.

162 *Crest Homes Limited v Ascott* [1980] FSR 396; *Bestobell Paints Limited v Bigg* [1975] FSR 421.

163 *Holley v Smyth* [1998] QB 726 at 748 (per Sir Christopher Slade).

164 [1989] VR 747.

165 [1891] 2 Ch 269.

166 [1989] VR 747 at 754.

167 *Ibid.*

168 *Ibid* at 763.

169 *Chappell v TCN Channel Nine Pty Ltd* (1988) 14 NSWLR 153 at 163.

As regards other defences, such as fair comment and qualified privilege, no injunction is granted under English law unless the court is convinced that the defence is hopeless. In other words, the claimant must demonstrate malice in the defendant. Thus, in *Quartz Hill Consolidated Gold Mining Company v Beall*[170], where a defence of qualified privilege was pleaded, the Court of Appeal made it clear that the claimant had a difficult task. On the facts there was no evidence of malice, but Jessel MR said that even if there had been some evidence,

> a Judge should hesitate long before he decides so difficult a question as that of privilege upon an interlocutory application, the circular being on the face of it privileged, and the only answer being express malice. Those are questions which really cannot be tried upon affidavit, or in the mode in which an interlocutory application is disposed of.[171]

The effect of this dictum could be seen in *Champion and Co (Limited) v The Birmingham Vinegar Brewery Company (Limited)*[172], where there was some evidence of malice in the defendant's wide circulation of a report of court proceedings, but the court was not 'absolutely satisfied that a wrong was being done'[173].

In relation to fair comment the same caution could be seen. For instance, in *Mulkern v Ward*[174] Wickens VC doubted that an injunction was appropriate to restrain a critique of building society balance sheets, saying that the criticisms were 'false as principles are false and not false as statements of fact are false'[175]. In *Armstrong v Armit*[176] the same caution took the orthodox form of denying an injunction on the ground of proof of lack of malice. As Lord Denning MR was to put it subsequently, fair comments were not to be restrained because of 'the importance in the public interest that the truth should out'[177].

4. CONCLUSION

The jurisdiction to grant injunctions for defamation, and the rules governing the exercise of that jurisdiction emerged as a result of intense judicial creativity in the 1870s and 1880s. They were settled by 1891. Inevitably those rules reflected contemporary assessments of the relative importance of reputation and freedom of speech, but they have been applied ever

170 (1882) 20 Ch D 501.
171 *Ibid* at 509.
172 (1893) 10 TLR 164.
173 *Ibid.*
174 (1872) LR 13 Eq 619.
175 *Ibid* at 622.
176 (1886) 2 TLR 887.
177 *Fraser v Evans* [1969] 1 QB 349 at 360.

since. Indeed, in 1998 the Court of Appeal described the provisions of the European Convention on Human Rights as being 'of a piece with the rationale of the English courts' rigorous application of the *Bonnard v Perryman* rule over the last hundred years'[178]. It seems that we can look forward to another hundred years of *Bonnard v Perryman*.

[178] *Holley v Smyth* [1998] QB 726 at 742–43.

Part II

The Defendant's Wrong

5

Fault in Ordinary Liability

WRITING HIS TREATISE on libel in 1812, Starkie used 'the defendant's fault' as a major organising category[1]. This was a sensible choice, which reflected the principles set out in the case law. The function of fault in the modern law of defamation, by contrast, is fragmentary and unprincipled. An author's liability requires no proof of fault[2], whilst a distributor escapes liability if he proves that he was not careless[3]. The defences of qualified privilege and fair comment are destroyed if the claimant can show that the defendant acted with some improper motive[4]. Damages may be increased by proof of malice, but only if the claimant's feelings were hurt as a result[5]. There is no unifying theory to explain this diverse and complex set of rules.

What has happened is not so much the disappearance of malice, but, as one writer has described it, its 'withering'[6]. It has lost its vitality, and its ability to give coherence and support to other, more detailed, rules. This chapter analyses the withering of malice in ordinary liability (ie, where no defence is pleaded) in three stages. The first examines the transition from fault to strict liability. The second considers the legal context of the transition, including a comparative analysis. The final section draws on the social context, particularly changes in newspapers, to offer an explanation of why the law developed as it did.

1. THE TRANSITION FROM FAULT TO STRICT LIABILITY

At the start of the nineteenth century the liability of an author (or publisher) had four ingredients: (1) publication of (2) defamatory matter (3) referring to the claimant (4) with malice. Although there was some element of fault in the requirement of publication—in the sense that entirely involuntary publications incurred no liability—the major source

[1] Starkie, *Law of Slander, Libel Scandalum Magnatum and False Rumours* (London, 1812).
[2] *E Hulton & Co v Jones* [1910] AC 20.
[3] Defamation Act 1996 s 1. See further, ch 6.
[4] *Horrocks v Lowe* [1975] AC 135. See further, chs 7 and 8 respectively.
[5] *Rookes v Barnard* [1964] AC 1122. See further, ch 3, above.
[6] Ibbetson, *A Historical Introduction to the Law of Obligations* (Oxford, 1999) at 185, n108.

of fault was the requirement of malice. From early in the history of the common law action for defamation it had been settled that proof of the publication of defamatory matter about the claimant gave rise to a rebuttable presumption of malice[7]. The defendant rebutted this presumption by proving that his motive in speaking (or writing) had not been to injure the claimant: for instance, defendants succeeded where they showed that the defamatory words had been spoken in 'Grief and Sorrow'[8], 'as good counsel'[9] and by way of admonition[10]. The position was encapsulated and explained by Park J in *Bromage v Prosser* at *nisi prius*:

> To support an action for words, malice is essential; but malice may be presumed by the jury, either from their being false, from the nature of the words themselves, from the manner of the speaking of them, or from other evidence; but then the absence of malice may be shown on the other side: and if it were not competent to the jury to consider the question of malice or no malice, and for the defendant to show that he was not actuated by any malice, the communications of society must be at an end.[11]

Where the defendant's motive was a matter of controversy the jury would be invited to draw their conclusion from the evidence. It is important to remember that the evidence would not include the defendant's sworn account of his own state of mind—parties could not give evidence until after 1851[12]. The main evidence of motive would, therefore, show when and how the words were spoken[13]. How a defendant could go about rebutting the presumption of malice in practice can be seen from the evidence produced in *Bromage v Prosser*[14]. The defendant had said that the claimants' bank had stopped payment. Since this was a defamatory statement about the claimant and had been published, the presumption of malice arose. The defendant sought to rebut the presumption by showing the circumstances surrounding the defamatory statement. He had heard a rumour that the bank had stopped payment, and was on his way there to try to get money on notes he held from the bank. After speaking the words he rode on to the bank and discovered that payment had not been stopped; on his return he told the one person to whom he had spoken that the story of payment being stopped was untrue. Park J permitted this evidence to go to the jury, who found for the defendant. However, counsel for the claimant obtained a rule for a new trial; the Court of King's Bench then gave judgment on this rule in a way that changed the law.

7 *Ibid* at 115.
8 *Crawford v Middleton* (1662) 1 Lev 82.
9 *Vanspike v Cleyson* (1597) Cro Eliz 541.
10 *Wilson v Stephenson* (1816) 2 Price 282.
11 (1824) 1 Car & P 475 at 476.
12 Lord Brougham's Act 1851 s 2.
13 Eg, *Smith v Richardson* (1737) Willes 20 at 24.
14 (1824) 1 Car & P 475.

Counsel's objection was that the judge ought not to have left the question of malice to the jury. He argued that the presumption of malice was a conclusion of law, and was, therefore, for the judge to determine. The complaint was essentially about procedure. But the King's Bench seized the opportunity to change the substance of the law:

> That *malice* in some sense, is the gist of the action, and therefore the manner and occasion of speaking the words is admissible in evidence to shew that they were not spoken with malice is said to have been agreed . . . but in what sense the words malice or malicious intent are here to be understood, whether in the popular sense, or in the sense the law puts upon these expressions, none of these authorities state. Malice in common acceptation means ill-will against a person, but in its legal sense it means a wrongful act, done intentionally, without just cause or excuse. If I give a perfect stranger a blow likely to produce death, I do it of *malice*, because I do it intentionally and without just cause or excuse.[15]

The Court held that only legal malice was required for ordinary liability, whereas malice in fact was required for qualified privilege[16]. Two points can be made about the Court's reasoning. First, in order to claim that the meaning of malice in ordinary liability was unclear, the King's Bench had to interpret all of those authorities where the meaning of malice was clear as being cases of qualified privilege. To impose such a rigid distinction between ordinary liability and qualified privilege on those earlier authorities was incorrect: when dealing with situations that today would be regarded as privileged occasions—such as employment references—eighteenth century courts applied the same principles as they did in cases of ordinary liability. The only difference was of emphasis: in the reference cases malice was not presumed from the publication of defamatory words, it had to be proved by the claimant[17]. Secondly, whilst the Court stated that the question of malice should not be left to the jury in cases of ordinary liability[18], there was no guidance as to how the defendant's intention should be ascertained. In a system where the parties could not give evidence, proof of intention was not straightforward.

Two later cases—*Haire v Wilson*[19] and *Fisher v Clement*[20]—made it clear that the defendant's intention could be established by means of a presumption: 'every man must be presumed to intend the natural and ordinary consequences of his own act'[21]. It followed that 'if the tendency of the publication was injurious to the plaintiff, then the law will presume that

[15] (1825) 4 B & C 247 at 254–55.
[16] See further, ch 7, below.
[17] Mitchell, 'Duties, Interests and Motives: Privileged Occasions in Defamation' (1998) 18 *Oxford Journal of Legal Studies* 381 at 387.
[18] (1825) 4 B & C 247 at 258.
[19] (1829) 9 B & C 643.
[20] (1830) 10 B & C 472.
[21] *Haire v Wilson* (1829) 9 B & C 643 at 645.

the defendant, by publishing it, intended to produce that injury which it was calculated to effect'[22]. The idea that a person must be presumed to have intended the natural consequences of his acts was also to be invoked to determine when a defendant was liable for the repetition of his defamatory words[23]. One judge paraphrased the test as being that the intention of the defendant was 'collect[ed] from the libel itself'[24]. Interestingly the question of malice was left to the jury in both later cases without adverse comment from the appellate court, despite the fact that Bayley J, who had delivered the judgment in *Bromage v Prosser*, was a member of the court on both occasions. The procedural objection which had made it possible for the King's Bench to intervene in *Bromage* seemed to have been completely forgotten.

Although these two cases gave some explanation of how the test of legal malice would function in practice they left two crucial questions unanswered. First, did the presumption of intention arise from the publication of any defamatory words? Some statements are not apparently defamatory, but may take on a defamatory meaning if those hearing them interpret them in a particular way. For instance, a statement about 'Frank Hough's curly-headed wife' may be defamatory: if Hough is married to a woman with straight hair, people hearing the statement might think that the straight-haired woman is only pretending to be his wife when she is really living with him in sin[25]. It is unclear whether the judges meant that the presumption of intention should apply to such secondary defamatory meanings because, in each of the cases where the presumption arose the allegation was obviously defamatory. That said, the language used by the judges suggested that the presumption was not meant to apply to secondary defamatory meanings: Littledale J spoke of the 'tendency of the publication'[26], Bayley J of the defendant's intention being collected 'from the libel itself'[27].

The point arose in *The Capital and Counties Bank v Henty & Sons*[28]. There the defendant had sent round a circular to all of its customers stating that it would not accept cheques drawn on the Capital and Counties Bank. The words did not in themselves impute financial instability, but they caused a run on the bank. Counsel for the defendant argued that because the words did not naturally carry an imputation of financial instability the court was required to ascertain 'what the writers of the circular meant, and not what inference might be drawn from it'[29]. This argument appeared to

22 *Ibid.*
23 *Ward v Weeks* (1830) 7 Bing 211.
24 *Fisher v Clement* (1830) 10 B & C 472 at 476.
25 *Hough v London Express Newspapers* [1940] 2 KB 507.
26 *Haire v Wilson* (1829) 9 B & C 643 at 645.
27 *Fisher v Clement* (1830) 10 B & C 472 at 476.
28 (1880) 5 CPD 514 (1882) 7 App Cas 741.
29 (1880) 5 CPD 514 at 518.

enjoy some success in the Divisional Court: Grove J stated that he had to decide whether 'those writing the circular intended to convey any such imputation as is mentioned in the statement of claim'[30]. However, when he came to decide the point his views seemed to be contradictory. He stated: 'I do not agree . . . that what is in the mind of a person is the test of this question, but that the test is what inference would be drawn by a person reasonably reading a circular of this description'[31]. This suggested that he considered the defendant's actual intention to be irrelevant. However, further down the same page he stated that:

> to send a general circular round to a large number of persons stating that the defendants will not receive, as I read it, from anybody cheques drawn on any branch of the Capital and Counties Bank seems to me evidence of an intention in the sense in which I use the word 'intention', viz. that this circular shall be read by the person reading it in a sense injurious to the interests of the Capital and Counties Bank.

Here the judge seemed to be saying that an intention to injure could be inferred from the widespread publication and broad language of the circular. Denman J did not deal with the point.

In the Court of Appeal a majority accepted that if the language was not obviously defamatory proof of the defendant's intention was needed. Thesiger LJ held that if the words of the circular were capable of a defamatory meaning it would be:

> a question for the jury, whether, looking to the particular circumstances of the case, the words spoken or written constituted merely an act done, carrying with it no statement of the motive leading to the act, involving no defamatory meaning, or were intended solely, or in conjunction with the act, to convey and did convey such a defamatory meaning.[32]

He contrasted the facts of the case with an imaginary situation where a circular was 'of such a clearly defamatory character as that it could and ought to be so held, whether those publishing it really meant it as such or not, upon the principle that persons must in law be presumed to intend the natural consequences of their acts . . .'[33]. Cotton LJ also emphasised the importance of intention: 'if there is not in the document itself that which on the fair interpretation of the language is defamatory, the special circumstances must be regarded and those circumstances may shew that it is defamatory and was intended so to be'[34]. He reinforced the point using a variation of the facts of the case: if the defendants had stuck up

[30] *Ibid* at 522.
[31] *Ibid* at 524–25.
[32] *Ibid* at 533.
[33] *Ibid* at 535.
[34] *Ibid* at 536.

posters in public with the same wording as the circular it would have demonstrated their intention to injure, since they had no justification for such widespread publication[35].

In the House of Lords, however, only Lord Selborne LC supported the idea that proof of an intention to injure was required[36]. Lords Penzance[37], Blackburn[38] and Bramwell[39] denied that proof of intention was necessary. So it seemed that the presumption of malice applied to all defamatory imputations, whether they were obviously defamatory or not.

Across the Atlantic, a different view was taken. There, in *Times Pub Co v Carlisle*[40] the Circuit Court of Appeals had clearly considered the reasoning in *Bromage v Prosser*[41], even though it did not cite the case directly. The Court's analysis of malice started by drawing the identical distinction between the 'ordinary' and 'legal' meanings of malice which the English reasoning had drawn. 'In many decisions', the Court then noted, 'it is laid down as a settled rule that malice is essential to a recovery in an action of libel, but that it is conclusively implied from the unprivileged publication of a false charge which is libelous in itself'[42]. It is submitted that the American view had much to recommend it. Quite simply, it did not make sense to assert that a person must have intended to injure the claimant's reputation by uttering words that were not obviously defamatory. The presumption of intention had to have some factual basis to be coherent, and by limiting the presumption to a publication 'libelous in itself' the American court ensured that the factual basis was there. The House of Lords' approach in *The Capital and Counties Bank v Henty & Sons*[43], by contrast, required a presumption of intention to be made without foundation.

The second question left unanswered was whether the presumption of intention could be rebutted; and if so, how? Some of the judicial language used in *Fisher v Clement* suggested that the presumption was irrebuttable: 'a person who publishes matter injurious to the character of another must be considered, in point of law, to have intended the consequences resulting from that act'[44]. However, *Day v Bream*[45] demonstrated one way in which the presumption could be rebutted. The defendant was the porter at a coach office who had delivered parcels of handbills defamatory of the claimant; the parcels had arrived on a coach. Patteson J

35 (1880) 5 CPD at 537.
36 (1882) 7 App Cas 741 at 747, 749.
37 *Ibid* at 767.
38 *Ibid* at 772.
39 *Ibid* at 790.
40 94 F 762 (Circuit Court of Appeals, 8th Circuit, 1899).
41 (1825) 4 B & C 247.
42 94 F 762 at 766.
43 (1882) 7 App Cas 741.
44 (1830) 10 B & C 472 at 475.
45 (1837) 2 M & Rob 54.

> left it to the jury to say whether the defendant delivered the parcels in the course of his business without any knowledge of their contents; if so, to find for him, observing that prima facie he was answerable, inasmuch as he had in fact delivered and put into circulation the libel complained of, and was therefore called upon to shew his ignorance of the contents.[46]

The jury found for the defendant. The defendant's knowledge that his action would injure the claimant's reputation was crucial: without such knowledge an intention to injure could not be presumed.

The same emphasis on the defendant's knowledge can also be found in *Harrison v Smith*[47]. There the defendant had published in the *Cornhill Magazine* an article about the Spanish exploits of a 'notorious swindler', General Plantaganet Harrison. The author had heard the story from a friend in Madrid, and had thought that 'General Plantaganet Harrison' was the swindler's alias. He had never heard of the claimant, whose real name was General Plantaganet Harrison, and who had been in Spain at the times mentioned in the article. The following exchange took place between counsel for the defendant and the judge:

> The *Solicitor-General* for the defendants—It is perfectly true that you have no right to write of a person that which is actually untrue. If you say of a person who is in existence that he did that which he never did do, you have no right to say you did not know that it would do him any damage, and you must pay damage. But in libel intention is everything. It implies an act of the mind; and if a person writes that of a living man, or under the name of a living man, that which is believed to be applied to a particular individual, it may be highly libellous. But if he does not know of the existence of that man and is not thinking of him, he cannot be and ought not to be made liable to an action of libel.
>
> LUSH, J—I must hold the contrary of that.
>
> The *Solicitor-General*—I may take an example from one of Thackeray's novels[48]. There is an absurd barrister called Cockle. There is also a living man, a most excellent, amiable, and distinguished barrister called Cockle, and he fills at this moment a most distinguished situation. Could he have brought an action against Mr Thackeray? If this is not an answer to the action, I confess I shall be extremely surprised.
>
> LUSH, J—If the character is a mere creation of the brain, then it would be no libel.[49]

In his direction to the jury Lush J repeated the point that a writer could not be liable because of a fictional character that was 'a creature of fancy'. Although the judge did not go into the precise legal analysis leading to his

[46] *Ibid* at 56.

[47] (1869) 20 LT 713.

[48] The choice of novelist and example was not at random: Thackeray edited the *Cornhill Magazine*, see Drabble (ed) *The Oxford Companion to English Literature* (Oxford, 1985) at 973–74.

[49] *Ibid* at 714–15.

conclusion, that conclusion was supported by the prevailing test for malice: the writer had published words that defamed the claimant but was unaware of the fact that they would cause injury. It was, therefore, impossible to infer that the defendant had *intended* to defame the claimant.

Further confirmation of the importance of the defendant's knowledge is provided by *The Capital and Counties Bank v Henty & Sons*[50]. The facts of the case are given in more detail above[51], but for present purposes it is enough to recall that it concerned the publication of a statement that was not defamatory on its face. In the Court of Appeal Brett LJ stated that the proper approach was to ask:

> whether there were facts known both to the person who framed the alleged libel, and to the persons to whom it was published, which would lead the latter reasonably to put upon the document the construction that, having a secondary defamatory sense, it was issued ironically or otherwise than in the primary sense of the language.[52]

He explained that the author of the statement must know the extrinsic facts, otherwise he would be 'liable for doing that which by the hypothesis he could have no reason to suppose would injure anybody'[53]. Liability without fault was clearly unacceptable. Lord Blackburn's speech in the House of Lords showed a similar concern with fault:

> The question is not whether the defendant intended to convey that imputation; for if he, without excuse or justification, did what he *knew or ought to have known was calculated to injure the plaintiff*, he must (at least civilly) be responsible for the consequences, though his object might have been to injure another person than the plaintiff or though he may have written in levity only.[54] (emphasis added)

In allowing an intention to injure to be presumed from matters that the defendant ought to have known Lord Blackburn was making explicit something implicit in earlier case law[55].

Knowledge of the circumstances that would lead to the defendant's act injuring the victim was also required in criminal law before a court would hold that the defendant intended the consequences of his act[56]. So the definition of malice in ordinary liability after *Bromage v Prosser*[57] did not represent a radical or unorthodox view. *Bromage v Prosser*[58] had simply substituted one definition of malice for another; the cases following

[50] (1880) 5 CPD 514, (1882) 7 App Cas 741.
[51] See p 104.
[52] (1880) 5 CPD 514 at 539.
[53] *Ibid.*
[54] (1882) 7 App Cas 741 at 772.
[55] *Shepheard v Whittaker* (1875) LR 10 CP 502.
[56] Holmes, *The Common Law* (Boston, 1881) at 51–57. The importance of the defendant's knowledge was made explicit by the House of Lords in *DPP v Smith* [1961] AC 290 at 331.
[57] (1825) 4 B & C 247.
[58] *Ibid.*

Bromage clarified and refined that new definition. The new definition was still firmly rooted in ideas of fault, since it required an awareness on the part of the defendant that his action was likely to injure a person's reputation. Only once that awareness had been proved could malice be presumed against the defendant. So it is difficult to understand why Odgers, for instance, felt able to assert, in relation to ordinary liability in defamation, that 'to say that defamatory words are malicious . . . simply means that they are unprivileged, not employed under circumstances which excuse them'[59]. Odgers' influential work contained no treatment of malice in ordinary liability. It is also difficult to see why Pollock endorsed Odgers' view[60], but this dismissive attitude may well have contributed to the eventual elimination of malice as part of the cause of action.

This elimination was effected by *Jones v E Hulton & Co*[61]. The words complained of formed part of a newspaper's fictional sketch of events at a Grand Prix in Dieppe, and depicted the slightly sleazy behaviour of a character called Artemus Jones, a churchwarden from Peckham. The claimant was a barrister called Artemus Jones, who claimed that readers had associated him with the fictional character[62]. Although there is strong evidence that the writer of the sketch knew the claimant and intended a spiteful jibe at him[63], that evidence was not at the forefront of the legal discussion. The legal point of significance was whether an author could be liable where his fictional character shared attributes with the claimant. There were dicta that purely fictional characters could not be a source of liability to their authors[64] and, as has been demonstrated[65], that authority was supported by the concept of malice that had been brought in by *Bromage v Prosser*[66]. However, at the trial counsel for the defendant failed to address the issue, to the judge's surprise:

> Now I rather thought that it was something in reference to malice that the defendants might be going to contend in this case. There are certain well recognised cases in law where the inference of malice which would otherwise be drawn is rebutted; then in those cases the plaintiff has got to prove actual malice, and it may well be that the inference of actual malice might be different—I do not know whether it is, because the point has not been argued, but this case may go elsewhere, and I want to make clear the reason why I further deal with

59 Odgers, *A Digest of the Law of Libel and Slander* (London, 1881) at 265.

60 Editor's note to de Villiers, 'Malice in the English and Roman Law of Defamation' (1901) 17 *LQR* 388 at 391.

61 [1909] 2 KB 444, [1910] AC 20. Mitchell, 'Malice in Defamation' (1998) 114 *LQR* 639 at 654–61.

62 See, for instance, the evidence that it was alluded to by an Assistant Official Receiver in Bankruptcy, just after the claimant had finished addressing a jury in a case at Chester Assizes. (*House of Lords Journal, Appeal Cases*, vol 573 (1909) Appendix at p 34.)

63 Mitchell, 'Artemus Jones and the Press Club' (1999) 20 *Journal of Legal History* 64.

64 *Harrison v Smith* (1869) 20 LT 713 at 714–15.

65 See above pp 107–108.

66 (1825) 4 B & C 247.

> the question of malice. I think it may well be that where there has been an intentional defamation, and where there has been an accidental defamation, the inference of malice might be different, and the inference of law would not apply.[67]

Instead of focusing on malice, counsel for the defendant had argued that the words could not be read as referring to the claimant because they were about a fictitious character. The judge's direction on this point was that it was a question of fact for the jury to decide. The jury decided that the words did refer to the claimant and awarded £1,750.

The Court of Appeal upheld the jury's verdict by a majority. Counsel for the defendant, perhaps taking the trial judge's hint, made submissions about malice[68]. But those submissions, at least as reported, did not go into how the presumption of malice could be rebutted. As the malice issue had not been properly presented to the Court, it is not surprising that the role of malice was not satisfactorily dealt with in the judgments. Lord Alverstone CJ held that the authorities established 'beyond dispute that . . . the intention or motive with which the words are used is immaterial, and that, if the article does refer, or would be deemed by reasonable people to refer to the plaintiff, the action can be maintained'[69]. He thought that Lord Blackburn's speech in *Capital and Counties Bank v Henty & Sons* was 'conclusive of the point'[70]. As shown above, the authorities—not least Lord Blackburn's speech in *Capital and Counties Bank v Henty & Sons*[71]—supported the requirement of a rebuttable presumption of malice.

Farwell LJ was not content to rely on authorities. He invoked the general principle that:

> the true intention of the writer of any document . . . is that which is apparent from the natural and ordinary interpretation of the written words, and this, when applied to the description of an individual, means the interpretation that would reasonably be put upon those words by persons who know the plaintiff and the circumstances.[72]

This general principle was completely different to the principle established in *Bromage v Prosser*[73] for ascertaining the author's intention. Under the *Bromage* principle, an intention to injure could only be presumed if the defendant had actual or constructive knowledge that his action would injure. Under Farwell LJ's principle, the intention to defame was presumed conclusively if readers understood the words to be defamatory of

67 *House of Lords Journal, Appeal Cases*, Vol 573 (1909), Appendix at 96.
68 [1909] 2 KB 444 at 447.
69 *Ibid* at 455.
70 *Ibid* at 456.
71 (1882) 7 App Cas 741.
72 *Ibid* at 478.
73 (1825) 4 B & C 247.

the claimant—the defendant's awareness of injury played no part. However, Farwell LJ went on to say that:

> the intention to libel the plaintiff may be proved not only when the defendant knows and intends to injure the individuals, but also when he has made a statement concerning a man by a description by which the plaintiff is recognized by his associates, if the description is made recklessly, careless whether it hold up the plaintiff to contempt and ridicule or not.[74]

Presumably this was meant to qualify the earlier statement of principle. The qualification brought Farwell LJ's statement of the law closer to the previous principle; in particular it brought it close to Lord Blackburn's exposition in *The Capital and Counties Bank v Henty & Sons*[75], which referred to a defendant being liable where he knew or ought to have known that injury would result.

However, this position was qualified yet further towards the end of the judgment when Farwell LJ considered what liability arose if published words referred to two or more different claimants. He held that if the allegation was true of one of them, none of the others referred to could sue. However, if the allegation was false in respect of all of them they could all sue. No principled explanation was put forward for this distinction, and the High Court of Australia subsequently rejected it[76]. The overall impression given by the judgment was of a lack of confidence as to what the relevant principles were.

The House of Lords unanimously upheld the Court of Appeal's decision. Lord Loreburn LC defined libel as 'using language which others knowing the circumstances would reasonably think to be defamatory of the person complaining and injured by it'[77]. In his view the defendant's intention was irrelevant. Lords Shaw, Atkinson and Gorrell concurred, although Lords Atkinson and Gorrell completely baffled courts[78] and commentators[79] alike by also concurring in the judgment of Farwell LJ. Farwell LJ had insisted on recklessness for liability, whilst Lord Loreburn LC imposed liability without fault. Furthermore, Lord Loreburn LC made no exception where the words were true of one of several claimants. Despite some subsequent authority that appeared to support Farwell LJ's

[74] *Ibid* at 480–81.

[75] (1882) 7 App Cas 741.

[76] *Lee v Wilson* (1934) 51 CLR 276.

[77] [1910] AC 20 at 23.

[78] *Newstead v London Express Newspapers Ltd* [1940] 1 KB 377 at 385–387. The Supreme Court of Victoria relied on Farwell LJ's judgment when deciding *Lee v Wilson*; the High Court of Australia, overruling the Supreme Court, emphasised the different approach of the House of Lords: (1934) 51 CLR 276 at 285, 296–97.

[79] (1910) 26 *LQR* 103; Holdsworth (1930) 46 *LQR* 133; Holdsworth, 'A Chapter of Accidents in the Law of Libel' (1941) 57 *LQR* 74 at 78; McKerron, 'Fact and Fiction in the Law of Defamation' (1931) 48 *South African Law Journal* 154; Paton, 'Reform and the English Law of Defamation' (1939) 33 *Illinois Law Review of Northwestern University* 669.

position[80], this latter point was finally settled in favour of the view that the truth of the allegation in relation to one potential claimant did not bar an action by other claimants to whom the words referred[81].

The range of liability created by the House of Lords' decision is nicely illustrated by *Cassidy v Daily Mirror Newspapers Ltd.*[82] The defamatory words were in a picture caption: 'Mr. Corrigan, the race horse owner, and Miss X, whose engagement has been announced.' This accurately reported what the subjects of the photograph had told the photographer. The claimant was Corrigan's existing wife. She argued that people reading the statement would conclude that she was masquerading as Corrigan's wife, whilst actually living in sin with him. The Court of Appeal held, by a majority, that an action lay. Both members of the majority regarded the conclusion as compelled by the House of Lords' earlier decision. Greer LJ, the dissenting judge, argued that *Jones v E Hulton & Co*[83] only applied to words that were defamatory on their face. Academic reaction was mixed. Pollock favoured the majority view; reasserting his earlier assessment that malice was irrelevant to ordinary liability[84], he argued that the dicta of Brett LJ in *The Capital and Counties Bank v Henty & Sons*[85] (quoted above[86]) stood alone and did not represent the law[87]. Holdsworth[88], responding to Pollock's analysis, invoked the criterion of recklessness put forward by Farwell LJ in *Jones v E Hulton & Co*[89]; for Holdsworth, the absence of recklessness should be decisive. He (and other commentators[90]) also supported Greer LJ's attempt to limit the application *Jones* by confining it to situations where the words were defamatory on their face.

So after the decisions in *Jones v E Hulton & Co*[91] and *Cassidy v Daily Mirror Newspapers Ltd*[92] ordinary liability was imposed without fault whether or not the words were explicitly defamatory. The transition from fault-based to strict liability, however, had been neither smooth nor

[80] *Shaw v London Express Newspaper Ltd* (1925) 41 TLR 475; *DC Thomson & Co v McNulty* (1927) 71 Sol Jo 744. The High Court of Australia interpreted these cases as turning on whether the words referred to the claimant in order to avoid having to accept Farwell LJ's position (*Lee v Wilson* (1934) 51 CLR 276 at 285–86, 294–95 and 298).

[81] *Newstead v London Express Newspapers Ltd* [1940] 1 KB 377.

[82] [1929] 2 KB 331.

[83] [1910] AC 20.

[84] See above, n 60.

[85] (1880) 5 CPD 514 at 539.

[86] See p 108.

[87] (1930) 46 *LQR* 1 at 2.

[88] (1930) 46 *LQR* 133.

[89] [1909] 2 KB 444.

[90] Anon, 'Libel and Slander—Extrinsic Facts Making the Publication Libelous—Defendant's Ignorance of Such Facts Not a Defense' (1929–1930) 14 *Minnesota Law Review* 186; Anon, 'Libel—Extraneous Facts—Knowledge of Publisher' (1929–1930) 78 *University of Pennsylvania Law Review* 568 at 570.

[91] [1910] AC 20.

[92] [1929] 2 KB 331.

unanimous. The appellate courts that decided *Jones v E Hulton & Co* were not told about the presumption of malice and how it could be rebutted. They drew on authorities that explained the presumption of malice—in particular Lord Blackburn's speech in *Capital and Counties Bank*—but mistakenly interpreted them as supporting strict liability. Members of the House of Lords concurred in judgments that were diametrically opposed, one judgment requiring fault, the other eliminating it. If there was a coherent rationale for the transition to strict liability, it did not appear in the cases.

2. THE LEGAL CONTEXT

The transition to strict liability appears even less convincing when seen in the context of contemporaneous defamation principles. For instance, just before it decided *Jones v E Hulton & Co*[93], the Court of Appeal had held that there was no liability for publication of a letter addressed to the claimant where the defendant did not know that the claimant's clerk would open it. In a judgment that emphasised the defendant's lack of awareness that a clerk would open the letter, Cozens-Hardy MR described the claimant's action as 'a case of libel gone mad'[94]. There were no doubts here about the role of fault. The fact that the decision in *Jones* made a defendant liable for inferences drawn from the words 'whether he foresaw them or not'[95] also appeared to be out of line with other principles. By way of contrast, a claimant could only be held liable for publications to those people to whom he intended to publish the words[96]; and any liability for repetition by those people required proof that the repetition was a natural consequence of the initial publication[97].

Perhaps the most striking contrast was with the law relating to the liability of distributors, such as newsagents[98]. As shown above[99], there was authority that a distributor of defamatory material could escape liability if he proved that he did not know that the material was defamatory. However, when the Court of Appeal considered the basis of a distributor's liability in *Emmens v Pottle*[100], this earlier authority was not discussed (although it was cited); the Court held that an innocent distributor escaped liability if he was ignorant of the libel despite using reasonable care. When the basis of a distributor's liability was considered again, in *Vizetelly v*

93 [1909] 2 KB 444.
94 *Sharp v Skues* (1909) 25 Times LR 336 at 337.
95 *Cassidy v Daily Mirror Newspapers Ltd* [1929] 2 KB 331 at 339.
96 *Powell v Gelston* [1916] 2 KB 615.
97 *Speight v Gosnay* (1891) 60 LJQB 231.
98 See further, ch 6.
99 See pp 106–107.
100 (1885) 16 QBD 354.

Mudie's Select Library Limited[101], Vaughan Williams LJ described *Emmens v Pottle*[102] as being 'in consonance with the whole history of the law of libel'[103]. He explained that a presumption of malice arose from the publication of defamatory words, but that the presumption was rebutted if the publication took place under the circumstances specified in *Emmens*. This perceptive analysis illustrated how far *Jones v E Hulton & Co*[104] and *Cassidy v Daily Mirror Newspapers Ltd*[105]—where the defendants were also unaware that their actions would defame the claimant—were in dissonance with the history of defamation. The fault-based liability of distributors was unaffected by *Jones*[106], and remains a part of modern law[107].

In other common law countries *Jones v E Hulton & Co*[108] also altered the course of legal development. In Australia, for instance, the High Court had said in 1904 that there would be no liability to a claimant who happened to share the same name as the intended target of a libel, because the reference to that claimant was 'an accident'[109]. Such reasoning was obsolete once a later High Court had decided to follow the House of Lords[110].

In the United States various state courts also adopted the new English approach[111]. In the period preceding *Jones v E Hulton & Co*[112], however, Holmes J had developed a very different approach that invoked the general, fault-based, principles of tort. According to Holmes' analysis, where the claimant happened to share the name of a fictitious character the defendant would have a defence only if his belief that there was no real person with that name was 'justifiable' or 'reasonable'[113]. By using a name the defendant was put 'on inquiry'[114] to ascertain whether some real person might be identified. Essentially the basis of liability was negligence, the burden of proof being on the defendant[115]. However, this rule applied only to 'manifestly hurtful statements'[116].

101 [1900] 2 KB 170.
102 (1885) 16 QBD 354.
103 *Ibid* at 178.
104 [1910] AC 20.
105 [1929] 2 KB 331.
106 *Weldon v 'The Times' Book Company (Limited)* (1911) 28 Times LR 143.
107 Defamation Act 1996 s 1.
108 [1910] AC 20.
109 *Godhard v James Inglis & Co Ltd* (1904) 2 CLR 78 at 87.
110 *Lee v Wilson* (1934) 51 CLR 276.
111 *Washington Post Company v Kennedy* 41 Am LR 483 (Court of Appeals of District of Columbia, 1925); *Larocque v New York Herald Company* (1917) 220 NY Rep 632. See also American Law Institute, *Restatement of the Law of Torts* (St Paul, 1938) s 579 and comment a.
112 [1910] AC 20.
113 *Hanson v Globe Newspaper Company* 159 Mass 293 at 301 and 303 (Supreme Judicial Court of Massachusetts, 1893).
114 *Ibid* at 304.
115 It is revealing that one American commentator who welcomed the Court of Appeal's decision in *Jones* believed that it imposed liability for negligence: Anon, 'Libel Without Intent' (1909–10) 23 *Harvard Law Review* 218.
116 *Peck v Tribune Company* 214 US 185 at 189 (Supreme Court of the United States, 1909).

Where the statement was not manifestly hurtful the American position was more complex, both before and after *Jones v E Hulton & Co*[117]. The case law was equivocal, but academic commentators argued that the importance of the defendant's culpability must not be overlooked[118] and that the appropriate standard of liability was negligence[119]. Indeed, one commentator thought that the decision in *Cassidy v Daily Mirror Newspapers Ltd*[120] would not be followed by American courts because there was no evidence of the defendant's lack of due care[121]. Despite this academic unanimity, the author of the *Restatement of the Law of Torts* took the view that the law of the United States was the same as English law:

> . . . one who publishes defamatory matter of another is not relieved of liability because
>
> (a) he did not intend the matter so published to be defamatory and neither knew nor by the exercise of every possible precaution could have known that it would be so understood.[122]

However, even assuming that the *Restatement* correctly aligned English and US law on this point, libels not defamatory on their face were dealt with significantly differently in some parts of the United States. Some States had adopted the rule of libel *per quod*[123], under which a libel not defamatory on its face was not actionable without proof of special damage, unless it made an allegation of the type that was actionable without proof of special damage in slander[124]. American claimants complaining of libels not defamatory on their face were, therefore, faced with an obstacle which similar English claimants did not have to negotiate. Enough states adopted the libel *per quod* rule that there was a proposal to amend the *Restatement*[125] which, as drafted, reflected the English rule that all libels were actionable without proof of special damage. The proposed amendment became 'something of a storm center'[126] with Prosser, the Reporter, becoming embroiled in a fierce debate over exactly how many states recognised libel *per quod*[127]. Among the arguments of principle put

117 [1910] AC 20.

118 Anon, 'Negligence in the Law of Defamation' (1915–16) 29 *Harvard Law Review* 533.

119 Above; Anon, 'Liability for Defamatory Words Intended to Apply to Another Person But Reasonably Applicable to the Plaintiff' (1924–25) 38 *Harvard Law Review* 1100.

120 [1929] 2 KB 331.

121 Hallows, 'Libel—Liability for Hidden Defamatory Meaning' (1930) 25 *Illinois Law Review* 98, noted at (1930) 46 *LQR* 263.

122 American Law Institute, *Restatement of the Law of Torts* (St Paul, 1938) s 580. See also comments b and c.

123 For more detail see chapter 1, pp 12–14.

124 Ie, unfitness for office, criminality, loathsome disease, female unchastity.

125 American Law Institute, *Restatement of the Law of Torts* (St Paul, 1938) s 569.

126 American Law Institute, *Restatement of the Law (Second) Torts, Tentative Draft No 12* (Philadelphia, 1966) at 29.

127 Prosser, 'Libel *Per Quod*' (1960) 46 *Virginia Law Review* 839; American Law Institute, *Restatement of the Law (Second), Torts, Tentative Draft No 11* (Philadelphia, 1966) at

forward for adopting the rule, it was said that it would 'protect publishers who make statements innocent in themselves, that are defamatory only because of extrinsic facts known to the reader'[128]. The importance of protecting innocent publishers was at the forefront in the formulation that the Institute provisionally adopted: it agreed to retain the general rule that libel was actionable without proof of special damage 'with a proviso that the publisher of a statement whose libelous character can be ascertained only by reference to extrinsic facts is liable only if he knew or should have known those facts'[129]. This amounted to a direct reversal of s 580 of the first *Restatement* (quoted above). Before it could be incorporated into the second *Restatement*, however, it was overtaken by events. In 1974 the Supreme Court held, in *Gertz v Robert Welch Inc*[130], that the First Amendment to the Constitution required that the standard of liability in defamation should be at least negligence; a higher degree of fault might be needed where the words were not apparently defamatory[131]. Paradoxically the Supreme Court was invoking constitutional reasoning in order to return the basis of liability to where the general theory of tort had located it over half a century earlier. The American experience of strict liability in defamation had been brief and unhappy.

The South African courts of the period drew on the English law of defamation to develop their own, but they rejected *Jones v E Hulton & Co*[132]. Although the foundation of the South African law of defamation was Roman, its superstructure was strongly influenced by English law. The Roman basis was the delict *iniuria,* which, in classical Roman law, required that an action was done deliberately to cause affront and with knowledge that it was not justified[133]. There was a close similarity between South African and English law before 1910 on the role of fault in ordinary liability: in South African law the fault element, *animus injuriandi,* was presumed from the utterance of defamatory words. The presumption could be rebutted in various ways[134]. Shortly after the decision in *Jones* the

83–89; Eldredge, 'The Spurious Rule of Libel *Per Quod*' (1966) 79 *Harvard Law Review* 733; American Law Institute, *Restatement of the Law (Second), Torts, Tentative Draft No 12* (Philadelphia, 1966) at 29–45; Prosser, 'More Libel *Per Quod*' (1966) 79 *Harvard Law Review* 1629.

128 *American Law Institute, Restatement of the Law (Second), Torts Tentative Draft No 12* (Philadelphia, 1966) at 44; Prosser, 'More Libel *Per Quod*' (1966) 79 *Harvard Law Review* 1629 at 1646; both quoting from Justice Traynor in *MacLeod v Tribune Co* 343 P2d 43–44 (Supreme Court of California, 1959).

129 American Law Institute, *Restatement of the Law (Second), Torts*, Appendix, Vol 4 (St Paul, 1981) s 569 at para 4. See also Eldredge, 'Variation on Libel *Per Quod*' (1972) 25 *Vanderbilt Law Review* 79.

130 418 US 323 (1974).

131 *Ibid* at 347–48.

132 [1910] AC 20.

133 De Villiers, 'Malice in the English and Roman Law of Defamation' (1901) 17 *LQR* 388 at 388–89.

134 *Botha v Brink* (1878) 8 Buch 118 at 130.

South African courts started to narrow down the ways in which the presumption could be rebutted by excluding situations where the defendant believed that his actions were justified[135]. In doing so they were strongly influenced by English law[136]. However, the courts were not prepared to presume an intention to injure when the defendant's innocent mistake was the cause of the words referring to the claimant; they expressly rejected *Jones'* case[137]. At the very least negligence, and probably recklessness, was required[138].

So strict liability outside England had a less than enthusiastic reception: no principled justification was found by the jurisdictions that adopted it, and another jurisdiction that was highly receptive to English rules rejected it. This caution about strict liability makes the English courts' adoption of it all the more puzzling. One option is simply to explain away the English cases as 'a chapter of accidents'[139]. A better explanation however, is to look beyond their analytical weaknesses and to see them as judicial responses to social change.

3. THE NEWSPAPER CONTEXT

What had changed between 1881, when the House of Lords thought that fault was relevant, and 1910, when the same court eliminated fault, was newspapers. The compulsory primary education introduced by the 1870 Education Act had created an enormous class of new readers with a rudimentary level of literacy. As one commentator put it, this was a generation of readers 'which had been taught to read but not to think'[140]. Newspaper proprietors quickly identified the potential of this enormous new market. The pioneer was Newnes, whose weekly *Tit-Bits* (1885–) reprinted interesting short facts for the diversion of its readers; the formula of 'Information as entertainment' was a massive success. Harmsworth (later Lord Northcliffe) followed it with *Answers* (1888–), which answered questions from readers (real or imagined) such as What the Queen Eats and Why Jews Don't Ride Bicycles[141].

[135] *Jooste v Claassens* 1916 TPD 723; *Laloe Janoe v Bronkhorst* 1918 TPD 165; *Kleinhans v Usmar* 1929 AD 121; McKerron, 'Fact and Fiction in the Law of Defamation' (1931) 48 *South African Law Journal* 154. The process was reversed in *Maisel v Van Naeren* 1960 (4) SA 836.

[136] Price, 'The Basis of the South African Law of Defamation' [1960] *Acta Juridica* 254, particularly at 261 and 263.

[137] *Ferreira v Sardinha* 1917 TPD 478; *Laloe Janoe v Bronkhorst* 1918 TPD 165 at 168–69. For a delighted reaction ('eschewing the mongrel breed of legal decisions') see De Villiers, '*Animus Injuriandi*: An Essential Element in Defamation' (1931) 48 *South African Law Journal* 308 at 310.

[138] *Nasionale Pers v Long* 1930 AD 87.

[139] Holdsworth, 'A Chapter of Accidents in the Law of Libel' (1941) 57 *LQR* 74.

[140] Pound and Harmsworth, *Northcliffe* (London, 1959) at 100.

[141] Pound and Harmsworth, *ibid* at 82. These two examples are taken from the first issue of *Answers*.

Daily newspapers were also adapting to the needs and tastes of the new reading public. In London this process was led by WT Stead, the editor of the *Pall Mall Gazette*, who produced sensational articles that responded vividly to the events of the day. Another key figure was T P O'Connor, who edited *The Star* (1888). O'Connor was strongly influenced by American popular journalism, which was concise and punchy[142]. But it was not only the style that was new: the choice of content was different too. In the first edition of *The Star* he promised his readers 'plenty of entirely unpolitical literature—sometimes humorous, sometimes pathetic; anecdotal, statistical, the craze of fashions and the arts of house-keeping—now and then a short, dramatic and picturesque tale . . .'[143]. As one recent commentator put it, O'Connor's emphasis on gossip was 'a seismic shock, an innovation to match the arrival of Page Three girls nearly a century later'[144]. Another commentator drily noted that it might be difficult for readers of *The Star* to tell the difference between reported facts and picturesque tales[145]. O'Connor also wrote an influential article in support of the new style of journalism[146]. In particular he extolled 'the more personal tone of modern methods'[147], comparing it with the use of personal detail made by historians such as Macaulay and Carlyle. He argued that 'the desire for personal details with regard to public men is healthy, rational, and should be yielded to'[148], and that newspapers should report good-natured gossip.

Later popular newspapers followed a similar model to O'Connor's *Star*. The *Daily Mail* (1896) was characterised by extreme brevity: when its founder, Lord Northcliffe, was invited to reproduce the effect in an edition of the New York *World*, he insisted that no story should be longer than 250 words[149]. The *Daily Express* (1900) had a similar style. Another of Northcliffe's newspapers, the *Daily Mirror* (1903), was initially a financial disaster, but was saved by the increased use of illustrations and gossip[150]. The tabloid press had arrived.

All these developments tended to increase the likelihood of defamation by newspapers. Each journal was competing for readers who expected their newspaper to entertain them. That entertainment was being provided by accounts of diverting incidents, personal details, gossip and a mixture of fact and fiction. When cases of defamation by newspaper

142 Small, *The Printed Word; An Instrument of Popularity* (Aberdeen, 1982) at 93–98. Wilkes, *Scandal: A Scurrilous History of Gossip* (London, 2002) at 87–90.

143 *The Star*, 1 January 1888.

144 Wilkes, *Scandal: A Scurrilous History of Gossip* (London, 2002) at 88.

145 Small, *The Printed Word; An Instrument of Popularity* (Aberdeen, 1982) at 97.

146 'The New Journalism' (1889) 1 *The New Review* 423.

147 *Ibid*.

148 *Ibid* at 428.

149 Pound and Harmsworth, *Northcliffe* (London, 1959) at 266.

150 *Ibid* at 277–80.

reached the courts it was clear that the popular press was not popular with everyone. O'Connor described 'a spirit of savage hatred to journalism'[151] among juries, leading to 'some scandalous damages', and he complained that some portions of the public thought that journalists set out to libel. Certainly O'Connor's complaint was not without foundation. Shortly before the decision in *Jones v E Hulton & Co*[152], for instance, there had been a strong manifestation of antipathy to the Press when Lever Brothers had sued the *Daily Mail* for defamatory allegations about cheating and the jury awarded £50,000, at that time the largest jury award ever made[153].

Set against this background, the decision in *Jones v E Hulton & Co*[154] becomes intelligible. Indeed, a dislike of the conduct of certain newspapers can be detected in the judgments. Rejecting the defendant's submission that the damages were excessive, Farwell LJ commented that 'Such newspapers as publish libellous statements do so because they find that it pays: many of their readers prefer to read and believe the worst of everybody, and the newspaper proprietors cannot complain if juries remember this in assessing damages'[155]. When Lord Loreburn LC rejected the same submission, he pointed out that the jury was entitled to condemn publications, and to decide 'whether they bear a stamp and character which ought to enlist sympathy and ensure protection'[156]. Both judges saw large damages awards as a means of curbing the excesses of popular journalism. Lord Alverstone CJ, who gave the leading judgment in the Court of Appeal, made clear his disapproval of 'certain low-class newspapers' extrajudicially[157].

The judgments in *Cassidy v Daily Mirror Newspapers Ltd*[158] revealed similar judicial disapproval. On the facts it was difficult to criticise the defendant's behaviour—as one commentator remarked, 'normally one may take the word of *two* people who say they are engaged'[159]. However, the *Daily Mirror's* general conduct was unlikely to have endeared it to the judiciary. Its unashamed policy at the time was to use salacious stories to increase circulation[160]; as one reporter reminisced, 'The Mirror wanted Sex . . . Sex . . . sold papers'[161]. Indeed, the fact that the case concerned an imputation about sexual morality by this particular newspaper may have made the

[151] *Lee v Wilson* (1934) 51 CLR 276 at 430.
[152] [1910] AC 20.
[153] Pound and Harmsworth, *Northcliffe* (London, 1959) at 302–4.
[154] [1910] AC 20.
[155] [1909] 2 KB 444 at 483.
[156] [1910] AC 20 at 24.
[157] See his evidence given in 1910 to the Royal Commission on Divorce (1912). Wilkes, *Scandal: A Scurrilous History of Gossip* (London, 2002) at 134.
[158] [1929] 2 KB 331.
[159] Paton, 'Reform and the English Law of Defamation' (1939) 33 *Illinois Law Review of Northwestern University* 669 at 677.
[160] Wilkes, *Scandal: A Scurrilous History of Gossip* (London, 2002) at 118.
[161] *Ibid.*

defendant's arguments about moral fault particularly unattractive. Certainly, given the context, it was not surprising to find that Russell LJ denied that strict liability imposed a hardship on the defendant newspaper:

> From a business point of view no doubt it may pay them not to spend time or money in making enquiries, or verifying statements before publication; but if they had not made a false statement they would not now be suffering in damages. They are paying a price for their methods of business.[162]

A remark by Greer LJ, who dissented, was particularly revealing: 'It must be remembered that there is no special law, for the purposes we are considering, applicable to libels by newspapers'[163]. This suggested that the majority did see the case as laying down a special law for newspapers.

Once the decisions in *Jones v E Hulton & Co*[164] and *Cassidy v Daily Mirror Newspapers Ltd*[165] are seen in the light of the newspaper revolution that preceded them, the introduction of strict liability can be understood. It is not surprising that the courts abandoned the previously accepted criteria of fault, because their underlying conception of the law of libel was changing. They no longer saw it as being a mere part of the law of tort, where justice to the defendant required fault for the imposition of liability. Rather, they saw it as part of the law relating to newspapers, and the behaviour of some newspapers called for a stricter standard of liability. Libel had become part of media law.

4. CONCLUSION

The basis of liability in the modern law of defamation remains strict[166]. As has been shown, the authorities have no principled basis, but are best understood as a judicial reaction to the expansion of the popular press. Even on the (dubious) assumption that the role of fault in ordinary liability is a question of media law, it is doubtful whether the balance struck in *Jones v E Hulton & Co*[167] and *Cassidy v Daily Mirror Newspapers Ltd*[168] is still appropriate today. The modern trend is towards making all professional liability turn on the absence of reasonable care[169]. As Lord Hoffmann has

162 [1929] 2 KB 331 at 354.
163 *Ibid* at 350.
164 [1910] AC 20.
165 [1929] 2 KB 331.
166 Statutory intervention has enabled defendants to avoid some of the effects of strict liability (see Defamation Act 1996 ss 2–4).
167 [1910] AC 20.
168 [1929] 2 KB 331.
169 *Arthur JS Hall & Co v Simons* [2002] 1 AC 615.

remarked, negligence actions, even vexatious ones, 'are an occupational hazard of professional men'[170]. In other words, all professionals should be liable for damage they cause through falling below the accepted standards of their profession. At the time of the decisions in *Jones* and *Cassidy* the general principle of liability for negligence had not been acknowledged[171], and recognition that professional liability should be governed by that principle was over thirty years away[172]. Today, however, there is no good reason why journalists should be treated differently: liability in damages should turn on negligence. In the United States it already does[173]. The best way to strike the balance between the media and claimants, therefore, is to make liability in damages depend on fault; reshaping the law in this way would be doing no more than repeating the balancing process that the courts used in *Jones* and *Cassidy*.

Furthermore, it may not be correct to assume that fault in ordinary liability is purely a question of media law: the statistical predominance of actions against the media should not lead us to overlook other defendants, who are equally deserving of fair treatment. One option might be to have two separate rules, one for media and one for non-media defendants[174]. Even if the theoretical objections to differential treatment can be overcome[175], an obvious problem with this approach is that it makes the law more complex and creates an immediate definitional difficulty: how do you define a 'media defendant'? The preferable option would be to formulate a test that, as a matter of principle, was sensitive to the factual matrix. The standard of reasonable care is admirably suited to this role: assessing whether the defendant has failed to act with reasonable care involves the delicate balance of a range of factors[176]. For instance, the high degree of harm that is likely to result from widespread publication would call for a higher standard of care than when the publication is to a limited audience[177]; the professional skills and expertise of media defendants would require them to go to greater lengths to verify the accuracy of statements than non-professional speakers[178]. This high standard of care might require media defendants to take steps to eliminate the risk of accidental defamation by checking that the descriptions of real or fictitious characters

[170] *Ibid* at 696–7.
[171] *Donoghue v Stevenson* [1932] AC 562.
[172] *Hedley Byrne & Co Ltd v Heller & Partners Ltd* [1964] AC 465.
[173] *Gertz v Robert Welch Inc* 418 US 323 (United States Supreme Court, 1974).
[174] *South African Broadcasting Corporation v O'Malley* 1977 (3) SA 394.
[175] See, for instance, *Philadelphia Newspapers, Inc v Hepps* 475 US 767 (United States Supreme Court, 1986) at 780: 'the inherent worth of . . . speech in terms of its capacity for informing the public does not depend upon the identity of the source, whether corporation, association, union or individual' (per Brennan and Blackmun JJ, concurring).
[176] *Qualcast (Wolverhampton) Ltd v Haynes* [1959] AC 743.
[177] *Paris v Stepney Borough Council* [1951] AC 367.
[178] *Wells v Cooper* [1958] 2 QB 265.

cannot be identified with unintended real people[179]. On the other hand, a praiseworthy motive, such as the exposure of corruption, might justify taking an otherwise unjustifiable risk of defaming the claimant[180]. The court could take all relevant factors into account. Indeed, in the recently developing law of qualified privilege for statements in the media[181], the courts have shown a readiness to engage in questions about the standard of responsible journalism.

So, whether the role of fault should be seen as a question of media law or not, the position set out in *Jones* and *Cassidy* no longer deserves support. The standard imposed on the media by those two cases is significantly more stringent than the standard imposed on other professions; it also applies to non-professional speakers, where there is no justification for it at all. A standard of reasonable care, by contrast, would be flexible, fair and in line with the level of conduct generally demanded in tort.

179 The current process of negative checking is described in Barendt, Lustgarten, Norrie and Stephenson, *Libel and the Media; The Chilling Effect* (Oxford, 1997) at 114–16.

180 *Watt v Hertfordshire County Council* [1954] 1 WLR 835.

181 *Reynolds v Times Newspapers Ltd* [2001] 2 AC 127.

6

Second Publishers

LIABILITY IN DEFAMATION is not restricted to authors: any person who takes part in making the defamatory matter known to another may also be liable[1]. The gist of the action is publication, not creation. This chapter examines the law relating to the liability of those publishers who are not also authors. For convenience the analysis is divided, as it is in the case law, into three separate classes: first, liability for repetition of allegations; second, liability for distributing defamatory material; and finally, liability for failing to prevent a person making a publication. Although the traditional approach has been to analyse these three classes of liability separately it can be seen that the classes deal with essentially the same problem: namely, the liability of publishers who did not create the defamation. The only difference between the classes is the degree of involvement of the second publisher, which ranges from the positively active (repetition) to the utterly passive (failure to prevent publication). The final section of the chapter draws together themes from the case law in all three classes and considers what the most convincing approach to the liability of second publishers would be.

1. REPETITION

In the modern law of defamation a defendant does not establish a defence purely by proving that he repeated words used by another[2]. Accurate reports of certain proceedings, such as a Parliamentary debate or a court hearing, may be protected by a defence of absolute or qualified privilege, but the scope of these defences is narrowly defined[3]. This modern position is much more restrictive than it was in the eighteenth and early nineteenth centuries. In that earlier period a defence based on repetition was recognised and applied.

[1] *Marchant v Ford* [1936] 2 All ER 1510.
[2] *Stern v Piper* [1997] QB 123.
[3] Defamation Act 1996 s 14 and s 15. See further ch 10 below.

The leading authority was *The Earl of Northampton's Case*[4], an action of *scandalum magnatum*[5] against six defendants, each of whom claimed that they had done no more than repeat a scandalous imputation they had previously heard. The panel of eleven judges resolved that:

> . . . in a private action for slander to a common person, if JS publish that he hath heard JN say, that JG was a traitor or thief; in an action of the case, if the truth be such, he may justify.

The court went on to make clear that it was crucial for the defendant to identify his source. Otherwise the defendant would not give the claimant a cause of action against anyone else. Furthermore, failure to name the source might cause unnecessary damage to the claimant's reputation. For instance if the source were identified as a drunkard the allegation would receive less credit than if the defendant could keep his source anonymous.

The defence set out in *The Earl of Northampton's Case*[6] was recognised, although often distinguished, by later courts on both sides of the Atlantic. For example, in *Davis v Lewis*[7] the Court of King's Bench acknowledged the defence, but held that it did not apply where the defendant had failed to identify his source until the pleadings. Similarly, in *Maitland v Goldney*[8] the same Court assumed the validity of the defence, but held that the defendant had not done enough to give the claimant a cause of action against the source of the allegation by pleading that the source had spoken words 'to the effect following'; the precise words should have been given. Both qualifications to the defence were approved in *Woolnoth v Meadows*[9], where Lawrence J also commented that the rule laid down in *The Earl of Northampton's Case* was 'good'[10]. In the United States the Superior Court of Delaware acknowledged that the defence was 'the settled rule of law whether reasonable or not'[11]; it was also discussed and applied by two decisions in the Supreme Court of New York[12] and one in the Supreme Court of Vermont[13].

As well as recognising the defence the courts explored whether it was consistent with the general principles of liability for defamation. In general they held that the defence was consistent with general principles,

[4] (1612) 12 Co Rep 132.

[5] A special claim available only to the King and other grandees when allegations had been made that might cause discord or slander between the rulers and the people. See further Kiralfy, *The Action on the Case* (London, 1951) at 115 ff.

[6] (1612) 12 Co Rep 132.

[7] (1796) 7 TR 17.

[8] (1802) 2 East 426.

[9] (1804) 5 East 463.

[10] *Ibid* at 472.

[11] *Tatlow v Jaquett* 1 Del 333 (Superior Court of Delaware, 1834).

[12] *Dole v Lyon* 10 Johns 447 (Supreme Court of New York, 1813); *Mapes v Weeks* 4 Wend 659 (Supreme Court of New York, 1830).

[13] *Skinner v Grant* 12 Vt 456 (Supreme Court of Vermont, 1840).

and in particular with the principle that liability was based on malice[14]. Thus, in *Maitland v Goldney*[15] the Court considered how the defence applied where the defendant repeated an allegation which he knew that the source had admitted was mistaken and had retracted. The Court disposed of the case on the point of pleading mentioned above, but Lord Ellenborough CJ hinted that the attempt to use the defence would have failed anyway. He remarked:

> The fact . . . of such previous uttering was merely used by the defendants as a pretence for publishing the same slander: that shews malice in the defendants and an injury to the plaintiffs.[16]

The Supreme Court of New York in *Dole v Lyon*[17] made more explicit that the defence from *The Earl of Northampton's Case*[18] should be seen as based on the absence of malice. Kent CJ observed that:

> . . . it may well be questioned, whether . . . this rule as to slanderous words ought not to depend upon the *quo animo* with which the words with the name of the author are repeated. Words of slander with the name of the author may be repeated with a malicious intent, and with mischievous effect.[19]

The same approach was taken by the Supreme Court of Vermont[20]. Perhaps the most forthright analysis was extrajudicial. Starkie, in his treatise on defamation, pointed out that the principle in *The Earl of Northampton's Case*[21] was 'not very apparent' and offered the following explanation:

> . . . since the conduct of a person who gives up the author of an injurious report, and enables the party calumniated to reach the author of the calumny, may be attributed to a good and friendly motive, that circumstance may operate to the defendant's advantage, though it does not seem, in strictness, to warrant any thing more than a *prima facie* presumption in his favour.[22]

This explanation was consistent with the hint in *Maitland v Goldney*[23] that the defence would fail where the defendant repeated an allegation he knew was untrue: such conduct was 'pregnant with malice'[24] and therefore rebutted any presumption of friendliness.

[14] For an analysis suggesting that *The Earl of Northampton's Case* was consistent with the principles of justification (truth) see the judgment of Paine J in *Sans v Joerris* 14 Wis 663 (Supreme Court of Wisconsin, 1861).
[15] (1802) 2 East 426.
[16] *Ibid* at 437.
[17] 10 Johns 447 (1813).
[18] (1612) 12 Co Rep 132.
[19] 10 Johns 447 (1813) at 449.
[20] *Skinner v Grant* 12 Vt 456 (1840).
[21] (1612) 12 Co Rep 132.
[22] Starkie, *Law of Slander, Libel Scandalum Magnatum and False Rumours* (London, 1812) at 219.
[23] (1802) 2 East 426.
[24] *Ibid* at 221.

However, it should be noted that, elegant as the explanation based on malice was, it was not entirely consistent with *The Earl of Northampton's Case*[25]. The Court had insisted that for a defendant to claim the defence he must have named his source at the time of speaking. If the defence was merely one way for a defendant to show that he was not malicious, as Starkie and others argued, it was difficult to see why the name of the source should be so important. Indeed in *Crawford v Middleton*[26] a case was referred to with approval where the defendant had said that he had heard that the claimant had been hanged for theft; Hobart J nonsuited the claimant because on the evidence it appeared that the words were spoken out of grief and sorrow, not malice. No significance appears to have attached to the defendant's failure to name his source.

So the defence set out in *The Earl of Northampton's Case*[27] was recognised by the courts and could be made consistent with the general principles of liability for defamation. However, neither factor could guarantee its continued existence and two decisions in 1829 eliminated it from English law. The first, *De Crespigny v Wellesley*[28] held that the defence had no application to libels. The Court was prepared to accept that the defence might be adequate for slander because 'the report is not heard of beyond the circle in which all the parties are known, and the veracity of the accuser, and the previous character of the accused, will be properly estimated.'[29] Libel, however, could be inserted in a journal and circulated throughout the world, to places where no estimation of the character of the accused or accuser could be made.

This distinction would in itself have justified the decision not to permit the defence to apply on the facts. However, Best CJ went on to assert two broader reasons of policy against the defence. The first was that it was open to abuse: it would be easy to pay 'wretches, who would be better off within the walls of a prison than they are without'[30] to make any defamatory statement. A defendant repeating such a statement could shelter behind the defence. Secondly, 'our moral duty'[31] on hearing something defamatory was to keep quiet about it unless it was a matter of public concern. Best CJ insisted that:

> We are on no account to report it to gratify our emnity to any particular person, or, for that more common cause of slander, to gratify the malice that exists by a desire to raise ourselves above, or keep ourselves upon an equality with our neighbours by injuring their characters.[32]

[25] (1612) 12 Co Rep 132.
[26] (1662) 1 Lev 82.
[27] (1612) 12 Co Rep 132.
[28] (1829) 5 Bing 392.
[29] *Ibid* at 402.
[30] *Ibid* at 403.
[31] *Ibid* at 405.
[32] *Ibid* at 405.

Both were powerful reasons. However, both reasons assumed that the defence would be available to a malicious defendant. As shown above, courts in England and the United States had seen *The Earl of Northampton's Case*[33] as being based on the principle that a defendant should escape liability by showing that he was not malicious. Best CJ implicitly rejected that view.

The second decision eliminating the defence from *The Earl of Northampton's Case*[34] was *McPherson v Daniels*[35], where the defendant had repeated a slander and named his source. Parke J rejected the defence on two grounds. First he criticised the accuracy and reliability of volume 12 of Coke's Reports, in which *The Earl of Northampton's Case*[36] was reported. Secondly he adopted the broad objections of policy that Best CJ had advanced in *De Crespigny v Wellesley*[37]. The reasoning of Bayley and Littledale JJ was more doctrinal. Their starting point was that any publication of slanderous matter was *prima facie* wrongful. Therefore once a plaintiff had shown that the defendant had published defamatory matter the defendant had to raise a defence. The only possibility on the facts was to show that the publication had taken place 'upon a justifiable occasion'[38]. Such occasions were determined on grounds of 'public policy and convenience'[39], and included speaking in a judicial proceeding or giving the character of a servant. There were no such grounds where a defendant merely repeated a slander.

At first glance it is surprising that neither Bayley J nor Littledale J dealt with the principled explanation of *The Earl of Northampton's Case*[40], ie that merely repeating the defamation and naming the source suggested that the defendant was not malicious. Their failure to deal with the point was both deliberate and significant. The principled explanation of *The Earl of Northampton's Case*[41] had been developed against the background that a defendant escaped liability by showing that his motive in speaking was not to injure the claimant's reputation[42]. At the time of the decision in *McPherson v Daniels*[43] that background assumption was no longer true. In *Bromage v Prosser*[44] the Court of King's Bench, in a judgment written by Bayley J, held that 'malice' in defamation did not refer to the defendant's motive; rather, 'malice' meant an intention to injure, and a person was presumed to intend

33 (1612) 12 Co Rep 132.
34 *Ibid.*
35 (1829) 10 B & C 263.
36 (1612) 12 Co Rep 132.
37 (1829) 5 Bing 392.
38 *Ibid.*
39 *Ibid.*
40 (1612) 12 Co Rep 132.
41 *Ibid.*
42 See further ch 5.
43 (1829) 10 B & C 263.
44 (1825) 4 B & C 247.

the natural consequences of his acts. However, the judgment in *Bromage v Prosser*[45] also stated that 'malice' in the sense of motive was still required for liability if the publication was made on an occasion privileged in law. Littledale J described the position in *McPherson v Daniels*:

> It is competent to a defendant, upon the general issue, to shew that the words were not spoke maliciously; by proving that they were spoken on an occasion, or under circumstances which the law, on grounds of public policy allows, as in the course of a parliamentary or judicial proceeding, or in giving the character of a servant.[46]

The decision in *Bromage v Prosser*[47] had enormous consequences for the liability of authors and the development of the defence of qualified privilege. It also destroyed the principled explanation for *The Earl of Northampton's Case*[48]: since liability no longer turned on proof of motive, facts suggesting the presence of a friendly motive were irrelevant.

The identical analysis can be seen more explicitly in South Africa and the United States. In South Africa the necessary mental element for liability in defamation—the *animus injuriandi*—is presently understood as requiring a consciously wrongful intent[49]. At the start of the twentieth century, however, the definition was less clear. In *Jooste v Claassens*[50] the defendant heard a defamatory rumour about the claimant, which he repeated to several others. The magistrate found that the defendant was 'not animated by any hostile feeling to the plaintiff.'[51] The question for the Supreme Court of the Transvaal was whether this finding rebutted the presumption of *animus injuriandi* which arose when a defendant published defamatory words. This, in turn, depended on what *animus injuriandi* meant: did it mean that the defendant's motive was to injure the claimant? The Court held that *animus injuriandi* was not limited to those situations where the defendant's motive was to cause damage; it also included situations where the defendant intended to cause damage. A defendant could intend to cause damage where he spoke not aiming to cause damage, but knowing that damage would result. On the facts the Court held that the defendant knew that speaking the words would cause damage; he was, therefore, liable, despite the absence of hostile motive. This definition of *animus injuriandi* in terms of intention and its application to the facts seems to have been very close to the definition of malice given in *Bromage v Prosser*; both definitions drew support from the criminal law[52].

45 *Ibid*.
46 *Ibid* at 272.
47 (1825) 4 B & C 247.
48 (1612) 12 Co Rep 132.
49 *Maisel v Van Naeren* 1960 (4) SALR 836. See below, p 165.
50 1916 TPD 723.
51 *Ibid* at 727.
52 *Ibid* at 736; *Bromage v Prosser* (1825) 4 B & C 247 at 254–55.

In the United States the link between motive and a defence based on repetition was explicitly acknowledged. Thus, in one case it was said that:

> The person libeled is as clearly entitled to full compensation for the loss he has sustained from a wrong inflicted with a laudable motive, or through mistake or inadvertence, as from one perpetrated from a bad motive or with a diabolical intent . . . It is a corollary to these rules that it is no justification for the publication of such a libel that another had spoken or written the false charge, and that the libeler simply repeated his statement, and that he gave the name of his informant.[53]

The resulting liability was seen as fair: 'He who originally published a slander inflicts an injury on his neighbour, and he is of equal guilt and malevolence who assists in the propagation of it.'[54]

However, some American courts were reluctant to apply the strict rule that repetition was never a defence. In *Layne v Tribune Co*[55] the Supreme Court of Florida refused to impose liability where the defendant newspaper had reprinted a defamatory article it had received from a reputable news agency. The Court explained that the reason why repetition was not generally a defence was that the party repeating the defamation usually endorsed it, and made it his own. On the facts there was no endorsement, so malice could not be presumed against the defendant. To succeed, the claimant would have to prove malice, which the Court defined as 'either wantonness, recklessness, or carelessness in its publication.'[56] Subsequently it was held that the principle in *Layne v Tribune Co*[57] also protected a newspaper that had reprinted a news agency dispatch and added an appropriate headline[58]. Admittedly, the analysis in *Layne v Tribune Co*[59] was problematic[60]—malice was generally understood to mean an intention to injure; the defendant must have known that printing defamatory allegations, whatever their source, would inevitably cause damage. But it may be missing the point to focus on the analytical detail. As one commentator pointed out, the merit of the decision in *Layne v Tribune Co*[61] was that it took a functional approach to the problem and produced a solution supported on policy grounds[62]. The tension between

[53] *Times Pub Co v Carlisle* 94 F 762 at 767 (Circuit Court of Appeals, 8th Circuit, 1899).

[54] *Haines v Campbell* 21 A 702 at 704 (Court of Appeals of Maryland, 1891).

[55] 146 So 234 (Supreme Court of Florida, 1933).

[56] *Ibid* at 239.

[57] *Ibid.*

[58] *MacGregor v Miami Herald Publishing Co* 119 So 2d 85 (District Court of Appeal of Florida, 2nd District, 1960).

[59] 146 So 234 (Supreme Court of Florida, 1933).

[60] Vold, 'The Basis For Liability for Defamation by Radio' (1935) 19 *Minnesota Law Review* 611 at 635, n 65.

[61] 146 So 234 (Supreme Court of Florida, 1933).

[62] Painter, 'Republication Problems in the Law of Defamation' (1961) 47 *Virginia Law Review* 1131 at 1162.

the analytical and functional approaches was also to dominate the rules relating to distributors, to which we now turn.

2. DISTRIBUTORS

Today the liability of distributors of defamatory material is governed by statute[63]. In contrast with the liability of authors, the liability of distributors turns on fault: if the distributor shows that he did not know that he was distributing defamatory material, and that ignorance was not due to negligence, he escapes liability. However, this special treatment of distributors was not the result of bold legislative intervention: both the current statute and its predecessor[64] were based on common law rules. This section examines how those special common law rules emerged and whether, as now embodied in statute, they continue to set an appropriate standard for liability.

Perhaps the most striking aspect of the early cases is that no special rules for distributors are to be found. Liability was determined using the ordinary general principles. After 1825 those general principles were to be derived from *Bromage v Prosser*[65], which held that a defendant was liable where he published defamatory words with an intention to injure the claimant's reputation. A person was presumed to intend the natural consequences of his acts, and the focus in the cases was on how a distributor might rebut this presumption. The most effective way to rebut the presumption was to show that the defendant had no idea that the material he was distributing was defamatory: it was then impossible to infer an intention to injure the claimant's reputation. Thus, in *Chubb v Flannagan*[66] where the defendants had sold a copy of a periodical containing a paragraph defamatory of the claimant, the judge directed the jury to decide 'did the defendants know what they were selling?'[67]. In *Day v Bream*[68], where the defendant was the porter of a coach office who had delivered three sealed parcels containing defamatory handbills, the direction to the jury explained the principles in more detail. Patteson J:

> . . . left it to the jury to say whether the defendant delivered the parcels in the course of his business without any knowledge of their contents; if so, to find for him, observing that prima facie he was answerable, insamuch as he had in fact delivered and put into publication the libel complained of, and was therefore called upon to show his ignorance of the contents.[69]

[63] Defamation Act 1996 s 1.
[64] Defamation Act 1952.
[65] (1825) 4 B & C 247.
[66] (1834) 6 Car & P 431.
[67] *Ibid* at 434.
[68] (1837) 2 M & Rob 54.
[69] *Ibid* at 56.

Special rules for distributors were not to emerge until the Court of Appeal's decision in *Emmens v Pottle*[70]. There the defendant was a newsvendor who had been found liable for one farthing damages at the trial despite the jury's findings that he did not know of the libel in the newspaper and that his ignorance was not due to negligence. *Day v Bream*[71] was cited in argument[72], but the Court seems to have treated the case as one of first impression. It held the defendant not liable. Lord Esher MR asserted that it was not enough for a defendant to show that he did not know of the particular libel; he must also show that he 'ought not to have known it, using reasonable care'[73]. Bowen LJ may have had a slightly narrower defence in mind: 'I by no means intend to say that the vendor of a newspaper will not be responsible for a libel contained in it if he knows, or ought to know, that the paper is one which is *likely* to contain a libel'[74] (emphasis added).

The major change effected by the decision in *Emmens v Pottle*[75] was the addition of negligence and reasonable care in determining liability. The prevailing general principles had focussed on whether the distributor defendant knew of the defamatory matter; if he did not, he escaped. After *Emmens v Pottle*[76] a distributor defendant ignorant of the defamatory matter might still be liable if he had negligently failed to make himself aware of it. The special rules for the liability of distributors were more stringent, not less, than the prevailing general rules for authors and other publishers.

Booksellers saw this differential treatment as an injustice, and sought to change the law by sponsoring an amendment to the Libel Law Amendment Bill, subsequently the Law of Libel Amendment Act. The proposed amendment limited a bookseller's liability to special damages if he had sold the book 'in ignorance of the existence of the libel complained of'[77]. Parliament, however, rejected the amendment. One objection was that a bookseller's assertion that he had never looked into the book would be impossible to disprove[78]. A second, more principled, criticism praised the effect of the current common law rule, asserting that: 'Booksellers ought to be careful as to the kind of literature they deal in'[79]. Over a century later booksellers were still pressing for a change in the law[80].

[70] (1885) 16 QBD 354; see the observation by Scrutton LJ in *Sun Life Assurance Company of Canada v WHSmith and Son Limited* (1933) 150 LT 211 at 214.

[71] (1837) 2 M & Rob 54.

[72] (1885) 16 QBD 354 at 356.

[73] *Ibid* at 357.

[74] *Ibid* at 358.

[75] *Ibid.*

[76] *Ibid.*

[77] *Hansard's Parliamentary Debates (3rd Series)*, vol 327, col 57, Mr Sydney Gedge (13 June 1888).

[78] *Ibid* at col 58, Mr Kelly.

[79] *Ibid* at col 59, Mr Darling.

[80] Law Commission, *Defamation and the Internet; A Preliminary Investigation* (London, 2002) at 2.27.

Why the Court of Appeal felt that distributors should be a special category is unclear. One contributory factor may have been that around the time of the decision in *Emmens v Pottle*[81] there seems to have been doubt about the precise role of malice in determining the liability of authors[82]: the Court of Appeal may well have shared these doubts and therefore not had a clear view of whether they were creating special rules. The fact that the Court only heard argument from the claimant in person would not have made it easy to get a sense of the wider legal picture. Even after full argument a subsequent Court of Appeal was unable to agree on whether *Emmens v Pottle*[83] created new law[84]. One Lord Justice said: 'The case of *Emmens* seems to me, when carefully read, to be in consonance with the whole history of the law of libel'[85]; another said: 'For many years it has been well-settled law that a man who publishes a libel is liable to an action, although he is really innocent in the matter and guilty of no negligence'[86].

A second factor may have been the judicial personnel involved: a dominant theme in the judgments of Lord Esher MR was the generalisation of liability for negligence[87]. It may not be a coincidence that he participated in the first case introducing negligence into defamation. Certainly one American commentator perceived a conceptual link, observing that the decision in *Emmens v Pottle*[88] was 'in complete harmony with the doctrine of unavoidable accident in the law of torts'[89].

A final factor may have been functional. Around the mid-1880s mass circulation newspapers were starting to take off[90], indeed the extraordinarily popular *Tit-Bits* commenced publication in the same year that *Emmens v Pottle*[91] was decided[92]. Perhaps the Court of Appeal already recognised the potential for reputations to be damaged in popular newspapers and formulated a rule to encourage all participants in the chain of supply to be vigilant.

Despite the assertion by Lord Esher MR that there was no intention to lay down a general rule, later English courts adopted the principles set out in *Emmens v Pottle*[93]. They were also adopted in South Africa[94],

[81] (1885) 16 QBD 354.
[82] See above, ch 5, p 109.
[83] (1885) 16 QBD 354.
[84] *Vizetelly v Mudie's Select Library Ltd* [1900] 2 KB 170.
[85] *Ibid* at 178 (per Vaughan Williams LJ).
[86] *Ibid* at 179 (per Romer LJ).
[87] *Heaven v Pender* (1883) 11 QBD 503; *Thomas v Quartermaine* (1887) 18 QBD 685; *Le Lievre v Gould* [1893] 1 QB 491.
[88] (1885) 16 QBD 354.
[89] Smith, 'Liability of a Telegraph Company for Transmitting a Defamatory Message' (1920) 20 *Columbia Law Review* 30 at 47.
[90] See above ch 5, pp 117–118.
[91] (1885) 16 QBD 354.
[92] Pound and Harmsworth, *Northcliffe* (London, 1959) at 53.
[93] *Ibid.*
[94] *Trimble v Central News Agency Ltd* 1934 AD 43.

the United States[95] and applied in Canada to telegraph companies too[96].

The longevity of the principles set out in *Emmens v Pottle*[97] in England is in some ways surprising. In 1910 the House of Lords' decision in *E Hulton & Co v Jones*[98] imposed liability irrespective of fault on authors of defamatory material. This might have been expected to have some impact on the rules for distributors. However, a year later counsel for the claimant in *Weldon v 'The Times' Book Company (Limited)*[99] did not even suggest that distributors' liability might also be strict; he simply focussed his submissions on how the test derived from *Emmens v Pottle*[100] should be applied. Clearly it was accepted that *Emmens v Pottle*[101] had created a special set of rules for distributors, distinct from the general principles of liability. As one writer put it when considering whether special rules for distributors applied in Scotland, 'The English rule seems to belong to the technicalities of 'publication' in the law of that country, and these have no equivalent in our law'[102]. There was a certain irony in the fact that the Court of Appeal in *Emmens v Pottle*[103] had subjected distributors to a more stringent liability than applied to authors; after *E Hulton & Co v Jones*[104] the effect of *Emmens v Pottle*[105] was to secure more favourable treatment for distributors than for authors. *Emmens v Pottle*[106] remained good authority, but its effect was reversed.

One consequence of the rules imposing different liabilities on authors and distributors was that it became crucial to distinguish between them. In other words, how little did a person have to do to count as an active participant? The question was potentially very difficult to answer when the courts were faced with new publishing methods such as radio broadcasting, where the

95 Cf *Cubby Inc v Compuserve* 776 F Supp 135 (United States District Court SD New York, 1991) at 139: 'The requirement that a distributor must have knowledge of the contents of a publication before liability can be imposed for distributing that publication is deeply rooted in the First Amendment . . .' To the extent that this was an historical claim it was incorrect: see, for instance, *Street v Johnson* 50 NW 395 (Supreme Court of Wisconsin, 1891), where *Emmens v Pottle* was cited and applied and there was no mention of the First Amendment. For further instances of the requirement before the courts recognised—in *New York Times Co v Sullivan* 376 US 254 (Supreme Court of the United States, 1964)—that the First Amendment could apply to defamation see *Balabanoff v Fossani* 81 NYS 2d 732 (Supreme Court, New York County, New York, 1948); *Sexton v The American News Company* 133 F Supp 591 (United States District Court ND Florida, Gainesville Division, 1955).

96 *Archambault v Great North Western Telegraph Co* (1886) 4 Montreal QB 122 at 132.

97 (1885) 16 QBD 354.

98 [1910] AC 20.

99 (1911) 28 Times LR 143.

100 (1885) 16 QBD 354.

101 *Ibid.*

102 Dykes, *Cooper on Defamation and Verbal Injury*, 2nd edn (Edinburgh, 1906) at 21–22.

103 (1885) 16 QBD 354.

104 [1910] AC 20.

105 (1885) 16 QBD 354.

106 *Ibid.*

roles of the various parties involved were ill-defined and developing in response to technological changes. In England, however, there were cultural reasons why radio broadcasting did not raise these difficulties of definition. The sole broadcaster was the BBC, and its Head of Talks, Hilda Matheson, saw the Corporation's role as a kind of co-author, assisting outside speakers to express themselves most effectively[107].

Across the Atlantic, however, the situation was to prove more problematic. In the United States it was common practice for radio stations to hire out their facilities to political speakers or companies, who would broadcast their own material. What was the radio station's position if that broadcast material was defamatory? Was it a main publisher, or a mere subordinate distributor?

In *Sorenson v Wood*[108] the Supreme Court of Nebraska held that the radio station was a main publisher. Goss CJ made it clear that, in his view, the appropriate analogy to draw was with a newspaper proprietor. Proof of due care did not excuse the newspaper from liability, so, he reasoned, it should not excuse a radio broadcaster either[109]. The main ground for choosing an analogy with the newspaper proprietor seems not to have been based on a comparison of respective roles in the publication process. Rather, the Court emphasised that treating newspapers and radio stations differently would create unfair competition between the two media:

> Radio advertising is one of the most powerful agencies in promoting the principles of religion and of politics. It competes with newspapers, magazines and publications of every nature. The fundamental principles of the law involved in publication by a newspaper and by a radio station seem to be alike. There is no legal reason why one should be favoured over another nor why a broadcasting station should be granted special favours as against one who may be a victim of a libelous publication[110].

The Court was not prepared to take sides in a press-radio war over advertising[111].

Commentators on *Sorenson v Wood*[112] focused less on the policy articulated in the decision and more on the legal analysis. Several were struck by the fact that the station could not be said to be an instigator or author of the statement, and argued that it should be treated like a newsvendor[113].

[107] Briggs, *The Golden Age of Wireless* (London, 1965) at 124–25.

[108] 243 NW 82 (1932).

[109] *Ibid* at 86.

[110] *Ibid*.

[111] For an analysis of one non-legal dimension of the press–radio war see Postol, 'America's Press–Radio Rivalry: Circulation Managers and Newspaper Boys during the Depression' in Harris and O'Malley (ed), *Studies in Newspaper and Periodical History 1995 Annual* (Westport, Connecticut) at 155.

[112] 243 NW 82 (Supreme Court of Nebraska, 1932).

[113] Anon, 'Defamation by Radio' (1932) 66 *United States Law Review* 637; Huston, 'Torts—Libel and Slander—Liability of Broadcasting Company' (1932) 12 *Oregon Law Review* 149.

This was not, however, a unanimous view. Vold[114], writing in 1935, praised the decision, arguing that it was supported by a close analysis of the process of broadcasting. The key point, in his view, was that radio broadcasting was not automatic. Considerable active participation was needed by the broadcaster, particularly in adjusting the modulation to ensure that the sounds were transmitted intelligibly and continuously. Broadcasting should, therefore, be seen as a a joint effort: 'it is only by the combination of the voluntarily controlled, deliberate and continuing efforts of both speaker and broadcaster, each doing his part in conjunction with the other as the speech proceeds, that the utterances delivered into the microphone can be effectively transmitted'[115].

This was a powerful analysis, but it was quickly overtaken by events. In 1938, a bright law student, who had been to visit his local radio station, could point out that the joint participation described by Vold was no longer the universal practice[116]. Modulation could now be done automatically[117]. Two years later Vold had to acknowledge that the facts of broadcasting had changed[118], and that the trend was towards 'an automatic process'[119]. Nonetheless, he insisted that the radio station was still distinct from a newsvendor. It could not be seen as taking 'only a secondary and subordinate part in a later republication of defamatory matter already published by others'[120].

The American Law Institute's attempts to formulate the general rule in its *Restatement of Torts* reflected these disagreements[121]. Bohlen's preliminary draft, submitted to the Council of the Institute, proposed that the station's liability should be based on lack of reasonable care. The Council, however, voted that the liability of radio and newspaper proprietors should be the same. Bohlen remained unconvinced[122].

Later courts tended to agree with Bohlen, and subjected radio stations to a fault-based standard, either because they were like newsvendors[123], or because of a broader notion of the importance of fault[124]. In the 1950s

114 'The Basis For Liability For Defamation by Radio' (1935) 19 *Minnesota Law Review* 611.

115 *Ibid* at 620.

116 Newhouse, 'Defamation by Radio: A New Tort' (1938) 17 *Oregon Law Review* 314.

117 *Ibid* at 316.

118 Vold, 'Defamatory Interpolations in Radio Broadcasts' (1940) 88 *University of Pennsylvania Law Review* 249.

119 *Ibid* at 263.

120 *Ibid* at 279. Strangely, a year later Vold seemed to have forgotten his admission about the changed nature of broadcasting, saying that a radio station's role was one of 'active participation': Vold, 'Extemporaneous Defamation by Radio: A Rejoinder' (1941) 25 *Marquette Law Review* 57 at 60.

121 Farnum, 'Radio Defamation and the American Law Institute' (1936) 16 *Boston University Law Review* 1.

122 Bohlen, 'Fifty Years of Torts' (1936–37) 50 *Harvard Law Review* 725 at 730–31.

123 *Kelly v Hoffman* 61 A 2d 143 (Court of Errors and Appeals of New Jersey, 1948).

124 *Summit Hotel Co v National Broadcasting Co* 8 A 2d 302 (Supreme Court of Pennsylvania, 1939).

the position finally became more settled, but this was not as a result of persuasive legal analysis. A campaign by the National Association of Radio and Television Broadcasters promoted a model statute, which, amongst other things, restricted the liability of broadcasters for statements by someone other than their own agents to cases where the claimant proved a lack of due care. Many state legislatures considerately passed the legislation as it stood; others amended it by altering the burden of proof[125]. All the academic analysis and judicial jurisprudence had culminated in law reform by lobbying.

In England the main focus of the case law following *Emmens v Pottle*[126] has been on what steps a defendant is required to take in order to satisfy the court that he had not been negligent in failing to know of the defamatory matter. Since liability today turns on the defendant having taken reasonable care in relation to the publication[127] the exploration of the negligence standard in the cases is crucial. Thus, where a distributor had failed to see notices recalling a defamatory book that had been placed in *Publishers' Circular* (a trade magazine) and the *Athaeneum* newspaper (a 'well-known medium of communication among literary people'[128]) he was held to have been negligent. Furthermore distributors had 'a reasonable obligation on them to find out'[129] about defamatory matter, an obligation which juries seem to have interpreted stringently on more than one occasion[130]. Indeed, in one case the judge refused to enforce the jury's damages award, stating that: 'there was a mere slip which involved no kind of moral obliquity'[131]. Negligence might also be found where the system of business operated by the defendant did not allow for the immediate suppression of defamatory material detected by employees[132].

Perhaps the most controversial issue was what a distributor should do about a controversial author or title. In *Emmens v Pottle*[133] Bowen LJ had suggested that a distributor would not escape liability if he ought to know that a newspaper was 'likely'[134] to contain a libel. This suggestion was taken up with approval in *Weldon v 'The Times' Book Company (Limited)*[135], where it was said that: 'There were some books as to which there might be

125 Leflar, 'Radio and TV Defamation: "Fault" or Strict Liability?' (1954) 15 *Ohio State Law Journal* 252 at 267 ff.
126 (1885) 16 QBD 354.
127 Defamation Act 1996 s 1(1)(b).
128 *Vizetelly v Mudie's Select Library Ltd* [1900] 2 KB 170 at 171.
129 *Haynes v De Beck* (1914) 31 TLR 115 at 116.
130 *Ibid*. In *Bottomley v FW Woolworth & Co Ltd* (1932) 48 TLR 521 the jury's finding of negligence against a distributor was held by the trial judge to be against the weight of the evidence; Scrutton LJ described it as 'absurd'.
131 *Haynes v De Beck* (1914) 31 TLR 115 at 116.
132 *Sun Life Assurance Company of Canada v WHSmith and Son Limited* (1933) 150 LT 211.
133 (1885) 16 QBD 354.
134 *Ibid* at 358.
135 (1911) 28 Times LR 143.

a duty on . . . distributing agents to examine them carefully because of the recognized propensity of their authors to scatter libels abroad'[136]. In *Goldsmith v Sperrings Ltd*[137] Lord Denning MR said that 'very strong evidence'[138] would be needed to establish that a title or author was of this character. He may even have intended to go further, saying slightly later that: 'Even though a publication may be contentious and controversial even though it may be scurrilous and give offence to many—it is not to be banned on that account'[139]. It is submitted that Lord Denning MR's caution was supported by powerful reasons. In practice it is impossible for wholesale distributors to check through the material before they distribute it. To impose a requirement that there were certain titles a distributor must look through would have the practical effect that those titles would not be distributed. Controversial authors or titles would be effectively suppressed[140].

The judgment of Lord Denning MR in *Goldsmith v Sperrings Ltd*[141] also contained a more radical challenge to the reasonable care standard:

> Common sense and fairness require that no subordinate distributor—from top to bottom—should be held liable for a libel contained in it unless he knew or ought to have known that the newspaper or periodical contained a libel on the plaintiff himself; that is to say, that it contained a libel on the plaintiff which could not be justified or excused: and I should have thought that it was for the plaintiff to prove this . . .[142]

This radical proposal has not received any judicial support; nor, however, has it been disapproved.

Although Lord Denning MR's remarks stand alone in the English law of defamation they are reflected in a different aspect of English law and in the law of defamation abroad. In the English law of copyright a person may be liable for infringement not only where he creates an infringing item, but also where he sells or otherwise deals with an infringing item made by another person[143]. The Copyright, Designs and Patents Act 1988 s 23 provides that:

> The copyright in a work is infringed by a person who without the licence of the copyright owner—(a) possesses in the course of business (b) sells . . . or offers . . . for sale . . . an article which is, and which he knows or has reason to believe is, an infringing copy of the work.

136 *Ibid* at 144.
137 [1977] 1 WLR 478.
138 *Ibid* at 488.
139 *Ibid.*
140 See *Report of the Committee on Defamation* (Cmnd 5909, 1975) at para 296.
141 [1977] 1 WLR 478.
142 *Ibid* at 487.
143 For more detail see Bently and Sherman, *Intellectual Property Law*, 2nd edn (Oxford, 2004) at 185–89.

The seller must know or have reason to know that the copy is *infringing*, in other words, that making the copy was not justified. A seller would not be liable where, for instance, he mistakenly believed that the copy had been made under a licence from the copyright owner.

Further support for the approach of Lord Denning MR can be found in the United States' law of defamation. There the principles from *Emmens v Pottle*[144] were applied to newsvendors, but when the courts had to consider the basis for imposing liability on telegraph companies for transmitting defamatory messages an entirely different approach was adopted. In essence the courts required the claimant to show that the telegraph company knew that the message was defamatory and that the sender was not protected by qualified privilege.

The early cases on the point do not seem to have been consistent: the formative event seems to have been a law review article by Young B Smith[145]. Smith took some of the analysis from the earlier cases[146] and combined it with ideas from qualified privilege. In particular he drew on English authorities such as *London Association for the Protection of Trade v Greenlands Ltd*[147], where it had been held that qualified privilege arose where the defendant believed that a person who had asked him for information had a duty or interest in receiving it. Smith argued that the same rule should apply where the sender of a telegraph asked the telegraph company to send it: if the company believed that the sender had a duty or interest to send the telegraph, it should be protected by qualified privilege.

Smith's analysis was adopted in the *Restatement of Torts*, s 612:

> A public utility whose duty it is to transmit messages for the public is privileged to transmit a message although it is obviously defamatory, unless the agents who transmit it know or have reason to know that the sender is not privileged to send it.[148]

The courts applied s 612 broadly. For instance they rejected the suggestion that a telegraph company should be presumed to know what situations gave rise to qualified privilege. As one court commented, 'Even lawyers, and the judges themselves, often have difficulty in defining what public or private interests are of sufficient importance to justify the recognition of a privilege to publish defamatory matter'[149]. It followed that the tele-

[144] (1885) 16 QBD 354.

[145] 'Liability of a Telegraph Company for Transmitting a Defamatory Message' (1920) 20 *Columbia Law Review* 30.

[146] Eg, *Nye v Western Union Tel Co* 104 F 628 (Circuit Court, D Minnesota, 4th Division, 1900); *Paton v Great Northwestern Telegraph Co of Canada* 170 NW 511 (Supreme Court of Minnesota, 1919).

[147] [1916] 2 AC 15.

[148] American Law Institute, *Restatement of the Law of Torts* (St Paul, 1938).

[149] *O'Brien v Western Union Telegraph Co* 113 F 2d 539 at 542 (Circuit Court of Appeals, 1st Circuit, 1940).

graph company would only be liable if it either knew that the message was spurious or that the sender was acting in bad faith[150]. The rule laid down in s 612 also gained support because it prevented the telegraph company being able to monitor or obstruct free communication[151].

Lord Denning MR's powerful objection and the position taken by the courts in the United States suggest that the 'reasonable care' standard should not be assumed to be appropriate. The Law Commission's recent call for the defence to be reviewed is, it is submitted, a powerful one[152]. One minor reform might be to place the burden of proof of lack of reasonable care on the claimant. However, a more far-reaching reform might be more appropriate, particularly in the light of recent developments in the law of qualified privilege. The House of Lords has recently recognised that political reports published to a wide audience may be protected by qualified privilege[153], so there is a real possibility that many defamatory publications in a newspaper are protected. The precise scope of the defence is, however, uncertain: its existence depends upon weighing various factors against each other, including whether the claimant was given an opportunity to respond to the allegations before publication[154]. If a defamatory political story about the claimant was drawn to the distributor's attention he might be (understandably) reluctant to take the risk of the story not being privileged. Under the present system of liability his genuine belief that the reports were privileged would be of no avail. The limited protection granted by the House of Lords in order to promote the wider availability of information of public importance could be rendered ineffective unless a corresponding and wider protection is extended to distributors.

3. OMISSION TO PREVENT DEFAMATION

Under English law a person may be made liable for failing to prevent a defamatory publication by a third party. Since a person failing to prevent the publication is neither the author, the editor, nor the publisher, his liability is governed by Defamation Act 1996 s 1: he can only avoid liability if he neither knew nor ought to have known that he was taking part in

[150] *O'Brien v Western Union Telegraph Co* 113 F 2d 539 (Circuit Court of Appeals, 1st Circuit, 1940); *Von Meysenbug v Western Union Telegraph Co* 54 F Supp 100 (District Court SD Florida, 1944).

[151] *Mason v Western Union Telegraph Company* 52 Cal App 3d 429 (Court of Appeal, SD California, 1975).

[152] Law Commission, *Defamation and the Internet; A Preliminary Investigation* (London, 2002) at 2.65–2.66.

[153] *Reynolds v Times Newspapers Ltd* [2001] 2 AC 127.

[154] *Ibid* at 205 (per Lord Nicholls).

a defamatory publication. The leading case is *Byrne v Dean*[155], where an unknown third party had put up a defamatory notice on the wall of a golf club. One of the defendants, the secretary of the golf club, was aware of the notice and failed to remove it. Under the rules of the golf club a notice could not be put up without the consent of the secretary. The Court of Appeal held that there had been a publication by the secretary. In its view the secretary had 'taken part'[156] in the publication in the same way that a house owner would take part if a defamatory notice were tied to the railings of his house. The crucial point seemed to be that the secretary had the power under the rules to remove it. It was also important that the notice could have been removed with minimal effort[157]. The High Court recently derived support from *Byrne v Dean*[158] when holding that there was no general rule that publication required active participation.[159]

In the United States the issue has received more attention, but a consistent position has not emerged. In *Hellar v Bianco*[160] a Californian court applied *Byrne v Dean*[161] where an anonymous author had written defamatory graffiti on the wall of the men's toilet in the defendant's tavern. The court explained the basis of liability:

> The theory is that by knowingly permitting such matter to remain after reasonable opportunity to remove the same the owner of the wall or his lessee is guilty of republication of the libel.[162]

It was a question for the jury how long a reasonable opportunity was. The same idea, but expressed in different language, could be seen in *Choctaw Coal & Mining Co v Lillich*[163], where it was held that an employer could not be liable for unauthorised defamatory writing on a board unless, having been informed that the writing had been done by its employee, 'its failure to repudiate the act with reasonable promptness would . . . have amounted to approval and ratification'[164].

However the reasoning in *Hellar v Bianco*[165] must now be read in the light of the decision in *Tacket v General Motors Corporation*[166]. There a small defamatory sign had been painted on the inside wall of one of the defendant's factories; it was eight months before the sign was painted

155 [1937] 1 KB 818.
156 *Ibid* at 829.
157 *Ibid* at 837.
158 *Ibid*.
159 *Godfrey v Demon Internet Ltd* [2001] QB 201 at 207.
160 244 P 2d 757 (District Court of Appeal, 3rd District, California, 1952).
161 [1937] 1 KB 818.
162 244 P 2d 757 (District Court of Appeal, 3rd District, California, 1952) at 759.
163 86 So 383 (Supreme Court of Alabama, 1920).
164 *Ibid* at 384.
165 244 P 2d 757 (District Court of Appeal, 3rd District, California, 1952).
166 836 F 2d 1042 (United States Court of Appeals, 7th Circuit, 1987).

over. The Court held that the defendant could be liable on the basis that it had adopted the defamatory statement:

> A person is responsible for statements he makes or adopts, so the question is whether a reader may infer adoption from the presence of a statement. That inference may be unreasonable for a bathroom wall or the interior of a subway car in New York City but appropriate for the interior walls of a manufacturing plant over which supervisory personnel exercised greater supervision and control.[167]

This reasoning casts considerable doubt on *Hellar v Bianco*[168]. An extreme factual situation would seem to be needed before a reader of graffiti would attribute it to the owner of the building.

Even if the analysis in *Byrne v Dean*[169] can be interpreted narrowly, in terms of adopting a statement, a fundamental objection remains: the court is imposing liability for an omission to act. Recently the House of Lords has reasserted that tortious liability for failure to act is very limited, for political, moral and economic reasons[170]. The courts insist on some special relationship to justify the imposition of this exceptional liability[171], and are reluctant to find it. For instance, there is no special relationship where a stranger allows a child to drown in a shallow pool of water even if it would be easy to effect a rescue[172].

The defamation examples could be made to fit within this framework of special relationships[173]. Thus, it may be that the best explanation for the decision in *Byrne v Dean*[174] is that the secretary occupied a position of responsibility which justified imposing liability for failure to act. Similarly, a householder's liability for failure to remove a defamatory notice from the railings of his house[175] should be seen in terms of the responsibility flowing from property ownership. However, the fundamental concerns over liability for an omission are not addressed anywhere in the English defamation cases.

Given the current general reluctance to impose liability for omissions in tort, the United States cases denying liability in defamation for an omission to act deserve more attention than they have previously received[176].

[167] *Ibid* at 1046–47.

[168] 244 P 2d 757 (District Court of Appeal, 3rd District, California, 1952).

[169] [1937] 1 KB 818.

[170] *Stovin v Wise* [1996] AC 923 at 930 (per Lord Nicholls) and 943–44 (per Lord Hoffmann).

[171] *Smith v Littlewoods Organisation Ltd* [1987] 1 AC 241; *Topp v London Country Bus (South West) Ltd* [1993] 1 WLR 976.

[172] *Stovin v Wise* [1996] AC 923 at 930 (per Lord Nicholls).

[173] For a helpful taxonomy of the situations in which the courts have imposed liability for a negligent failure to act see Lunney and Oliphant, *Tort Law: Text and Materials* 2nd edn (Oxford, 2003) at 427–8.

[174] [1937] 1 KB 818.

[175] *Ibid* at 829.

[176] Cf *Godfrey v Demon Internet Ltd* [2001] QB 201 at 204: 'Care has to be taken before American cases are applied in English defamation cases.'

For instance, in *Scott v Hull*[177] the court refused to hold liable the owner of a building on which defamatory graffiti had been written. The court distinguished *Hellar v Bianco*[178] on the basis that there the defendant had committed a positive act by continuing to invite customers onto his premises after he knew of the graffiti. The court proceeded to lay down the following general principle:

> . . . liability to respond in damages for the publication of a libel must be predicated on a positive act, on something done by the person sought to be charged, malfeasance in the case of an intentional defamatory publication and misfeasance in the case of a negligent defamatory publication. Nonfeasance, on the other hand, is not a predicate for liability.[179]

Perhaps the most persuasive authorities deal with the liability of providers of means of communication. In *Anderson v New York Telephone Company*[180] the claimant sought to impose liability on a telephone company that knew that its service was being used to make defamatory allegations. The Court of Appeals of New York approved the analysis that there had been no publication by the telephone company because its role had been 'merely passive'[181]; to be liable the provider must have had 'a direct hand'[182] in the publication. So, for instance, there would also be no liability on a company that hired out a typewriter or photocopier to a person who produced defamatory material using it.[183]

The importance of the analysis in *Anderson v New York Telephone Company*[184] can be seen in its later application to Internet service providers. In *Lunney v Prodigy Services Co*[185] the claimant sought to impose liability on an Internet service provider whose system had been used to send defamatory email. In the Appellate Division Bracken JP remarked that the analysis in *Anderson* was 'as persuasive'[186] for email and messages on computer bulletin boards as it was for messages heard over the telephone. The Court of Appeals, affirming, commented that the principles established by *Anderson* 'accommodate the technology comfortably'[187]. It found the application of the *Anderson* principles easy where email was concerned: the service provider acted as a 'conduit'[188], just like a telephone

177 259 NE 2d 160 (Court of Appeals of Ohio, 1970).
178 244 P 2d 757 (District Court of Appeal, 3rd District, California, 1952).
179 259 NE 2d 160 at 162.
180 320 NE 2d 647 (Court of Appeals of New York, 1974).
181 *Ibid* at 648.
182 *Ibid* at 649.
183 *Ibid.*
184 *Ibid.*
185 683 NYS 2d 557 (New York Appellate Division 2nd Department, 1998); 701 NYS 2d 684 (New York Court of Appeals, 1999).
186 683 NYS 2d 557 at 560.
187 701 NYS 2d 684 at 686.
188 *Ibid* at 687.

company. Bulletin board messages posted by subscribers were more problematic, but the 'essentially passive role'[189] of the service provider convinced the Court that there would be no liability there either[190]. By contrast, where a service provider had assumed a more active role the courts were not afraid to impose liability[191].

In England the appropriate analysis where a defendant's contribution was essentially passive has not been properly considered. Cases have been rare—partly because the Post Office, an obvious passive defendant, has an immunity[192]. There is now also a statutory immunity for certain information technology services[193]. However, these statutory provisions operate against a background assumption made pretty much by default and contrary to the general principles of tortious liability, that a negligent failure to prevent defamation is actionable. This assumption has led, for instance, to the imposition of liability on an internet service provider for hosting a website where defamatory allegations were posted[194]. The decision may well be unaffected by later statutory Regulations[195] and, if so, its consequences should not be underestimated. As with other distributors, it is practically impossible for a service provider to monitor all of the material distributed, and juries have tended to interpret the standard of reasonable care exactingly[196]. A rational, and conventional response on the part of the service provider is to close down controversial bulletin boards[197], thereby chilling the freedom to discuss controversial matters. Indeed, such was the concern in the United States over imposing liability that legislation was passed preventing a service provider being 'treated as the publisher or speaker of any information provided by another information content provider'[198].

[189] *Ibid.*

[190] Cf *Godfrey v Demon Internet Ltd* [2001] QB 201 where a service provider was held liable for defamatory bulletin board postings. Morland J observed that the service provider's role was not 'purely passive' (at 210) because it chose to store and transmit the postings.

[191] *Stratton Oakmont Inc v Prodigy Services Company* (Supreme Court, Nassau County, New York, 24 May 1995; motion for renewal denied, 11 December 1995); noted by Luftman, 'Defamation for On-Line Services: The Sky is Not Falling' (1997) 65 *George Washington Law Review* 1071 and Miranda, 'Defamation in Cyberspace: *Stratton Oakmont Inc v Prodigy Services Co*' (1996) 5 *Albany Law Journal of Science and Technology* 229. The decision has now been reversed by the Communications Decency Act 1996 s 230.

[192] Post Office Act 1969 s 29. See further, Milmo and Rogers (eds), *Gatley on Libel and Slander*, 9th edn (London, 1998) at 6.8.

[193] Electronic Commerce (EC Directive) Regulations (SI 2002/2013) regs 17–19.

[194] *Godfrey v Demon Internet Ltd* [2001] QB 201.

[195] Law Commission, *Defamation and the Internet; A Preliminary Investigation* (London, 2002) at 2.18–2.23.

[196] See above pp 136–137. See also *Reynolds v Times Newspapers Ltd* [2001] 2 AC 127: 'it may now be over-romantic to conceive of juries as champions of free speech' (per Lord Cooke of Thornden at 226).

[197] Law Commission, *Defamation and the Internet; A Preliminary Investigation* (London, 2002) at 2.4.

[198] Communications Decency Act 1996 s 230 (c)(1).

4. CONCLUSION

The class of publishers is a wide one, embracing defendants with a degree of involvement ranging from authorship to acquiescence. Before the imposition of strict liability a requirement of fault served to separate out those publishers who were particularly deserving of legal liability: either their motive (pre-*Bromage v Prosser*[199]) or their intention (post-*Bromage v Prosser*) was to injure. Once the general requirement of fault had been eliminated some other method was needed to identify publishers who ought to be liable. The method that emerged was to divide publishers into categories according to their level of involvement, although English courts failed to recognise that in principle those who had an essentially passive role should be allocated a separate category. Differential fault requirements formulated before the introduction of strict liability were then applied to the categories.

A more elegant and rational process could be imagined. Fundamentally the problem is, as Bayley J put it in *McPherson v Daniels*[200], that any publication of slanderous matter is *prima facie* wrongful. The class of all publishers, irrespective of fault, is just too big. It has to be cut down, but the current approach involves using artificial rules badly suited to the purpose. First, distributors' liability is based on a common law rule that was formulated against the background of a completely different scheme of liability to the one now prevailing. It needs to be reconsidered. Secondly, no attention has been paid to the position of those who have an essentially passive role. A more functional, conceptually coherent approach is needed in order to distinguish more accurately between different degrees of involvement and to take account of the policies that should guide the law's current development.

[199] (1825) 4 B & C 247.
[200] (1829) 10 B & C 263.

7

Qualified Privilege

THE LIABILITY OF an author of defamatory words is strict[1], but it is not absolute. English law recognises that there are some situations where defamation should be permitted. The remaining chapters of this book deal with the defences that define these situations. As a moment's perusal of any current tort textbook will show, the defences to defamation are regarded today as a being a disparate list: truth, fair comment, qualified privilege, absolute privilege, reports of proceedings. There is no conceptual scheme, and certainly no unifying principle.

The contrast with Starkie's approach to the matter in the first edition of his textbook[2] (1812) could not be greater. Truth was dealt with separately, because it effectively defined what kind of damage was actionable[3]. What we would recognise today as the other defences were dealt with in terms of the defendant's fault[4]. The principle underlying them all was that they rebutted the presumption that the defendant's utterance of defamatory words was prompted by a malicious motive. The major theme of the remaining chapters of this book is an analysis of why the conceptual coherence identified by Starkie fragmented, and what the consequences of that fragmentation were.

In this chapter the focus is on qualified privilege. Whilst the early nineteenth century analysis was in terms of rebutting malice, today it would be utterly inaccurate to describe the defence as based on fault: malice does have a role, but only a subordinate one. A successful plea of qualified privilege requires the defendant to show that he had a duty to utter the words or an interest to protect by uttering them, and that the person to whom he spoke had a corresponding duty or interest to receive the information. Malice is only relevant in that the defence is lost if the claimant proves that the defendant spoke the words maliciously. In short, the emphasis is on the existence of the relevant duties and interests, not the defendant's state of mind.

[1] See ch 5, above.
[2] Starkie, *Law of Slander, Libel Scandalum Magnatum and False Rumours* (London, 1812).
[3] *Ibid* at 175.
[4] *Ibid* at 171–74.

This chapter explores how and why the analysis in terms of duties and interests came about, and also explores its significance. The first section deals with the analysis based on fault; the second with the leading case that introduced the duty-interest test. The third section of the chapter examines the various attempts by English judges to make sense of that case, and to construct their own formulae for qualified privilege. The final section introduces a comparative element. The South African courts, faced with the same difficulties that had confronted their English counterparts, articulated those difficulties more clearly and reached opposite conclusions. Their illuminating analyses throw a not entirely flattering light on the English decisions.

1. THE ANTECEDENTS TO QUALIFIED PRIVILEGE

By the middle of the eighteenth century it was settled that the publication of defamatory words gave rise to a presumption of malice against the defendant. To avoid liability the defendant had to rebut this presumption. He could do so by producing evidence to convince the jury[5] that he did not utter the words out of spite. For instance, in one case a defendant avoided liability for saying that the claimant had been hanged for stealing a horse by showing that the words had been spoken 'out of grief and sorrow' at the news[6]. Similarly a verdict was found for the defendant where he had said that the claimant was likely to be bankrupt soon because the words were spoken 'in confidence and friendship' to a person who was considering selling a horse on credit to the claimant[7]. In certain exceptional situations the presumption of malice might not apply, as, for instance, where a witness made defamatory allegations in the course of litigation[8], or a barrister made an imputation in court 'pertinent to the matter in question'[9]. Such a barrister was described as having 'a privilege'[10]. However, the court was careful to point out that irrelevant defamatory allegations made by a barrister would be actionable, 'for it shall be intended as spoken maliciously'[11].

From the mid-1760s onwards the courts were faced with the question how these general principles applied to references given by masters about the characters of their servants. This novel legal point was of enormous political and social significance. At the time relations between masters and

[5] *Robinson v May* (1804) 2 Smith 3.
[6] *Crawford v Middleton* (1662) 1 Lev 82.
[7] *Herver v Dowson* (1765); Buller, *Introduction to the Law Relative to Trials at Nisi Prius* (London, 1772) 8.
[8] *Weston v Dobniet* (1617) Cro Jac 432.
[9] *Brook v Montague* (1605) Cro Jac 90.
[10] *Ibid.*
[11] *Ibid.*

servants were particularly tense. In the early 1760s employers had organised a campaign against the practice of house guests giving large tips (or 'vails') to servants. The sums given were significant—vails might effectively double a servant's wages[12]—and were virtually obligatory: servants reportedly abused and ill-treated any guest who had not been sufficiently generous on his previous visit[13]. Employers' objections to the practice were twofold. First, it was claimed that social visits became prohibitively expensive[14]. Secondly, it was feared that vails allowed servants more independence, and made them less easy to control[15]. Feelings ran high. Servants organised protests before the premiere of a play that claimed to expose servants' malpractices[16] and, following the presentation by employers of a petition to the House of Commons, servants rioted[17]. Eventually the employers prevailed by adopting a unanimous attitude against vails, although the practice may have survived in the houses of the clergy and the judiciary[18].

The dispute over vails was not only significant in bringing tensions between masters and servants to a head, it also served to consolidate the opposing economic groups. As one leading historian has commented:

> The war on vails proved highly successful. It was plainly not merely a question of servants' gratuities. The object was to render all servants one class, and all masters another. Just as countless middle-class men and women sought to attain a life of gentility which made them morally if not materially the equals of the first gentlemen in the land, so they sought to employ their inferiors on the same terms.[19]

Employers of servants might have come from a diverse range of social positions, but on matters such as vails they were capable of acting together in a common interest.

Character references had an important part to play in relations between masters and servants, since a servant's independence and bargaining power depended on his ability to obtain a position in another household. In the mid-eighteenth century the huge demand for servants outstripped supply, so the employer's only means of curtailing his servants' independence was to hold over them the threat of an unfavourable reference. In practice few employers seem to have written unfavourable references[20], and even when they did, there was a small industry supplying forgeries[21].

[12] Hecht, *The Domestic Servant in Eighteenth-Century England* (London, 1980) 160.
[13] *Ibid* at 162.
[14] Langford, *Public Life and the Propertied Englishman 1689–1798* (Oxford, 1991) 505.
[15] Hecht, *The Domestic Servant in Eighteenth-Century England* (London, 1980) 162.
[16] *Ibid* at 164.
[17] *Ibid* at 167.
[18] *Ibid* at 165.
[19] Langford, *Public Life and the Propertied Englishman 1689–1798* (Oxford, 1991) 505.
[20] Hecht, *The Domestic Servant in Eighteenth-Century England* (London, 1980) 83.
[21] *Ibid* at 84.

Such was the level of employers' dissatisfaction with the system of references that proposals were made for a general registry of characters to be controlled by the government. Eventually an Act of 1791 made it a criminal offence for anyone to impersonate an employer, give a false or forged character reference, or supply misinformation in a character reference[22].

The first reported case of a servant suing in defamation for a bad reference was heard in 1766, just after the conflict over vails had reached its height. In *Edmondson v Stevenson*[23] the claimant's employer had given a character reference to a prospective employer who had inquired about the claimant's character. Lord Mansfield is reported as holding that:

> this is not to be considered as an action in the common way for defamation by words; but that the gist of it must be malice which is not implied from the occasion of speaking, but should be directly proved.

In a later case, *Weatherston v Hawkins*[24], Lord Mansfield expanded slightly on this reasoning. There the defamatory statement was contained not in an employment reference, but in a letter written by the defendant to the claimant's brother-in-law. The story was a complicated one. First, the defendant, who employed the claimant, had given an unfavourable character reference of him to a prospective employer. No action was brought in respect of this reference. The claimant's brother-in-law then seems to have started to harass the defendant, and this drove the defendant to write a letter explaining why he had acted as he had. The defendant succeeded at nisi prius and in the King's Bench. Lord Mansfield set out the relevant principles in terms similar to his earlier judgment:

> To every libel there may be a necessary and implied justification from the occasion. So that what, taken abstractedly, would be a publication, may from the occasion prove to be none; as if it were read in a judicial proceeding.[25]

The circumstances of the case before him showed that, rather than the imputation being malicious, it was 'incident to the application by [the prospective employer] to the master of the servant'[26].

These two authorities demonstrated that the ordinary rules of defamation did not apply to employer's references. However, the rules for references were only slightly different to the normal rules: the difference was merely that the burden of proof of malice was on the claimant rather than being presumed in the defendant's favour. Even this minor change was not unprecedented—it had already been applied in the earlier cases on liability for statements in litigation. On the other hand, the scope of

22 *Ibid* at 92–96.
23 (1766), Buller, *An Introduction to the Law Relating to Trials at Nisi Prius* (London, 1772) 8.
24 (1786) 1 Term Rep 110.
25 *Ibid* at 111.
26 *Ibid*.

this exception—turning on the 'occasion'—was more vague than the litigation exception.

'Occasion' was not a word devoid of ambiguity. The third edition of Johnson's *Dictionary*[27], published in 1765, gives four senses:

1. Occurrence; casualty; incident
   The laws of Christ we find rather mentioned by occasion in the writings of the Apostles, than any solemn thing directly written to comprehend them in legal sort. (Hooker)
2. Opportunity; convenience
   I'll take th' occasion which he gives to bring/Him to his death. (Waller)
3. Accidental cause
   Her beauty was the occasion of the war (Dryden)
4. Reason, not cogent, but opportune
   Your own business calls on you,
   And you embrace th' occasion to depart (Shakespeare)

Of these four senses, only the second can be ruled out immediately. It was clear that a master would be liable if he used a reference as the pretext to make malicious defamatory allegations. The real difficulty is to ascertain whether the defence is based on the incident (sense 1) or the cause or reason for speaking (senses 3 and 4). There is strong persuasive evidence that the latter was both intended by Lord Mansfield and accepted by the courts.

The evidence that Lord Mansfield meant that the reason or cause of speaking gave a defence can be seen in his emphasis on the need for a request. In *Lowry v Aikenhead* he is said to have distinguished between cases where a request for a character was received and those where it was not:

> Where a person intending to hire a servant applies to his former master for a character, the master is not bound to prove the truth of the character which he gives; for what he speaks of the servant he does not speak officiously, but only discloses that which rests in his own knowledge alone; but that where a master speaks ill of a servant who has quitted his place, without any previous application having been made to him, there he must plead and prove the truth of the character in justification.[28]

Similarly, in *Weatherston v Hawkins* Lord Mansfield related the defamatory letter to '*the application* by [the prospective employer]'[29] (emphasis added). Again, in *Hargrave v Le Breton*, a slander of title case, Lord Mansfield summarised the rule in defamation as being that:

[27] Johnson, *A Dictionary of the English Language*, 3rd edn (London, 1765).
[28] *Rogers v Clifton* (1803) 3 B & P 587, 594.
[29] (1786) 1 Term Rep 110 at 111.

> No action lies for giving the true character of a servant, upon application made to his former master, to inquire into his character, with a view of hiring him: unless there should be extraordinary circumstances of express malice.[30]

The obvious explanation for this insistence on a request being made is that Lord Mansfield quite literally meant that there must be a tangible cause or reason for the defamatory reference being given before he regarded a case as falling outside the ordinary rules of defamation.

Furthermore, it is clear that courts had no difficulty in understanding 'occasion' in the literal sense of 'reason' or 'cause'. In *Rogers v Clifton*[31] Chambre J cited and applied Lord Mansfield's statement in *Lowry v Aikenhead*; Lord Alvanley CJ modified the rule slightly, allowing a master to warn others where the servant had committed a felony. In *Bromage v Prosser*[32] the court described the defence as being based on the 'cause of speaking'[33]. Lord Mansfield's approach also gained the approval of the Scottish treatise writer Borthwick, who cited *Lowry's* case and added that 'The rule laid down by Lord Mansfield may be applied in this country as uniformly as it has been in England . . .'[34].

So the intense social pressures resulting from the conflicts between employers and servants seem, on the face of it, to have had little influence on the development of the law of defamation. The innovation that the courts introduced—namely, to reverse the burden of proof of malice in one closely defined situation—was hardly a radical approach. However, the effect of the courts' innovation should not be underestimated: because neither party could give sworn evidence[35] it would be very difficult for a claimant to convince a jury that the defendant had been malicious. Indeed it may be that the courts' use of a subtle and apparently modest reform was a direct result of the surrounding social circumstances. Given that servants had already rioted when a satirical play was being staged, and also after a petition about tips had been presented to Parliament, there would be a grave risk of the same response to a court decision creating a new defence for masters writing character references. The importance of references was such that servants were likely to have followed cases; at least one litigant thought that servants were sufficiently interested to help fund his case[36]. Social instability seems to have drawn an overtly cautious, stabilising response from the judiciary[37].

30 (1769) 4 Burr 2423 at 2426.

31 (1803) 3 B & P 587.

32 (1825) 4 B & C 247.

33 *Ibid* at 256.

34 Borthwick, *A Treatise on the Law of Libel and Slander* (Edinburgh, 1826) 223.

35 Neither party in civil proceedings could give evidence until 1851 (Lord Brougham's Act 1851, s 2).

36 *Rogers v Clifton* (1803) 3 B & P 587.

37 For a similar analysis of the judiciary's response to the Black Act 1723, see Thompson, *Whigs and Hunters* (London, 1975).

2. THE EMERGENCE OF QUALIFIED PRIVILEGE

It was not until the 1830s that a distinct defence of qualified privilege emerged. In *Toogood v Spyring*[38] Parke B, delivering the judgment of the Court of Exchequer, laid down the following general principle:

> In general, an action lies for the malicious publication of statements which are false in fact, and injurious to the character of another (within the well-known limits as to verbal slander), and the law considers such publication as malicious, unless it is fairly made by a person in the discharge of some public or private duty, whether legal or moral, or in the conduct of his own affairs, in matters where his interest is concerned. In such cases, the occasion prevents the inference of malice, which the law draws from unauthorized communications, and affords a qualified defence dependent on the absence of actual malice. If *fairly* warranted by any reasonable occasion or exigency, and honestly made, such communications are protected for the common convenience and welfare of society; and the law has not restricted the right to make them within any narrow limits.[39]

He went on to discuss the position where, as on the facts of the case before him, there was a casual bystander:

> If made with honesty of purpose to a party who has any interest in the inquiry (and that has been very liberally construed) the simple fact that there has been some casual bye-stander cannot alter the nature of the transaction.[40]

These statements of principle are generally recognised as founding the defence of qualified privilege[41]. Their power as legal precedent has not been diminished by the curious fact that they were unnecessary for the decision in *Toogood v Spyring*[42] itself. The facts of the case concerned a statement made to the claimant himself; such a publication was not actionable in any event, and so no question of privilege arose[43].

The striking novelty about the principles set out in *Toogood v Spyring*[44] was their use of the defendant's performance of a duty or conduct of his affairs as the test for a defence. Neither of these criteria had been used in previous cases, except for Parke B's earlier nisi prius decision in *Cockayne v Hodgkisson*[45]. In previous cases the test had been simply whether the defendant had succeeded in rebutting the presumption of malice[46], with

38 (1834) 1 C M & R 181.
39 *Ibid* at 193.
40 *Ibid* at 193–94.
41 *London Association for Protection of Trade v Greenlands Ltd* [1916] 2 AC 15.
42 (1834) 1 C M & R 181.
43 *White v J and F Stone (Lighting and Radio) Ltd* [1939] 2 KB 827.
44 (1834) 1 C M & R 181.
45 (1833) 5 C & P 543.
46 Eg, *Delany v Jones* (1802) 4 Esp NC Cas 191; *McDougall v Claridge* (1808) 1 Camp 267.

the burden of proof sometimes being reversed, as it was in the servants' reference cases[47].

The intellectual roots of this novel defence lay outside the case law, in moral philosophy and legal treatises. At a general level an analysis of duties to speak could be seen at least a century earlier in the works of the great natural law scholars, such as Pufendorf and Barbeyrac[48]. Pufendorf, arguing that there was no general duty to disclose one's thoughts, asserted that disclosure was only required where there was 'another Obligation . . . arising either from some particular Covenant, or from the general command of the Law of Nature.'[49] In his view, it was morally acceptable to lie 'where no body else is injured in his Right, and where the Advantage or the Safety of myself, or of some other Person, cannot be otherwise procured.'[50] It is easy to see in this analysis the seeds of legal or moral duty and interest. Barbeyrac's analysis took the matter further, asserting that 'Speech . . . is to be govern'd by three great Principles of Duty . . . viz. Religion, Self-Love and Sociability.'[51] Procuring an innocent advantage for oneself would justify dissembling.

The natural law scholars, however, were primarily moral philosophers seeking to define moral precepts. Their focus was not on legal liability. The first signs of something resembling the modern defence of qualified privilege in a legal text can be found in the first edition of Starkie's treatise on defamation, published in 1812[52]. Starkie explained the treatment of servant's reference cases, where the burden of proof of malice moved to the claimant, as being based on the master's moral duty to speak. He also invoked the notion of duty to explain why defamatory literary criticism did not incur liability: it was the critic's duty to correct errors of taste[53]. However, Starkie's analysis did not use the criterion of interest as an alternative basis for the defence. The introduction of 'interest' seems to have been the work of the Scots writer, Borthwick. In his 1826 treatise on libel Borthwick[54] made copious reference to Starkie's earlier work, but extended and developed Starkie's test of privilege. After discussing servants' references and literary criticism (as Starkie had also done) he introduced a new category of privileged communications, those made to someone 'who has an interest in the matter or for whose material benefit

[47] Eg, *Edmondson v Stevenson* (1766), Buller, *An Introduction to the Law Relating to Trials at Nisi Prius* (London, 1772) 8.

[48] Cf the source of the concept of duty of care in negligence as identified by Ibbetson, ''The Law of Business Rome': Foundations of the Anglo-American Tort of Negligence' (1999) 52 *CLP* 74 at 84–86.

[49] Pufendorf, Kennet (tr), *The Law of Nature and Nations: Or, A General System of the Most Important Principles of Morality, Jurisprudence and Politics*, 5th edn (London, 1749) at 320.

[50] *Ibid* at 322.

[51] *Ibid* at 320.

[52] Starkie, *Law of Slander, Libel, Scandalum Magnatum and False Rumours* (London, 1812).

[53] *Ibid* ch XIV.

[54] Borthwick, *A Treatise on the Law of Libel and Slander* (Edinburgh, 1826).

it is that the fact should be made known.'[55] His illustrations of this category included two English cases[56].

Starkie adopted Borthwick's analysis wholeheartedly. In the second edition of his treatise[57], published in 1830, he referred in the general introduction to Borthwick's category of privilege based on interest[58]. In the substantive chapter on privilege he then added two new categories of privilege to his previous analysis. The first was 'where a party acts fairly, and bona fide in the prosecution of his own, or even of another's interest.'[59] The second was 'where a communication is made in confidence, either by or to a person entrusted in the communication, supposing it to be true, or by way of admonition or advice.'[60] Starkie prefaced his analysis with the following general statement of principle:

> The extensive principle which governs this class of cases, where the existence of express malice is a test of civil responsibility, comprehends all where the author of the alleged mischief acted in the discharge of any public or private duty, whether legal or moral, which the ordinary exigencies of society, or his own private interest, or even that of another called upon him to perform.[61]

Parke B copied out this exact passage into his commonplace book with a reference to Starkie's treatise[62]. He seems to have more or less copied it out again, without the reference, in his judgment in *Toogood v Spyring*[63].

It is important to notice that when Parke B introduced Starkie's formulation as the test for qualified privilege, he went further than Starkie himself had gone. Starkie recognised that there were some earlier cases that could not be explained using the duty and interest test. For those cases he had developed the further category of communications made in confidence or by way of admonition or advice. The criteria were interpreted broadly: Starkie included within it a case where the defamatory publication was an advertisement to the public[64]. In essence, it was a miscellaneous category. Parke B made no reference to this category at all, so it seemed as if the authorities contained in it were no longer authoritative.

It is also important to realise the nature of Starkie's project, which was reflected in his approach to qualified privilege. Starkie was not content with mere description. He was committed to the study and teaching of law

55 *Ibid* at 236.

56 *McDougall v Claridge* (1808) 1 Camp 267; *Dunman v Bigg* (1808) 1 Camp 269.

57 Starkie, *A Treatise on the Law of Slander and Libel and incidentally of Malicious Prosecutions*, 2nd edn (London, 1830).

58 *Ibid* at lvi.

59 *Ibid* at 315.

60 *Ibid* at 320.

61 *Ibid* at 292.

62 p339a. Baron Parke's commonplace book is held in the manuscripts section of the Squire Law Library, University of Cambridge.

63 (1834) 1 C M & R 181.

64 *Ibid* at 321; *Delany v Jones* (1802) 4 Esp NC Cas 191.

through the extraction of principles[65]. As the Supreme Court of Vermont put it, Starkie was 'an eminent writer and one who endeavored to draw his principles from decided cases'[66]. 'Endeavored' was perhaps not the gushing endorsement that his publishers might have liked, but it underlined the sophisticated use that Starkie made of authorities. The principles were not always obvious on the surface of the case law, but Starkie's method was to come to the cases seeking support for a framework of general principles he had constructed in advance[67].

Thus, the second edition of his treatise began with a lengthy 'Preliminary Discourse' in which he set out, at great length, 'the general principles' for liability for defamatory words. These were the principles for which he would seek support in the English case law in the main part of the book. He made reference, among others, to the laws of Egypt, Rome, Athens, Scotland, the ancient law of the Burgundians and the Psalms of David. When he came to consider the general principles underlying the role of fault, however, the citations were less exotic and the focus more on legal policy. He argued that good motive or intention should not, in itself, be a ground for 'limitation, exemption or privilege' because 'wherever a man uses noxious and injurious means, he must be presumed to have intended the natural consequences of using such means.'[68] Furthermore, unless reference was made to the 'occasion and circumstances' of speaking the defence would be 'far too uncertain and precarious for practical purposes.'[69] It was

> essential, therefore, that the law itself should define, in reference to the occasion, to what extent the acting on such intentions should be privileged. Where boundaries have been defined and appointed by the law, the wilful transgression of them cannot be justified in foro conscientiae, still less in foro humano; for no man has a right, even morally speaking, to act on his own opinion in derogation of the legal right of another, and in opposition to the municipal law of the country. To allow him to do so, because in his own opinion his act was meritorious and expedient, would, in effect, be to permit every man to act on his own judgment, in opposition to the law, and that not only in the particular instance but in all cases, which, in effect, would be to substitute every man's own vague notion of what is right and expedient, for the certain rules established by the supreme power of the state.[70]

[65] Starkie, 'Introductory Law Lecture', in *The Legal Examiner and Law Chronicle, Vol. II* (London, 1833) 437 at 438 and passim.

[66] *Colby v Reynolds* 6 Vt 489 (Supreme Court of Vermont, 1834) at 494.

[67] Cf the methodology of Sir William Jones in his treatise on bailments as described in Ibbetson, 'Sir William Jones as Comparative Lawyer' in Murray (ed), *Sir William Jones 1746–1794; A Commemoration* (Oxford, 1998) 19.

[68] Starkie, *A Treatise on the Law of Slander and Libel, and incidentally of Malicious Prosecutions*, 2nd edn (London, 1830) lxxv.

[69] *Ibid* at lxxvi.

[70] *Ibid* at lxxvi–lxxvii.

This exposition of principles shaped Starkie's treatment of the English case law. For instance, decisions based on the absence of malice—such as *Edmondson v Stevenson*[71] and *Weatherston v Hawkins*[72]—conflicted with the principle that malice was an adequate legal basis to determine liability. Such cases were reclassified, and seen as turning on the defendant's duty to speak. This re-classification had profound effects on the structure of defamation: rather than seeing cases like *Edmondson v Stevenson*[73] as situations where no tort was committed because the necessary element of fault was lacking, such cases were now to be seen as examples of a separate defence to a tort. The focus had shifted from liability to justification.

3. THE RESPONSES TO *TOOGOOD v SPYRING*

The radically innovative approach in *Toogood v Spyring*[74] was clear, but the precise limits of the defence remained vague. For instance, in *Toogood v Spyring*[75] there was no mention of a defence arising where a defendant spoke in order to protect another's interest, whereas in *Cockayne v Hodgkisson*[76] Parke B had said that:

> when the writer is acting on any duty, legal or moral, towards the person to whom he writes, or where he has, by his situation, to protect *the interests of another*, that which he writes under such circumstances is a privileged communication.[77] (emphasis added)

The reason for the different formulations was likely to be that *Cockayne v Hodgkisson*[78] concerned a defendant speaking to protect another's interest, whereas *Toogood v Spyring*[79] case did not. However, the different formulation should make us sceptical about *Toogood's* canonic status: the attractive abstract principles contained in the judgment were expounded with the facts of the case in mind and were not, apparently, meant to be definitive. Similarly, *Toogood v Spyring*[80] hinted that the person to whom the words were spoken must have had a duty or interest in hearing them for the defence to be established. This requirement was not set out as part of Parke B's general formulation, but it was implicit in his remarks. The

[71] (1766) Buller, *An Introduction to the Law Relating to Trials at Nisi Prius* (London, 1772) 8.
[72] (1786) 1 Term Rep 110.
[73] (1766) Buller, *An Introduction to the Law Relating to Trials at Nisi Prius* (London, 1772) 8.
[74] (1834) 1 C M & R 181.
[75] *Ibid*.
[76] (1833) 5 C & P 543.
[77] *Ibid* at 548.
[78] *Ibid*.
[79] (1834) 1 C M & R 181.
[80] *Ibid*.

point was settled in *Harrison v Bush*[81], where the court accepted that a corresponding duty or interest was necessary.

The wider issue left open, which included both of these more detailed points, was what link, if any, there was between qualified privilege and the test of malice it had supplanted. The question was made more important by the fact that the general role of malice in defamation had recently been recast. In *Bromage v Prosser*[82] the Court of King's Bench had split malice into two. What had been a single, simple test of motive had now become two distinct questions. Where there was no privilege malice mean an intention to injure. A person was presumed to intend the natural consequences of his acts, and it was legally recognised that the natural consequence of speaking defamatory words was injury to the claimant's reputation. Where privilege was relevant, on the other hand, malice meant an injurious motive, and had to be proved by the claimant. In this new scheme of malice set up by *Bromage v Prosser*[83] a person's motive for speaking could only provide a defence if he satisfied the requirements for qualified privilege. Thus, for instance, it became crucial to know whether a person had a defence if he made a defamatory statement in the mistaken belief that he had a duty or interest to protect. Such a belief demonstrated a lack of bad motive in the speaker, but did not appear to satisfy the test for a duty or interest. On the face of it such a person was liable: he failed to meet the requirements for qualified privilege, and was presumed to intend the natural consequence of speaking defamatory words. This apparently simple point took over eighty years to resolve, because the courts adopted a range of mutually incompatible responses to, and interpretations of, *Toogood v Spyring*[84].

One response was to see a very close conceptual connection between malice and privileged occasion. Thus, Parke B in *Wright v Woodgate*[85] stated that:

> The proper meaning of a privileged communication is only this; that the occasion on which the communication was made rebuts the inference prima facie arising from a statement prejudicial to the character of the plaintiff, and puts it upon him to prove that there was malice in fact—that the defendant was actuated by motives of personal spite or ill-will, independent of the occasion on which the communication was made.[86]

This approach relegated the importance of the test of duty or interest: situations where a defendant had a duty to speak or interest to protect by

[81] (1855) 5 E & B 344.
[82] (1825) 4 B & C 247.
[83] *Ibid*.
[84] (1834) 1 C M & R 181.
[85] (1835) 2 C M & R 573.
[86] *Ibid* at 577.

speaking became mere illustrations of the wider principle that the circumstances rebutted malice. It followed that, for instance, a petition making defamatory allegations against an official would be protected despite being sent by oversight to the wrong government minister[87].

This approach to *Toogood* was espoused most emphatically by Erle J, later Chief Justice. In *Coxhead v Richards*[88] he rejected the argument that defamatory publications were only protected if a duty or interest could be shown and continued:

> The principle upon which communications may be said to be protected,—the presumption of malice being rebutted,—appears to me to be not restricted in the manner so contended for. Among such protected communications, there are some in which the protection is derived from the subject-matter alone, without regard to any relation in which the author may stand, such as criticism and public comments . . .
>
> There are others in which the protection is derived from the relation in which the giver of the information stands to the person who is the subject of it; as in the case of a communication by a party in the conduct of his affairs where his interest is concerned . . .
>
> There is also another class in which the protection appears to me to be derived from the relation in which the receiver of the information stands to the person who is the subject of it; and for this class I think it is not essential that the giver of the information should stand in any relation to the other parties.[89]

Such a broad approach allowed a defence to be found where there was no obvious duty or interest, but where other evidence suggested the absence of malice. In *Hibbs v Wilkinson*[90], for instance, Erle CJ was prepared to find that a publication in the press responding to the claimant's earlier press attack was privileged.

A second approach to *Toogood's* case was to see it as setting out a definitive test: a duty or interest had to exist before the publication was privileged. This approach denied any link between the privileged occasion and malice. The trouble was that the concepts of duty and interest were so vague that both narrow and wide interpretations were possible. For instance, in *Coxhead v Richards*[91] the issue arose whether a communication of the suspected misconduct of a ship's captain to the ship-owner was privileged. Coltman and Cresswell JJ took the view that the duty not to blacken the captain's reputation with unsubstantiated allegations outweighed any duty to communicate the suspicions. Tindal CJ, on the other hand, felt that there was a duty to communicate the information because

[87] Parke B ruled that such a publication was privileged when hearing *Blagg v Sturt* at *nisi prius*. A brief summary of the ruling at *nisi prius* is given at (1846) 10 QB 899.

[88] (1846) 2 CB 569.

[89] *Ibid* at 607–8.

[90] (1859) 1 F & F 608.

[91] (1846) 2 CB 569.

otherwise the defendant would have made himself 'responsible, in conscience, if his neglect of the warnings [communicated to him] brought destruction upon the ship or crew'[92]. In the same case Erle J took the view that the overall circumstances negatived malice, so the result was a stalemate: two judges found the communication privileged, two others did not. The same court split again, but this time by a majority, when a similar issue about the existence of an interest in speaking arose in *Blackham v Pugh*[93]. Cresswell J took a strict approach, requiring an immediate financial interest to justify speaking; the majority took a broader view.

Similarly, courts showed a range of creativity in discovering the requisite duties or interests. In *Blagg v Sturt*[94], for instance, the Court of Queen's Bench reversed the ruling of Parke B at nisi prius and found that there was no privilege where a petition complaining about a town clerk had been sent to the Home Secretary. The Court held that the Secretary of State had no direct authority in the matter complained of, and that the petition had therefore not been sent to the correct tribunal. On the other hand, in *Harrison v Bush*[95] a defamatory petition sent to the wrong government minister was held to be privileged. The court held that the Queen would have had the power to investigate the allegation and that the petition could be regarded as addressed to her *via* the minister. In current law the more creative approach to interests to hear complaints still prevails[96].

By the mid-1860s the broad approach to duties and interests seems to have been sufficiently dominant for Blackburn J to comment on it[97]. Indeed, even Erle CJ seemed to abandon his previous approach in order to adopt the broad test of duty and interest. In *Whiteley v Adams*[98] he set out the principles in a very different way to his earlier judgments:

> The rule has been laid down in the Court of Exchequer, and again lately in the Court of King's Bench, that, if the circumstances bring the judge to the opinion that the communication was made in the discharge of some social or moral duty, or on the ground of an interest in the party making or receiving it, then, if the words pass in the honest belief on the part of the person writing or uttering them, he is bound to hold that the action fails.[99]

However, any appearance of consensus was misleading. A third approach adopted by judges was to take the duty and interest test as a basis, but to find that a privileged occasion existed if the defendant believed that the

[92] *Ibid* at 598.
[93] (1846) 2 CB 611.
[94] (1846) 10 QB 899.
[95] (1855) 5 E & B 344.
[96] *Beach v Freeson* [1972] 1 QB 14.
[97] *Cowles v Potts* (1865) 34 LJQB 247 at 250.
[98] (1863) 15 CB (NS) 392.
[99] *Ibid* at 414. Cf the judgment of Erle CJ in *Fryer v Kinnersley* (1863) 15 CB (NS) 422, of which Blackburn J said 'I do not quite understand the *ratio decidendi*' (*Cowles v Potts* (1865) 34 LJQB 247 at 248).

duties or interests were present. Superficially such an approach was close to the test of privileged occasion set out in *Toogood v Spyring*[100]. However, the focus on the defendant's state of mind brought it closer to the concept of malice: a defendant who believed that he had a duty or interest to speak did not look as if he was motivated by spite. Thus, in *Woodward v Lander*[101] the jury was told that the publication was privileged because it was written 'bona fide to a person whom *the defendant believed* to have the power of giving him redress for a grievance'[102] (emphasis added). Similarly, in *Jenoure v Delmege*[103] the Privy Council held that a defence of privilege was available where a letter had been sent to the inspector of constabulary under an 'honest unintentional mistake'[104] that he was the proper authority to deal with the complaint. In *Tompson v Dashwood*[105] a defence of privilege was upheld where the defendant had written a defamatory letter to a person with an interest in reading the allegations, but had accidentally put the letter in the wrong envelope, so its actual recipient had no interest.

Perhaps the most emphatic exposition of the position that the occasion was privileged if the defendant believed there were duties or interests can be seen in the majority reasoning in *Waller v Loch*[106]. There a request had been made to the defendant, the secretary of the Charity Organisation Society, for a report on whether the claimant was deserving of charity. The unfavourable report was passed on by the person who made the request to a person who was contemplating giving charity to the claimant. Jessel MR stated that a communication was privileged where the defendant 'bona fide thinks that he is discharging a social or moral duty.'[107] Cotton LJ took the same view:

> . . . it is the duty of those who have knowledge as to persons seeking charitable relief to communicate it, when asked by persons who wish to know whether the applicants are deserving objects. The secretary might well believe that he was asked for that purpose. The occasion then was a privileged occasion . . .[108]

A similar, but slightly different approach could be seen in the judgment of Byles J in *Whiteley v Adams*[109]. There the defendant claiming to have spoken the words out of a moral duty was a 'zealous and conscientious'[110] clergyman; Byles J used the clergyman's belief that there was a duty as the basis for his conclusion that there was in fact a duty.

100 (1834) 1 C M & R 181.
101 (1834) 6 C & P 548.
102 *Ibid* at 550.
103 [1891] AC 73.
104 *Ibid* at 77.
105 (1883) 11 QBD 43.
106 (1881) 7 QBD 619.
107 *Ibid* at 621.
108 *Ibid* at 622.
109 (1863) 15 CB (NS) 392.
110 *Ibid* at 420.

The approach to qualified privilege that allowed beliefs as to duties or interests to establish the defence came under a barrage of criticism in the 1890s. In *Stuart v Bell*[111] Lindley LJ claimed that the remarks of Sir George Jessel MR in *Waller v Loch* failed to distinguish a privileged occasion from malice[112]. Lopes LJ described the same remarks as 'opposed to all the authorities, ... against common sense, and ... lamentably far-reaching and unjust in the consequences [they] would produce'[113]. The Court of Appeal in *Pullman v Walter Hill & Co*[114] affirmed the requirement that the duty must actually exist. In *Hebditch v MacIlwaine*[115] Lord Esher MR scornfully summarised the approach as being that 'the belief of the defendants that the occasion is privileged makes it privileged'[116], before rejecting the argument based on it.

In spite of these fierce criticisms, however, the approach survived, being adopted by two (of a panel of four) Law Lords in *London Association for Protection of Trade v Greenlands Ltd*[117]. Lord Atkinson stated that it had been established for almost a century that

> ... if one person makes an inquiry of another touching the position or character of a third, and the person inquired of makes a reply which he bona fide believes to be true, and also believes that the inquirer desires the information, not merely to gratify idle curiosity, but for some purpose in which he, the inquirer, has a legitimate interest of his own, the occasion upon which the answer is communicated to him is a privileged occasion. This will be so, I think, whether either of the beliefs so formed by the person inquired of be reasonable or not ... and also whether the inquirer, in fact, desired the information for the purpose mentioned. It will be sufficient if the other person honestly believes he does so require it ...[118]

Lord Parker's formulation was in almost identical terms[119].

In the United States the approach to qualified privilege set out by Lords Atkinson and Parker proved influential even after the English courts had rejected it. Young B Smith argued that since there was qualified privilege in the circumstances described by Lord Atkinson, it followed that there should also be qualified privilege where a telegraph company received a request to transmit a defamatory telegraph and believed that the sender was privileged to send it[120]. This proposition was adopted by

[111] [1891] 2 QB 341.
[112] *Ibid* at 349.
[113] *Ibid* at 356.
[114] [1891] 1 QB 524.
[115] [1894] 2 QB 54.
[116] *Ibid* at 59.
[117] [1916] 2 AC 15.
[118] *Ibid* at 35–36.
[119] *Ibid* at 42.
[120] Smith, 'Liability of a Telegraph Company for Transmitting a Defamatory Message' (1920) 20 *Columbia Law Review* 30.

the *Restatement of the Law of Torts*[121], and subsequently applied by the courts[122].

A final, and entirely distinct, approach was to focus on Parke B's allusion in *Toogood's* case to the welfare and convenience of society, and to take that as the basis of the defence. The leading analysis was advanced by Blackburn J in *Davies v Snead*[123], where he paraphrased the defence of qualified privilege as being 'such occasion as would render it right for a person to speak'[124]. He then expanded on this, saying that 'where a person is so situated that it becomes right in the interests of society that he should tell to a third person certain facts, then if he bona fide and without malice does tell them it is a privileged communication'[125].

Blackburn J's analysis was enthusiastically endorsed by Brett LJ (later Lord Esher MR) in *Waller v Loch*[126] as being 'the best, it leaves out all misleading words, saying nothing about 'duty' and states in plain terms what I conceive to be the true rule'[127]. On the facts of *Waller* a request had been made to the defendant, the secretary of a charity society, by a person whom the defendant mistakenly believed intended to make a donation. Brett LJ held that such a situation came within Blackburn J's formulation:

> It is not material whether the information was really wanted for that purpose or not, it is enough if the defendant reasonably supposed the questioner to be asking for it for that purpose. He could not reasonably suppose that the question was asked for any other purpose, and that being so, I think it was right and for the benefit of society that he should answer it.[128]

A similar approach was adopted by Earl Loreburn in *London Association for Protection of Trade v Greenlands Ltd*[129] where he held that the 'welfare of society' might require that qualified privilege should only be given where care had been taken to verify the defamatory allegation.

This approach also had its detractors. For instance, Lord Atkinson in *London Association for Protection of Trade v Greenlands Ltd*[130] described the analysis in *Davies v Snead* as 'only another way of saying'[131] that there must be a duty or interest. More surprisingly, the test was abandoned by Lord Esher MR, who, in *Waller v Loch*[132] had sung its praises. In *Pullman v Walter Hill & Co*[133] he asserted that

121 American Law Institute, *Restatement of the Law of Torts* (St Paul, 1938), s 612.
122 For more detail see chapter 6, above at 138–9.
123 (1870) 5 LRQB 608.
124 *Ibid* at 611.
125 *Ibid*.
126 (1881) 7 QBD 619.
127 *Ibid* at 622.
128 *Ibid*.
129 [1916] 2 AC 15.
130 *Ibid*.
131 *Ibid* at 35.
132 (1881) 7 QBD 619.
133 [1891] 1 QB 524.

> An occasion is privileged when the person who makes the communication has a moral duty to make it to the person to whom he does make it, and the person who receives it has an interest in hearing it. Both of these conditions must exist in order that the occasion may be privileged.[134]

In *Hebditch v MacIlwaine*[135] he said of the defendants that

> They had no interest in the matter, . . . and . . . they had no duty or power to take any action upon the communication made to them. Under these circumstances I think it clear that the occasion was not privileged.

It is difficult to believe that this was the same judge who had praised Blackburn J's definition of qualified privilege because it did not mention duty[136].

The overall picture was one of confusion. There were at least four distinct and mutually incompatible approaches to the defence of qualified privilege. Sometimes judges endorsed one approach only to discard it later in favour of a different approach. Other judges, while remaining loyal to one approach might well find themselves in disagreement with judges apparently adopting an identical approach. The level of confusion and uncertainty was not due merely to differences of interpretation, although the concepts of duty and interest employed in *Toogood's* case and Starkie's treatise were open-textured.

The real source of the confusion was more profound: there was no clear view about the relationship between qualified privilege and malice. A clear view of the relationship would determine which formulation of qualified privilege was appropriate. If, for instance, it was decided that qualified privilege was a separate justification for defamation, those formulations of the defence referring to the defendant's state of mind would be inappropriate. On the other hand, if qualified privilege were seen as merely a way of rebutting the presumption of malice the defence should be seen in terms of the defendant's state of mind.

Without really getting to grips with this difficult conceptual issue English law has now settled down into the position that mutual duties or interests must actually exist between the speaker and hearer[137]. Rather than the judge applying his own ideas of morality in assessing whether a 'moral duty' to speak existed, he must look for 'a duty recognised by English people of ordinary intelligence and moral principle'[138]. The theoretical distinction between the judge's own morality and the morality of

[134] *Ibid* at 528.
[135] [1894] 2 QB 54.
[136] Perhaps Lord Esher MR changed his mind about the importance of duty as a result of his developing ideas about the role of duty in the tort of negligence. See further, Mitchell, 'Duties, Interests and Motives: Privileged Occasions in Defamation' (1998) 18 *OJLS* 381 at 405–7.
[137] *Adam v Ward* [1917] AC 309.
[138] *Stuart v Bell* [1891] 2 QB 341 at 350. See similarly *Watt v Longsdon* [1930] 1 KB 130.

ordinary people was, however, easily blurred in practice. As Scrutton LJ pointed out, 'The judge is supposed to find what the great majority of reasonable men would think without any evidence except his own intuition'[139]. In effect qualified privilege is likely avail those people whose sense of duty and interest corresponds with that of the judge hearing their case. Ironically, it was this very element of personal judgment in the simple malice test that had prompted Starkie to formulate his alternative duty-interest approach in the first place[140]. Starkie had wanted to achieve 'certain rules established by the supreme power of the state'[141]. What had resulted from his analysis however, was a mere substitution of personal judgments: now it was the judge's sense of duty, not the defendant's, that determined liability. The law was no more predictable than it had been before Starkie's ideas were adopted.

Indeed, in some ways it was less predictable. There was still a sense, in some quarters, that a mistaken belief that the recipient had a duty to receive information gave rise to the defence[142]. Furthermore, factors other than duty and interest were invoked to justify qualified privilege, such as provocation[143] and consent[144]. Bringing in provocation suggested a link back to rebutting malice, but consent seemed to go further, hinting at a broader idea of excuse. And even where the courts have confined themselves to duties and interests, the open-ended nature of the criteria was such that definite boundaries were impossible. Most recently, for instance, the House of Lords in *Reynolds v Times Newspapers Ltd*[145] felt able to discern a (previously overlooked) duty in the media to publish matters of public interest to the population at large. The duty is to be identified in future cases by examining at least ten different factors, which is hardly likely to promote certainty. The standard complaint that several of the factors seem more obviously linked to malice than to the occasion[146] simply serves to underline that, even today, English law has not coherently defined the relationship between privilege and fault.

139 *Ley v Hamilton* (1934) 151 LT 360.

140 See above, p 154.

141 Starkie, *A Treatise on the Law of Slander and Libel, and incidentally of Malicious Prosecutions*, 2nd edn (London, 1830) at lxxvi.

142 *Smith v National Meter Co Ltd* [1945] KB 543.

143 *Adam v Ward* [1917] AC 309.

144 *Chapman v Lord Ellesmere* [1932] 2 KB 431.

145 [2001] 2 AC 127.

146 *Lange v Atkinson* [2000] 3 NZLR 385; *Loutchansky v Times Newspapers Ltd* [2002] QB 783 at [26]; Mitchell, 'Political Qualified Privilege' (2000) 11 *King's College Law Journal* 114 at 116–17.

4. THE CONTRAST WITH SOUTH AFRICA

The importance of the relationship between the defendant's mental state and the defence of qualified privilege can be seen by contrasting the development of English law with South African law. In the South African law of defamation liability is not imposed unless the defendant had a consciously wrongful intention to injure (*animus injuriandi*), but the intention is presumed from the publication of the defamatory words. This presumption is rebuttable, but how exactly it could be rebutted has proved controversial. Early cases took the view that the intention could be rebutted either by establishing a set defence, such as qualified privilege, or—taking a lead from Roman law[147]—in some other way[148]. Under this approach it was clear that there was a very strong conceptual link between *animus injuriandi* and privilege. Indeed, it would have been of no legal significance whether a defendant who believed he had a duty was treated as having qualified privilege or not: the crucial question was whether the presumption of *animus injuriandi* was rebutted.

However during the first half of the twentieth century the South African position changed. A series of decisions held that a defendant could only rebut the presumption of *animus injuriandi* by establishing one of the recognised defences, such as privilege, fair comment on a matter of public interest, or that the words were true and on a matter of public interest[149]. As one case described it, the defendant was limited to 'certain definite grooves'[150]. The South African courts in this period took a similar approach to qualified privilege to that currently taken by the English courts: they borrowed the test for ascertaining a moral duty from the English cases[151], and asserted that the defendant's belief that there was a duty was irrelevant to establishing privilege[152]. The Appellate Division in *Basner v Trigger*[153] described the development of the law as going from the position where the defendant was 'at large' to rebut the inference of *animus* to a situation where

> there have become crystallised in our legal system certain set or stereotyped defences whereby the law recognises that the inference of *animus injuriandi* following from the use of defamatory words can be rebutted . . .[154]

[147] See eg Justinian's *Digest* 47.10.20.
[148] *Botha v Brink* (1878) 8 Buch 118, 128.
[149] *Jooste v Claassens* 1916 TPD 723; *Laloe Janoe v Bronkhorst* 1918 TPD 165; *Kleinhans v Usmar* 1929 AD 121; *Barry v Bayer* 1937 SWA 73.
[150] *Mankowitz v Geyser* 1928 OPD 138 at 139.
[151] *De Waal v Ziervogel* 1938 AD 112 at 121, citing *Watt v Longsdon* [1930] 1 KB 130.
[152] *Ibid* at 122.
[153] 1946 AD 83.
[154] *Ibid* at 94.

As a result of this process 'some beneficial elasticity is lost but there is a gain in certainty'[155].

The academic commentary prompted by this change demonstrated a keen grasp of what was at stake. McKerron argued that by confining the defendant to certain stereotyped defences the centre of gravity of the tort had shifted away from *animus injuriandi*; in his view the gist of the action was now publication[156]. Melius de Villiers replied that no responsible person would argue that South African law had moved away from its Roman law roots[157]. When McKerron pointed out that he was simply describing the case law[158], de Villiers was driven to asserting that any cases conflicting with the Roman law were wrong[159]. Another commentator adopted a more modest approach to circumventing these decisions[160].

In 1960 the previous half-century of development was reversed by the decision in *Maisel v Van Naeren*[161]. The case concerned a defamatory publication that had been made in the mistaken belief that it was required by statute. If the defendant had been limited to the stereotyped defences he could have had no defence, but the court held that he was not so limited. In its view the basis of liability was *animus injuriandi*, a 'consciously wrongful intent'[162] which was presumed from the utterance of the defamatory words but could be rebutted by the circumstances. Occasions of qualified privilege in English law were 'mere examples, and nothing more, of sets of circumstances which would prima facie indicate an absence of *animus injuriandi*'[163]. Since the focus was on the state of mind of the defendant,

> the enquiry . . . would not be assisted by a narrow or technical approach confined to ascertaining whether an interest or duty to speak in truth existed; for a bona fide error as regards a conceived interest or duty must surely be as relevant to the enquiry as the technical existence of such interest or duty.[164]

This broad approach was, in the court's view, preferable to the English approach, which produced 'difficulty and inconsistency' by confining a defendant to 'the grooves of established and somewhat casuistic defences'[165].

155 *Ibid.*
156 'Fact and Fiction in the Law of Defamation' (1931) 48 *SALJ* 154.
157 '*Animus Injuriandi*: An Essential Element in Defamation' (1931) 48 *SALJ* 308.
158 'Correspondence' (1931) 48 *SALJ* 457.
159 'On Fundamentalism in Law' (1932) 49 *SALJ* 199.
160 Price, '*Animus Injuriandi* in Defamation' (1949) 66 *SALJ* 17.
161 1960 (4) SALR 836.
162 *Ibid* at 840.
163 *Ibid* at 841.
164 *Ibid.*
165 *Ibid* at 842.

Maisel v Van Naeren[166] was a radical departure from the previous fifty years of case law, and some commentators found it difficult to accept[167]. However, the cogency of reasoning commended it to the Appellate Division, who endorsed it in a 'well-known trilogy'[168] of cases[169]. Today it remains the basis of South African law and has also been applied to liability for other types of offensive behaviour.

The contrast between English and South African law is revealing for several reasons. First, it demonstrates that a test for liability based purely on the defendant's state of mind was not too uncertain or impractical. Having experimented with the English approach to liability, the South African courts found that the test based purely on the defendant's state of mind was more certain and less arbitrary. Secondly, and more profoundly, the South African courts and commentators focussed their efforts on the question that English courts tended to sidestep: what was the relation between fault and privilege? The result was a more probing and coherent analysis of the issues than the English courts had been capable of.

In particular the South African courts were able to draw upon the basic definition of fault derived from classical Roman law[170], which they could be confident applied in defamation. English courts had no such firm basis to work from because there was not one general concept of fault that applied in defamation: in *Bromage v Prosser*[171] the Court of King's Bench had split off malice in ordinary liability from malice in qualified privilege. There were therefore two different definitions of malice—one for ordinary liability and one for qualified privilege. With the benefit of hindsight it can be seen that the decision in *Bromage v Prosser*[172] contributed directly to the confusions over qualified privilege, because by fragmenting the definition of malice the Court of King's Bench had made it almost impossible to discern the link between privilege and fault. The decision in *Bromage v Prosser* effectively cut loose qualified privilege from the main part of defamation, leaving judges to develop the principles of qualified privilege in isolation.

This inevitably threw up new, difficult questions about the nature of qualified privilege. For instance, if two people published defamatory material jointly on a privileged occasion and only one of them was malicious, did the other one also lose his defence? In *Smith v Streatfeild*[173]

[166] 1960 (4) SALR 836.

[167] Eg, McKerron, *The Law of Delict*, 7th edn (Cape Town, 1971) 190 at n 56 ('cannot be regarded as good law'). For a more welcoming reaction see Price, 'The Basis of the South African Law of Defamation' (1960) *Acta Juridica* 254 at 275 ('a long and careful analysis of the basic principles').

[168] Neethling, Potgieter and Visser, *Law of Delict*, 2nd edn (Durban, 1994) 327.

[169] *Jordaan v van Biljion* 1962 (1) SA 286; *Craig v Voortrekkerpers Bpk* 1963 (1) SA 149; *Nydoo v Vengtas* 1965 (1) SA 1.

[170] See, for instance, the use of D47.10.3.2. in *Maisel v Van Naeren* 1960 (4) SALR 836 at 840.

[171] (1825) 4 B & C 247.

[172] *Ibid.*

[173] [1913] 3 KB 764.

Bankes J held that he did, explaining that 'Qualified privilege in one sense may be said to be the privilege of the individual . . . but as a defence it is attached to the publication'[174]. Pollock commented, revealingly, that 'The point appears to be new; the decision seems clearly right on principle'[175]. The point was new, but only because when the emphasis was placed on the defendant's state of mind, as had been done in earlier cases, there was no difficulty. Only if one insisted on analysing the privilege as something separate from malice was it necessary to decide if 'the privilege' was destroyed by the state of mind of one joint tortfeasor. As to the principle, Pollock was not alone in approving the decision[176], but it was later reversed by the Court of Appeal[177] on grounds of fairness rather than analysis. The courts were having to solve difficult questions about the nature of qualified privilege in the abstract, with no sense of where it belonged in a broader conceptual scheme.

5. CONCLUSION

Although the groundwork of qualified privilege was laid in cases concerning servants' references from the mid-eighteenth century onwards, the decisive formative influence was not social pressure, but an academic treatise. The treatise writer had his reasons for formulating the legal principle as he did: he thought that liability based purely on fault was impractical and uncertain; and he believed that the state should determine when defamatory words were justified. However, the courts did not adopt these reasons as enthusiastically as they had adopted his legal proposition. The result was a lengthy period of uncertainty as the courts struggled to make sense of the new defence. Their task was doubly difficult because the key issue—the relationship between privilege and fault—was obscured by the fragmentation of fault into two separate definitions.

So the modern law of qualified privilege was made by two contrasting events. The first was the sudden, abrupt introduction of Starkie's test for privileged communications. The second was the eighty-year delay whilst the courts uncertainly groped their way towards a consensus over what *Toogood v Spyring*[178] had achieved. Ultimately Starkie's form of words triumphed in the competition for acceptance, but it was not the victory its author had hoped for: the defence still in effect turned on a personal judgment, and the law was less predictable than ever. Recent developments in qualified privilege have only tended to underline those problems.

[174] *Ibid* at 770.
[175] (1914) 27 *LQR* 15.
[176] Paton, 'Reform and the English Law of Defamation' (1939) 33 *Illinois Law Review of Northwestern University* 669 at 681.
[177] *Egger v Viscount Chelmsford* [1965] 1 QB 248.
[178] (1834) 1 C M & R 181.

8

Fair Comment

TODAY A PERSON making a fair comment on a matter of public interest is not liable in defamation, provided that he was not malicious. There is, for instance, no liability for sincere hostile literary criticism. Each element of this defence—fair comment, public interest and malice—has undergone changes and refinements over the last two centuries. More fundamentally, there was also a change in where the defence was located in the wider scheme of liability. For Starkie[1], cases about critical book reviews belonged with decisions about servants' references and other types of qualified privilege[2]: the common theme linking them was that the circumstances rebutted the presumption of malice that arose automatically on proof that defamatory words had been spoken. In the middle of the nineteenth century, however, this categorisation was overturned by the Court of Queen's Bench decision in *Campbell v Spottiswoode*[3]. The subsequent history of the defence was dominated by efforts to find it a new home. Textbook writers eventually categorised it as a partner to the defence of truth, an academic arranged marriage that was to change the appearance, if not perhaps the fundamental character, of the defence.

In investigating these developments this chapter adopts, with one slight amendment, the division of the history of fair comment into three distinct phases as originally put forward by Diplock KC in *Kemsley v Foot*[4]:

> (1) from the beginning of the nineteenth century; (2) from the middle of the nineteenth century: *Campbell v Spottiswoode*; (3) from the beginning of the twentieth century . . .

1. FROM THE END OF THE EIGHTEENTH CENTURY

The earliest example of a recognisable defence of fair comment dates from the 1790s. *Dibdin v Swan and Bostock*[5] concerned a critical review in a

[1] Starkie, *Law of Slander, Libel, Scandalum Magnatum and False Rumours* (London, 1812).
[2] *Ibid*, ch XIV, 'Where the Defendant gives the Character of a Servant, & c', p 223.
[3] (1863) 3 B & S 769.
[4] [1952] AC 345 at 349.
[5] (1793) 1 Esp 28.

newspaper of a place of public entertainment owned by the claimant. Lord Kenyon directed the jury that:

> [t]he editor of a public newspaper may fairly and candidly comment on any place or species of public entertainment; but it must be done fairly and without malice or view to injure or prejudice the proprietor in the eyes of the public. That if so done, however severe the censure, the justice of it screens the editor from legal animadversion; but if it can be proved that the comment is unjust, is malevolent, or exceeding the bounds of fair opinion, that such is a libel, and therefore actionable.[6]

The reporter did not record the jury's verdict.

This direction set out the principled basis of the defence very clearly. The key point was that malice could not be presumed from a fair criticism. When the case was heard malice was still a substantive element of liability[7]: proof that defamatory words had been spoken created a presumption of malice, but that presumption could be rebutted by the defendant. He would have to put before the jury evidence showing that the circumstances[8] demonstrated a lack of malice—for instance, that the words were spoken out of sorrow[9], or to give a requested reference about a servant[10]. Making a genuine criticism of a place of public entertainment could equally be seen as rebutting the presumption of malice. A further confirmation that proof of fair comment was seen as rebutting the presumption of malice could be seen in relation to pleading: the correct plea to raise fair comment was the general issue ('not guilty'), which denied that all of the basic elements of liability were present[11]. Formally fair comment was seen as negativing malice rather than as a separate defence.

Whilst *Dibdin v Swan*[12] set out an orthodox, principled doctrinal basis for fair comment, it was not until fifteen years later that the courts articulated policy reasons to support it. In *R v White*[13] a newspaper proprietor was prosecuted for libel for publishing an article abusing LeBlanc J and a jury for acquitting in a murder trial. Grose J directed the jury that they should acquit if the writer had merely discussed 'with decency and candour . . . the propriety of the verdict of a Jury, or the decisions of a Judge'[14]. However, there should be a conviction 'if the extracts from the newspaper . . . contained no reasoning or discussion, but only declamation and invective, and were written not with a view to elucidate the truth . . .'[15]. The jury convicted.

6 *Ibid* at 29.
7 See further, ch 5.
8 The defendant was not permitted to give evidence until Lord Brougham's Act 1851, s 2.
9 *Crawford v Middleton* (1662) 1 Lev 82.
10 *Edmondson v Stevenson,Buller's Nisi Prius*, p 8 (1766).
11 *Earl of Lucan v Smith* (1856) 1 H & N 481.
12 (1793) 1 Esp 28.
13 (1808) 1 Camp 359.
14 *Ibid*.
15 *Ibid*.

The emphasis on reasoning and elucidating the truth was amplified in *Tabart v Tipper*[16], where the claimant was a publisher of children's books and the defendant had said he published immoral poetry. In the course of argument, Lord Ellenborough CJ interjected that 'The main question here is, quo animo the defendant published the article complained of; whether he meant to put down a nuisance to public morals, or to prejudice the plaintiff'[17]. The doctrinal basis was clear, but Lord Ellenborough CJ went on, in a passage later applauded as 'bold and noble'[18] to assert that

> Liberty of criticism must be allowed, or we shall have neither purity of taste nor of morals. Fair discussion is essentially necessary to the truth of history, and the advancement of science. That publication, therefore, I shall never consider as a libel, which has for its object, not to injure the reputation of any individual, but to correct misrepresentations of fact, to refute sophistical reasoning, to expose a vicious taste in literature, or to censure what is hostile to morality.[19]

The same rhetoric was developed further by Lord Ellenborough CJ in *Carr v Hood*[20]. There the publication was a satire on an earlier work by the claimant, *The Stranger in Ireland*. Apparently the claimant was now unable to sell the copyright to the sequel, about a tour through Scotland. Lord Ellenborough CJ was unimpressed by this evidence of loss, asking (rhetorically):

> Is he to be indemnified by receiving a compensation in damages from the person who may have opened the eyes of the public to the bad taste and inanity of his compositions? Who would have bought the works of Sir Robert Filmer after he had been refuted by Mr Locke? But shall it be said that he might have sustained an action for defamation against that great philosopher, who was labouring to enlighten and ameliorate mankind?[21]

Unless authors and their works could be criticised, he continued, 'the first who writes a book on any subject will maintain a monopoly of sentiment and opinion respecting it. This would tend to the perpetuity of error'[22]. However, that was not to say that it was open season on authors. If the criticism reflected on the author's personal private character there would be liability; similarly, if the commentator introduced 'fiction for the purpose of condemnation'[23] he was not protected.

[16] (1808) 1 Camp 350.
[17] *Ibid* at 351.
[18] Anon (Foster or Finlason), 'The Law of Libel, As Applied to Public Discussion' (1863) 15 *The Law Magazine and Law Review* 193 at 224. The attribution of authorship stems from the note to *Morrison v Belcher* (1863) 3 Foster and Finlason's Reports 619, where 'the reporter' refers to his article in the 'Law Review' for 1863.
[19] *Ibid* at 351–52.
[20] (1808) 1 Camp 355.
[21] *Ibid* at 357.
[22] *Ibid*.
[23] *Ibid* at 358.

One later commentator described *Carr v Hood*[24] as 'the foundation of the law of literary criticism'[25]. To the extent that this description suggested that the case laid down new law it was misleading: the doctrinal basis for protecting literary criticism was the traditional one; only the rhetoric was new. This rhetoric was, however, of enormous significance. It emphasised the importance of discussion and argument in furthering understanding of any public subject. This, in turn, implied the entitlement of every citizen to contribute to the debate: a 'monopoly of sentiment and opinion' was to be avoided. Whilst the courts had dealt with literary disputes and a murder trial, the subject-matter of public debate could legitimately extend to the most fundamental questions, including the foundations of government. The example given by Lord Ellenborough in *Carr v Hood* was particularly revealing in this respect: Sir Robert Filmer had advanced an extreme version of the divine right of kings[26], which Locke demolished in his *First Treatise of Government* (1690). In short, the rhetorical side of the decisions in *R v White*[27], *Tabart v Tipper*[28] and *Carr v Hood*[29] was describing what would later be called the 'public sphere'[30]: an ideal space where contributors of equal status could use their reasoning and analytical powers freely on artistic and political subjects.

The courts, and particularly Lord Ellenborough CJ, had used the traditional, flexible defamation rules in order to protect this public sphere. It was, perhaps, a happy coincidence that the orthodox rules about malice could be applied to achieve the result that the courts wanted. However, the emphasis placed on protecting the public sphere could also be seen in the approach taken in contemporary copyright cases, where the existing doctrine was not so malleable as it was in defamation. For instance, in *Wilkins v Aikin*[31] the claimant was seeking an injunction against the defendant, asserting that the defendant's book (*An Essay on the Doric Order of Architecture*) was a copy of the claimant's (*The Antiquities of Magna Graecia*). By his answer the defendant denied that the books were identical, but acknowledged some quotations and abridgments. The Lord Chancellor held that an injunction should be maintained until the trial, and analysed the question for decision in terms of motive:

24 (1808) 1 Camp 355.
25 Hallen, 'Fair Comment' (1929–30) 8 *Texas Law Review* 41 at 44.
26 *Patriarcha, or the Natural Power of Kings* (1680). Drabble (ed), *The Oxford Companion to English Literature* (Oxford, 1985) at 349.
27 (1808) 1 Camp 359.
28 (1808) 1 Camp 350.
29 (1808) 1 Camp 355.
30 Habermas, Burger (tr), *The Structural Transformation of the Public Sphere* (1989).
31 (1810) 17 Ves Jun 422.

> There is no doubt, that a man cannot under the pretence of quotation, publish either the whole or part of another's work; though he may use, what it is in all cases very difficult to define, fair quotation.[32]

The defendant's motive was even more explicitly emphasised in an example given by the Lord Chancellor, where he imagined a book on the history of maps of a county, which reproduced such maps.

> If it was a fair history of the maps of the county, which had been published, and the publication of the individual map was merely an illustration of that history, that is one way of stating it: but if a jury could perceive the object to make a profit by publishing the map of another man, that would require a different consideration.[33]

Sixteen years later, in *Mawman v Tegg*[34], the emphasis was still on the defendant's intentions. The Lord Chancellor held that the question for the jury was whether matter copied from one encylopedia to another:

> Has, upon the whole, been used in such a manner as to shew . . . that the party meant to give to the public what might fairly be called a new work; or whether, on the other hand, in robbing the former author of much of his work, he acted . . . *animo furandi*.[35]

What is immediately striking about these copyright cases is how similar they were to the defamation decisions already discussed: both made the key test the defendant's motive (or *animus*) in publishing. The similarity was surprising, for breach of copyright did not require malice or intention to injure to be actionable. Nevertheless, the courts seem to have decided that use of another's work in a discussion or review in good faith was an exception to breach of copyright. Perhaps the earlier defamation cases were an unacknowledged influence[36]. Such influence may even have been reciprocal, with one contemporary author describing the defence of fair comment as 'the fair use of the defendant's own judgment in the criticism of works of art or literature'[37]. But whether there was a direct influence or not, the copyright cases highlighted a judicial determination to protect the public sphere using whatever means were to hand.

[32] *Ibid* at 424.

[33] *Ibid* at 425.

[34] (1826) 2 Russ 385.

[35] *Ibid* at 401. For further illustrations see *Whittingham v Wooler* (1817) 2 Swans 428 and *Bell v Whitehead* (1839) 8 LJ Ch 141.

[36] Burrell, 'Reigning in Copyright Law: Is Fair Use the Answer?' [2001] *Intellectual Property Quarterly* 361 at 365–67, convincingly demonstrates that *Gyles v Wilcox* (1740) 2 Atk 141, sometimes seen as an early example of the fair use defence, is better seen as a question of statutory interpretation.

[37] Holt in notes to *Wyatt v Gore* (1816) Holt 299 at 307.

The structure of the defence of fair comment had been fixed by *Dibdin v Swan*[38] in 1793, and its foundation explained in *Tabart v Tipper*[39] and *Carr v Hood*[40] fifteen years later. Both the structure and its foundation remained stable until the middle of the nineteenth century; the case law developed details.

The first question requiring detailed analysis was what, exactly, came within the category of fair criticism. Lord Ellenborough CJ took a broad approach, saying that one public writer could criticise another 'exerting his talents in all the latitude of free communication belonging to a public writer'[41]. He reiterated his view that protection ceased where the defamation concerned 'the private character of the individual'[42]. It was also made clear that a 'fair' criticism did not mean one that the jury agreed with: in *Soane v Knight*[43] Lord Tenterden CJ directed the jury to find for the defendant 'although [the criticism] may not be correct'[44]. Lord Tenterden CJ also seemed to introduce a different requirement, or at least a different emphasis, when he told the jury that the criticism had to be 'fair, reasonable and temperate'[45] in order to be protected. A year later, in *Thompson v Shackell*[46], Best CJ made the same point, telling the jury that 'the question for you is whether the publication is a fair and temperate criticism on the painting of the plaintiff'[47]. Best CJ then went on to make clear that in his view some of the analysis in *Carr v Hood*[48] had gone too far. In particular he singled out a passage where Lord Ellenborough had said that authors 'should be liable to criticism, to exposure, and even to ridicule, if their works be ridiculous'[49]. Best CJ took the view that 'no personal ridicule of the author is justifiable'[50].

The change of emphasis was subtle but significant. Lord Ellenborough's position had been, essentially, that a defendant who confined himself to the work and spoke in good faith had a defence. A defendant who fulfilled those two conditions had complete freedom of discussion. The view put forward by Lord Tenterden CJ and Best CJ was more restrictive: it sought to regulate the public sphere by requiring contributions to be 'reasonable' and 'temperate'. On their view only certain types of good faith discussions of the work were protected. How far the courts should regulate the public

38 (1793) 1 Esp 28.
39 (1808) 1 Camp 350.
40 (1808) 1 Camp 355.
41 *Stuart v Lovell* (1817) 2 Stark 93 at 96.
42 *Ibid.*
43 (1827) M & M 74.
44 *Ibid* at 76.
45 *Ibid.*
46 (1828) M & M 187.
47 *Ibid* at 188.
48 (1808) 1 Camp 355.
49 *Ibid* at 357.
50 (1828) M & M 187 at 188.

sphere was clearly a difficult question of policy; it was not to be settled for over fifty years[51].

Cases in the first half of the nineteenth century also explored the nature of comment or criticism. The most revealing was *Dunne v Anderson*[52], which concerned a published criticism of the claimant doctor's petition to Parliament. Best CJ explained to the jury that if the defendant 'without ostensible cause for attack, had come forward, as of his own knowledge, to impute to the Plaintiff ignorance'[53] there would have been liability. But,

> if [the defendant] had not imputed ignorance to the Plaintiff, except in so far as he had collected the existence of ignorance from the contents of the Plaintiff's petition; if the attack was only through the sides of the petition, and not spontaneous; in short, if what had been written was no more than a fair comment on that petition, the Defendant was entitled to a verdict[54].

The jury found for the defendant. The key point was that a comment was a response or reaction to the defendant's publication.

Further light was cast on the nature of comment in *Cooper v Lawson*[55]. There a newspaper had published an article about an election petition to which the claimant was surety. The article set out an affidavit made by the claimant at the time of becoming surety, affidavits showing that the claimant was insolvent, and the claimant's counter-affidavit. It then went on to question why the claimant was taking such an interest in an election miles from where he lived, and concluded 'There can be but one answer . . . he is hired for the occasion'. Lord Denman CJ directed the jury that if they found that the claimant was unfit to be a surety they should consider whether the comments imputing that he was hired were fair. The jury having found for the claimant, the defendant claimed a new trial on the ground of misdirection.

The defendant's argument was that the issue of fairness should not have been left to the jury at all, as there was no basis to say the comment was unfair. It was, counsel submitted, like writing 'He murdered his father, and therefore is a disgrace to human nature'[56]: no one could deny that the latter words were a fair comment.

The Court of King's Bench refused the motion for a new trial. All of its members agreed that counsel's hypothetical example would not have been left to a jury to determine its fairness. As Coleridge J put it, there were some comments 'where the inference is so fair, that, if you prove the fact, you prove the correctness of the comment'[57]. However, the Court was also

51 See below, p 178.
52 (1825) 3 Bing 88.
53 *Ibid* at 97.
54 *Ibid*.
55 (1838) 8 Ad & E 746.
56 *Ibid* at 749.
57 *Ibid* at 753.

unanimous in its view that the facts of the case were distinguishable from the hypothetical example. Here the inference was not so obvious: 'the comment raises an imputation of motives that may or may not be a just inference from the proceeding statement'[58]. Lord Denman CJ expressed the general rule that:

> a comment may be the mere shadow of the previous imputation; but, if it infers a new fact, the defendant must abide by that inference of fact, and the fairness of the comment must be decided upon by a jury.[59]

Cooper v Lawson[60] brought out three important themes. First, the defence was not narrowly defined to subjective matters of literary judgment: it embraced specific factual inferences drawn from the available data. Second, a successful defence depended upon the inference being fairly drawn; in other words, there had to be sufficient foundation for the comment. Third, it was assumed in the court's analysis that a publication protected by fair comment would first set out the basis for the comment, then express the comment itself. The much discussed statement 'He murdered his father, and is therefore a disgrace to human nature' was a perfect illustration of this assumption. In other words, it was not enough that the defendant meant the defamatory language as a comment, he must also have made clear to his audience that it was a comment. All three themes reinforced the sense that fair comment was a broad, flexible defence that aimed to facilitate informed and genuine public discussion.

The final aspect of the defence to receive attention in the early nineteenth century was the subject-matter of the comment. Clearly artistic subjects such as literature[61], architecture[62] and painting[63] were protected, but the boundaries were unpredictable. In *Dunne v Anderson*[64], for instance, the defendant commented on a petition to the House of Commons. Best CJ directed the jury that such a petition was suitable for comment, since 'where a man obtruded himself on the public by proposing measures to affect the interests of the community at large, his proposals were legitimate objects of observation and criticism'[65]. The Court of Exchequer, however, disagreed: a petitioner to Parliament was not in the same position as a published author, so *Carr v Hood*[66] did not apply[67].

58 *Ibid* at 752 (per Patteson J).
59 *Ibid* at 754.
60 (1838) 8 Ad & E 746.
61 *Carr v Hood* (1808) 1 Camp 355.
62 *Soane v Knight* (1827) M & M 74.
63 *Thompson v Shackell* (1828) M & M 187.
64 (1825) 3 Bing 88.
65 *Ibid* at 97.
66 (1808) 1 Camp 355.
67 (1825) 3 Bing 88 at 98.

Criticism of a floriculturist's decision no longer to exhibit his flowers in public[68] was also held to fall outside *Carr v Hood*.

The case that most clearly demonstrated the difficulty in drawing the line was *Gathercole v Miall*[69]. The comment touched on two matters: the claimant clergyman's sermons, and the principles upon which he managed a local charity. The Court of Exchequer held that neither matter was covered by the defence. It found the charity point easier to dispose of, saying that the management of the charity was not like publishing a literary work[70] and was 'essentially private'[71]. Protection for comments on unpublished sermons divided the Court: Parke B and Pollock CB held that there was no protection, whereas Alderson and Rolfe BB inclined to the opposite view.

All three cases manifested a narrow view of what was a 'public' matter, and seemed to be based on the idea that only those things which the defendant deliberately placed before the public as a whole counted. In *Gathercole v Miall*, for example, Parke B said that whilst an unpublished sermon could not be commented on, a published sermon was 'offered . . . as a subject for general criticism'[72]. In the same case Pollock CB suggested that there was no privilege for comments on a privately circulated book[73]. It was a very literal and literary approach, which severely curtailed the defence. How a clergyman administered a charity, for instance, would cast light on his character and suitability for his public role. One commentator captured the nuances neatly: 'though, no doubt what is parochial is not strictly public, it certainly is not private'[74]. What was missing from these decisions was a recognition that it might be important for a matter to be brought to the public's attention by the commentator. One could comment on public matters, but not matters of public interest.

2. FROM THE MIDDLE OF THE NINETEENTH CENTURY: *CAMPBELL v SPOTTISWOODE*

The development of fair comment in the second half of the nineteenth century was shaped by two influences. The first was a series of rulings at nisi prius in the 1860s, which amounted to a restatement of the law. The second was the decision in *Campbell v Spottiswoode*[75], which effectively relocated fair comment within the scheme of the tort of defamation.

[68] *Green v Chapman* (1837) 4 Bing NC 92.
[69] (1846) 15 M & W 319.
[70] *Ibid* at 328 (per Parke B).
[71] *Ibid* at 343 (per Rolfe B).
[72] *Ibid* at 321.
[73] *Ibid* at 334.
[74] Anon (Foster or Finlason), 'The Law of Libel, As Applied to Public Discussion' (1863) 15 *The Law Magazine and Law Review* 193 at 238.
[75] (1863) 3 B & S 769.

The series of decisions at nisi prius in the 1860s explored every aspect of the defence of fair comment. Most prominent was the development of what counted as a public matter. In *Turnbull v Bird*[76] Erle CJ set the scene for expansion by ruling that 'Every person has the right to comment on the acts of a public man, which concern him as a subject of the realm'[77]. This included anyone holding 'any public employment'[78], such as a calendarer of foreign state papers. A bolder expansion was made the following year in *Seymour v Butterworth*[79]. There a writer had commented on a Member of Parliament's censure by the Benchers of Middle Temple. Cockburn CJ emphatically rejected the defendant's argument that this was a private matter:

> Seymour held a position in which integrity, honesty and honour were essential, and if in his private conduct he showed himself destitute and devoid of those essential qualities, surely it could not be said that it was not a fair matter for public animadversion, so long as the writer keeps within the bounds of truth and the limits of just criticism.[80]

This wider approach became the dominant view of matters of public interest[81], although not without dissent. In *Henwood v Harrison*[82], for example, the comment related to proposals submitted to the Admiralty for improving ships. The majority held that the matter was clearly of public interest because the improvement of the Navy was a matter of national importance. Grove J dissented: in an analysis that echoed the narrower approach of the early nineteenth century he emphasised that the proposals had not been published generally.

The developments surrounding the idea of 'fair comment' were more subtle, but of equal significance. One consistent theme was the emphasis on comment as inference or deduction from public facts. Thus, for instance, in *Morrison v Belcher*[83] Cockburn CJ paraphrased the defence, for the benefit of the jury, as whether the defendant's 'observations and inferences were fair and legitimate under the circumstances'[84]. Later, in *Hedley v Barlow*[85], the same judge described it as the 'right of public discussion on matters of public interest'[86]. Again, in *Hunter v Sharpe*[87] the emphasis was clear: 'if a public writer . . . discussing the subject in the exercise of his

[76] (1861) 2 F & F 508.
[77] *Ibid* at 524.
[78] *Ibid*.
[79] (1862) 3 F & F 372.
[80] *Ibid* at 382.
[81] Eg, *Kelly v Tinling* (1865) LR 1 QB 699.
[82] (1872) LR 7 CP 606.
[83] (1863) 3 F & F 614.
[84] *Ibid* at 619.
[85] (1865) 4 F & F 224.
[86] *Ibid* at 230.
[87] (1866) 4 F & F 983.

vocation, falls into error as to the facts or the inferences, and goes beyond the limits of strict truth, he is nevertheless privileged'[88]. This emphasis on inference and discussion was important because it showed that what identified a comment was simply that it was a reaction or response. As a contemporary commentator put it, a comment was limited to 'what naturally arose out of what was already public'[89]. It seems to have been a satisfactory test, being applied in England[90], Ireland[91] and America[92].

A further important development occurred in relation to the assumption that any publication protected by fair comment should contain an account of the data on which the comment was based. In *O'Brien v Marquis of Salisbury*[93] Field J made explicit what had been implicit in earlier case-law: it was essential to show the reader what materials formed the basis of the comment[94]. These materials did not need to be set out in full if they were general knowledge, when a reference sufficed. This apparently modest requirement helped to distinguish protected inferences from unprotected assertions of fact. But, more importantly, it also promoted and encouraged the operation of the public sphere in two ways. First, it prioritised expressions of reasoning and analysis—the key forms of expression in the public sphere[95]. Second, it facilitated participation by protecting only those contributions that set out their premises explicitly: to engage with such contributions was relatively simple. By requiring that the basis for the comment be made explicit the courts both imposed and encouraged a minimum standard of reasoned debate.

The range of that debate could be extensive, as one Victorian commentator realised:

> Criticism, comment, discussion—these are the three degrees, so to speak, of the right of discussion. Criticism—which merely describes or denounces the tone or character of the plaintiff's publication, as appears on the fact of it; as to say a book is obscene or immoral. Comment—which from these observations deduces obvious inferences; as that an immoral writer is a man of immoral mind, or that he who writes immoral books must do so for some bad purpose. Discussion—which, in regard to public matters, blends inferences, or opinion, or suggestions, as to facts, with the expression of other opinions.[96]

[88] *Ibid* at 1005–6.

[89] Anon (Foster or Finlason), 'The Law of Libel, As Applied to Public Discussion' (1863) 15 *The Law Magazine and Law Review* 193 at 218.

[90] *Popham v Pickburn* (1862) 7 H & N 891; *Davis & Sons v Shepstone* (1886) 11 App Cas 187.

[91] *Lefroy v Burnside (No 2)* (1879) 4 LR Ir 556.

[92] *Burt v Advertiser Newspaper Co* 28 NE 1 (Supreme Judicial Court of Massachusetts, 1891).

[93] (1889) 54 JP 215.

[94] *Ibid* at 216.

[95] Habermas, Burger (tr), *The Structural Transformation of the Public Sphere* (1989) at 27.

[96] Anon (Foster or Finlason), 'The Law of Libel, As Applied to Public Discussion' (1863) 15 *The Law Magazine and Law Review* 193 at 224.

At each stage of this classification the defendant's role became more prominent. In theory each type of response was entitled to protection, provided it was fair; but fairness was a slippery concept to define.

At one extreme there was a minimalist approach based on the idea that 'fairness' meant simply 'not malicious'. Thus, in *Hedley v Barlow*[97] Cockburn CJ stated that 'The word "fair" is used with reference to the question of malice'[98]. The same judge, in *Strauss v Francis*[99], formulated the question for the jury as 'whether, as a whole, it was fair or prompted by motives of another character'[100]. To underline the point, it was made clear in *Morrison v Belcher*[101] that for a defendant to lose the defence the comments had to be not merely unfair, but 'so unfair as to be reckless, and thus, in law, malicious'[102]. This minimalist approach to fairness had a coherence and consistency with earlier cases such as *Carr v Hood*[103]: essentially it left the public sphere free to operate by protecting any genuine result of the judgment of the critic.

At the same time there were suggestions of a more stringent test of fairness. In a note to *Turnbull v Bird*[104] the reporter suggested that a defendant needed reasonable grounds for his belief in order to claim the defence[105]. Either the same reporter or his partner later recanted[106], but traces of the same opinion started appearing in judicial language. In *Hunter v Sharpe*[107], for instance, Cockburn CJ told the jury that protection was given to 'a public writer, using a reasonable degree of temper and moderation, as behoves any one who makes imputations upon others'[108]. Two years later, in *Risk Allah Bey v Whitehurst*[109], the same judge went even further, saying that the defence was available where a writer 'has acted in good faith in discharge of his duty, bringing to it the amount of care, reason, and judgment which a man who takes upon himself to discuss public questions is bound to bring, so that the jury is of opinion that he has acted reasonably and properly'[110]. Later on in his summing up he alluded to the need for a writer to show a 'calm, fair and dispassionate exercise of . . . judgment'[111]. These requirements came close to imposing a standard of reasonable care.

97 (1865) 4 F & F 224.
98 *Ibid* at 231.
99 (1866) 4 F & F 1107.
100 *Ibid* at 1115–16.
101 (1863) 3 F & F 614.
102 *Ibid* at 620.
103 (1808) 1 Camp 355.
104 (1861) 2 F & F 508.
105 *Ibid* at 524.
106 Anon (Foster or Finlason), 'The Law of Libel, As Applied to Public Discussion' (1863) 15 *The Law Magazine and Law Review* 193 at 249.
107 (1866) 4 F & F 983.
108 *Ibid* at 1105.
109 (1868) 18 LT(NS) 615.
110 *Ibid* at 620.
111 *Ibid*.

The more stringent test of fairness could also be traced back to earlier cases, such as *Thompson v Shackell*[112], where Best CJ had doubted whether personal ridicule of an author could ever be justified. The significance of this more stringent approach was fully appreciated: it regulated what opinions could be expressed. One contemporary commentator[113] was particularly troubled by the fact that this test would be applied by the jury. In their hands, he argued, it would become a test of what they agreed with: 'to expect a jury to be able to draw a line between what they approve of, and what they think fair, as to opinions they disapprove of, is what no one at all acquainted with trial by jury will be so deluded as to dream of'[114]. The commentator forcefully argued that it was precisely where an opinion was unpopular that the defence was needed.

The uncertainty over fairness was eventually resolved in favour of the minimalist approach in *Merivale v Carson*[115]. Lord Esher MR asserted that the 'meaning' of 'fair comment' was 'is the article in the opinion of the jury beyond that which any fair man, however prejudiced or however strong his opinion may be, would say of the work in question?'[116] The House of Lords later diluted this test even further, saying that the reference should be to an 'honest', not a 'fair' man, so as to eliminate any possible suggestion of reasonableness[117].

Whilst these general principles were being elaborated during the second half of the nineteenth century, one situation highlighted the inevitable vagueness inherent in a test of fairness, and the potential for the general principles to harden into strict rules. The problem arose where a defendant imputed corrupt motives for a public act, and its resolution caused a difference of opinion between England and America. Courts in both jurisdictions were reluctant to grant protection, but had an important disagreement over the basis for doing so.

In England protection was denied by applying the general principle that the comment must fairly arise from the public act. Thus, in *Campbell v Spottiswoode*[118] it was said that a defendant should only impute corrupt motives where 'there is so much ground for the imputation that the jury shall find, not only that he had an honest belief in the truth of his statements, but that his belief was not without foundation'[119]. In other words, it had to have a sufficient factual basis[120]. As one commentator explained,

112 (1828) M & M 187.
113 Anon (Foster or Finlason), 'The Law of Libel, As Applied to Public Discussion' (1863) 15 *The Law Magazine and Law Review* 193.
114 *Ibid* at 211.
115 (1887) 20 QBD 275.
116 *Ibid* at 280.
117 *Turner (otherwise Robinson) v Metro-Goldwyn Mayer Pictures Ltd* [1950] 1 All ER 449 at 461.
118 (1863) 3 B & S 769.
119 *Ibid* at 776.
120 *Douglas v Stephenson* (1898) 29 Ontario 616 at 624.

one could not fairly infer corruption from the mere performance of a public duty: the only fair presumption in such a situation would be that the duty was performed honestly[121].

Some American courts, by contrast, adopted an independent rule that an imputation of corrupt motives could never be a fair comment. In one leading Maryland case[122], for instance, it was said that there was a 'broad distinction' between fair comment and imputation of motives; anyone imputing corrupt motives 'must do so at his peril'[123].

This independent rule had inconvenient consequences[124], its major disadvantage being that it arbitrarily excluded discussion of matters of public importance that might arise from the facts. As a matter of authority it was also unconvincing: the case cited by the Maryland court was, surprisingly, *Campbell v Spottiswoode*[125]. The underlying explanation of the rule, however, seemed to be that it was an application of the general statements in literary criticism cases that an author's private character should not be attacked. The difficulty with this was that literary criticism and discussion of political activities involved different segments of the public sphere. As Veeder explained[126], it might not be fair criticism of a book to attack the author's motives and character, but it did not follow that it was also unfair to impugn the motives behind a dubious official act: the author's character was not a legitimate subject of public interest, the official's was. The tendency to apply generalisations about literary works to official acts was particularly well illustrated by *Hamilton v Eno*[127]. The defendant's criticism of an official report contained the hint that the author of the report must have been bribed to recommend a particular manufacturer of pavements. The New York Court of Appeals approached the question purely as a matter of literary criticism, stating that the defendant had a free hand to discuss the report 'as a work'[128]. The fact that there was also an official act, raising different dimensions of public interest, was not considered. Strikingly, when there was no element of literary criticism on the facts, a lower New York court was happy to protect imputations of motive as a fair comment[129].

121 Anon (Foster or Finlason), 'The Law of Libel, As Applied to Public Discussion' (1863) 15 *The Law Magazine and Law Review* 193 at 229–30.

122 *Negley v Farrow* 60 Md 158 (Court of Appeals of Maryland, 1883).

123 *Ibid* at *11 (Westlaw transcript).

124 Chase, 'Criticism of Public Officers and Candidates for Office' (1889) 23 *American Law Review* 346 at 368; Veeder, 'Freedom of Public Discussion' (1910) 23 *Harvard Law Review* 413 at 429–32.

125 (1863) 3 B & S 769.

126 Veeder, 'Freedom of Public Discussion' (1910) 23 *Harvard Law Review* 413 at 429.

127 81 NY 116 (Court of Appeals of New York, 1880).

128 *Ibid* at *5 (Westlaw transcript).

129 *Howarth v Barlow* 99 NYS 457 (Supreme Court of New York, Appellate Division, 1906).

Campbell v Spottiswoode[130] has been referred to above in relation to imputations of corrupt motives for official acts. Its analysis of this factual situation was indeed illuminating, but it also made two general claims about the nature of the defence of fair comment that had long-term and fundamental consequences. These claims were, in essence, that fair comment was not part of qualified privilege; and that a person pleading fair comment raised the question 'libel or no libel'.

Taking the first claim first, Crompton J explained that qualified privilege was confined to cases of 'real necessity or duty'[131]. The implication was that a person making a criticism of some public matter was not performing a duty. This, however, was not self-evident. Starkie, for instance, had classified protection for criticisms of books with qualified privilege precisely because the commentator was performing 'a most difficult and important public duty'[132]. A second explanation, put forward by both Crompton and Blackburn JJ, was that 'privilege' was the wrong term to use. 'Privilege' meant that 'a person stands in such a relation to the facts of the case that he is justified in saying or writing what would be slanderous in any one else'[133]. Fair comment, however, concerned 'a general right which belongs to the public'[134].

Having removed fair comment from the category of qualified privilege, the Court then relocated it as part of the question 'libel or no libel'[135]. It was not immediately apparent what this meant. One possibility was that it related to interpreting the defamatory language: a fair comment on a matter of public interest was not truly defamatory. Some support for this interpretation existed: in one New York case, for instance, it was said that abstract criticisms of a work were not generally actionable because 'the book cannot be plaintiff'[136]. There was also a useful analogy in the earlier English decision that it was not defamatory to impute unfitness for purpose to a seller's goods[137]. However, the explanation based on interpreting language had major weaknesses. For one thing, it was artificial to say that criticism of the work cast no aspersion on the author: indeed, it was accepted that an inaccurate attribution of authorship could be defamatory[138]. The more realistic view was that criticism of the work was an 'indirect reflection'[139] on the author. Furthermore, it should be emphasised

130 (1863) 3 B & S 769.
131 *Ibid* at 779.
132 Starkie, *A Treatise on the Law of Slander and Libel* 2nd edn (1830) vol 1 at 305.
133 (1863) 3 B & S 769 at 780.
134 *Ibid* at 781.
135 *Ibid* at 780.
136 *Cooper v Stone* 24 Wend 434 (Supreme Court of Judicature of New York, 1840).
137 *Evans v Harlow* (1844) 5 QB 624.
138 *Archbold v Sweet* (1832) 5 Car & P 219.
139 Anon (Foster or Finlason), 'The Law of Libel, As Applied to Public Discussion' (1863) 15 *The Law Magazine and Law Review* 193 at 200.

that the facts of *Campbell v Spottiswoode*[140] did not concern abstract criticism; the imputation was that the claimant's motives were corrupt. It is difficult to believe that the Court meant to say that such an allegation was not defamatory.

Another problem with the explanation in terms of interpretation was the role of malice. It had been, and continued to be, accepted that a defence of fair comment was lost by proof of malice in the defendant. But if the defence was based on interpreting language, it was not clear why this should be so[141]. If the words were not defamatory, they were not actionable; saying them maliciously should make no difference.

A second possibility was that 'libel or no libel' meant simply 'actionable'[142]. If this was what the Court meant in *Campbell's* case, it had not so much transferred fair comment from one category to another as put fair comment in a category of its own.

The categorisation of fair comment was dismissed as a mere 'metaphysical'[143] question by Bowen LJ, but it had important practical and theoretical consequences. The practical consequences flowed from the general rule that libel or no libel was a question for the jury[144]. If fair comment was part of the question 'libel or no libel' it followed that it was for the jury to decide whether all the elements of fair comment were present. In *Henwood v Harrison*[145], however, Willes J responded to a submission to this effect with utter horror: 'A jury, according to their individual views of religion or policy, might hold the church, the army, the navy, parliament itself, to be of no national or general importance . . .'[146]. He made it clear that fair comment had to be seen as a branch of qualified privilege, where the existence of a privileged occasion was a matter of law for the judge. Although this attempt to reclassify fair comment with qualified privilege was later disapproved[147], the significance of the point for the powers of the jury seems not to have resurfaced.

A second practical consequence, also relating to the role of the jury, arose in relation to the rule that a judge could withdraw from the jury's consideration anything that was not capable of being a libel. Did the classification of fair comment mean that if a judge thought that a defence of fair comment was certain to succeed he should withdraw the case from the jury? In *Jenner v A'Beckett*[148] the judges could not agree: a majority

140 (1863) 3 B & S 769.

141 Radcliffe, 'The Defence of "Fair Comment" in Actions for Defamation' (1907) 23 *LQR* 97 at 98.

142 *Speight v Syme* (1895) 21 VLR 672 at 675–76.

143 *Merivale v Carson* (1887) 20 QBD 275 at 282.

144 *Campbell v Spottiswoode* (1863) 3 B & S 769 at 781.

145 (1872) LR 7 CP 606.

146 *Ibid* at 628.

147 *Merivale v Carson* (1887) 20 QBD 275.

148 (1871) LR 7 QB 11.

thought that the case could not be withdrawn, but Hannen J contributed a powerful dissent.

In essence, then, the courts dealt with the practical consequences of *Campbell v Spottiswoode*[149] by denial and suppression. The theoretical consequences, by contrast, were long-term. The immediate theoretical consequence of the decision was uncertainty: clearly fair comment no longer belonged with qualified privilege, but where it should be classified now was less obvious. Folkard updated Starkie's textbook by transplanting the discussion of fair comment from the chapter on qualified privilege to a chapter entitled 'Libels Affecting Persons in Their Official Capacity, Profession, Trade or Business'[150]. Odgers dealt with fair comment adjacent to his treatment of defamatory words[151]. Pollock's approach was different again: he appeared to act on the more convincing reading of *Campbell v Spottiswoode*, and discussed fair comment under a general heading of 'exceptions' to defamation[152].

The most radical approach was taken by Fisher and Strahan[153]. They dealt with truth and fair comment together, under the heading 'Justification'. In their view,

> If it be matter of fact, the defendant may justify it by proof that it is in substance and in fact true. If it is matter of opinion, he may justify it by proof that it is fair and honest comment on a matter of public interest.[154]

A lengthy footnote (quoted here only in part) defended their position:

> The authors are, of course, aware that it is the usual—though not the invariable practice . . . to apply the term 'justification' only to proof of the truth of a statement of fact. They are also aware of the somewhat profitless controversy as to whether fair comment is a case of privilege, or of no libel, or of no defamation (see *Henwood v Harrison*). It is submitted, however, that using the word 'justify' in its ordinary sense, the above is a simple and accurate statement of the law. Justification by proof of truth, and justification by proof of fairness are practically the same. If matter *prima facie* defamatory is published, an action founded on it must go to the jury. If it is a matter of fact, the defendant may prove it is true, and that will be an answer to the action. If it is a matter of opinion the test of truth cannot apply. In matters of opinion, the test of truth cannot apply. In matters of opinion the corresponding test is honesty and fairness.[155]

Fisher and Strahan's analysis was perhaps the crucial moment in the history of fair comment; it was the first attempt to pair fair comment with

[149] (1863) 3 B & S 769.

[150] Folkard (ed), *Starkie's Treatise on the Law of Slander and Libel*, 3rd edn (London, 1869) at 245 ff.

[151] Odgers, *A Digest of the Law of Libel and Slander* (London, 1881) at 34.

[152] Pollock, *The Law of Torts* (London, 1887) at 219.

[153] Fisher and Strahan, *The Law of the Press*, 2nd edn (London, 1898) at 181.

[154] *Ibid*.

[155] *Ibid*.

justification, and to explain the protection for comment in relation to the protection for truth. The pairing was so novel because justification and fair comment were entirely different in both form and function. Justification was pleaded specially; it admitted that all of the elements of liability existed, but put forward an excuse. Fair comment, by contrast, was pleaded under the general issue ('not guilty'); it denied the existence of malice, a requirement of liability. Fisher and Strahan may well have been inspired to put the two together by a new form of pleading[156], later named the rolled up plea[157], which also paired truth and fair comment. The typical form of the rolled up plea was that

> In so far as [the words complained of] consist of allegations of fact, the said words are true in substance and in fact, and in so far as they consist of expressions of opinion they are fair comment made in good faith and without malice upon the said facts, which are a matter of public interest.[158]

It was particularly striking that this plea, like Fisher and Strahan's analysis, did not attempt to justify matters of opinion as being true. But whatever their inspiration, at the end of the nineteenth century these two authors had articulated a controversial position that was rapidly to become the academic orthodoxy.

3. FROM THE START OF THE TWENTIETH CENTURY

The essential features of the defence of fair comment, as established in the nineteenth century, remained unchanged in the twentieth. What counted as a matter of public interest was again viewed broadly—it now embraced matters as diverse as the closure of a West End play[159] and the dismissal of a law professor[160]. Similarly, the need to indicate the basis for any comment was underlined by the House of Lords[161]; the Court of Appeal emphasised that the reader should be in no doubt what was basis and what was comment[162]. Minute factual analyses of what could be evidence of malice were undertaken by both appellate courts[163].

The nineteenth-century sense of coherence and purpose surrounding the defence fared differently. As the twentieth century progressed uncertainty over the nature of the defence of fair comment provoked contrasting

156 *Penrhyn v The 'Licensed Victuallers' Mirror'* (1890) 7 TLR 1.
157 *The Aga Khan v Times Publishing Company* [1924] 1 KB 675 at 681 (per Scrutton LJ).
158 *Penrhyn v The 'Licensed Victuallers' Mirror'* (1890) 7 TLR 1.
159 *London Artists Ltd v Littler* [1969] 2 QB 375.
160 *Clark v McBaine* 252 SW 428 (Supreme Court of Missouri, 1923).
161 *Kemsley v Foot* [1952] AC 345.
162 *Hunt v The Star Newspaper Company* [1908] 2 KB 309.
163 *Turner (otherwise Robinson) v Metro-Goldwyn Mayer Pictures Ltd* [1950] 1 All ER 449; *Broadway Approvals Ltd v Odhams Press Ltd (No 2)* [1965] 1 WLR 805.

judicial and academic responses. The judiciary continued to apply the nineteenth-century principles in a taxonomical vacuum. Academic writers, for whom classification was a major concern, adopted a new theoretical explanation for fair comment which, unfortunately, did not quite fit with the case law.

From the very start of the twentieth century there was a sense of uncertainty about where exactly fair comment belonged in the conceptual scheme of things. This uncertainty was a continuation of the difficulties caused by certain judicial remarks in the 1860s[164], and it seemed to deepen as the years passed. In *Thomas v Bradbury, Agnew & Co*[165] Collins MR tried to bury the whole question by saying that all the rules governing fair comment were 'precisely the same'[166] as those for qualified privilege. But less than two years later, in *Peter Walker & Son, Limited v Hodgson*[167], the Court of Appeal showed that the problem had not gone away. Vaughan Williams LJ said that the fair comment defence was 'a denial that the words complained of are really defamatory'[168]. Buckley LJ said the opposite: 'Fair comment does not negative defamation, but establishes a defence to any right of action founded on defamation'[169]. Even as late as 1948, juries were being told that fair comment was a matter of interpreting the words used[170]. In 1912, when the South African courts adopted a defence of fair comment from English law, they inherited, then reproduced, the same problems of classification[171].

The sense of uncertainty would not have been lessened by the decision in *E Hulton & Co v Jones*[172] that malice had no substantive role in ordinary liability for defamation[173]. The original doctrinal explanation for fair comment had been that it rebutted the usual presumption of malice that arose from speaking defamatory words[174]. After the decision in *E Hulton & Co v Jones*[175] there was no scope for rebutting any presumption: the presumption of malice was irrebuttable. So the doctrinal basis of the cases founding the defence was no longer useful for anyone seeking to make sense of fair comment.

The explanation of fair comment that prevailed focussed on the relationship with justification, and emphasised that justification was for facts, fair comment for opinions. Thus, for example, the first sentence of Gatley's

164 *Campbell v Spottiswoode* (1863) 3 B & S 769.
165 [1906] 2 KB 627.
166 *Ibid* at 640.
167 [1909] 1 KB 239.
168 *Ibid* at 250.
169 *Ibid* at 253.
170 *Braddock v Bevins* [1948] 1 All ER 450 at 457.
171 Burchell, *The Law of Defamation in South Africa* (Cape Town, 1985) at 219–20.
172 [1910] AC 20.
173 See further, ch 5.
174 See eg *Tabart v Tipper* (1808) 1 Camp 350.
175 [1910] AC 20.

treatment of 'comment' stated 'The words must be the expression of an opinion, and not the allegation of a fact'[176]. As Fisher and Strahan, the earliest exponents of this explanation, acknowledged, it rested on the assumption that the test of truth did not apply to comments[177]. In essence, the explanation of fair comment was that it was needed to supplement justification.

Some judicial support for this view was forthcoming. In *Stopes v Sutherland*[178], for example, Bankes LJ set out the following general principle:

> In ordinary circumstances . . . where justification and fair comment are pleaded . . . the questions for the jury are: . . . are [the words] statements of fact or expressions of opinion, or partly one or partly the other? . . . In so far as you find that they are statements of fact, are they true? . . . In so far as you find that they are expressions of opinion, do they exceed the limits of fair criticism on matter of public interest?[179]

He described the submission that justification could apply to matters of comment as 'unusual and not . . . universally sound'[180]. In the House of Lords, Lord Wrenbury took the same view[181]. The most emphatic support and exposition was, however, academic. In the first edition of his textbook, Winfield began his discussion of fair comment with the statement that '*It must be an expression of opinion and not an allegation of fact*'[182]. He illustrated the point by imagining that a defendant had said that a particular line of verse was 'the worst in English poetry'. Such a statement was, he explained, obviously comment, 'for verification of it as a fact is impossible'[183]. The role of fair comment as a supplement to justification could not have been clearer. Winfield's exposition must have been enormously influential on generations of students, for it was repeated in every subsequent edition of his work[184]. At the very end of the century one could still hear echoes of Winfield in one commentator's observation that 'verifiability' was 'a factor that arguably explains why English law has the two defences of justification and fair comment'[185].

176 Gatley, *Law and Practice of Libel and Slander* (London, 1924) at 334. See similarly *Stephen's Commentaries on the Laws of England*, vol III (London, 1928) at 411, where it was said that the defendant must show that the statement was 'an expression of opinion and not an allegation of facts'.

177 See quotation from Fisher and Strahan at n 153 above.

178 (1923) 39 TLR 677.

179 *Ibid* at 678–79.

180 *Ibid* at 679.

181 [1925] AC 47 at 87.

182 Winfield, *A Text-Book of the Law of Tort* (London, 1937) at 294.

183 *Ibid*.

184 See eg Rogers (ed), *Winfield and Jolowicz on Tort*, 15th edn (London, 2002) at 422.

185 Young, 'Fact, Opinion and the Human Rights Act 1998: Does English Law Need to Modify its Definition of "Statements of Opinion" to Ensure Compliance with Article 10 of the European Convention on Human Rights?' (2000) 20 *Oxford Journal of Legal Studies* 89 at 102.

The idea that fair comment was the defence for unverifiable statements could be expressed with clarity and force in textbooks, but it was not easy to reconcile with all the cases. An inference of corrupt motives, for example, was capable of being protected under fair comment[186], but it was an allegation that clearly could be verified as a fact. Similarly, in *Dakhyl v Labouchere*[187] the alleged comment was that the claimant doctor was a 'quack'. The House of Lords held that such an allegation was capable of being a comment. As Lord Atkinson explained, 'A personal attack may form part of a fair comment upon facts truly stated if it be warranted by those facts—in other words, . . . if it be a reasonable inference from those facts'[188]. There was no mention of verifiability. Winfield's treatment of the case was revealing: he avoided going into the detailed reasoning, opting instead to say that it was an illustration of the difficulty in distinguishing fact from comment[189].

A further, and fundamental difficulty in the case law was presented by the House of Lords' decision in *Sutherland v Stopes*[190]. The facts and course of the trial occupied much of their Lordships' attention[191], but the important point of principle to emerge was that justification covered both facts and comments: an expression of opinion could be proved to be true. This position was a convincing one. Allegations of accepting a bribe or corruption, for instance, could be comment, but could clearly be justified as facts if the evidence was available. The same could be said of comments expressing value-judgments where the jury could agree that the claimant's conduct had been accurately described. For instance, a comment that the defendant was 'cruel' could be proved true by evidence showing conduct that no one could deny was cruel[192]. Even a statement that a line of poetry was 'the worst . . . in the English language' might be capable of being proved true in the relative sense that a jury might be persuaded to agree with it. Of course, it would be easier for a defendant to use fair comment in such a situation, but that was not the same thing as saying that justification was unavailable. The declaration of principle in *Sutherland v Stopes*[193], therefore, falsified the assumption that comments could not be dealt with under justification. This, it should be remembered, was the assumption behind the theory that fair comment was needed as a

[186] *Hunt v The Star Newspaper Company* [1908] 2 KB 309; *Peter Walker & Son Limited v Hodgson* [1909] 1 KB 239.

[187] [1908] 2 KB 325 n.

[188] *Ibid* at 329.

[189] Winfield, *A Text-Book of the Law of Tort* (London, 1937) at 294–95.

[190] [1925] AC 47.

[191] Pollock described it as 'a mass of controversial matter which is of little profit to lawyers': (1925) 42 *LQR* 126.

[192] Young, 'Fact, Opinion and the Human Rights Act 1998: Does English Law Need to Modify its Definition of "Statements of Opinion" to Ensure Compliance with Article 10 of the European Convention on Human Rights?' (2000) 20 *Oxford Journal of Legal Studies* 89 at 103.

[193] [1925] AC 47.

supplement to justification. Again, it is interesting to see what Winfield did: he dealt with other aspects of *Sutherland v Stopes*, but omitted this one[194].

What had emerged by the second half of the twentieth century was a curious dichotomy. A reader approaching the subject through the authorities would find the emphasis on reasoning and inference. On turning to the textbooks, however, he would be told that the key points were opinion and verifiability. The textbooks did not entirely omit inference, but tended to relegate its importance. Thus, for example, the eighth edition of Gatley stated that 'while a comment is usually a statement of opinion . . . an inference of fact may also be a comment'[195]. This statement was subsequently adopted by the Privy Council[196]. Later editions of Winfield cryptically remarked that equating opinion and comment might be 'an over-simplification'[197], without explaining why. This friction between the cases and the theoretical framework they inhabit continues today.

The final twentieth-century development of importance was the withering of malice from organising principle to, perhaps, disappearance. Early fair comment cases identified the defendant's motive as the key factor[198]. In doing so they were consistent with the general principles of defamation: malice was presumed from speaking the defamatory words, but could be rebutted by contrary evidence[199]. In 1909 the House of Lords altered the general principle so as to make the presumption of malice irrebuttable[200]. The rules about malice in fair comment remained unchanged, but the idea that the fair comment defence was merely an illustration of general principle was no longer tenable. For instance, in the nineteenth century a fair comment on an accurate report of legal proceedings did not cause analytical difficulty: both the accurate report and the fair comment on it rebutted the general presumption of malice[201]. In the mid-twentieth century, however, the rebuttable presumption of malice had disappeared. Fair comment was now seen as a supplement to truth. It was, therefore, much harder to explain how a fair comment on an untrue defamatory statement made in court proceedings could be protected[202].

Until very recently the courts assumed that the test for malice in fair comment and qualified privilege was the same: was the dominant motive

194 Winfield, *A Text-Book of the Law of Tort* (London, 1937) at 297.
195 *Gatley on Libel and Slander*, 8th edn (London, 1981) para 697, p 294.
196 *Jeyaretnam v Goh Chok Tong* [1989] 1 WLR 1109 at 1113.
197 Rogers (ed), *Winfield and Jolowicz on Tort*, 15th edn (London, 2002) at 422.
198 Eg, *Tabart v Tipper* (1808) 1 Camp 350.
199 See further, ch 5.
200 *E Hulton & Co v Jones* [1910] AC 20.
201 *Lewis v Levy* (1858) 27 LJ (QB) 282.
202 *Grech v Odhams Press Ltd* [1958] 1 QB 310, [1958] 2 QB 275; *Brent Walker Group plc v Time Out Limited* [1991] 2 QB 33.

something other than that for which the defence was conferred?[203] In *Cheng v Tse*[204], however, Lord Nicholls questioned this assumption. His view was that a more appropriate definition of malice for fair comment was genuine belief in the comment; the new definition would, therefore, protect people making genuine comments with unattractive motives such as self-interest or spite. Lord Nicholls' view might lead to some unfortunate consequences[205]: for instance, it seems to deny a defence to a newspaper editor printing articles or letters expressing opposing views on a matter of public interest. For such an editor the test of motive or purpose seems more appropriate. The decision also has an important historical dimension: it is a further stage of disintegration in the general principle of liability based on malice. Indeed, Lord Nicholls even suggested that it would be simpler to drop the word 'malice' altogether, and just ask the jury whether the defendant genuinely believed what he said[206].

4. CONCLUSION

The history of the defence of fair comment and its current state are the result of the interplay of grand ideas about the function of the defence and its place in the scheme of classification. Its origins can be seen in the desire to keep discussion in the public sphere free from legal interference and its early classification was on the basis of rebutting malice. Whilst the idea about its function remained constant, and inspired detailed rules such as the requirement to set out the basis of one's comment, the classification changed. The key case was *Campbell v Spottiswoode*, which created an uncertainty about classification that had to be resolved in some way by academic commentators. A defence designed for allegations *unverified* except by the premises given was now said to be for *unverifiable* remarks. It was a subtle but crucial change that aligned fair comment with truth, thus establishing the approach to fair comment that prevails today.

[203] *Horrocks v Lowe* [1975] AC 135. For an isolated exception see *Slim v Daily Telegraph Ltd* [1968] 2 QB 157 at 170 (per Lord Denning MR).

[204] (2000) 3 Hong Kong Court of Final Appeal Reports 339.

[205] Trindade, 'Malice and the Defence of Fair Comment' (2001) 117 *LQR* 169 at 173–74.

[206] (2000) 3 Hong Kong Court of Final Appeal Reports 339 at 361.

9

Absolute Privilege

THERE ARE THREE situations where a person making defamatory allegations cannot be held liable in defamation. They are: where words are uttered in the course of parliamentary proceedings, communications by one high official of state to another, and statements in judicial proceedings. The modern tendency is to regard each situation as an application of the defence of 'absolute privilege'. This modern tendency implicitly assumes that the general category of absolute privilege is coherent and principled, an assumption that the courts have supported during the course of the twentieth century. For instance, in Australia the High Court held that the unifying rationale of absolute privilege was that it applied to situations where freedom from liability for defamation was 'indispensable to the effective performance of judicial, legislative or official functions'[1]. Fleming sought to provide a further principled explanation by stating that absolute privilege was designed to facilitate improved performance in each of the three branches of government—legislative, executive and judicial[2]. The High Court subsequently adopted Fleming's explanation and at the same time added the further rationale that the categories of absolute privilege were grounded in 'necessity'[3].

A comparative historical investigation of absolute privilege reveals a very different and less elegant picture. The most striking feature emerging from the historical investigation is the lack of a coherent category of absolute privilege for most of the modern period. In place of a coherent category, each situation where there was no liability in defamation was analysed separately; the reasons justifying the absence of liability were different in each case; and there were fundamental differences of view both within and between jurisdictions. This chapter therefore focuses on each situation in turn, reserving comments on unifying themes for the concluding section.

[1] *Gibbons v Proctor* (1932) 47 CLR 520 at 528.

[2] Fleming, *The Law of Torts*, 8th edn (1992) at 557–58.

[3] *Mann v O'Neill* (1997) 191 CLR 204 at 258 (per Kirby J); 213 (per Brennan CJ, Dawson, Toohey and Gaudron JJ). The same point had been made in England two centuries earlier in *Curry v Walter* (1796) 1 B & P 525 at 528.

1. PARLIAMENTARY PROCEEDINGS

Immunity from liability in defamation for words spoken in Parliamentary proceedings is a vital part of the law of Parliamentary privilege[4]. The 'great leading case'[5] is *R v Elliot*[6]. There the House of Lords resolved that the conviction of the defendant for seditious libel and assault committed in the Chamber of the House of Commons was unlawful, because the trial judge had overruled the defendant's plea that he spoke the seditious words in Parliament. However, it would be wrong to say that *R v Elliot* created new law. The House of Lords in its reasoning explained that it was applying a statute of 1512:

> extending to indemnify all and every the members of both Houses of Parliament, in all Parliaments, for and touching any bills, speaking, reasoning or declaring of any matter or matters in and concerning the Parliament to be communed and treated of.[7]

The statute itself, it said, was 'a declaratory law of the ancient and necessary rights and privileges of Parliament'[8].

Whilst it remains the position that Parliament's inherent rights and privileges are not limited by the terms of declaratory statutes[9], one statutory provision has become central in litigation over the scope of Parliamentary privilege in defamation. Article 9, Bill of Rights 1689 states that:

> *Freedom of Speech*—That the freedome of speech and debates or proceedings in Parlyament ought not to be impeached or questioned in any court or place out of Parlyament.

There seems to be no doubt that this provision prevents a person from being made liable for defamatory statements made in Parliamentary proceedings. A private remark by one Member to another, however, would not be part of the 'proceedings'[10]. The protection is not confined to Members of Parliament: other participants in Parliamentary processes, such as those petitioning Parliament[11] and witnesses giving evidence

[4] The Privy Council once observed that any colonial legislature set up by the British Parliament would have the same privilege of freedom of speech as its parent out of 'inherent necessity' (*Chenard and Company v Arissol* (1948) 65 TLR 72 at 73).

[5] *Bradlaugh v Gossett* (1884) 12 QBD 271 at 283 (per Stephen J).

[6] (1668) Cro Car 605.

[7] *Ibid* at 609.

[8] *Ibid*.

[9] For examples of the courts applying a test for Parliamentary privilege set out in Blackstone's *Commentaries* see *Bradlaugh v Gossett* (1884) 12 QBD 271 at 278 (per Stephen J) and *Church of Scientology of California v Johnson-Smith* [1972] 1 QB 522 at 530.

[10] Leopold, 'Parliamentary Privilege and the Broadcasting of Parliament' (1989) 9 *Legal Studies* 53 at 60.

[11] *Lake v King* (1668) 1 Wms Saund 120.

before a Parliamentary Select Committee[12] are also protected. Where any question arises about whether a process is a 'proceeding in Parliament' the current position is that the courts are free to form their own view[13], which risks a conflict between the courts and Parliament[14]. The risk of conflict is heightened by the absence of a principled test for 'proceedings in Parliament'[15].

However, the main controversy has centred on whether Parliamentary privilege went beyond merely protecting people against actions for words uttered in Parliamentary proceedings. In a narrow sense this controversy might appear to be beyond the scope of the present chapter, which is concerned with immunity from liability in Parliament. However, the cases on the scope of the privilege consider its justifications in depth. These cases are, therefore, crucial because they cast light on the fundamental basis for the immunity.

In *Church of Scientology of California v Johnson-Smith*[16] the claimant sued for a defamatory statement made outside Parliament and the defendant raised the defence of fair comment. The question for the court was whether the claimant could rely on speech by the defendant in Parliament as evidence of malice. The English High Court held that using such evidence would infringe Parliamentary privilege. Browne J first identified two bases for Parliamentary privilege. The first was that the Houses of Parliament should be left to control their own Members. The second was that 'a member must have a complete right of free speech in the House without any fear that his motives or intentions or reasoning will be questioned or held against him thereafter'[17]. He then referred to Blackstone's statement that proceedings in Parliament could not be 'examined, discussed and adjudged'[18] in court, and concluded that 'questioned' in Article 9 should be interpreted 'in a wide sense'[19]. Investigating the motives behind Parliamentary speech would 'question' freedom of speech in this wide sense.

A similarly wide approach to what constituted 'questioning' could be seen subsequently in *Rost v Edwards*[20], where it was held that evidence showing that the claimant had not been offered the chairmanship of a Select Committee as a result of a libel infringed the privilege. The decision in *Rost* also elaborated on the idea that the privilege was justified by fear of litigation. Popplewell J suggested that it was open to the claimant to ask

12 *Goffin v Donnelly* (1881) 6 QBD 307; *R v Murphy* (1986) 64 ALR 498.
13 *Rost v Edwards* [1990] 2 All ER 641 at 653.
14 Contrast the approach in *Lake v King* (1668) 1 Wms Saund 120 at 133.
15 See further Leopold, "Proceedings in Parliament": The Grey Area' [1990] *PL* 475.
16 [1972] 1 QB 522.
17 *Ibid* at 530.
18 Blackstone, *Commentaries*, 17th edn (1830), vol 1 at 163.
19 [1972] 1 QB 522 at 530.
20 [1990] 2 All ER 641.

Parliament to waive the privilege, and that Parliament could agree to the request[21]. Clearly the judge believed that the privilege only needed to be co-extensive with the fear of litigation.

The most searching analysis of privilege was made by the Privy Council in *Prebble v Television New Zealand*[22]. There the defendant was seeking to support a defence of justification with evidence that the claimant, a Member of Parliament, had been motivated by personal and political gain when contributing to Parliamentary debates and introducing legislation. The Privy Council held that such evidence would infringe Parliamentary privilege. The key point was that the defendant was seeking to impute impropriety in relation to Parliamentary utterances[23]; this questioned freedom of speech. If there had been no imputation of improper motives or intentions the privilege would not have been infringed. It therefore followed that the evidence of loss of chairmanship in *Rost's case*, which did not impute impropriety, did not question freedom of speech, and that case had been wrongly decided.

The most important aspect of the *Prebble* decision, for present purposes, was the analysis of the nature of the privilege. Adopting the submissions of the Attorney-General of New Zealand[24] Lord Browne-Wilkinson held that the privilege was a jurisdictional rule that avoided conflicts between the courts and Parliament and promoted mutual respect between the two institutions[25]. For instance, if a member was accused of misleading Parliament the matter would potentially raise an issue of contempt of Parliament to be determined by Parliament, and an action for defamation to be determined by the courts. If there were no Parliamentary privilege to make clear that Parliament alone had jurisdiction, there was the potential for conflict, with Parliament upholding the allegation and the courts dismissing it, or vice versa[26].

In characterising the privilege as a jurisdictional rule Lord Browne-Wilkinson had the support of authority[27] and his approach was also consistent with general constitutional principles of mutual respect and non-intervention[28]. Furthermore, since the privilege related to jurisdiction it could not be waived or conceded by either party[29]. It was therefore impossible to admit evidence infringing the privilege even if the member concerned had no fear of litigation.

21 *Ibid* at 651.
22 [1995] 1 AC 321.
23 *Ibid* at 337.
24 *Ibid* at 326.
25 *Ibid* at 332.
26 *Ibid* at 334.
27 Eg, *R v Lord Abingdon* (1794) 1 Esp 226 at 228.
28 *Bradlaugh v Gossett* (1884) 12 QBD 271.
29 [1995] 1 AC 321 at 335.

The approach taken in two Australian jurisdictions was very different. In New South Wales it was held that the privilege was effective only to prevent proceedings being brought for things said or done in Parliament[30]. Where Parliamentary matters were being used for some other purpose there was no infringement of privilege. For instance, it was permissible to challenge a defendant's credibility by proving that his evidence at a trial was inconsistent with his previous statement to a Parliamentary Select Committee: the Parliamentary speech was being used against the defendant, but it was not the basis of the cause of action. Similarly the New South Wales court held that *Church of Scientology of California v Johnson-Smith*[31] was wrongly decided. There the cause of action was not based on Parliamentary speech; rather, the Parliamentary speech was being used as evidence of malice. The defendant would be liable not for what he said in Parliament, but for the malicious speech outside Parliament. As Hunt J put it in *R v Murphy*[32]: 'To resort to the language of causation, what the defendant said or did in Parliament may possibly be thought to be the *causa sine qua non*, but it was not the *causa causans* of those legal consequences'[33]. The real cause of the liability was the defendant's malice 'which was revealed by what he said or did in Parliament, but which existed in any event'[34].

The Supreme Court of South Australia took yet a different approach. It held that the privilege only applied where the Member of Parliament was being sued[35]. So where a Member of Parliament brought an action for defamation for criticisms of his Parliamentary conduct the defendant was entitled to prove any Parliamentary activity to support a defence of justification. In contrast with the Supreme Court of New South Wales, the Supreme Court of South Australia held that the *Church of Scientology* case[36] had been rightly decided because the claimants were seeking to use Parliamentary speech against the defendant Member of Parliament[37].

The approaches taken by these two Australian jurisdictions were put before the Privy Council in *Prebble's case* but both were rejected. Some commentators were disappointed by this[38]. However these Australian approaches were not free from difficulty. For instance in the New South Wales case the Supreme Court emphasised that its approach was based on a close reading of the Bill of Rights 1689. But the Bill of Rights was merely

30 *R v Murphy* (1986) 64 ALR 498.
31 [1972] 1 QB 522.
32 (1986) 64 ALR 498.
33 *Ibid* at 514.
34 *Ibid*.
35 *Wright and Advertiser Newspapers Limited v Lewis* (1990) 53 SASR 416.
36 [1972] 1 QB 522.
37 *Ibid* at 447.
38 Eg, Marshall, 'Impugning Parliamentary Impunity' [1994] *PL* 509; Sharland and Loveland, 'The Defamation Act 1996 and Political Libels' [1997] *PL* 113 at 119–20.

declaring an existing privilege that had been given statutory recognition as early as 1512, so a close reading of the 1689 Act should not have been seen as conclusive of the scope of the privilege. Furthermore, the analysis of the *Church of Scientology* case[39] was very artificial. Where an allegation of malice is made against a defendant the claimant must produce some evidence, or no finding of malice can be made. Commonly evidence of malice takes the form of a series of details with—the claimant hopes—a cumulative persuasive power[40]. Given this background it seems incorrect to say that the evidence of malice is not the real cause of the defendant's liability. A more accurate application of the principles of causation would suggest that the finding of malice is typically made as a result of the cumulative contribution of evidential details. On the orthodox principles of causation, every factor making a material contribution to the consequence should be regarded as a cause in law[41].

The major criticism that can be made of both Australian approaches is that they fail to give effect to the role of Parliamentary privilege in defining the respective jurisdictions of Parliament and the courts. Ultimately the difference between the approach in *Prebble* and the Australian approaches flowed from the emphasis in *Prebble's case* on the jurisdictional aspect of the privilege.

The decision in *Prebble's case* prompted contrasting statutory responses both in New Zealand and in England. In New Zealand there was acceptance of the wide privilege defined by *Prebble*. The statutory response aimed to reform Parliamentary procedures so as to reduce the likelihood of unfounded defamatory allegations being made in Parliament[42]. By Clause 8 of the Parliamentary Privilege Bill 1994 a Member of Parliament intending to make an allegation of 'breach of duty, dishonesty or criminal conduct' against a person not a Member was required to give notice in advance to the Speaker. The Member would only be permitted to make the allegation if the Speaker was satisfied that there were 'grounds' for it. However, support for the measure dwindled and it has not been enacted.

The English response was more radical: the Defamation Act 1996 s 13 permitted a Member of Parliament to choose to waive Parliamentary privilege in a defamation action. This is unlikely to happen where the Member of Parliament is the defendant. So in effect the Act widens the potential for Members of Parliament to sue their critics, not an obviously desirable policy result[43]. But more important, for present purposes, was

39 [1972] 1 QB 522.

40 Eg, *Broadway Approvals Ltd v Odhams Press Ltd* [1965] 1 WLR 805.

41 *Bonnington Castings Ltd v Wardlaw* [1956] AC 613.

42 For more detail see Harris, 'Sharing the Privilege: Parliamentarians, Defamation and Bills of Rights' (1996) 8 *Auckland University Law Review* 45 at 57–66.

43 Williams, '"Only Flattery is Safe": Political Speech and the Defamation Act 1996' (1997) 60 *MLR* 388.

the effect of s 13 on the nature of the privilege. First, it transformed the privilege from being a privilege of the House into a personal privilege. Second, it modified the basis of the privilege. The privilege now seemed to be based on the individual Member's fear of adverse legal consequences: where the Member had no such fear, or calculated that it was worth taking the risk of adverse consequences, the privilege vanished.

So the current position in relation to Parliamentary speech in England represents a choice on the part of Parliament. By enacting s 13 the basis for Parliamentary privilege has been fixed as the fear of adverse consequences in litigation, and the jurisdictional basis expounded in *Prebble's case* has been rejected. At the same time, however, because the theoretical consequences of s 13 are not made explicit in the statute, the courts have continued to refer to the jurisdictional rationale. For instance, the House of Lords referred to its importance in *Hamilton v Al Fayed*[44]. Very recently the European Court of Human Rights recognised that one function of Parliamentary privilege was the regulation of relations between the legislature and the courts[45]; it regarded this function as one reason why Parliamentary privilege pursued a legitimate aim and was therefore consistent with Article 6 of the Convention on Human Rights. Given that the privilege only applies where a Member of Parliament chooses not to waive it, the jurisdictional aspect of Parliamentary privilege seems to have been overstated in cases following the 1996 Act. It is perhaps better described as an occasional fortuitous side-effect rather than a rationale. Certainly in defamation cases its availability will turn on the relevant Member's calculation of potential adverse consequences, not on the proper extent of Parliament's own jurisdiction.

2. THE EXECUTIVE

A very limited absolute privilege has been conferred on statements by one high-ranking official of State to another, and also on reports by military officers. The origin of the first category is relatively late, being the Court of Appeal's decision in *Chatterton v Secretary of State for India in Council*[46]. There it was held that there was an absolute privilege in respect of a communication by the Secretary of State for India to the Under-Secretary of State for India, made in order to enable the Under-Secretary to answer a Parliamentary question.

Lord Esher MR approached the matter as one of policy, asserting that 'it would be injurious to the public interest [to allow an action] because it

[44] [2000] 2 All ER 224 at 234.
[45] *A v United Kingdom* [2002] All ER (D) 264 (Dec) at para 76.
[46] [1895] 2 QB 189.

would tend to take from an officer of state his freedom of action in a matter concerning the public weal'[47]. Nor was it sufficient to grant a defence of qualified privilege to the official, because he would then have to deny malice to escape liability.

> That he should be placed in such a position, and that his conduct should be so questioned before a jury, would clearly be against the public interest, and prejudicial to the independence necessary for the performance of his functions as an official of state.[48]

As to the precise limits of the privilege, Lord Esher MR was content to adopt the formulation from Fraser's textbook, which stated that absolute privilege applied to 'anything in the nature of an act of state, for example, to every communication relating to state matters made by one minister to another, or to the Crown.'[49] The reference to 'act of state' was puzzling. 'Act of state' in its technical sense referred to an act which had been committed outside the United Kingdom against an alien and had been subsequently ratified by the British government; the 'act of state' defence barred an action by the alien[50]. Clearly this could not have been the sense of the phrase understood by Lord Esher MR. Unfortunately, however, neither Fraser nor Lord Esher MR gave neither a special definition of the phrase, nor illustrative examples of what he meant, an omission that caused difficulties for later courts seeking to identify what activities were covered by the decision in *Chatterton*[51].

The reasoning adopted by the other two judges was more complex. Kay LJ referred to two cases on the admissibility of official communications in evidence[52]. Although he recognised that these cases had been decided under the evidence rules, Kay LJ concluded that they both 'involve[d] the conclusion'[53] that absolute privilege applied. He said that he could have dismissed the case on the basis that the evidence was not admissible, but instead preferred to apply the absolute privilege. AL Smith LJ also drew on the law of evidence, holding that, although absolute privilege applied, the 'conclusive'[54] ground for the decision was inadmissibility of evidence. Neither judge sounded as confident as the Master of the Rolls had done.

The decision in *Chatterton's case*[55] was based, to the extent that it was not a complete innovation, on the view expressed in Fraser's textbook. That

47 *Ibid* at 191.

48 *Ibid*.

49 Fraser, *Principles and Practice of the Law of Libel and Slander*, 1st edn (London, 1893) at 95.

50 Grubb (ed), *The Law of Tort* (London, 2002) at 2.19, referring to leading 19th century authorities.

51 See, for example, *Gibbons v Duffell* (1932) 47 CLR 520 at 530 (per Starke J).

52 *Anderson v Hamilton* 2 B & B 156, n; *Home v Bentinck* 2 B & B 130.

53 [1895] 2 QB 189 at 193.

54 *Ibid* at 195.

55 *Ibid*.

view was, in turn, derived from the treatment of a military report in *Dawkins v Lord Paulet*[56]. There the Court of Queen's Bench had held, by a majority, that no action lay in respect of a report written by the claimant's senior officer in the Coldstream Guards to the adjutant-general. The report had been written because the claimant had made a formal complaint about an order that the defendant had given; it was the defendant's duty to forward the complaint to the adjutant-general with his own written report. As with the reasoning in *Chatterton's case* the Court of Queen's Bench did not rely solely on absolute privilege.

Mellor J advanced three lines of reasoning. The first was that it was a complete defence that the defendant was performing his duty; proof of malice would be irrelevant, since 'the law regards the doing of the duty and not the motives under which it is done'[57]. Whilst perfectly tenable as a matter of logic this argument was flatly contradicted by the law of qualified privilege: there a defendant uttering defamatory words required by duty lost his defence if the claimant proved malice[58]. In defamation, the law did regard the motives with which the duty was performed[59].

The second line of reasoning advanced by Mellor J was that absolute privilege should apply by analogy with that conferred upon jurors. Essentially the point was that the efficiency of upholding discipline in the army would be impaired by actions, particularly since officers might be inhibited from acting by the threat of a vexatious suit[60].

The third line of reasoning was that military matters ought to be determined by a military tribunal alone, because a common law jury was ill-equipped to assess military matters[61]. Lush J, the second member of the majority, concurred only in this final line of reasoning[62]. *Dawkins v Lord Paulet*[63] was not, therefore, authority for any claim about absolute privilege in defamation, and its dicta on the respective roles of malice and duty were wrong. What it was actually authority for was the proposition that defamatory military reports should be dealt with in military tribunals. It was, in short, a decision on jurisdiction, not defamation. But it had been creatively re-interpreted by a textbook writer whose work was then relied on by the Court of Appeal. The result was a new category of absolute privilege.

56 (1869) LR 5 QB 94.
57 *Ibid* at 114.
58 See ch 7.
59 For an analysis of the position in the law of tort as a whole see Ames, 'How far an Act may be a Tort because of the Wrongful Motive of the Actor' (1904–5) 18 *Harvard Law Review* 411.
60 (1869) LR 5 QB 94 at 114–15.
61 *Ibid* at 117.
62 *Ibid* at 120.
63 *Ibid*.

The key question for the courts after the decisions in *Chatterton v Secretary of State for India in Council*[64] and *Dawkins v Lord Paulet*[65] was the extent to which a general category of absolute privilege could be deduced from them. The answer tended to be that no general principle existed. In a New York predating *Chatterton's case*, for instance, the Court of Appeals agreed that absolute privilege applied to military reports to superiors and acts of state, but refused to extend it to a report by the claimant's immediate superior to the board of the institution that employed her. The Court admitted that 'it would perhaps be difficult to make a satisfactory distinction, founded upon principle'[66].

A similarly cautious approach could be seen in the Australian case of *Gibbons v Duffell*[67]. There the claimant was a police officer who had requested a transfer. The defendant was an inspector of police whose duty it was to forward the request accompanied by his own report. The accompanying report was the defamatory publication complained of. The defendant claimed absolute privilege on the basis of *Chatterton* and *Dawkins*.

The claim under *Chatterton* was rejected both by the Supreme Court of New South Wales and the High Court of Australia. The State Court held that *Chatterton's case* did not apply to communications between people of all ranks of Government: the privilege was granted 'because of the high dignity and responsibility of the officer making the request or for whose information the report is prepared'[68]. The High Court of Australia agreed, Starke J commenting that although 'act of State'—the phrase used by Fraser and adopted in *Chatterton's case*—was obscure, it did not include a report by a police inspector[69].

The claim based on *Dawkins' case* succeeded before the State court but was rejected by the High Court. The State court was impressed by the close factual analogy between *Dawkins' case* and the case before it. In particular it held that the importance of preserving discipline in the army could be equated with the importance of preserving discipline in the police[70]. Furthermore, like the army, the police preserved the state and was organised on military lines, at least in New South Wales.

The High Court's rejection of absolute privilege based on *Dawkins' case* was emphatic and multi-faceted. First the judges challenged the authority of *Dawkins*, citing Pollock's view that it was 'not received as conclusive'[71]

64 [1895] 2 QB 189.
65 (1869) LR 5 QB 94.
66 *Hemmens v Nelson* 34 NE 342 at 344 (Court of Appeals of New York, 1893).
67 (1931) 32 SR (NSW) 31; (1932) 47 CLR 520.
68 (1931) 32 SR (NSW) 31 at 36.
69 (1932) 47 CLR 520 at 530–31.
70 (1931) 32 SR (NSW) 31 at 39.
71 (1932) 47 CLR 520 at 531 (per Starke J).

and Spencer Bower's that it was 'undoubtedly wrong'[72]. Second, they distinguished *Dawkins' case* on a variety of grounds: for instance, the organisation and functions of the police were different to the army[73]. Most importantly, for our purposes, the High Court attacked the use of reasoning by analogy in absolute privilege cases altogether. In its view analogy was not enough, there had to be 'clear grounds of public policy . . . [showing that] complete freedom from suit appear[ed] indispensable to the effective performance of judicial, legislative or official functions'[74].

The approach to recognising novel applications of absolute privilege set out by the High Court in *Gibbons' case* has been influential both in Australia and in England. In Australia two members of the High Court in *Jackson v Magrath*[75] followed the very cautious approach to *Chatterton's case* that required the official making the defamatory communication to be at a 'high level'[76]. Subsequently the High Court in *Mann v O'Neill*[77] confirmed that 'necessity' was required for new situations of absolute privilege—analogy was not good enough.

In England the decision in *Gibbons v Duffell*[78] was crucial in persuading the Court of Appeal that a defamatory minute sent by the Deputy Commissioner of the Metropolitan Police to the Commissioner was not a clear case of absolute privilege[79]. Salmon LJ observed that 'The categories of absolute privilege are not closed'[80], but gave no indication of how a defendant could benefit from their being open.

Today the pressures to limit the defence of absolute privilege have been increased further by the European Convention on Human Rights which, by Article 6, grants the right to a fair trial. The exposition of Article 6 by the European Court of Human Rights has established that the right to a fair trial embraces a right of access to court[81]. Any immunity denying access must satisfy the tests of legitimate aim and proportionality[82]. Whilst the fact that an immunity is absolute does not automatically bring it into conflict with the Convention, the European Court of Human Rights

[72] *Ibid* at 534 (per Evatt J).

[73] *Ibid* at 527 (per Gavan Duffy CJ, Rich and Dixon JJ). McTiernan J preferred to emphasise that the libel in *Dawkins' case* reflected solely on the claimant's abilities as a soldier; the libel in *Gibbons' case* was more general (see 535–37).

[74] *Ibid* at 528.

[75] (1947) 75 CLR 293.

[76] *Ibid* at 306 (per Latham CJ); see Rich J at 309 to similar effect.

[77] (1997) 191 CLR 204.

[78] (1932) 47 CLR 520.

[79] *Merricks v Nott-Bower* [1965] 1 QB 57.

[80] *Ibid* at 73. Salmon LJ seemed to be alluding to the famous statement by Lord Macmillan in *Donoghue v Stevenson* [1932] AC 562 that 'The categories of negligence are never closed' (at 619). On the composition of the speech see Rodger, 'Lord Macmillan's Speech in *Donoghue v Stevenson*' (1992) 108 *LQR* 236, particularly at 242.

[81] Eg, *Osman v United Kingdom*, 28 October 1998, at para 147.

[82] *A v United Kingdom* [2002] All ER (D) 264 (Dec), at para 74.

gives particularly close scrutiny to absolute immunities. Therefore it is likely that in future English courts wary of the Convention's requirements will be even less likely to develop new categories of absolute privilege than they were under the common law.

3. JUDICIAL PROCEEDINGS

The current position relating to absolute privilege for participants in judicial proceedings is as stated by Lord Mansfield CJ in *R v Skinner*[83]: 'neither party, witness, counsel, jury or judge, can be put to answer, civilly or criminally, for words spoken in office'[84]. Behind this succinct formulation, however, lies a complex pattern of historical development in which the scope and justifications for the privilege shifted and different jurisdictions pursued their own variations on the basic rule.

(a) Judicial immunity

Judicial immunity has been recognised by the common law since the early modern period. In *Bushell's Case*[85], for instance, Hale CJ asserted that no action for false imprisonment could lie against a judge whose judgment and sentence had been reversed by a higher court. As Hale CJ pointed out, reversing the earlier judgment did not make the earlier proceedings void, 'and the matter was done in a course of justice'[86]. *Hamond v Howell*[87], which seemed to be related to *Bushell's case*[88]—although how is not obvious from the report, fleshed out the judicial immunity rule. The defendant was the Recorder of London; he had imprisoned members of a jury who rejected his direction on the law in a trial for riot. The immediate response of the Court of King's Bench was that no action would lie[89]. After further argument the Court was unanimously of this opinion and provided reasons[90]. The Recorder clearly had jurisdiction of the riot prosecution, and also had power to punish any misdemeanour committed by the jury. He had mistakenly identified the jury's action as a misdemeanour—it was merely an error of judgment on his part, for which no action lay. Furthermore, the King's Bench thought that the Recorder's error was reasonable, 'because it might be supposed very inconvenient for the jury

[83] (1772) Lofft 55.
[84] *Ibid* at 56.
[85] (1674) 1 Mod 119.
[86] *Ibid.*
[87] (1674) 1 Mod 184; (1677) 2 Mod 218.
[88] *Sirros v Moore* [1975] QB 118 at 134 (per Lord Denning MR).
[89] (1674) 1 Mod 184.
[90] (1677) 2 Mod 218.

to have such liberty to give what verdicts they please'[91]. The reasoning was cautious and closely linked to the facts[92].

The same emphasis on actions being within jurisdiction and the absence of liability for errors of judgment can be found subsequently[93]. However, this cautious approach was cast aside in *Miller v Seare*[94]. There the question was whether commissioners of bankrupt could claim judicial immunity. The Court of King's Bench held that the commissioners were not judges, but the dicta of de Grey CJ (with whose judgment Blackstone and Nares JJ concurred) were to be remarkably influential. De Grey CJ asserted that it was uncontroversial that judges of 'the King's Superior Courts of Justice'[95] and courts of general jurisdiction were not liable to answer personally for their 'errors in judgment'. In courts of special and limited jurisdiction the position was different: 'While acting within the line of their authority, they are protected as to errors in judgment; otherwise they are not protected'[96]. To underline the distinction de Grey CJ concluded that 'The protection, in regard to the Superior Courts, is absolute and universal; with respect to the Inferior, it is only while they act within their jurisdiction'[97].

Whilst de Grey CJ presented his analysis as uncontroversial it was in fact a radical innovation. No authority was cited in the judgment; the only authority cited in argument was *Hamond v Howel* where, as has been shown above[98], the court emphasised that the Recorder had made an error of judgment on a matter within his jurisdiction. Furthermore, there seemed to be no compelling reason why the rule for courts of limited jurisdiction should be different. Nevertheless, the distinction remains a landmark in the present law of judicial immunity: an attempt by the Court of Appeal to eliminate it[99] was rejected by the House of Lords[100] because the distinction was 'so deeply rooted'[101].

Miller v Seare[102] had established the basic structure of judicial immunity, but many of the details remained to be worked out. In particular the relationship between fault and the immunity was problematic. The first form in which the difficulty emerged related to the jurisdiction test which had to be satisfied by judges of inferior courts. In *Calder v Halket*[103], an appeal

[91] *Ibid* at 220.
[92] Cf the interpretation in *Sirros v Moore* [1975] QB 118 at 134–35 (per Lord Denning MR).
[93] Eg, *Groenvelt v Burwell* (1700) 1 Salk 396.
[94] (1777) 2 Wm Bl 1141.
[95] *Ibid* at 1145.
[96] *Ibid*.
[97] *Ibid*.
[98] p 204.
[99] *Sirros v Moore* [1975] QB 118.
[100] *In re McC (a minor)* [1985] AC 528.
[101] *Ibid* at 550.
[102] (1777) 2 Wm Bl 1141.
[103] (1840) 3 Moore PC 28.

to the Privy Council from the Supreme Court of Bengal, the defendant was acting as judge and magistrate of a local criminal court in Bengal. He received a report that the claimant had been involved in a riot and ordered that he be arrested. In fact the claimant did not fall under the court's jurisdiction because he was not a native. Parke B, giving the Council's advice, held that the statute conferring protection on judges of Native Courts gave the same protection that the common law offered to judges of limited jurisdiction. This protection did not extend to all acts done without jurisdiction in good faith[104]. However, it was 'well settled'[105] that a judge of limited jurisdiction was not to be held liable for acting outside his jurisdiction 'unless he had the knowledge or means of knowledge of which he ought to have availed himself, of that which constitutes the defect of jurisdiction'[106]. On the facts the defendant did not know, and had no means of knowing, that the claimant was European; so the immunity applied. The same test was applied by the Court of Queen's Bench in *Houlden v Smith*[107] to a situation where a County Court judge had ordered the imprisonment for contempt of a person who lived outside the Court's jurisdiction. Patteson J pointed out that the defendant could not have been ignorant of where the claimant lived and carried on business; he could not therefore claim a common law immunity.

The judicial concern to link the question of jurisdiction with fault is perhaps most strikingly illustrated by the judgments in *Polley v Fordham (No 2)*[108]. There a magistrate had convicted and fined the claimant for the offence of failing to have his child vaccinated within six months of birth. The High Court quashed the conviction because the prosecution had not been brought within the statutory time limit, as was apparent on the face of the documents before the magistrate. In deciding whether the magistrate could claim immunity the Court of Appeal had to apply Justices Protection Act 1848 s 2 which provided that an action lay against a justice of the peace for any act 'in which he has exceeded his jurisdiction'. The section made clear that a claimant did not need to allege malice or lack of probable cause. The Court of Appeal held that s 2 applied to the facts before them. However, both judges made clear that their decision was based on the defect of jurisdiction being evident on the documents. Kennedy J suggested that s 2 might well not apply where a magistrate had not been informed of all the facts and came to an erroneous conclusion about his jurisdiction[109]. Even when the statutory provision

104 *Ibid* at 74.
105 *Ibid* at 77.
106 *Ibid*.
107 (1850) 14 QB 841.
108 (1904) 68 JP 504.
109 *Ibid* at 508.

seemed to make good faith and fault irrelevant the court sought to reintroduce them into the equation.

The determination to link fault and lack of jurisdiction could also be seen in the United States. In *Grove v Van Duyn*[110], for instance, the court considered the scope of immunity of a justice of the peace. It reasoned that a test based solely on jurisdiction was 'as unreasonable as it is impolitic'[111] since it made liability turn on finely balanced legal questions. A better, preferable test, was to accord immunity to all proceedings '*colorably*'[112] under the justice's jurisdiction. It followed that a justice would only be liable where he proceeded with a case in which 'no facts are present, or only such facts as have neither legal value nor color of legal value in the affair'[113]. In *Broom v Douglass*[114] the Supreme Court of Alabama amplified the test set out in *Grove's case*, emphasising that the immunity extended to situations where a magistrate to whom a colorable case was presented made a bona fide determination that he had jurisdiction[115].

A second, related manifestation of the relationship between the immunity and fault is the one that has come to light the most recently. In *Sirros v Moore*[116] the Court of Appeal considered in what circumstances the judge of a superior court could be said to be acting judicially so as to come within the immunity. According to Lord Denning MR the test was, essentially, good faith[117]. Buckley LJ added a requirement of acting 'reasonably'[118]. Although certain aspects of *Sirros v Moore* were overruled by the House of Lords in *In re McC (a minor)*[119], the observations about the superior courts remain good law[120].

The statements in *Sirros v Moore*[121] and the cases on the role of fault in relation to jurisdiction did not threaten the basic structure of judicial immunity. However, an emphasis on fault could be taken further and amount to a direct challenge to the existence of judicial immunity. A series of defamation cases in the mid-nineteenth century provided the context for this challenge.

The first case was *Kendillon v Maltby*[122], where a police officer sought to make a magistrate liable for a defamatory remark made in the course of a

110 43 Am Rep 412 (Court of Errors and Appeals of New Jersey, 1882).
111 *Ibid* at *3.
112 *Ibid.*
113 *Ibid.*
114 57 So 860 (Supreme Court of Alabama, 1912).
115 *Ibid* at 862.
116 [1975] QB 118.
117 *Ibid* at 135.
118 *Ibid* at 140.
119 [1985] AC 528.
120 Grubb (ed), *The Law of Tort* (London, 2002) at 2.62.
121 [1975] QB 118.
122 (1842) Car & M 402.

case about the officer's credibility. Lord Denman CJ expounded the law as follows:

> I have no doubt on my mind, that a magistrate, be he the highest judge in the land, is answerable in damages for slanderous language, either not relevant to the cause before him or uttered after the cause is at an end; but of words uttered in the course of his duty no magistrate is answerable, either civilly or criminally, unless express malice and the absence of reasonable or probable cause be established.[123]

As there was no evidence of malice on the facts, a nonsuit was directed. In the formulation of the law judicial immunity had been replaced by a stringent fault requirement.

Lord Cockburn CJ took the challenge forward in *Thomas v Churton*[124], where the defendant was a coroner whose address to a jury had made defamatory observations about the claimant. The Court of Queen's Bench found for the defendant. Although no reasoned judgment was given, remarks made by Cockburn CJ in the course of argument were very revealing. In particular he asserted: 'I am reluctant to decide, and will not do so until the question comes before me, that if a Judge abuses his judicial office, by using slanderous words maliciously and without reasonable and probable cause, he is not liable to an action'[125].

This would not be the last time that Lord Cockburn CJ expressed scepticism and reservations about absolute privilege. In *Dawkins v Lord Paulet*[126] where a majority of the Court of Queen's Bench conferred absolute privilege on a military report[127] Cockburn CJ was the dissenter, expressing trenchant doubts about the fairness and effectiveness of absolute immunity[128]. Later, in *Seaman v Netherclift*[129] he refused to confer a wide immunity on a witness[130]. The source of his views may have been his own independent analysis, but he may well have found inspiration in Roman law. As has been shown, Cockburn CJ had an impressive knowledge of Civil law concepts[131], and it may well be no coincidence that in classical Roman law a judge was liable if he 'made the case his own'[132].

[123] (1842) Car & M at 409.
[124] (1862) 2 B & S 475.
[125] *Ibid* at 479.
[126] (1869) LR 5 QB 94.
[127] See above, p 201.
[128] (1869) LR 5 QB 94 at 109–10.
[129] (1876) 2 CPD 53.
[130] *Ibid* at 56–57.
[131] Ibbetson, '"The Law of Business in Rome": Foundations of the Anglo-American Tort of Negligence' (1999) 52 *Current Legal Problems* 74 at 106–7.
[132] See further Schrage, 'The Judge's Liability for Professional Mistakes' (1996) 17 *Journal of Legal History* 101.

The denial of judicial immunity in *Kendillon v Maltby*[133] and *Thomas v Churton*[134] provoked equally emphatic assertions that it existed. In *Fray v Blackburn*[135], decided less than a year after *Thomas v Churton*, the Court of Queen's Bench refused leave to amend a claim against a judge for wrongly awarding costs by adding an allegation of malice to the claim. Crompton J made it clear that the allegation of malice was irrelevant, and went on to assert the reason for judicial immunity:

> The public are deeply interested in this rule, which, indeed, exists for their benefit, and was established in order to secure the independence of the Judges, and prevent their being harassed by vexatious actions . . .[136]

In *Scott v Stansfield*[137] the relationship between malice and judicial immunity was finally made clear. The Court of Exchequer held that judicial immunity protected a county court judge against an action for slander for a remark made to the claimant, a party in a case being heard. Kelly CB held that malice, probable cause and relevance were of no significance when identifying the immunity. He went on to explain why:

> It is essential in all courts that the judges who are appointed to administer the law should be permitted to administer it under the protection of the law independently and freely, without favour and without fear. This provision of the law is not for the protection or benefit of a malicious or corrupt judge, but for the benefit of the public, whose interest it is that the judges should be at liberty to exercise their functions with independence and without fear of consequences. How could a judge so exercise his office if he were in daily and hourly fear of an action being brought against him . . .[138]

This reasoning revealed the complex and paradoxical relationship between the immunity and malice: whilst the aim of the immunity was to protect judges acting in good faith, that aim could only be achieved by a rule that did not discriminate between malice and bona fides. Otherwise judges who acted in good faith would be pestered by actions accusing them of malice.

The Court also gave a further reason for the immunity: if the rule was based on malice a jury would be placed in the position of reviewing a judge's motives. In the view of Kelly CB it was 'impossible to overestimate the inconvenience of such a result'[139]. This was a very different reason from the first. Its main concern seemed to be the undesirability of judges having to explain themselves and be accountable to juries; usually the power relationship was

133 (1842) Car & M 402.
134 (1862) 2 B & S 475.
135 (1863) 3 B & S 576.
136 *Ibid* at 577.
137 (1868) LR 3 Exch 220.
138 *Ibid* at 223.
139 *Ibid*.

the other way round. This reason also found favour in Scotland, where the Court of Session[140] emphasised that judges were responsible to the King, not to other judges or juries. Making judges liable for things done in their judicial capacity would 'expose them to be dealt with as servants not of [the King] but of the public'[141], and nobody wanted that.

So the challenge to the doctrine of judicial immunity had been answered. Not everyone was convinced. In *Seaman v Netherclift*[142], a case on witness immunity, Lord Coleridge CJ went out of his way to express his agreement in principle with those judges 'who were disposed to hold a judge liable for words spoken even in office, if spoken in abuse of office, with express malice and without reasonable cause'[143]. He intimated that the law could be changed by a higher court.

However, any potential for influence that *Thomas v Churton* might continue to exert was extinguished in *Anderson v Gorrie*[144]. Lord Esher MR dismissed Cockburn CJ's earlier doubts about judicial immunity: 'had the question come before that learned judge he must and would, after considering the previous authorities, have decided that the action would not lie'[145]. This scarcely did justice to Cockburn CJ's principled objections to absolute privilege, but it certainly ended the debate.

A similar immunity to that enjoyed by judges was accorded to jurors and grand jurors. In *Floyd and Barker's case*[146], for instance, the Star Chamber held that no action for conspiracy would lie against a grand juror where a grand inquest had indicted the claimant for murder and he had been acquitted. However, the case cannot be seen as establishing an absolute immunity: the Star Chamber also held that a jury acquitting against manifest proof could be charged with partiality.

More modern authorities from the United States show a close parallel between the English judicial immunity and juror's immunity. There is an emphasis on the judicial nature of the jury's role[147], and even occasional reference to English judicial immunity authorities[148]. Most importantly, the same justification for the immunity is advanced: jurors should be free to carry out their duties without fear of vexatious actions. The Supreme Court of Indiana[149], like the English Court of Exchequer in *Scott v Stansfield*[150], acknowledged that the immunity shielded corrupt jurors,

[140] *M'Creadie v Thomson* 1907 SC 1176.
[141] *Ibid* at 1182.
[142] (1876) 1 CPD 540.
[143] *Ibid* at 544.
[144] [1895] 1 QB 668.
[145] *Ibid* at 671.
[146] (1607) 12 Co Rep 23.
[147] Eg, *Dunham v Powers* 42 Vt 1 (Supreme Court of Vermont, 1869).
[148] Eg, *Turpen v Booth* 56 Cal 65 at 69 (Supreme Court of California, 1880) referring to *Scott v Stansfield*.
[149] *Hunter v Mathis* 40 Ind 356 (Supreme Court of Indiana, 1872).
[150] (1868) LR 3 Exch 220.

but, it asserted, 'the evils which would result from any other rule would be far more frequent and pernicious than the rules resulting from this'[151].

(b) Lawyers, witnesses and litigants

Whilst judicial immunity has been treated by the courts as a separate, self-defined topic, the privileges attaching to lawyers, witnesses and litigants have tended to be treated together. Although the precise justifications for absolute privilege differ in each case, the treatment here follows that of the courts, highlighting differences where appropriate.

Before the common law courts assumed jurisdiction over defamation, the ecclesiastical courts had acknowledged that liability in defamation was unlikely to attach to those giving evidence in court. However, the reason for this absence of liability was not a special defence of absolute privilege. Rather, it was based on the rule that liability required malice; the fact that a defendant spoke the words in evidence suggested that he was speaking 'for the discharge of his conscience'[152], not maliciously.

The early common law cases, on the other hand, often emphasised the policy reasons against liability. In *Cutler v Dixon*[153], for instance, it was held that no action lay where the defendant had applied to justices of the peace for the claimant to be bound to good behaviour and supported his application with documents. The reason given was that 'if actions should be permitted in such cases, those who have just cause for complaint, would not dare to complain for fear of infinite vexation'[154]. The same reason was given in *Ram v Lamley*[155].

However, the courts had not forgotten the justification based on malice. In *Weston v Dobniet*[156] it was invoked directly when holding that no action lay for an imputation against the credibility of a witness made in court by one of the parties. Malice also seemed to be at the root of the reasoning in *Moulton v Clapham*[157]. There the claimant had sworn an affidavit in proceedings to have the defendant bound to good conduct. The defendant, commenting on the affidavit at the hearing, said 'There is not a word true in the Affidavit, and I will prove it by forty witnesses'. The Court of King's Bench held that no action for slander lay 'because the answer to the said affidavit was a justification in law, and spoken solely in defence of himself, and this in a legal and judicial way to the extent that he wished to prove it

[151] 40 Ind 356 at *2 (Westlaw transcript).
[152] *Richardes* c. *Rutter* (1566) 101 Selden Society 26.
[153] (1585) 4 Co Rep 14b.
[154] *Ibid.*
[155] (1632) Hut 113.
[156] (1617) Cro Jac 432.
[157] (1639) 1 Rol Abr 87 M pl 4.

by forty witnesses'. As the New York Court for the Correction of Errors later observed, the reasoning in *Moulton v Clapham* was inconsistent with a general absolute privilege for parties to litigation[158].

The protection for advocates was subtly different. In *Brook v Montague*[159] the Court of King's Bench made an important distinction between allegations relevant to the case and those not. The advocate had a 'privilege'[160] to make defamatory allegations 'pertinent to the matter in question'. Allegations that were not pertinent should not be made. If they were made 'it shall be intended as spoken maliciously and without good cause; which is a good ground for an action'[161]. The Court's reasoning contained elements of 'privilege' or immunity and reasoning based on malice. It therefore represented an attempt to combine the two different explanations for the absence of liability for judicial participants.

Eighteenth-century developments suggested that for judicial speech in general the reason for the absence of liability was an immunity. In *Astley v Younge*[162] the defendant had made an affidavit stating that another affidavit, made in support of his opponent in litigation, was false. The Court of King's Bench did not feel it necessary to hear argument from the defendant 'as the matter was so plain'[163]. Lord Mansfield CJ, giving the judgment of the Court, held that no action lay. He emphasised 'the reason of the thing': 'There can be no SCANDAL if the allegation is material: and if it is not, the court before whom the indignity is committed by immaterial scandal, may order satisfaction, and expunge it out of the record . . .'[164]. This approach seemed implicitly to reject the malice-based explanation for the absence of liability. However, Lord Mansfield CJ went on to quote *Moulton v Clapham* in its entirety[165] and to refer to it with approval. As has been shown above[166], *Moulton's case* conferred only a limited protection from liability and seemed to be based on malice. The outcome on the facts of *Astley's case* may have been 'plain', but the principle was not.

By the end of the eighteenth century, however, the immunity explanation seemed to be prevailing. For instance, in *Johnson v Evans*[167] Lord Eldon CJ could assert that 'words used in the course of legal or judicial proceeding' could not give rise to an action for slander. Allowing an action 'would be a matter of public inconvenience, and operate to deter persons from preferring their complaints against offenders'[168].

158 *Hastings v Lusk* 22 Wend 410 at *6 (Westlaw transcript).
159 (1605) Cro Jac 90.
160 *Ibid*.
161 *Ibid*.
162 (1759) 2 Burr 807.
163 *Ibid* at 810.
164 *Ibid*.
165 *Ibid* at 811.
166 See pp 211–212.
167 (1799) 3 Esp 32.
168 *Ibid* at 33.

However, the immunity explanation was still not universally embraced. In *Hodgson v Scarlett*[169] the Court of King's Bench considered the matter in depth. It held unanimously that counsel would be liable for a malicious and irrelevant allegation. The conclusion was supported by authorities such as *Brook v Montague*[170] and *Moulton v Clapham*[171], but the Court made clear that it was also justified by principle. Lord Ellenborough CJ viewed statements by counsel in litigation as being subject to the same rules as character references about servants: in both 'the convenience of mankind'[172] required protection for fair communications made bona fide. In subsequent cases the importance of malice in imposing liability on counsel seems to have disappeared, but the requirement of relevance was retained[173]. The protection for counsel could therefore be seen as an immunity for words spoken in court, provided they were relevant. In 1821, the Court of King's Bench was still insisting that the privilege attached only where counsel spoke 'conscientiously according to his instructions'[174].

By 1875, at the latest, the immunity explanation was universally accepted. When, in a case decided that year, Kelly CB stated that the protection for a witness giving evidence in court did 'not proceed on the ground that the occasion rebuts the *prima facie* presumption that words disparaging to another are maliciously spoken'[175], it was by way of preamble, introducing the controversial issue for decision.

In the United States the path of development was very different. The emphasis was on the malice-based explanation of liability rather than the immunity explanation. In Vermont the Supreme Court was of opinion that there should be no protection for statements in judicial proceedings that the defendant did not believe to be true[176]. However, the Court felt constrained to follow the English authorities. The only rationale that it could see for granting absolute privilege to litigants was so as not to deter 'humble suitors' from bringing actions. Whilst there might be societies 'of such unequal relations of ranks and castes, as to require such immunity to protect the humble against the mighty'[177], Vermont society, the Court felt, was less stratified.

Other jurisdictions were not content to parrot English law. In Pennsylvania, for instance, the Supreme Court explained the matter in

[169] (1818) 1 B & Ald 232.
[170] (1605) Cro Jac 90.
[171] (1639) 1 Rol Abr 87 M pl 4.
[172] *Ibid* at 239–40.
[173] Eg, *Needham v Dowling* (1845) 15 LJ (CP) 9 (per Maule J); *Mackay v Ford* (1860) 5 H & N 792.
[174] *Lewis v Walter* (1821) 4 B & Ald 605 at 613 (per Bayley J).
[175] *Dawkins v Lord Rokeby* (1875) LR 7 HL 744 at 752.
[176] *Torrey v Field* 10 Vt 353 at *38 (Supreme Court of Vermont, 1838) (Westlaw transcript).
[177] *Ibid* at *40.

terms of first principles[178]. The law implied malice from speaking defamatory words; the burden then lay on the defendant to show that he was not malicious. One way to rebut this legal presumption of malice was to show that the words were spoken 'when examined as a witness in a court of justice; or when I was concerned in a prosecution, as attorney for the Commonwealth'[179]. The analysis mirrored precisely the approach taken by the English ecclesiastical courts over two hundred years earlier[180].

In New Hampshire[181], Kentucky[182] and Massachusetts[183] the emphasis on malice and good faith took a slightly different form. Courts in these jurisdictions recognised protection for statements made in judicial proceedings provided that the speaker had *invoked the legal process* in good faith 'for the assertion of a right or the redress of a wrong'[184].

The most direct and fundamental attack on the English approach came from the federal Supreme Court. In *White v Nicholls*[185] the Court held that there was no such thing as absolute privilege. Mr Justice Daniel sought to distinguish and interpret the English cases in a way that was not very convincing[186], but the real power of his reasoning lay in his analysis of principle:

> It is difficult to conceive how, in society where rights and duties are relative and mutual, there can be tolerated those who are privileged to do injury legibus soluti ; and still more difficult to imagine, how such a privilege could be instituted or tolerated upon the principles of social good.[187]

A judge of the Virginian Supreme Court of Appeals later said that he knew 'of no treatise or decision where this subject is treated with more clearness and precision than in the opinion . . . in *White v Nicholls*'[188].

Ultimately this challenge to absolute privilege fizzled out[189]. One reason for its failure was the weight of English authority on absolute privilege, which many American courts were not prepared to discard[190]. In States where there was no disposition to follow English cases, the motive-based approach to words spoken in judicial proceedings continued. In

[178] *M'Millan v Birch* 1 Binn 178 (Supreme Court of Pennsylvania, 1806).
[179] *Ibid* at 185.
[180] See above, p 211.
[181] *Hill v Miles* 9 NH 9 (Superior Court of Judicature of New Hampshire, 1837).
[182] *Forbes v Johnson* 11 B Mon 48 (Court of Appeals of Kentucky, 1850).
[183] *Kidder v Parkhurst* 85 Mass 393 (Supreme Judicial Court of Massachusetts, 1862).
[184] *Forbes v Johnson* 11 B Mon 48 at *2 (Court of Appeals of Kentucky, 1850).
[185] 44 US 266 (Supreme Court of the United States, 1845).
[186] See the criticisms in *Johnson v Brown* 13 W Va 71 at 21–28 (Supreme Court of Appeals of West Virginia, 1878).
[187] 44 US 266 at 287 (Supreme Court of the United States, 1845).
[188] *Dillard v Collins* 25 Gratt 343 at *6 (Supreme Court of Appeals of West Virginia, 1874).
[189] In 1952 one commentator described the authority challenging absolute privilege as 'most of it now old and forgotten' (Barnett, 'The Privilege of Defamation by Private Report of Public Official Proceedings' (1952) 31 *Oregon Law Review* 185 at 187).
[190] Eg, *Johnson v Brown* 13 W Va 71 (Supreme Court of Appeals of West Virginia, 1878).

Louisiana, for instance, the courts held that an allegation in judicial proceedings was privileged only if 'founded on probable cause'[191]; the doctrine of absolute privilege was 'simply intolerable'[192].

A second reason for the failure seems to have been that the courts recognised that absolute privilege was not designed to allow particular individuals to commit torts without responsibility. On the contrary, it was designed to ensure that those with a well-founded complaint were not deterred from bringing it 'for fear of being pursued with 'infinite vexation''[193]. Although it was ultimately unsuccessful, the challenge to absolute privilege had two consequences that permanently affected American law. The first was that the courts would refuse to recognise any new categories of absolute privilege[194]. The second was a firm rule that absolute privilege was only granted to pertinent allegations. Malice had gone, but it had left its mark.

Parallel developments in Scotland showed that the malice and immunity bases could happily co-exist in the same system. In his treatise published in 1826, Borthwick[195] had included only statements by judges and witnesses in his category of 'cases where the capacity alone in which the defender has acted may amount to a complete justification'[196]. Statements by counsel and litigants could give rise to liability if the pursuer (claimant) proved malice. Borthwick described the rule relating to counsel as 'one which reason and propriety would seem to prescribe in every country'[197]; he was pleased to see that the rule applied in England[198].

Later cases relating to the liability of litigants confirmed the rule set out by Borthwick and emphasised the important role of malice[199]. In particular the courts developed stringent pleading rules, which required pursuers to set out in detail precisely how they proposed to establish malice against the defender[200]: a mere allegation of malice was not enough. In relation to the liability of advocates, however, the Scots courts changed their approach and recognised absolute immunity. The immediate catalyst for the change was the English decision in *Munster v Lamb*[201], in which

191 *Lescale v Joseph Schwartz Co* 40 So 708, 43 So 385 (Supreme Court of Louisiana, 1905–7); *Dunn v Southern Ins Co* 40 So 786 (Supreme Court of Louisiana, 1906).

192 *Lescale v Joseph Schwartz Co* 40 So 708 at 711 (Supreme Court of Louisiana, 1905).

193 *Bartlett v Christhilf* 14 A 518 at 520 (Court of Appeals of Maryland, 1888).

194 Eg, *Maurice v Worden* 54 Md 233 at 253–254 (Court of Appeals of Maryland, 1880); *Hemmens v Nelson* 34 NE 342 at 344 (Court of Appeals of New York, 1893).

195 *A Treatise on the Law of Libel and Slander* (Edinburgh, 1826).

196 *Ibid* at 198.

197 *Ibid* at 214.

198 *Ibid*, citing *Hodgson v Scarlett* (1818) 1 B & Ald 232 (discussed above, at p 213).

199 Eg, *Mackellar v The Duke of Sutherland* (1862) 24 D 1124.

200 *Scott v Turnbull* (1884) 11 R 1131 at 1134 (per Lord President Inglis), and 1135 (per Lord Shand); *Gordon v British and Foreign Metaline Company* (1886) 14 R 75 at 84 (per Lord Justice-Clerk); *M v H* [1908] SC 1130.

201 (1883) 11 QBD 588.

the Court of Appeal had confirmed that absolute privilege attached to words spoken by a solicitor when examining a witness in court. The Court of Session in *Williamson v Umphray*[202] held that *Munster's case* was good law in Scotland so far as advocates were concerned. Advocates, like judges and witnesses, it reasoned, deserved absolute protection because it was 'essential to the ends of justice that persons in such positions should enjoy freedom of speech without fear of consequences, in discharging their public duties in the course of a judicial inquiry'[203]. However, the Court made it clear that *Munster's case* did not affect the position of litigants: they were not performing a public function, they were just advancing their private interests[204].

The change effected by the Court of Session was obviously based on policy, not analysis. A different policy view was taken in England. Even the specific reasoning used—that advocates' immunity was based on performing a public function—was not watertight. In Vermont, for instance, the Supreme Court had held that advocates should not receive the same level of protection as jurors, because jurors 'acted in obedience to the requirement of law and on oath'[205] whilst advocates acted 'from motives of interest and pecuniary gain'. Subsequently the absolute privilege for Scots advocates was confirmed[206], although there was some hesitancy about applying it where advocates defamed each other[207]; later commentators remained unconvinced that the correct policy choice had been made[208].

(c) Assessment

The fundamental basis on which absolute privilege had established itself in English law was that it was the only reliable way to protect participants in litigation from vexatious actions. The courts emphasised that they were not trying to protect those who had spoken maliciously. As one judge pointed out, to the extent that the label 'absolute privilege' suggested a right to be malicious it was 'misleading'[209]. The true basis of the doctrine was that 'in the public interest it is not desirable to inquire whether the words or acts of certain persons are malicious or not'[210]. It might seem to be in the public interest to expose malice or improper motives in participants in litigation. However, as another judge pointed out, one could not

202 (1890) 17 R 905.
203 *Ibid* at 911.
204 *Ibid*.
205 *Dunham v Powers* 42 Vt 1 (Supreme Court of Vermont, 1869).
206 *Rome v Watson* (1898) 25 R 733.
207 *Clark v Haddon* (1895) 3 Scots Law Times 85 (no 128).
208 Normand, 'The Law of Defamation in Scotland' [1938] 6 *CLJ* 327 at 335.
209 *Bottomley v Brougham* [1908] 1 KB 584.
210 *Ibid*.

view the issue in the abstract[211]. A jury might well make a mistaken attribution of malice; even if it correctly absolved the defendant he would still have suffered the vexation and expense of defending himself. The prospect of incorrect exposure and damages at worst, and vexation and expense at best, risked deterring participants from performing their roles in an independent and fearless way.

This justification for the immunity was not limited to actions for defamation. In order to be sure that participants were not being influenced by a fear of subsequent litigation other actions were also barred. So, for instance, actions alleging that witnesses had conspired to give false evidence at trials were held to be subject to the immunity[212]. The High Court of Australia was unanimous in emphasising that the rule against liability for words spoken as a witness applied irrespective of the form of action[213]. Similarly, an attempt to bring a civil action for perjury was dismissed as 'an obvious 'try on''[214]. The courts also extended the immunity to actions for negligence against witnesses preparing forensic reports for trial[215] and, for a time, to counsel conducting a case in court[216]. Recently the immunity has been applied to misfeasance in public office[217].

On the other hand, it has never been true that participants in litigation faced no consequences if they abused their position. Judicial immunity was expressed in sufficiently wide terms that the consequences of abuse of position by a judge were unlikely to be actions at law; petitions for the judge's removal were the more likely means of redress. Against other participants a range of criminal or civil remedies might be available. The criminal law offered contempt of court or perjury, the civil law had malicious prosecution, malicious institution of proceedings and others.

The courts were clearly aware of these alternative remedies. In *Henderson v Broomhead*[218], for example, the Court of Exchequer viewed an attempt to sue in defamation for evidence given on oath as raising the question 'whether, instead of prosecuting for perjury the party injured may bring an action for damages'[219]. American courts were equally aware of the criminal law possibilities. In *Bartlett v Christhilf*[220] the Court of Appeals of Maryland incorporated the availability of criminal redress into its justification for absolute privilege. It said:

211 *Dawkins v Lord Rokeby* (1875) LR 7 HL 744 at 756 (per Lord Penzance).
212 *Cabassi v Vila* (1940) 64 CLR 130; *Marrinan v Vibart* [1963] 1 QB 234, [1963] 1 QB 528.
213 *Cabassi v Vila* (1940) 64 CLR 130 at 141 (per Starke J), 144 (per McTiernan J) and 149 (per Williams J).
214 *Hargreaves v Bretherton* [1959] 1 QB 45 at 54.
215 *Evans v London Hospital Medical College* [1981] 1 WLR 184.
216 *Rondel v Worsley* [1969] 1 AC 191; *Rees v Sinclair* [1974] 1 NZLR 180. See now *Arthur JS Hall & Co v Simons* [2002] 1 AC 615.
217 *Silcott v Commissioner of Police for the Metropolis* (Court of Appeal, 24 May 1996).
218 (1859) 28 LJ (Ex) 360.
219 *Ibid* at 361.
220 14 A 518 (Court of Appeals of Maryland, 1888).

> It is better . . . where the statements are false, and knowingly false, to leave the party injured to the redress which the criminal courts may apply, than to open the door for the institution of civil suits which may be successfully used as an efficient means to obstruct the full and fearless pursuit and administration of justice.[221]

The courts were also aware of the many civil law alternatives. For instance, in *Roy v Prior*[222] the House of Lords pointed out that the immunity did not apply to actions for malicious prosecution or malicious arrest[223]. In *Lilley v Roney*[224] the Divisional Court held that no action lay for defamation where a letter had been sent complaining about the professional conduct of a solicitor; the claim should have been made for maliciously instituting proceedings[225]. An action for malicious prosecution was a particularly attractive alternative, since harm to reputation was sufficient damage to found the claim[226].

Judges might even suggest new alternative actions. In a note to *Hodgson v Scarlett*[227] Holroyd J[228] suggested that the form of redress for damage done b words spoken in litigation was to bring an action on the case alleging malice and lack of probable cause. He reiterated the suggestion in his judgment in *Flint v Pike*[229], but when a claimant acted upon it[230] the claim failed. The main objection to it seemed to be its novelty[231].

This wide range of alternative options led one academic commentator to observe that 'underlying this whole doctrine of absolute immunity is the conception of an alternative remedy'[232]. 'Undermining' might have been a better word to use. Absolute privilege in defamation was supposed to be justified by the need to protect participants in litigation against the risk of liability for what they said or did in court. But what was the point of protecting participants against liability in defamation and leaving open other means of redress? Who was going to feel free to act independently because of an immunity in defamation when they were at risk of liability for contempt, perjury, malicious prosecution, etc? The risks of an incorrect finding of guilt and of vexation and expense were all present to the same extent in these alternatives as they were in defamation. Indeed, in perjury

221 *Ibid* at 520.
222 [1971] AC 470.
223 *Ibid* at 477.
224 (1892) 61 LJQB 727.
225 *Ibid*.
226 *The Quartz Hill Consolidated Gold Mining Company v Eyre* (1883) 11 QBD 674.
227 (1818) 1 B & Ald 232.
228 Holroyd J was identified as the author of the anonymous note in *Gibbs v Pike* (1842) 9 M & W 351 at 358 (per Alderson B).
229 (1825) 4 B & C 473 at 481.
230 *Revis v Smith* (1856) 18 CB 126.
231 *Ibid* at 141 (per Crowder J) and 142 (per Willes J).
232 Veeder, 'Absolute Immunity in Defamation: Judicial Proceedings' (1909) 9 *Columbia Law Review* 463 at 470.

and contempt of court there was the added risk of imprisonment. But the immunity did not apply to those alternatives.

In fact the alternative options for redress cast an entirely different light on absolute privilege in defamation. They demonstrate that the true nature of the privilege is a method of classification or organisation: claims relating to words spoken in litigation are not to be dealt with by the general tort of defamation, but must be dealt with under the specialised, specific wrongs designed to deal with dishonesty in litigation. Today absolute privilege for defamatory words in litigation is no guarantee of immunity; it is nothing more than an organising device.

(d) The scope of the privilege

It now remains to examine the precise scope of absolute privilege in judicial proceedings. The privilege only applies to words spoken during proceedings; words spoken after the end of proceedings are not protected. This rule seems not to have caused great difficulty, the courts having taken a realistic pragmatic approach. For example, words spoken by a magistrate were held to be within proceedings when he first dismissed the case, then added a defamatory criticism of one of the parties[233]. On the other hand words fell outside the proceedings where a disappointed litigant wrote a letter of complaint about the judge after the judgment had been given[234].

The privilege was not confined to courts of justice. In *Dawkins v Lord Rokeby*[235], for instance, it was held that the privilege applied to the proceedings of a military tribunal inquiring into allegations that officers had made false statements about the claimant. The Exchequer Chamber asserted that the tribunal had 'all the qualities and incidents of a court of justice'[236]. In particular the tribunal was recognised by law and military witnesses could be compelled to attend[237]. Furthermore a witness who took advantage of his position to commit malicious defamation could be punished by Court-martial; this was similar to the availability of indictments for perjury or contempt in the ordinary courts[238].

In *Royal Aquarium and Summer and Winter Garden Society v Parkinson*[239] Lord Esher MR summarised the position as being that absolute privilege applied 'wherever there is an authorised inquiry which, though not before

233 *Law v Llewellyn* [1906] 1 KB 487. Cf *Barry v Bayer* 1937 SWA 73.
234 *Mann v O'Neill* (1997) 191 CLR 204.
235 (1873) LR 8 QB 255; (1875) LR 7 HL 744.
236 (1873) LR 8 QB 255 at 266.
237 *Ibid*.
238 *Ibid* at 267.
239 [1892] 1 QB 431.

a court of Justice, is before a tribunal which has similar attributes'[240]. On the facts of the case before him Lord Esher MR held that the test was not satisfied. The privilege was being claimed for words spoken at a local council meeting in deciding whether to grant a licence for music and dancing to the claimant. What distinguished the council meeting from a court was that the council was performing an administrative function not a judicial one. Fry LJ amplified the point, underlining that it was not enough that the council had a duty to act 'judicially' in the sense of fairly or impartially[241]. He also added a further ground of distinction: the risks of abuse of absolute privilege in court were reduced by the control of the judge and the 'fixed and dignified course of procedure'[242].

The history of the law on this point since the *Royal Aquarium* case can hardly be described as a development. The Court of Appeal has made clear that a tribunal 'recognised by law' need not be established by statute[243], but no test or principle has modified the *Royal Aquarium* position. The main reason for this lack of development has been the courts' reluctance to identify any crucial factor or factors showing that a tribunal is sufficiently similar to a court to qualify for absolute privilege.

Thus, it is clear that the courts are not influenced by how the proceedings are described. In *Dawkins v Lord Rokeby*[244] for instance, it was not relevant that the Queen's Regulations stated that military tribunals were 'not to be considered in any light as a judicial body'[245]. Various substantive factors have been considered only to be rejected. Thus, a 'fixed procedure' seemed to be important[246]; but there was no fixed procedure in the military tribunal held to qualify in *Dawkins' case*[247]. The power to hear evidence on oath might be important[248], but in *Barratt v Kearns*[249] and *Dawkins' case* tribunals not having that power were given absolute privilege. The fact that a tribunal could only make recommendations to a final decision maker might suggest that it was not like a court[250]; but that did not deter the courts in *Dawkins'* and *Barratt's cases*. As Lord Diplock pointed out in *Trapp v Mackie*[251], if the crucial test was the limited power to make recommendations, technically the Judicial Committee of the Privy

240 *Ibid* at 442.
241 *Ibid* at 447.
242 *Ibid.*
243 *Lincoln v Daniels* [1962] 1 QB 237 at 250 (per Sellers LJ), 253–55 (per Devlin LJ), 269 (per Danckwerts LJ).
244 (1873) LR 8 QB 255; (1875) LR 7 HL 744.
245 (1873) LR 8 QB 255 at 257.
246 *Royal Aquarium and Summer and Winter Garden Society v Parkinson* [1892] 1 QB 431 at 447.
247 (1873) LR 8 QB 255; (1875) LR 7 HL 744.
248 *Trapp v Mackie* [1979] 1 WLR 377 at 381.
249 [1905] 1 KB 504.
250 *Barratt v Kearns* [1905] 1 KB 504 at 507 (argument of Hugh Fraser, author of *Fraser on Libel*, acting as counsel for the claimant).
251 [1979] 1 WLR 377.

Council would not qualify as a court, since its decisions are in the form of advice to the sovereign[252]. Similarly, an attempt to identify public hearings as the key factor for a court failed[253].

A more promising candidate seemed to be the nature of the inquiry: a contest between two parties raising a specific question looked similar to a court case[254]. Conversely, where a tribunal had to decide whether to uphold a claim for unemployment benefit the fact that it was 'not a body deciding between parties'[255] was important. However, in *Copartnership Farms v Harvey-Smith*[256] a tribunal deciding whether to grant an exemption from military service was held to be sufficiently similar to a court to receive absolute privilege.

In the most recent authority the House of Lords has had to acknowledge that 'there is no single element the presence or absence of which will be conclusive in showing whether [the tribunal] has attributes sufficiently similar to those of a court of law to create absolute privilege'[257]. The ultimately fruitless search for one key element has also distracted attention from the wider question of whether the *Royal Aquarium* test was satisfactory. Certainly the application of the test provoked some disquiet—in *Peter Walker & Son Ltd v Hodgson*[258] the High Court gave a preliminary ruling that the *Royal Aquarium* test was not satisfied by a panel of licensing justices. Legislation was introduced into Parliament designed to reverse this ruling[259]. In the event no statutory change was made, and the Court of Appeal later confirmed the result from the *Peter Walker* case[260].

The Scots courts, however, favoured a wider approach. In *Williamson v Umphray*[261], for example, again case of defamation before a panel of licensing justices, the Court of Session held that absolute privilege applied. It was sufficient that the position of advocates addressing the justices was 'parallel'[262] to advocates in a court of law. In *Slack v Barr*[263] the Court of Session went further, suggesting that the *Royal Aquarium* case should be confined to its own facts. Lord Anderson argued that since the absolute privilege rule was based on 'public policy'[264] it should apply to anyone

252 *Ibid* at 383.
253 *Addis v Crocker* [1961] 1 QB 11.
254 *Trapp v Mackie* [1979] 1 WLR 377 at 380.
255 *Collins v Henry Whiteway and Company, Limited* [1927] 2 KB 378.
256 [1918] 2 KB 405.
257 *Trapp v Mackie* [1979] 1 WLR 377 at 388.
258 Not reported, but carefully summarised in Williams, 'Absolute Privilege for Licensing Justices' (1909) 25 *LQR* 188.
259 *Ibid* at 199.
260 *Attwood v Chapman* [1914] 3 KB 275.
261 (1890) 17 R 905.
262 *Ibid* at 910.
263 (1918) 82 JP 91.
264 *Ibid* at 92.

giving evidence 'before any public body, whether that body is purely judicial, or quasi-judicial or exists merely for licensing purposes'[265].

The current approach in New Zealand also demonstrates a refusal to get caught up in the technicalities of whether a given tribunal is sufficiently like a court. There the Defamation Act 1992 s 14 went where the English courts feared to tread and identified two key factors. Absolute privilege attached to 'any proceedings' where the tribunal had power to compel witnesses to attend or had the duty to act judicially.

New Zealand also provides some guidance on a related point where there is no direct English authority: do statements made in proceedings before a court enjoy absolute privilege even if the court lacked jurisdiction? The New Zealand Court of Appeal has held that absolute privilege still applied[266]. Its reasoning was based mainly on the construction of the phrase 'any proceedings' in s 14 Defamation Act 1992. However, the reasons given for adopting that construction were of direct relevance to English law. Richardson J urged that it could not be correct that the absolute privilege depended on the outcome of 'extensive argument . . . appeal, or . . . other subsequent challenges'[267], and that absolute privilege applied 'where a matter which is of a statutorily recognised character is brought before the Court'[268]. Blanchard J seemed to be prepared to go further, saying that absolute privilege would apply to proceedings that were 'plainly misconceived or fatally flawed'[269].

On the other hand, there was powerful American authority the other way. In *Johnson v Brown*[270] the Supreme Court of Appeals of West Virginia pointed out in a trenchant analysis that the public policy behind absolute privilege was to allow litigants access to courts established to hear their causes; the policy did not extend to allowing litigants access to courts not established to hear those causes. Arguably the West Virginian approach is more consistent with current English law because it gives no emphasis to the defendant's reasonable belief that jurisdiction exists. Even in relation to qualified privilege the English courts seem to have rejected the idea that the privilege could be based on the defendant's reasonable, genuine belief that the requirements for the privilege were met[271].

The privilege was not confined to words spoken during proceedings, it also extended earlier in time to statements closely related to the proceedings. How far back it went, and how close a relationship to the proceedings was needed, have proved controversial. It was clear that the privilege

265 *Ibid.*
266 *Rawlinson v Oliver* [1995] 3 NZLR 62.
267 *Ibid* at 68.
268 *Ibid.*
269 *Ibid* at 71.
270 13 W Va 71 (Supreme Court of Appeals of West Virginia, 1878).
271 *Hebditch v MacIlwaine* [1894] 2 QB 54. See further, ch 7.

covered pleadings and other communications initiating proceedings[272], but in *Watson v M'Ewan*[273] the House of Lords extended it to cover statements made by a witness to a solicitor before the trial in order to inform the solicitor what evidence was going to be given. The reason for this extension was that the same public policy protecting witnesses in respect of their evidence applied to 'that which is a step towards and is part of the administration of justice'[274]. If the policy did not apply, witnesses might justifiably refuse to reveal their evidence in advance, which would make it impossible for the parties to know who to call as witnesses[275].

The Court of Appeal later held that statements made in an interview between a potential witness and a solicitor to establish whether the potential witness should be called at the trial were also absolutely privileged[276]. On the other hand, where accusations of criminality were made against the Acting Czechoslovak Minister in Egypt to the Military Office of the President of Czechoslovakia, the Court of Appeal refused to apply *Watson's case*[277]. The Court emphasised that at the time there were no courts in Czechoslovakia that could have heard the case, and the complaints were in the nature of a dossier: in essence the allegations were too remote from any legal proceedings to be covered by absolute privilege.

In *Lincoln v Daniels*[278] the scope of *Watson's case* was put directly in issue. The defendant had made defamatory allegations about the claimant's professional conduct as a barrister. He had addressed these complaints to the Bar Council, having been informed by the Bar Council that it was the appropriate recipient. However the only way in which the allegations could be used in a judicial proceeding was if the Bar Council forwarded them to the claimant's Inn of Court and the Benchers of the Inn held an inquiry. The question for the courts was whether the complaint to the Law Society was sufficiently connected to an inquiry by the Inn of Court so as to attract absolute privilege.

At first instance Salmon J held that the connection was not close enough. In his view, 'the document must be addressed to a body which has judicial, or quasi-judicial functions, and the document must be a step in setting in motion judicial or quasi-judicial proceedings'[279]. This test seemed to state the rule too narrowly: the solicitor to whom the statements had been

272 Eg, *Cutler v Dixon* (1585) 4 Co Rep 14b (articles exhibited to justices of the peace); *Astley v Younge* (1759) 2 Burr 807 (statement in affidavit).
273 [1905] AC 480.
274 *Ibid* at 487.
275 *Ibid*.
276 *Beresford v White* (1914) 30 TLR 591.
277 *Szalatnay-Stacho v Fink* [1947] KB 1.
278 [1960] 1 WLR 852; [1962] 1 QB 237.
279 [1960] 1 WLR 852 at 854.

addressed in *Watson v M'Ewan*[280] had had no judicial or quasi-judicial functions.

The Court of Appeal's analysis was more elaborate, although it reached the same result. Sellers LJ held that *Watson's case* should be confined to its own facts[281]. The only basis on which the defendant could claim absolute privilege here, therefore, was that his complaint initiated proceedings. Devlin and Danckwerts LJJ took a less restrictive view of *Watson's case*. Danckwerts LJ regarded it as authority for extending absolute privilege to 'preliminaries *such as* the taking of a proof from a prospective witness'[282] (emphasis added). Devlin LJ found it 'difficult . . . to define'[283] what *Watson's case* covered and noted that a 'reasonably close' connection with judicial proceedings was essential[284]. He finally settled on the test that absolute privilege applied to matters outside the court proceedings only where it was 'strictly necessary . . . in order to protect those who are to participate in the proceedings from a flank attack'[285]. The same degree of necessity found on the facts of *Watson's case* did not exist in relation to a complaint to the Bar Council.

Until very recently the courts took a strict view of the necessity for absolute privilege and the need for a 'reasonably close' connection. In *McCarrick v Metropolitan Borough of St Helens*[286] for instance, the Court of Appeal refused to say that sending a letter to establish an issue in pending proceedings before the Lands Tribunal was absolutely privileged: the letter was not 'a prescribed or formal stage in the proceedings'. In *Waple v Surrey County Council*[287] the defendant had issued a contribution notice under the Children Act 1989 against the claimants. Essentially this notice demanded a financial contribution from the claimants to the cost of looking after their foster son, who had been taken into local authority care. The claimants disputed their liability to pay. Their solicitor wrote to the defendants' solicitor asking who had initiated the boy's removal into care; the defamatory allegation was contained in the defendants' solicitor's reply. At first instance[288] French J held that the statement was absolutely privileged because it was closely connected with the contribution notice proceedings. However, this conclusion was reversed on appeal. For the Court of Appeal the crucial point seemed to be that a contribution notice would not necessarily result in legal proceedings at all—the parties might be able to agree the amount and method of payment. Since all that had

280 [1905] AC 480.
281 [1962] 1 QB 237 at 251.
282 *Ibid* at 269.
283 *Ibid* at 257.
284 *Ibid* at 261.
285 *Ibid* at 263.
286 CA, 20 November 1992.
287 [1997] 2 All ER 836; [1998] 1 All ER 624.
288 [1997] 2 All ER 836.

happened was that the contribution notice had been issued there was no 'immediate link with possible proceedings'[289].

The House of Lords' recent decision in *Taylor v Director of the Serious Fraud Office*[290] represents a radical departure from the cautious approach. The defendants had spoken words defamatory of claimant to the Attorney-General of the Isle of Man and to a Law Society employee when they were investigating the claimant's conduct. The allegations came to the claimant's attention when a letter and 'file note' recording them were disclosed on the prosecution of a third party. Neither the letter nor the file note were read in court. The Court of Appeal focussed most of its attention on whether the defamation action breached an implied undertaking not to use disclosed documents for a purpose other than conducting the accused's defence. It held with reluctance that earlier authority[291] precluded recognition of such an implied undertaking[292]. However, it also held that the defendants enjoyed immunity from suit because what had been done was 'in the context of the investigation of suspected crime'[293]. Millett LJ regarded the immunity from suit as an imperfect solution because it would 'not extend to pre-existing documents, that is to say documents which are not brought into existence in the course of the criminal investigation'[294]. Sir Brian Neill appeared to share the view of Millett LJ: he said that the defendants had a defence because 'the documents *came into existence* and the discussion took place in the context of the investigation of suspected crime'(emphasis added)[295]. This limitation to pre-existing documents was difficult to understand. Liability in defamation turned on publication of defamatory material, not its creation. On an orthodox application of the defamation principles a publication of any defamatory document, whether its existence predated the investigation or not, should be protected.

The House of Lords unanimously dismissed the appeal by holding that there was an implied obligation not to use the documents for any purpose other than the accused's defence. They also dealt with the absolute privilege point. Lord Hoffmann, with whom Lords Goff, Hope and Hutton agreed, held that absolute privilege applied to statements by, to and between investigators[296]. In his view new applications of absolute privilege could only be justified by necessity[297], and an extension of absolute

289 [1998] 1 All ER 624 at 631.
290 [1999] 2 AC 177.
291 *Mahon v Rahn* [1998] QB 424.
292 [1999] 2 AC 177 at 197 (per Kennedy LJ), 198–199 (per Millett LJ) and 200 (per Sir Brian Neill).
293 *Ibid* at 200.
294 *Ibid* at 198.
295 *Ibid* at 200.
296 *Ibid* at 215.
297 *Ibid* at 213.

privilege beyond statements to witnesses passed that test[298]. The policy behind the immunity was to promote freedom of speech in the legal process; this policy would not be furthered if the availability of the privilege depended on who happened to be called as a witness at the trial[299]. Lord Hutton added that investigating a crime was 'a step towards the administration of justice'[300], like the preliminary examination of a witness.

Despite expressing agreement with Lord Hoffmann[301], Lord Hope may have taken a slightly different approach more limited to the facts of the case. He expressed the rule as follows: 'The requirement therefore is to extend to informants, investigators and prosecutors *whose statements are revealed by the operation of the disclosure rules* the benefit of absolute privilege'[302] (emphasis added). An intention to limit his reasoning to cases where the statements have come to light as a result of disclosure was also suggested by Lord Hope's statement that the 'central' issue in the case was whether absolute privilege should be adjusted 'in order to keep pace with the widening disclosure rules'[303]. If this limitation was intended its rationale is difficult to see. Why should the privilege depend on how the claimant found out about the defamatory statements? As Kennedy LJ had noted in the Court of Appeal, the privilege was not traditionally seen as arising out of the way in which the claimant obtained the information[304].

The impact of the decision in *Taylor's case* may be widespread. Certainly the cases according only qualified privilege to reports of crime to the police look shaky[305]. But *Taylor's case* may also prompt the courts to look again at what counts as a 'sufficiently close connection'[306] with judicial proceedings. If statements made when investigating whether or not a crime has been committed or not are absolutely privileged it is difficult to explain why statements defining an issue for a tribunal hearing[307] or explaining the basis for a legally enforceable claim[308] are not.

Finally, there is the question whether absolute privilege extends to irrelevant statements made by participants in litigation. For judges the answer is likely to be that absolute privilege applies. Their immunity covers actions within jurisdiction[309], and it is difficult to see how irrelevant words uttered in a matter within their jurisdiction would deprive them of jurisdiction. However, the possibility cannot be entirely ruled out: in *In re*

298 *Ibid* at 214.
299 *Ibid*.
300 *Ibid* at 221.
301 *Ibid* at 220.
302 *Ibid* at 219.
303 *Ibid* at 217.
304 *Ibid* at 188.
305 Eg, *Padmore v Lawrence* (1840) 11 Ad & E 380.
306 *Lincoln v Daniels* [1962] 1 QB 237 at 272 (per Devlin LJ).
307 Eg, *McCarrick v Metropolitan Borough of St Helens*, CA, 20 November 1992.
308 Eg, *Waple v Surrey County Council* [1997] 2 All ER 836; [1998] 1 All ER 624.
309 See above, pp 204–205.

McC Lord Bridge said that judges might lose jurisdiction of a matter initially within their jurisdiction if there was a 'gross and obvious irregularity of procedure'[310].

For other participants the common law position has evolved and diverged. In England *Brook v Montague*[311] had established that if counsel made irrelevant allegations malice would be presumed against him in the same way it was presumed where there were no special circumstances. *Brook's case* was followed in *Hodgson v Scarlett*[312]. In relation to the parties a requirement of relevance was assumed, but interpreted liberally in the defendant's favour[313].

The matter was examined more closely in *Seaman v Netherclift*[314]. There the defendant had been an expert witness in a case about a will; the trial judge had publicly criticised his evidence. In a later, unrelated, criminal prosecution for forgery the defendant—appearing again as an expert on handwriting—was asked by counsel whether he had read the public criticisms made of his evidence by the trial judge in the earlier case. The defendant replied that he had, but that he maintained his view that the will in the earlier case was a 'rank forgery'. He was sued by one of the witnesses to the will.

The Divisional Court held that the absolute privilege applied: the words were part of the witness' evidence, and he was entitled to respond to the implicit suggestion of incompetence. The Court was careful not to endorse the position that relevance did not matter. In relation to counsel it hinted that there would be liability for irrelevant words spoken maliciously[315], and it avoided pronouncing on relevance for witnesses by holding that, on the facts, the defendant's words were relevant[316].

The Court of Appeal affirmed the Divisional Court's decision and elaborated on the role of relevance for witnesses. Cockburn C J made it clear that the absolute privilege for witnesses did not turn on relevance. However, it did not extend to words that 'a witness states altogether out of the character and sphere of a witness, or what he may say dehors the matter in hand'[317]. Bramwell JA thought that the test was whether the words spoken had 'reference to the inquiry'[318]. This was wider than a strict test of relevance[319]. As an example of something not protected Bramwell JA suggested the following: 'Suppose while the witness is in the

[310] [1985] AC 528 at 546.
[311] (1605) Cro Jac 90.
[312] (1818) 1 B & Ald 232.
[313] *Doyle v O'Doherty* (1842) Car & M 418.
[314] (1876) 1 CPD 540; (1876) 2 CPD 53.
[315] (1876) 1 CPD 540 at 545.
[316] *Ibid* at 547.
[317] (1876) 2 CPD 53 at 56.
[318] *Ibid* at 59.
[319] *Ibid* at 60.

box, a man were to come in at the door, and the witness were to exclaim "that man picked my pocket"[320].

In *Munster v Lamb*[321] the scope of advocate's immunity was before the Court of Appeal. Brett MR asserted that absolute privilege applied even assuming that the words were not spoken to advance the client's interest, were spoken maliciously and 'were irrelevant to every issue of fact which was contested in the court where they were uttered'[322]. 'Nevertheless', he continued, 'inasmuch as the words were uttered with reference to, and in the course of, the judicial inquiry which was going on, no action will lie against the defendant'[323].

It was subsequently argued that *Munster v Lamb* established a rule that anything said by participants was protected[324], and that *Munster's case* prevailed over *Seaman v Netherclift*[325]. However, both arguments seem to be overstated. Brett MR in *Munster* explicitly retained the requirement that the words be spoken 'with reference to' the inquiry. In the light of this, the rejection of the argument that everything said by a participant was protected was clearly correct[326]. As for the conflict with *Seaman's case*, it was striking that Brett MR saw no conflict—and he was unlikely to have been unaware of *Seaman*, since he heard it in the Divisional Court. Other courts did not see a conflict either[327]. Nor is it surprising that Brett MR saw no conflict: the requirement that the words had 'reference to the inquiry' was identical to the test put forward by Bramwell JA in *Seaman's case*. In fact the true relationship between *Munster's case* and *Seaman's case* seems to be that Brett MR was seeking to put advocates' immunity on the same footing as that of witnesses.

Recently, in *Taylor v Director of the Serious Fraud Office*[328] the question of relevance resurfaced. Lord Hoffmann stated that the absolute privilege for statements made to and by those investigating crime was confined to matters that 'can fairly be said to be part of the process of investigating a crime with a view to a prosecution or a possible prosecution in respect of the matter being investigated'[329]. He borrowed this language from *Evans v London Hospital Medical College*[330], a case on witness immunity from actions in negligence. Lord Hoffmann went on to spell out the conse-

320 *Ibid.*

321 (1883) 11 QBD 588.

322 *Ibid* at 599.

323 *Ibid.*

324 *Peter Walker & Son Ltd v Hodgson*, unreported but summarised in Williams, 'Absolute Privilege for Licensing Justices' (1909) 25 *LQR* 188; see in particular the exchange between counsel for the defendant and Ridley J transcribed at 193–96.

325 *Hercules v Phease* [1994] 2 VR 411 at 446 (per Ormiston J).

326 *Peter Walker & Son Ltd v Hodgson*, see n 324 above.

327 Eg, *Hunckel v Voneiff* 14 A 500 at 502–4 (Court of Appeals of Maryland, 1888).

328 [1999] 2 AC 177.

329 *Ibid* at 215.

330 [1981] 1 WLR 184 at 192.

quences for defamation: 'statements which are wholly extraneous to the investigation—irrelevant and gratuitous libels'[331] were excluded. Lord Lloyd, who dissented on the absolute privilege point, argued that the requirement of being 'fairly part' of the investigation stuck out: advocate's immunity contained no such restriction. He wondered whether the majority were trying to create a new, 'intermediate level of privilege'[332].

Whilst Lord Lloyd was correct to say that the precise formulation advanced by Lord Hoffmann had not been applied to defamation before, the difference between Lord Hoffmann's test and the established one—'reference to the inquiry'—was superficial. The essential point is to see which statements were excluded from protection: Lord Hoffmann's reference to 'gratuitous' libels seemed to indicate the same kind of statements as those identified by the Court of Appeal in *Seaman v Netherclift*[333].

In other common law jurisdictions divergent positions have emerged. At one end of the spectrum the courts in New Zealand have held that no test of relevance applies. Their method of reasoning, however, was dubious. The Court of Appeal took the point to be settled as a matter of authority[334], but the authority on which it relied dealt with judicial privilege[335]. As shown above[336], because the judicial privilege is expressed in terms of acting within jurisdiction irrelevant words will usually be insignificant: such words are very unlikely to deprive the judge of jurisdiction over the matter.

The courts in the United States have occupied a range of positions towards the opposite end of the spectrum. The most strict instance of a requirement of relevance was in Tennessee, where the Supreme Court at one stage asserted that only relevant statements made about another party to the litigation attracted absolute privilege; relevant statements about a stranger enjoyed only qualified privilege[337]. The position was, however, seen elsewhere as inconsistent with the policy of absolute privilege[338] and subsequently abandoned[339].

Some courts stated the test simply in terms of protection for words that 'pertained to the case'[340]. Others elaborated on the test. One particularly

[331] [1999] 2 AC 177 at 215.

[332] *Ibid* at 204.

[333] (1876) 2 CPD 53. See in particular the example given by Bramwell JA at 60.

[334] *Teletax Consultants Ltd v Williams* [1989] 1 NZLR 698 at 701; *Rawlinson v Oliver* [1995] 3 NZLR 62 at 69.

[335] *Fitzherbert v Acheson* [1921] NZLR 265.

[336] At pp 226–227.

[337] *Ruohs v Backer's next friend* 6 Heisk 395 (Supreme Court of Tennessee, 1871).

[338] *Johnson v Brown* 13 W Va 71 (Supreme Court of Appeals of West Virginia, 1878).

[339] *Cooley v Galyon* 70 SW 607 (Supreme Court of Tennessee, 1902).

[340] Eg, *Gilbert v The People* 1 Denio 41 (Supreme Court of New York, 1845); *Barnes v McCrate* 32 Me 442 (Supreme Judicial Court of Maine, 1851); *Hart v Baxter* 10 NW 198 (Supreme Court of Michigan, 1881); *Hollis v Meux* 11 P 248 (Supreme Court of California, 1886).

significant addition was made by the Supreme Court of Wisconsin in *Calkins v Sumner*[341], when it held that absolute privilege for a witness extended to statements

> he may make which are responsive to questions put to him, and which are not objected to and ruled out by the court, or concerning the impertinency or impropriety of which he receives no advice from the court or tribunal.[342]

The Supreme Court's concern was that witnesses should not be put in the position of having to assess the legal relevance of a matter about which they were tempted to speak.

The general approach to pertinence was liberal. The Supreme Court of Pennsylvania, for instance, held that if the issue was contested, 'all doubt should be resolved in favor of relevancy and pertinency'[343]. The Court of Appeals of New York took a similar line, holding that absolute privilege only ceased where matters were 'so obviously impertinent as not to admit of discussion'[344]; one commentator saw this decision as 'the vanishing point of relevancy'[345].

Perhaps the most liberal approach to relevancy was seen in Tennessee both before and, confusingly, simultaneously with the strict approach (described above) also adopted briefly in the same State. In *Lea v White*[346] the Supreme Court analysed the position as follows. It started from the proposition that a statement made in judicial proceedings with probable cause could not be slander, which it took from a leading textbook[347]. In an analysis that would strike fear into the heart of any academic author, the Court continued:

> The pertinency of the matter to the occasion is that which is meant by probable cause . . . Then, the question is presented in the case before us, Was there probable cause? or, in other words, Could the defendant have reasonably supposed it necessary to his defence to return, on the writ . . . the alleged libellous matter?[348]

It seems likely that what the textbook author meant was that a statement made with probable cause *to believe it was true* was protected. Such, at any rate, was the meaning of the phrase in the tort of malicious prosecution. But the Supreme Court had transcended the author's intentions. *Lea v White* was followed in *Shodden v McElwee*[349], where the Supreme Court

341 13 Wis 193 (Supreme Court of Wisconsin, 1860).
342 *Ibid* at 4.
343 *Kemper v Fort* 67 A 991 at 995 (Supreme Court of Pennsylvania, 1907).
344 *Youmans v Smith* 47 NE 265 at 267 (Court of Appeals of New York, 1897).
345 Veeder, 'Absolute Immunity in Defamation: Judicial Proceedings' (1909) 9 *Columbia Law Review* 463, 600 at 611.
346 4 Sneed 111 (Supreme Court of Tennessee, 1856).
347 *Cooke on Defamation* at 49.
348 4 Sneed 111 at *2 (Westlaw transcript).
349 5 SW 602 (Supreme Court of Tennessee, 1887).

held that absolute privilege covered matter 'pertinent to the issue, or fairly supposed to be'[350]. Later, however, the Court seemed to abandon this position, adopting instead the test for witnesses that the matter must be pertinent or 'fairly responsive to the questions propounded'[351].

Against this background of options the English rule seems a sensible choice. Too strict a requirement of relevance risks subjecting participants in litigation to frequent defamation actions, for, as Cockburn CJ observed, 'questions might be, and are, constantly asked which are not strictly relevant to the issue'[352]. On the other hand, no limitation invites abuse. Between these extremes there is little practical difference between 'having reference to the inquiry' and a liberally applied test of pertinence.

4. CONCLUSION

Absolute privilege abruptly deprives claimants of their cause of action. It must therefore be justified by compelling policy reasons[353]. The historical investigation of the defence reveals two major recurring themes. First, despite absolute privilege applying irrespective of fault or malice, the courts paradoxically seek to justify it in terms of protecting those acting in good faith. Thus, judicial immunity for high court judges applies to those acting reasonably in good faith; the corresponding test for judges of lower courts brings fault into the question of jurisdiction. Participants in litigation acting in good faith need protection against a mistaken jury finding of malice and the vexation of actions. This emphasis on fault led some courts to go a step further and say that protection should only be given to those acting in good faith.

Second, when a broader view is taken, absolute privilege can be seen to function as a classification device. For instance, Parliamentary matters should be determined by Parliament, not the courts; military matters should be heard by military tribunals; dishonesty in litigation should be dealt with under the specific wrongs dealing with litigation. Here the justification for the privilege is not based on the defendant's good faith, but rather on the integrity and coherence of the system of legal rules.

Both of these justifications for absolute privilege now face a new challenge. The day after *Taylor v Director of the Serious Fraud Office*[354] was decided the European Court of Human Rights handed down its judgment in *Osman v United Kingdom*[355]. Although the main point of the decision

[350] *Ibid* at 604.
[351] *Cooley v Galyon* 70 SW 607 at 610 (Supreme Court of Tennessee, 1902).
[352] *Seaman v Netherclift* (1876) 2 CPD 53 at 56.
[353] Williams, 'Absolute Privilege for Licensing Justices' (1909) 25 *LQR* 188 at 191–92.
[354] [1999] 2 AC 177.
[355] European Court of Human Rights, 28 October 1998.

related to the duty of care in negligence[356], its more general message was that any immunity potentially infringed the right to a fair trial, and the Court was prepared to police immunities in English law far more aggressively than it had ever done before. To satisfy Article 6 of the European Convention on Human Rights any immunity must pursue a legitimate aim and be proportionate. Parliamentary privilege seems to have passed the test[357], but it remains to be seen how the other categories of absolute privilege will fare.

[356] Lord Hoffmann may well have anticipated the European Court's approach when, in his speech in *Taylor's case*, he suggested that witness immunity from an action in negligence might have to be analysed as part of the duty of care rather than as an immunity in future (see p 215). Such anticipation would have been possible given the Commission's decision in *Osman's case* (European Commission of Human Rights, 17 May 1996).

[357] *A v United Kingdom* [2002] All ER (D) 264 (Dec).

10

Reports

IN GENERAL IT is no defence for a defendant to prove that he was merely repeating defamatory language first uttered by someone else[1]. The reporter, copyist, printer, actor and even bookseller are all prima facie liable as publishers of defamatory material; the fact that they did not create the material is irrelevant.

However, there are exceptions: fair and accurate reports of judicial proceedings, Parliamentary proceedings, public meetings and public documents all give rise to a defence. Each exception emerged separately in the course of the nineteenth century, and was justified by different detailed reasons, including the absence of malice. Malice, however, quickly became overshadowed by tests based on the public benefit accruing from publication of reports and, more elusively, on what ought to be in the public domain. Reports of judicial proceedings are dealt with first since they were the first exception to become established, and were subject to the most sophisticated judicial analysis.

1. REPORTS OF JUDICIAL PROCEEDINGS

In a 1960 defamation trial[2] Salmon J told the jury that the principle of report of judicial proceedings was 'one of the principles upon which our whole system of administering justice is based'[3]. He went on to direct the jury that, since the case concerned a report of judicial proceedings, the only question was whether it was fair and accurate. Whilst those general statements may have been accurate in 1960 they would not have been true, without considerable qualification, in 1860. In 1820 they would have been wrong.

The story of the defence for fair reports of judicial proceedings begins in 1796. In *Curry v Walter*[4] the *Times* had published a report of an unsuccessful application to the Court of King's Bench containing defamatory

[1] See ch 6.
[2] *Burnett & Hallamshire Fuel Ltd v Sheffield Telegraph & Star Ltd* [1960] 1 WLR 502.
[3] *Ibid* at 504.
[4] (1796) 1 B & P 525.

language used by the applicant. The defendant pleaded the general issue (in other words, a non-specific denial of liability), and proved at the trial that its account was accurate. Eyre CJ directed the jury that although the matter complained of was defamatory 'he was of opinion that, being an account of what took place in a court of justice which is open to all the world, the publication of it was not unlawful'[5]. The jury found for the defendant.

The claimant moved for a new trial on two grounds. First, that the evidence of accuracy did not establish a valid defence in law. Second, that even if there was a valid defence of accurate report on the facts, it ought to have been pleaded specifically. The Court of King's Bench was of opinion that the action did not lie, but was undecided as to whether the defence should have been pleaded specially. The reporter tells us that 'the case stood over . . . no judgment was ever given'[6].

Despite the absence of a judgment the case is very informative. The emphasis by Eyre CJ on the report being of proceedings 'open to all the world' enunciated a basis for the protection of reports of judicial proceedings that remained influential for over a century[7]. Furthermore the arguments of counsel cast light on the wider question of where a defence for reports of judicial proceedings fitted into the general scheme of the law of defamation. Counsel for the defendant seemed to classify the defence of report of judicial proceedings with the privilege attaching to participants in the proceedings[8]. The claimant's counsel responded that the privilege for participants arose 'ex necessitate' and should be 'construed strictly'[9]. At a broader level, however, counsel shared common ground: both agreed that fundamentally a report of judicial proceedings might exclude liability if it showed that the defendant was not malicious. Counsel for the defendant compared the report of proceedings with cases where a mistress gave a reference about a servant[10] and a person spoke defamatory words in sorrow[11] in order to show how the reason for speaking could rebut the presumption of malice that automatically arose when a person uttered defamatory words. Counsel for the claimant seemed to agree with this basic position and elaborated it in a way that highlighted the defendant's motive:

[5] *Ibid* at 526.

[6] *Ibid* at 529.

[7] See eg *Andrews v Chapman* (1853) 3 Car & K 286 at 289; *Macdougall v Knight* (1889) 14 App Cas 194 at 200; *Furniss v The Cambridge Daily News (Limited)* (1907) 23 TLR 705 at 706; *Chapman v Lord Ellesmere* [1932] 2 KB 431 at 475.

[8] (1796) 1 B & P 525 at 527.

[9] *Ibid* at 528.

[10] *Edmondson v Stevenson* (1766) Bull NP 8.

[11] *Crawford v Middleton* (1662) 1 Lev 82.

> Copying a scandalous matter is according to Lord Holt sufficient to constitute a libel, for it perpetuates the memory of the scandal; though if the copy be made by a clerk in writing an indictment, or a student a note, it is not so, because not done ad infamiam.[12]

Over fifty years later the fact that a fair report of a trial rebutted malice persuaded the Court of Common Bench that the pleading point raised in *Curry v Walter* should be decided in favour of allowing the general issue[13]. In the later court's view, proof of fair report of judicial proceedings challenged the basic presumption of malice; malice was a basic element of liability; the general denial of liability was therefore sufficient.

A very different basis for the defence of fair report of judicial proceedings was advanced three years later in *R v Wright*[14]. The case was a prosecution for libel contained in a House of Commons report republished by the defendant. Lawrence J was the only one of three judges to make a comparison with reports of judicial proceedings. He explained the protection for reports of judicial proceedings as follows:

> Though the publication of such proceedings may be to the disadvantage of the particular individual concerned, yet it is of vast importance to the public that the proceedings of Courts of Justice should be universally known. The general advantage to the country in having these proceedings made public, more than counterbalances the inconveniences to the private persons whose conduct may be the subject of such proceedings.[15]

This basis for protecting court reports made no mention of the defendant's presumed motive. Nor did it rest on the fact that the courts were open to the public as a whole. Instead, Lawrence J emphasised the importance of reports to the public, and undertook a balancing analysis, with a flavour of utilitarianism, as a result of which he concluded that the benefits of reports outweighed their disadvantages. It was an analysis that bypassed the traditional arguments and categories.

The scene was set for progress, but instead the judiciary retreated. In *Stiles v Nokes*[16] Lord Ellenborough CJ, in argument, said that he would 'hesitate' to say that a report of defamatory matter uttered by a witness would escape liability 'merely because the matter had been given in a Court of Justice'[17]. Counsel reminded his Lordship of *Curry v Walter*[18], to which Lord Ellenborough replied that *Curry v Walter* only protected a 'fair,

12 (1796) 1 B & P 525 at 529.
13 *Hoare v Silverlock* (1850) 9 CB 20.
14 (1799) 8 D & E 293.
15 *Ibid* at 298.
16 (1806) 7 East 493.
17 *Ibid* at 503. Compare the same judge's judgment in *R v Fisher* (1811) 2 Camp 563 at 570: 'The publication of proceedings in courts of justice, where both sides are heard, and matters are finally determined, is salutary, and therefore it is permitted.'
18 (1796) 1 B & P 525.

plain, unvarnished account of proceedings'[19]. In the case before the court the account was distorted, so *Curry v Walter* could be easily distinguished.

Writing in 1812, Starkie was uncertain what the governing principle now was: he set out the law from *Curry v Walter*[20] and *R v Wright*[21] but also quoted the dicta from *Stiles v Nokes*[22]. His minimalist introduction to the latter was the non-committal and rather uninformative phrase, 'But in Styles *v* Nokes . . .'[23]. In 1819 the doubts suggested in *Stiles v Nokes* were reasserted more trenchantly. *R v Carlile*[24] concerned the report of a trial in which arguments and statements 'of a most blasphemous and indecent description'[25] had been used. The publisher of the report, prosecuted for libel, argued unsuccessfully that it was lawful to publish a correct account of what took place in court. Abbott CJ denied that there was any privilege to report defamatory matter uttered in court[26]. Best J said that judicial proceedings could be reported, but 'what is contained in the publication must be neither defamatory of an individual, tending to excite disaffection, nor calculated to offend the morals of the people: for, if it contains that which is calculated to produce any of those effects, instead of disseminating useful knowledge, it will produce great mischief'[27].

A year later Abbott CJ was still not prepared to recognise a privilege[28]. By the following year, however, his view seemed to have changed: he was now prepared to hold that a full account of judicial proceedings containing defamatory matter could be protected[29]. Bayley J, however, held to the view articulated earlier in *R v Carlile*[30]. For him it was not enough to show that the report was accurate—the publisher would have to show that the defamatory allegations he published were true[31].

Duncan v Thwaites[32] continued the retreat: in the context of a report of an *ex parte* proceeding the Court of King's Bench observed that *Curry v Walter*[33] had 'not received the sanction of subsequent judges'[34]. The Court also found grounds on which to distinguish the earlier case[35]. Finally, in

19 (1806) 7 East 493 at 504.
20 (1796) 1 B & P 525.
21 (1799) 8 D & E 293.
22 (1806) 7 East 493.
23 Starkie, *Law of Slander, Libel, Scandalum Magnatum and False Rumours* (London, 1812) at 198. The book was, coincidentally, dedicated to Lord Ellenborough CJ.
24 (1819) 3 B & Ald 167.
25 *Ibid*.
26 *Ibid* at 168.
27 *Ibid* at 171.
28 *Lewis v Clement* (1820) 3 B & Ald 702 at 710.
29 *Lewis v Walter* (1821) 4 B & Ald 605 at 612.
30 (1819) 3 B & Ald 167.
31 *Ibid* at 613.
32 (1824) 3 B & C 556.
33 (1796) 1 B & P 525.
34 (1824) 3 B & C 556 at 583.
35 See below, p 239, for details.

1825 the Court of King's Bench held that there was no privilege for a report of counsel's speech unaccompanied by a report of the evidence on which the speech was based[36]. Although parts of the judgment of Bayley J focussed on the failure to report the evidence, other parts of the judgment went further, and the conclusion was emphatic:

> A party is at liberty to publish a history of the trial, viz. of the facts of the case, and of the law of the case as applied to the facts, but . . . he is not at liberty to publish observations made by counsel injurious to the character of individuals.[37]

Holroyd J agreed, emphasising that the report lacked privilege because it was not in the course of the administration of justice[38].

By 1825 a consensus seemed to be established that reports of judicial proceedings were not privileged. However in 1829 the authorities from the early 1820s were thrown aside when Tindal CJ asserted that it was 'generally received doctrine, that newspapers and other publications which narrate what passes in courts of justice are, to a certain extent, privileged'[39]. On the facts of the case before him he found that the report was not fair. Park J agreed, but pointed out that the privilege did not extend to the publication of offensive or indelicate material, and cited *R v Carlile*[40] in support of his view[41].

It is as difficult to explain the change of position in 1819–1825 as it is to explain the later change in 1829. Neither change claimed an analytical compulsion. One obvious point is that the law was at a formative stage and different judges took different views. The prevailing view in the early 1820s, when the King's Bench was dominated by Abbott CJ, Bayley J and Best J, was against privilege; Tindal CJ took the opposite view. However, even this personnel-based explanation cannot account for Tindal CJ's description of privilege for reports of judicial proceedings as the 'generally received doctrine'. It was as if nothing had happened between 1819 and 1825. Nor can it explain why Park J referred to *R v Carlile* in support of his views, when the case contained most emphatic statements against his position. Perhaps individual judicial conviction was permitted greater weight than it is today.

In any event, the position taken by Tindal CJ and Park J in *Saunders v Mills*[42], affirmed by the same two judges in *Roberts v Brown*[43], remained the basic common law position until legislative intervention in 1888[44]. The

36 *Flint v Pike* (1825) 4 B & C 473.
37 *Ibid* at 480.
38 *Ibid* at 481.
39 *Saunders v Mills* (1829) 6 Bing 213 at 218.
40 (1819) 3 B & Ald 167.
41 (1829) 6 Bing 213 at 221–22.
42 *Ibid*.
43 (1834) 10 Bing 519.
44 Law of Libel Amendment Act s 3.

standard reason given for the privilege was that first put forward by Eyre CJ in *Curry v Walter*[45], ie, that the report merely gave further publicity to proceedings that had taken place in public[46]. Within this basic position, however, there were detailed difficult questions that forced the courts to consider the precise justifications for the privilege and its scope.

The first such detailed question to trouble the courts was whether reports of *ex parte* proceedings were protected. *Curry v Walter*[47] had involved an *ex parte* application to the Court of King's Bench, but in the absence of a reasoned judgment the point remained open. Immediately after *Curry v Walter* the general view seemed to be that reports of *ex parte* proceedings did not enjoy qualified privilege. In *R v Lee*[48], for example, it was held to be 'highly criminal'[49] to publish reports of depositions taken by a magistrate on a murder charge before the murder trial had taken place. A similar situation, in *R v Fisher*[50], was analysed at length by Lord Ellenborough CJ. His Lordship rejected the argument that he should just apply *Curry v Walter*. In his view, the key point was that the trial jury should hear the case 'with minds pure and unprejudiced'[51]; it would be difficult for a jury to do so if its members had read earlier statements of evidence against the accused 'which the latter had no opportunity to disprove or controvert'[52]. He contrasted reports of contested trials with reports of *ex parte* evidence:

> The publication of proceedings in courts of justice, where both sides are heard, is salutary, and therefore it is permitted. The publication of these preliminary examinations has a tendency to pervert the public mind, and, to disturb the course of justice; it is therefore illegal.[53]

The identical analysis was repeated in England[54] and the United States[55]. It revealed two important points. First, that one reason for protecting reports of court proceedings was that readers of such reports could learn the truth about the parties to contested litigation. Second, and more importantly, the scope of protection for reports of judicial proceedings was not controlled by whether the presumption of malice had been rebutted, or whether the proceedings had taken place in a court open to

[45] (1796) 1 B & P 525.
[46] See, eg, argument of Serjeant Ludlow in *Saunders v Mills* (1829) 6 Bing 213 at 216; *Andrews v Chapman* (1853) 3 Car & K 286 at 289.
[47] (1796) 1 B & P 525.
[48] (1804) 5 Esp 123.
[49] *Ibid* at 125.
[50] (1811) 2 Camp 563.
[51] *Ibid* at 570.
[52] *Ibid*.
[53] *Ibid*.
[54] *R v Fleet* (1818) 1 B & Ald 379.
[55] *The Cincinnati Gazette Company v Timberlake* 10 Ohio St 548 (Supreme Court of Ohio, 1860); *Todd v Every Evening Printing Co* 62 A 1089 (Superior Court of Delaware, 1906).

the public. Rather, the benefits of reports were being balanced against the potential disadvantages, with the courts reaching a conclusion as to where the public's interest lay. As Lord Ellenborough CJ put it in *R v Fisher*: 'It is of infinite importance to us all, that whatever has a tendency to prevent a fair trial should be guarded against. Every one of us may be questioned in a Court of Law, and called upon to defend his life and character . . .'[56]

The reasoning in *R v Fisher*[57] had avoided discussing *Curry v Walter*[58]. In *Duncan v Thwaites*[59], by contrast, *Curry v Walter* received close attention. Again the context was a report of preliminary proceedings before a magistrate on a criminal charge. Counsel for the defendant urged the Court of King's Bench to follow *Curry*'s case[60], but the Court declined. Abbott CJ delivering the judgment of the Court doubted whether *Curry v Walter* was good law at all and identified two grounds to distinguish the present case[61]. First, the proceedings reported in *Curry* had taken place in the King's Bench, which was open to the public; proceedings before a magistrate could be conducted in private. Second, the proceeding in *Curry* ended in refusal of the application; the proceedings reported in *Duncan v Thwaites* ended in the accused being committed for trial. Both grounds of distinction were revealing. The first continued the idea that a report was privileged because it did no more than extend the area of publicity of the court, but it introduced a new variation. On the facts of *Duncan v Thwaites* the proceedings were held in public, but the *power* to hold them in private was emphasised in the Court's reasoning. The second ground of distinction underlined the concern that reports of preliminary proceedings could prejudice a later trial; it also suggested that reports of preliminary proceedings might be permissible if there was no future trial to prejudice.

This second ground of distinction came to the fore in *Lewis v Levy*[62], where the report concerned preliminary criminal proceedings ending with the charge being dismissed. Lord Campbell CJ emphasised that no trial was imminent, and distinguished *Duncan v Thwaites*[63]. He concluded his analysis with a cautious suggestion that even where the accused had been committed for trial, preliminary proceedings might be reported. The reason he gave was significant: he thought that the 'benefit arising from these reports [should be] fully experienced'[64] before their legal status was determined. Again, as with the dicta in *R v Wright*[65] and the analysis in

56 (1811) 2 Camp 563 at 571.
57 *Ibid.*
58 (1796) 1 B & P 525.
59 (1824) 3 B & C 556.
60 *Ibid* at 575.
61 *Ibid* at 583.
62 (1858) 27 LJ (QB) 282.
63 *Ibid* at 288–89.
64 *Ibid* at 290.
65 (1799) 8 D & E 293 at 298.

R v Fisher[66], the argument moved beyond questions of malice, motive or whether the court was public, and attempted to calculate whether protecting reports was more beneficial to society than not protecting them.

The task of identifying the greatest benefit where preliminary *ex parte* proceedings were reported and the accused committed for trial was taken on by the Court of Queen's Bench in Ireland. In *R v Gray*[67], a prosecution for contempt, the Court held that the greater good lay in protecting reports. The language used by Lefroy CJ was most revealing. He spoke of it being 'most expedient for the public'[68] that reports of magistrates' proceedings be published. It was 'very important' not to prejudice later trials, but it was 'of the utmost importance for the public to know that the magistrates do their duty impartially and without influence of any sort'[69]. Fitzgerald J also made clear that his reasoning was based on a calculation of the greatest public benefit. He acknowledged that reports could be a source of 'inconvenience' to individuals, but 'this inconvenience is infinitesimal in comparison to the great public advantage given by . . . publicity'[70]. The dissenting judgment of Hayes J highlighted that the calculation of public benefit involved a large element of subjective valuation. For him 'the first duty of this Court, and before all others . . . is to see that a fair trial shall be ensured to every accused person'[71]; this duty should not be abandoned for the benefits of publicity.

In England the tendency was also to expand the protection given to reports. In *Wason v Walter*[72] Cockburn CJ doubted that any action would lie for an accurate report of *ex parte* proceedings 'published with a view to the information of the public, and innocent of all intention to do injury to the reputation of the party affected'[73]. Although Cockburn CJ expressed this doubt shortly, in a case about reports of Parliamentary proceedings, it was enormously influential: even courts in the United States saw it as a turning point[74]. Later English courts seemed to regard the matter as settled. In *Usill v Hales*[75], for example, the point was taken by counsel that a report was of *ex parte* proceedings. Lord Coleridge CJ, rejecting the argument, commented that 'if this argument had been addressed to a Court some sixty or seventy years ago, it might have met with a different result

66 (1811) 2 Camp 563 at 570–71.
67 (1865) 10 Cox Cr Cas 184.
68 *Ibid* at 189.
69 *Ibid*.
70 *Ibid* at 193.
71 *Ibid* at 190.
72 (1868) LR 4 QB 73.
73 *Ibid* at 94.
74 *Storey v Wallace* 60 Ill 51 (Supreme Court of Illinois, 1871); *McBee v Fulton* 47 Md 403 (Court of Appeals of Maryland, 1878); *McDermott v The Evening Journal Association* 43 NJL 488 (Supreme Court of New Jersey, 1881).
75 (1878) 3 CPD 319.

from that which it is about to meet with to-day'[76]. He went on to quote from Cockburn CJ's judgment in *Wason v Walter*[77] and held, reluctantly, that the report was privileged. Lopes J held that no action lay for an impartial report of a judicial proceeding 'on principles of public convenience'[78]. He mentioned in passing preliminary proceedings leading to committal of the accused, but doubted whether the earlier authorities dealing with reports of such proceedings would be followed 'in the present day'[79].

So far as reports in newspapers were concerned, all doubts about *ex parte* proceedings were removed by the Law of Libel Amendment Act 1888 s 3. This provision stated that a 'fair and accurate report . . . of proceedings publicly heard before any court exercising judicial authority' was 'privileged' if published contemporaneously. The effect on reports of *ex parte* proceedings was deliberate, the House of Commons having rejected an amendment to exclude reports of such proceedings from s 3[80]. Once the Act was in force there was no need for newspapers to consider whether the report might affect later proceedings[81]. The Press felt liberated, publishing reports of *ex parte* proceedings with such frequency that if became a source of complaint, and was commented on judicially[82].

In relation to reports not in newspapers one further development was important. This related to the rule that reports of *ex parte* proceedings before magistrates were privileged only if the proceedings ended in the charges being dismissed. The rule had been doubted in *Wason v Walter*[83] and *Usill v Hales*[84], but in *Kimber v The Press Association, Limited*[85] the Court of Appeal chose to recognise it and then interpret it in a way that effectively deprived it of content. The case concerned the report of an informal application to a panel of magistrates for them to issue a summons for perjury against the claimant. Lord Esher MR formulated the general rule as follows: 'where the proceedings are such as will result in a final decision being given, a fair and accurate report, made bona fide, of those proceedings is privileged'[86]. He then went on to consider whether, on the facts of the case before him, the proceedings were 'such as will result in a final decision being given'. If the justices refused to issue the summons that was clearly a final decision. If they issued the summons there might be a further inquiry and a trial, but in his Lordship's view this still indicated

[76] *Ibid* at 325.
[77] (1868) LR 4 QB 73.
[78] (1878) 3 CPD 319 at 328.
[79] *Ibid* at 329.
[80] *Hansard's Parliamentary Debates*, 3rd Series, vol 326, col 1273–74 (6 June 1888).
[81] Eg, *McCarey v Associated Newspapers Ltd* [1964] 1 WLR 855.
[82] *R v Parke* [1903] 2 KB 432 at 438.
[83] (1868) LR 4 QB 73.
[84] (1878) 3 CPD 319.
[85] [1893] 1 QB 65.
[86] *Ibid* at 71.

finality, because 'at one stage or another of the proceedings, there must be a final decision of some kind or other'[87]. Lopes LJ put it more concisely—'if the proceedings were such as must ultimately lead to a final decision there may be a report of those proceedings which is privileged'[88]. The Supreme Court of Rhode Island described the reasoning in *Kimber v The Press Association, Limited* as 'remarkable'[89], seldom a judicial compliment. Certainly the application of the rule was at odds with the principle underlying it—namely that a later trial should not be prejudiced by publicity given to preliminary proceedings. In effect the Court of Appeal had taken a complex and circuitous route to abolish a rule that had been out of favour for over twenty years.

The next detailed issue that the courts had to address was whether the standard reason given for the privilege—that it merely allowed proceedings transacted in public to reach more people—defined the extent of privilege. The issue arose in two distinct shapes. First, did the privilege apply to the report of any defamatory matter uttered in a public courtroom? Second, could the privilege ever apply to proceedings that were not open to the public in general?

The first attempt to define the privilege in relation to defamation uttered in a courtroom out of turn took a strict line. In *Delegal v Highley*[90] the Court of King's Bench held that the report 'must be strictly confined to the actual proceedings in court, and must contain no defamatory observations or comments from any quarter whatever, in addition to what forms strictly and properly the legal proceedings'[91]. It followed that there was no privilege for a report of an impromptu interjection made by the clerk to the magistrates. The decision illustrated that the standard reason given for the privilege did not tell the whole story: anyone in court would have heard the clerk's interjection, but the privilege did not protect a reporter who put his readers in the same position as if they had been present. *Delegal v Highley* was approved and applied by the Exchequer Division in Ireland[92] to a report of an interjection by a member of the public at a coroner's inquest.

Later cases took a slightly more relaxed view. In *Hope v Sir WC Leng and Co (Sheffield Telegraph) (Limited)*[93] the Court of Appeal held that a report of a litigant's statement made in court, but not in the witness-box, was protected. However, the decision should not be seen as protecting reports of any defamatory utterance in court: the Court of Appeal emphasised

[87] *Ibid*.
[88] *Ibid* at 74.
[89] *Metcalf v Times Pub Co* 40 A 864 at 865 (Supreme Court of Rhode Island, 1898).
[90] [1837] 3 Bing NC 950.
[91] *Ibid* at 960–61.
[92] *Lynam v Gowing* (1880) 6 LR Ir 259.
[93] (1907) 23 TLR 243.

that the litigant was still sitting in the same place where he had given his evidence, and was still under the obligation of his oath. The real motivating reason behind the decision seems to have been that it would be unfair to reporters to expect them in such circumstances to be able to identify what was strictly part of the proceedings.

The final case on this point, *Farmer v Hyde*[94], similarly eschewed a technical, strict approach but stopped short of allowing privilege for a report of any defamatory utterance. There a spectator in the public gallery, whose behaviour was being criticised in the case being heard, stood up and said that he wished to make an application to the judge in order to contradict the lies being told. The defendant reported these events. Counsel for the defendant argued that the report should be privileged because 'members of the public who cannot attend a court should be put in the same position, through reading a report of the proceedings in a newspaper, as those members of the public who were present in court'[95]. The Court of Appeal found that there was a privilege, but took a more cautious approach. Its view was that reports of privileged 'proceedings' under Law of Libel Amendment Act 1888 s 3 included 'something . . . done in the course of proceedings which is in any way related to the proceedings as such, and can be done in the proceedings'[96]. It approved the Irish decision mentioned above as there the defamatory remarks were 'wholly irrelevant to the proceedings', and emphasised that in *Hope v Sir WC Leng* it was crucial that the speaker had been a witness who was still under oath[97].

What this line of cases showed was that whilst the courts were happy to use the justification that reports of judicial proceedings simply gave extra publicity to what happened in a public courtroom, they were not prepared to use that justification to define the limits of the privilege. The report should be a cleaned-up version of events, giving perhaps a misleading impression of order and calm. The reporter was not a mere conduit through which the court's proceedings reached the outer world, but a filter, responsible for removing from his report 'irrelevant' matter. Under these rules the wider public were entitled to receive only an idealised account of what had happened in court.

Reports of proceedings not open to the general public also challenged the assumption that reports were privileged because they extended existing publicity. If the assumption was correct reports of proceedings not open to the public should not be protected: there was no publicity to extend. However, in *Ryalls v Leader*[98] the Court of Exchequer took a different view. The proceedings in question were an examination of a gaoled

94 [1937] 1 KB 728.
95 *Ibid* at 733.
96 *Ibid* at 741.
97 *Ibid*.
98 (1866) LR 1 Exch 296.

debtor conducted in gaol by the registrar in bankruptcy. The registrar had statutory powers to adjudge the debtor bankrupt. If the debtor refused to co-operate in the examination the registrar could report the refusal to the court and the court could sentence the debtor to a month's imprisonment. Only creditors were entitled to be present at the examination. Counsel for the claimant emphasised that the proceedings were not public[99], but the Court held that the report was privileged. Martin B asserted that the registrar's power of adjudication 'ought to be exercised in public'[100], and he concluded his analysis with two powerful rhetorical questions:

> Can any one contend, that a matter for which one month's imprisonment may be given, is not one for the public to have reported to them? Is not an adjudication in such a matter properly to be held in public?[101]

Channell B took a similar approach, stating that the registrar's powers showed that the proceedings were in a public court.

The analysis in *Ryalls v Leader*[102] was enormously significant. It demonstrated that the courts were not content to rely on the principle that reports enlarged the existing area of publicity when defining the limits of the privilege. Instead, as with reports of irrelevant defamatory matter, the courts decided what ought to be in the public sphere. When making that decision it was neither sufficient nor necessary that the matter reported could have been witnessed at first hand by a member of the public. Whether the matter was public—and therefore protected if reported—had become a question of value, not fact.

A further important point about the analysis in *Ryalls v Leader*[103] was that it articulated a new reason for protecting reports of judicial proceedings: the public ought to be informed how judicial power was being exercised. In England this reason co-existed with the other reasons until the enactment of the privilege in statutory form[104] rendered common law justifications irrelevant. In the United States, however, monitoring judicial activity came to be seen as the dominant justification for the privilege and triggered further common law developments.

The context in which monitoring judicial activity came to prominence was reports of initial statements of claim and pleadings filed by the parties. In England such reports were not protected[105] because the Law of Libel Amendment Act 1888 s 3 was limited to 'proceedings publicly heard', wording deliberately introduced to exclude reports of plead-

[99] *Ibid* at 298.
[100] *Ibid* at 299.
[101] *Ibid.*
[102] *Ibid.*
[103] *Ibid.*
[104] Law of Libel Amendment Act 1888, s 3.
[105] *English and Scottish Co-Operative Properties Mortgage and Investment Society, Limited v Odhams Press, Limited* [1940] 1 KB 440 at 458 (per Goddard LJ).

ings[106]. Across the Atlantic the point remained open. The first American authorities were tentative, with courts rejecting privilege on the basis either of intuition[107] or absence of English authority[108]. The first landmark decision was *Cowley v Pulsifer*[109], where Holmes J explained the basis for protecting reports of judicial proceedings as follows:

> It is desirable that the trial of causes should take place under the public eye, not because the controversies of one citizen with another are of public concern, but because it is of the highest moment that those who administer justice should always act under the sense of public responsibility, and that every citizen should be able to satisfy himself with his own eyes as to the mode in which a public duty is performed.[110]

Reports of preliminary documents lodged with the court did not attract protection, because 'knowledge of them throws no light upon the administration of justice'[111]. Under this theory reports of defamatory allegations made by the parties and counsel were protected only because judicial activity could not be monitored without stating the facts and issues of cases decided. As a later court put it, protection for reports of defamatory allegations in court was 'an incidental result' of telling the public 'what its court does'[112]. One commentator advocated carrying the theory to its logical conclusion, and protecting only reports of court proceedings where the parties were identified solely by initials, or were anonymised[113].

The justification put forward by Holmes J gained widespread acceptance[114], and accumulated some complexities. For instance, it was held that there was no privilege for a report of proceedings where a judge acted in an administrative rather than judicial capacity[115]. Similarly, one case insisted that there must have been some judicial examination of the defamatory allegation: there was therefore no privilege for the report of a claim which the court had permitted to be filed late on the consent of the defendant[116]. On the other hand, a later decision in the same jurisdiction

[106] *Hansard's Parliamentary Debates,* 3rd Series, vol 326, col 1272–73 (6 June 1888).

[107] *Scripps v Reilly* 35 Mich 371 (Supreme Court of Michigan, 1877).

[108] *Barber v St Louis Dispatch Company* 3 Mo App 377 (St Louis Court of Appeals, Missouri, 1877).

[109] 137 Mass 392 (Supreme Judicial Court of Massachusetts, 1884).

[110] *Ibid* at 394.

[111] *Ibid.*

[112] *Ilsley v Sentinel Co* 113 NW 425 at 426 (Supreme Court of Wisconsin, 1907).

[113] Barnett, 'The Privilege of Defamation by Private Report of Public Official Proceedings' (1952) 31 *Oregon Law Review* 185.

[114] Eg, *Ilsley v Sentinel Co* 113 NW 425 (Supreme Court of Wisconsin, 1907); *Nixon v Dispatch Printing Co* 112 NW 258 (Supreme Court of Minnesota, 1907); *Meeker v Post Printing & Publishing Co* 135 P 457 (Supreme Court of Colorado, 1913). See also *Gazette Printing Company v Shallow* (1909) 41 Can Sup Ct 339 at 364.

[115] *Mannix v Portland Telegram* 23 P 2d 138 (Supreme Court of Oregon, 1933).

[116] *Lundin v Post Pub Co* 104 NE 480 (Supreme Judicial Court of Massachusetts, Suffolk, 1914).

held that a report of the issue of a warrant by a court was protected despite the fact that no judge was present[117].

Whilst the justification advanced in *Cowley v Pulsifer*[118] came to dominate, other justifications did not disappear entirely. In particular, there was a bold attempt to use the theory that reports should be protected if they dealt with matter already open to the general public. Defendants in some reports of pleadings cases argued that because any person was entitled to inspect documents filed in a court, any report of those documents must be privileged. The courts rejected this argument, and their reasons revealed a sophisticated approach to questions of publicity. The Supreme Court of Minnesota explained that the right of an individual to inspect documents filed with the court 'does not authorize the person inspecting the record to make an improper use thereof, or to publish to the world through the medium of the press libelous matter contained in the record'[119]. The Supreme Court of Wisconsin took a similar line, saying that the right to examine pleadings had 'no bearing on the question'[120] whether a report of proceedings was privileged[121]. As with the analysis of reports of irrelevant defamatory matter in England, there was a reluctance to allow public accessibility automatically to guarantee a privileged report. There was also here an implicit recognition that there were different types of publicity: pleadings might be public documents in the sense that they were open to inspection, but they were not public property to be circulated generally.

The rule that reports of pleadings were not privileged seems to have gone unchallenged in England, and seems to have been assumed in the most recent leading case[122]. In the United States, by contrast, there have been legislative and common law alterations. Texas presents a good example of the former. There *Cowley v Pulsifer*[123] was accepted by the Court of Civil Appeals as 'establishing the prevailing American doctrine'[124]. The same year the legislature intervened by enacting that qualified privilege applied to 'A fair, true and impartial account of the proceedings in a court of justice . . . or any other official proceedings authorized by law in the administration of law'[125]. The Court of Civil Appeals subsequently held,

117 *Thompson v Boston Pub Co* 189 NE 210 (Supreme Judicial Court of Massachusetts, Suffolk, 1934); contrast *Finnegan v Eagle Printing Co* 179 NW 788 (Supreme Court of Wisconsin, 1920), where there was no privilege for a report of the issue of a writ of attachment by the court because the issue had received no judicial attention.

118 137 Mass 392 (Supreme Judicial Court of Massachusetts, 1884).

119 *Nixon v Dispatch Printing Co* 112 NW 258 (Supreme Court of Minnesota, 1907).

120 *Ilsley v Sentinel Co* 113 NW 425 at 427 (Supreme Court of Wisconsin, 1907).

121 See also *Sanford v Boston Herald-Traveler Corporation* 61 NE 2d 5 at 6 (Supreme Judicial Court of Massachusetts, Essex, 1945): 'we are not prepared to concede that the general right of inspection of public records enables one in every instance to publish such records broadcast without regard to the truth of defamatory matter contained in them.'

122 *Stern v Piper* [1996] 3 All ER 385.

123 137 Mass 392 (Supreme Judicial Court of Massachusetts, 1884).

124 *Sutton v AH Belo & Co* 64 SW 686 at 687 (Court of Civil Appeals of Texas, 1901).

125 Gen Laws Tex (Acts, 1901, p 30, c 26) s 3.

in *AH Belo & Co v Lacy*[126], that this formulation protected the report of a pleading. However, the whole matter was thrown into doubt when a later Court of Civil Appeals, to which *AH Belo & Co v Lacy* was not cited, reached the opposite conclusion[127].

It is difficult to know why the Texas legislature chose to intervene—although it may be significant that one contemporary commentator expressed alarm about the influence of the press over legislation[128]. Where common law change to the rule took place, however, the reasons had to be given. One interesting early attempt to alter the rule was the dissenting judgment of Girouard J in a leading Canadian case[129]. He argued that the key question was whether the filed pleading was 'a document of a private or of a public nature'[130]. He concluded that it was generally public because under the Quebec Code of Procedure the office where pleadings were filed was declared to be a part of the court. However, there would be no privilege if a newspaper reported pleadings 'when private interests alone are at stake, for instance, in cases of seduction, filiation, separation from bed and board (although, even in such cases, there may be exceptions where public men are concerned) . . .'[131]. What was most striking about this analysis was the complexity surrounding the question whether the document was 'public': it involved an assessment not only of the form of the document, but of the content as well.

A more influential alteration of the rule was accomplished by the Court of Appeals of New York in *Campbell v New York Evening Post, Inc*[132]. New York, like many other states, had initially accepted the rule as set out in *Cowley v Pulsifer*[133], but the Court in *Campbell* preferred to start from first principles and create a rule 'consistent with practical experience'[134]. The Court emphasised the minimalism of the requirement of judicial action—it was difficult to see why the document being read 'on an ex parte application for an injunction, an order of arrest, an attachment, or an order of publication' should make the difference[135]. Furthermore, in New York at least, a lawsuit was a 'judicial proceeding' from the start.

[126] 111 SW 215 (Court of Civil Appeals of Texas, 1908).

[127] *Houston Chronicle Pub Co v McDavid* 173 SW 467 (Court of Civil Appeals of Texas, 1914).

[128] Bryan, 'Publication of Record Libel' (1918) 5 *Virginia Law Review* 513 at 524: 'the press is so powerful that restrictive legislation cannot be enacted at the present time without its consent'.

[129] *Gazette Printing Company v Shallow* 41 Can Sup Ct 339 (1909).

[130] *Ibid* at 341.

[131] *Ibid* at 352.

[132] 157 NE 153 (Court of Appeals of New York, 1927).

[133] *Stuart v Press Pub Co* 82 NYS 401 (Supreme Court, New York, 1903); *Williams v New York Herald Co*, 150 NYS 838 (Supreme Court, New York, 1914).

[134] 157 NE 153 at 156.

[135] *Ibid* at 155. See also, RP, 'Libel—A Limitation on the Privilege of Publishing Reports of Judicial Proceedings' (1925–26) 24 *Michigan Law Review* 489, particularly at 491.

The New York court's reasoning was not enthusiastically received by commentators[136], but it persuaded courts in other jurisdictions. Both the Supreme Court of South Carolina[137] and the Court of Appeals of Kentucky[138], for example, chose to follow the New York decision over *Cowley v Pulsifer*[139], the latter court emphasising that once a petition had been filed in the court office, 'the controversy is no longer a private one'[140]. But everyone was not convinced: in Massachusetts they stood by the rule in *Cowley*'s case[141].

The developments flowing from *Campbell v New York Evening Post, Inc* highlighted a general theme which ran through the history of protecting reports of court proceedings. The courts abandoned specific rationales for the privilege (such as that the privilege extended the area of publicity or that it allowed monitoring of judicial activity) when faced with cases where a strict application of the rationale produced an undesirable result. The courts then justified their preferred conclusion by appealing to the wider notion of the public sphere. Whether a report was protected depended on whether it was essentially public; deciding what satisfied this test involved a range of both factual and evaluative considerations.

The protection for reports of judicial proceedings was at various times subject to three conditions. First, after 1888, the report had to be published contemporaneously. Second, before 1888 it had to be published without malice. Third, it had to be fair and accurate.

The first two conditions require an examination of the background to and effects of the Law of Libel Amendment Act 1888 s 3. The relevant part of this section, as enacted, provided that:

> A fair and accurate report in any newspaper of proceedings publicly heard before any court exercising judicial authority shall, if published contemporaneously with such proceedings, be privileged:

The clause in the initial Bill was rather different:

> A fair and accurate report published in any newspaper of proceedings of and in any court exercising judicial authority shall be absolutely privileged.[142]

The privilege was said to be absolute, and there was no requirement of contemporaneous publication.

136 Eg, Anon, 'Libel and Slander—Privilege of Newspaper to Publish Complaint Filed in a Civil Action' (1927) 27 *Columbia Law Review* 225; Nadelmann, 'The Newspaper Privilege and Extortion by Abuse of Legal Process' (1954) 54 *Columbia Law Review* 359.

137 *Lybrand v The State Co* 184 SE 580 (Supreme Court of South Carolina, 1936).

138 *Paducah Newspapers, Inc v Bratcher* 118 SW 2d 178 (Court of Appeals of Kentucky, 1937).

139 137 Mass 392 (Supreme Judicial Court of Massachusetts, 1884).

140 118 SW 2d 178 at 180.

141 *Sanford v Boston Herald-Traveler Corporation* 61 NE 2d 5 (Supreme Judicial Court of Massachusetts, Essex, 1945).

142 *House of Commons Parliamentary Papers 1887*, vol III, p 141 (Bill 340).

The requirement of contemporaneous publication was introduced when the Bill was read in Committee in the House of Commons. Sir Algernon Borthwick, who had brought forward the Bill, proposed the amendment to prevent 'the raking up of old trials which might be highly disagreeable and injurious to individuals'[143]. On the face of it, it was strange to see the promoter of the Bill seeking to amend it—after all, he had had plenty of time to come up with wording he was happy with before he presented the Bill to Parliament. The explanation was that the Attorney General, Sir Richard Webster, had suggested amendments which would make the Bill acceptable to the Government. Sir Algernon Borthwick put forward these amendments, although in relation to another section, he put forward an amendment that he said he did not support[144]!

Members of the House of Commons expressed some disquiet about the requirement of 'contemporaneous publication', but their concerns were that the precise words used were unclear[145]. The Attorney General explained that the phrase should be 'construed with reference to the issue of the paper'[146] so that the report should appear in the next issue, whether that was the following day or week[147]. It was surprising that the amendment did not provoke more fundamental objections: an accurate report of earlier proceedings might well serve the public interest. It might, for instance, expose the criminal past of a candidate for elected office, or provide a point of comparison with contemporary judicial behaviour[148]. Two factors may explain the absence of fundamental objections. The first was the peculiar Parliamentary setting, in which Government support was conditional on the amendments being made. A Member favouring the Bill might damage its chances of becoming law by advocating a rejection of amendments that the Government regarded as significant. The second factor was that Scots law had a requirement of contemporaneous publication[149], and it was acknowledged that the Bill would bring English law closer to the Scottish position[150]. At the very least this factor may explain the acquiescence of the Lord Advocate and another Scottish Member, who both took the opportunity to contrast English and Scots law in relation to another clause in the Bill[151].

[143] *Hansard's Parliamentary Debates,* 3rd Series, vol 326, col 1274 (6 June 1888).

[144] See discussion of cl 4 of the Bill, below.

[145] *Hansard's Parliamentary Debates,* 3rd Series, vol 326, col 1275 (Addison) and 1276 (Cameron) (6 June 1888).

[146] *Ibid* at 1276.

[147] See similarly Fisher and Strahan, *The Law of the Press,* 2nd edn (London, 1898) at 167.

[148] Johnsen, 'When Truth and Accuracy Diverge: The Fair Report of a Dated Proceeding' (1982) 34 *Stanford Law Review* 1041 at 1056–57.

[149] Dykes, *Cooper on Defamation and Verbal Injury,* 2nd edn (1906) at 142.

[150] See eg, *Hansard's Parliamentary Debates,* 3rd Series, vol 329, col 502 (26 July 1888).

[151] *Hansard's Parliamentary Debates,* 3rd Series, vol 327, col 48–49 (13 June 1888).

Subsequently the requirement of publication in a newspaper was widened[152], then dropped altogether[153]. The requirement of contemporaneous publication, however, remained. Although the 1888 Act did not expressly preserve common law protection for reports of dated proceedings[154], it did not expressly abolish it either, and it is submitted that the common law protection is still available. The special considerations that might apply to reports of dated proceedings are discussed further below.

The second condition of protection was the absence of malice. This condition could be seen right from the start of protection for reports of court proceedings[155]. Malice was a key concept in the eighteenth- and early nineteenth-century law of defamation: it was presumed from speaking defamatory words, but could be rebutted by proof of circumstances showing no malicious motive in the speaker. In some situations, such as references for servants requested by potential employers, the courts took the view that the initial presumption of malice from proof of the defamatory words being spoken did not hold true. The burden of proof of malice was then on the claimant from the outset of the case[156].

Reports of court proceedings could be fitted into this structure of general rules about malice. Where, for instance, a student took down a note of a case he had heard in court for the purposes of study there was nothing from which malice could be inferred[157]. The same could be said of a law report published in a newspaper. When formal categories of qualified privilege (based on situations where malice could not be presumed from speaking defamatory words) emerged in the 1830s, reports of judicial proceedings were included.

A claimant seeking to prove malice against the publisher of a report of judicial proceedings might point to various factors. If, for instance, the defendant had gone to the trouble of printing the report as a pamphlet a court might start to suspect malice[158]. Similarly, an editor of a newspaper who inserted a report of the same trial every day for several weeks was unlikely to be inspired by the purest motives[159]. The fact that the reporter was also the person who had uttered the defamatory matter at the trial would likewise prompt suspicion[160]. However, where a newspaper published a report of the proceedings the following day there was nothing to

152 *Report of the Committee on the Law of Defamation* (Cmd 7536, 1948) at paras 100–3, Defamation Act 1952 s 7(5).

153 Defamation Act 1996, s 14.

154 Cf Law of Libel Amendment Act 1888 s 4, and its modern equivalent, Defamation Act 1996, s 15.

155 *Curry v Walter* (1796) 1 B & P 525.

156 For a more detailed historical analysis see above, chs 5 and 7.

157 *Curry v Walter* (1796) 1 B & P 525 at 529.

158 *Milissich v Lloyds* (1877) 46 LJ (CP) 404 at 406 (per Mellish LJ).

159 *Salmon v Isaac* (1869) 20 LT (NS) 885 at 886.

160 *Stevens v Sampson* (1879) 5 Ex D 53.

suggest malice. As one later commentator remarked, proof of malice was so rare and out of the ordinary that the privilege for newspapers was practically absolute[161].

In its original form, section 3 of the 1888 Act made the practical reality of absolute privilege into law. The word 'absolutely' was, however, deleted by the House of Commons in Committee as a result of an amendment stipulated by the Attorney General[162]. He took the view that the amendment had substantive effect: under the amended section, 'the protection would only be given where no malice was shown'[163]. Commentators construing the section took the opposite view. They pointed out the contrast between section 3 and the next section, where the privilege for reports of public meetings was expressly made subject to malice. They also drew attention to the fact that no 'amendment' to the law of libel would be accomplished if the privilege were qualified, which was at odds with the title of the Act. But the most powerful argument, as encapsulated by Fisher and Strahan, was that if the section did not give absolute privilege it was 'altogether useless, for newspapers had already, like everybody else, partial privilege with regard to the publication of such reports' [164].

The Court of Appeal also seemed to share the view that the statute conferred absolute privilege when it described section 3 as giving 'complete protection'[165] to fair and accurate reports; and the Porter Committee regarded the point as settled[166]. Today there is no room for doubt: the current provision reinserts the word 'absolutely' for the sake of clarity[167].

The position that prevails today is therefore the exact opposite of that intended by the 1888 legislature; ironically it is also the position that the Government's Attorney General had, he thought, been careful to avoid. The main reason behind this frustration of legislative intention was the interpreters' assumption that each section of the 1888 Act must effect change in the common law. The assumption may have gained some support from the title of the Act, but the details of the parliamentary debates revealed that it was mistaken. In relation to section 3, at least, Parliament's aim in 1888 was better described as being to codify and lay down with certainty what newspapers were entitled to report.

161 Barnett, 'The Privilege of Defamation by Private Report of Public Official Proceedings' (1952) 31 *Oregon Law Review* 185 at 186.

162 *Hansard's Parliamentary Debates*, 3rd Series, vol 326, col 1276–77 (6 June 1888).

163 *Ibid* at col 1277.

164 Fisher and Strahan, *The Law of the Press*, 2nd edn (London, 1898) at 164.

165 *Farmer v Hyde* [1937] 1 KB 728 at 744.

166 *Report of the Committee on the Law of Defamation* (Cmd 7536, 1948) at para 92.

167 Defamation Act 1996, s 14. Cf the position in Ireland, where the Defamation Act 1961 re-enacted the 1888 Act. The Dail assumed that s 3 gave absolute privilege. For a fascinating explanation and analysis see McDonald, *Irish Law of Defamation*, 2nd edn (1989) at 170–72.

Although the synchronisation between the legislative process and the interpretation of its products left something to be desired, it is submitted that the end result was beneficial. The protection initially conferred on reports of court proceedings may have been grounded on the fact that the circumstances suggested that the defendant was not malicious. By 1888, however, this rationale based on malice had been superseded by a rationale based broadly on the interest of the community as a whole in having reports. Since the reason for protecting accurate reports was the benefit they gave to the community, it was difficult to see why the defendant's motive should be relevant: the benefit to the community in receiving the reports was the same whether the reporter was motivated by malice or not. Ultimately s 3 could be seen as in effect (if not intent) removing a restriction on privilege which had become irrelevant as the common law had developed.

The third condition, fairness and accuracy, was, at a general level, uncontroversial. A helpful paraphrase was given by the Supreme Court of Tennessee[168]. Accuracy required that the report 'contain the substance of the thing it undertakes to present'[169]. Fairness was easier to explain in negative terms:

> [The report] must not give undue prominence to inculpatory facts, and depress or minify such facts as would explain or qualify the former . . . and must not omit material points in favour of the complaining party, or introduce extraneous matters of a nature injurious to him.[170]

Fairness and accuracy might seem to be self-evident, but their application to specific factual situations revealed a surprising degree of complexity.

Accuracy, for instance, required not only a correct statement of allegations, but also that it be made clear that the defendant was merely reporting. Otherwise the defendant might seem to be adding his own authority to the statements[171]. Furthermore, the standard of accuracy was that of 'literatim et verbatim'[172] transcription. As one court put it, 'The only interest the plaintiff has in the accuracy of the report is that it shall be so far accurate as not to be more injurious to him than a verbatim report would be'[173].

Judging the accuracy and fairness of a report by reference to a complete transcription coloured the reporter's obligation. There was no need for him to describe the effect of what was said on hearers; and, although he was not prohibited from doing so[174], including such a description could

[168] *American Publishing Co v Gamble* 90 SW 1005 (Supreme Court of Tennessee, 1906).
[169] *Ibid* at 1008.
[170] *Ibid.*
[171] *Ilsley v Sentinel Co* 113 NW 425 (Supreme Court of Wisconsin, 1907).
[172] *Macdougall v Knight & Son* (1886) 17 QBD 636 at 640.
[173] *Boogher v Knapp* 11 SW 45 at 47 (Supreme Court of Missouri, 1889).
[174] *Cook v Alexander* [1974] QB 279.

make the report unfair[175]. On the other hand, the standard of verbatim transcription made omissions from the report perilous. It had never been a requirement that the report be verbatim[176], indeed the courts had acknowledged that 'omissions and abridgments were essential'[177]. A fair report might even consist of a bare statement of the result of the case[178]. But such concessions to brevity had to be seen alongside the assertion that '*Prima facie*, being incomplete [a report] is unfair, but this presumption may be rebutted'[179].

A further facet of fairness and accuracy was that the report only had to be fair and accurate in so far as it affected the claimant's reputation[180]. As the Court of Appeal put it in relation to the report of Parliamentary proceedings (where the identical rule applied), 'The [report] may be unfair to the government; it may be unfair to the opposition; it may be unfair to the speakers. But that is irrelevant in an action for defamation in which the sole question is, was it unfair to the plaintiff?'[181]

The limitation of fairness and accuracy to matters affecting the claimant's reputation could lighten the burden on reporters. If, for instance, a report omitted part of proceedings that did not relate to the claimant, the privilege was not lost[182]. On the other hand, the emphasis on the claimant's reputation could be unhelpful to defendants. In *Milissich v Lloyds*[183] the defendants published an account of the trial of an associate of the claimant containing the speech for the prosecution, a summary of the speech for the defence, the judge's summing up, the verdict and the sentence. The evidence was not summarised, but the defendant argued that the summing up should be presumed to give a fair summary of it. The Court of Appeal disagreed. Mellish LJ sympathised with the reporter's decision to use 'the Judge's abstract [of the evidence] instead of his own', but he was not prepared 'to lay it down as law that the summing up is necessarily fair, especially when the party aggrieved is a third person and not the prisoner, of whom the Judge, so far as fairness is concerned, is mainly thinking'[184]. Brett JA agreed that the summing up was not 'necessarily fair'[185]. It seemed that a report could be a fair summary of the proceedings as a criminal trial, but fail to be a fair summary as regards the claimant's reputation.

175 *Risk Allah Bey v Whitehurst* (1868) 18 LT(NS) 615 at 618.

176 *Lewis v Levy* (1858) 27 LJ (QB) 282 at 287 ('a fair an impartial (though not *verbatim*) report'), *Pinero v Goodlake* (1867) 15 LT (NS) 676.

177 *Turner v Sullivan* (1862) 6 LT (NS) 130 at 131.

178 *Duncan v Associated Scottish Newspapers Limited* 1929 SC 14 at 19 and 21.

179 *Milissich v Lloyds* (1877) 46 LJ (CP) 404 at 406 (per Baggallay JA).

180 *Ibid* at 407 (per Brett JA). Cf the approach of Lord Denman in the debates on the Newspaper Libel and Registration Act 1881, below p 263.

181 *Cook v Alexander* [1974] QB 279 at 291.

182 *Stone v Hutchinson Daily News* 266 P 78 (Supreme Court of Kansas, 1928).

183 (1877) 46 LJ (CP) 404.

184 *Ibid* at 406.

185 *Ibid* at 407.

The greatest controversy over fairness and accuracy arose where the reporter had chosen to report only the judgment of the court. In *Macdougall v Knight* the Court of Appeal and House of Lords could not agree, and the Court of Appeal refused to yield. When the question first came before the Court of Appeal[186], Lord Esher MR began his analysis by drawing an analogy with *Lewis v Levy*[187]. One point decided in *Lewis v Levy* had been that a publisher was justified in making three separate reports of proceedings that had taken place over three days; there was no need for the publisher to wait until the proceedings had ended[188]. Lord Esher MR deduced from the decision in *Lewis v Levy* that 'a fair report of any one distinct part of a trial'[189] was privileged. Bowen and Fry LJJ both concurred in this analogy with *Lewis v Levy*, but both judges prefaced their analyses with remarks about the benefit to the community in publishing what judges had said in court.

The House of Lords decided the case on a procedural point[190], but made some observations on the question of privilege for reports of judgments. Lord Halsbury LC was 'not prepared'[191] to say that such a report was privileged, because the judgment might not deal with all the evidence affecting the claimant's reputation. He was not even prepared to recognise a rebuttable presumption that the judgment gave a complete and impartial account of the evidence[192]. Lord Bramwell expressed similar doubts[193].

The claimant then brought a second action against the same defendant for different passages in the same reported judgment. The second action came before the Court of Appeal[194]. Lord Esher MR and Fry LJ made it clear that their views had not changed. Lord Esher MR reiterated the analysis based on *Lewis v Levy*[195]. So far as the doubts expressed in the House of Lords were concerned, he was dismissive: 'To speak candidly, I cannot make up my mind what their doubt was'[196]. Fry LJ emphasised the policy reasons supporting the privilege, stating that it was in line 'with the ordinary practice of the public press, with the usages of society, and with the convenience of Her Majesty's subjects'[197].

From a strictly analytical perspective the Court of Appeal's view was unconvincing. In particular, the use of *Lewis v Levy*[198] was questionable. There a full account of proceedings had been published in instalments.

186 *Macdougall v Knight & Son* (1886) 17 QBD 636.
187 (1858) 27 LJ (QB) 282.
188 *Ibid* at 290.
189 (1886) 17 QBD 636 at 639.
190 (1889) 14 App Cas 194.
191 *Ibid* at 200.
192 *Ibid*.
193 *Ibid* at 203.
194 (1890) 25 QBD 1.
195 (1858) 27 LJ (QB) 282.
196 *Ibid* at 9.
197 *Ibid* at 11.
198 *Ibid*.

That was very different from publishing only an incomplete account, but the Court of Appeal seemed content to derive a general proposition from the result of the former case to apply in the latter. Indeed, from a strictly analytical perspective one could criticise Lord Esher MR for failing to follow (or at least trying to distinguish) his own earlier, binding judgment in *Milissich v Lloyds*[199]. However, from a less strict perspective the policy reasons invoked by the Court of Appeal were convincing. They were also consistent with many earlier decisions in favouring privilege where it was for the benefit of the community[200]. The case is best seen as another attempt by the English courts to map the boundaries of the public sphere.

One further source of friction between partial coverage and fairness emerged in relation to proceedings that were remanded or appealed. The difficult question was whether reports of those proceedings would fail to be fair if they omitted later events. For example, in *Grimwade v Dicks*[201] the claimant was charged with a deception offence before magistrates and his case was remanded for three days. On his second appearance before the magistrates the case was dismissed. Three days later the defendant published a report of the claimant's first appearance. Field J did not give a special direction to the jury, simply asking them whether the report was fair and accurate[202]. They found that it was not, but we cannot be certain of the grounds for their finding because there was some evidence that the report was inaccurate in other respects than its failure to mention the later dismissal of the charge. In the United States, however, the point received more attention. One commentator elegantly pointed out that requiring reference to subsequent events effectively imposed a strict duty of investigative journalism on all reporters without addressing the desirability of such a duty as a matter of policy[203]. Her proposed solution was to impose liability only for a reckless disregard of subsequent events.

In England today the position is unclear. The statutory provision protecting reports covers only those 'published contemporaneously with the proceedings'[204]. Reports published later would therefore seem to be subject to the common law. It is submitted that the courts already have the tools at hand from earlier cases to determine whether such reports should be protected. The approach should be to assess fairness as at the date of proceedings, and then to apply a test of public benefit[205].

199 (1877) 46 LJ(CP) 404.

200 See discussion of, *inter alia, R v Wright* (1799) 8 D & E 293; *Ryalls v Leader* (1866) LR 1 Exch 296 above, at pp 253 and 243–244 respectively.

201 (1886) 2 TLR 627.

202 *Ibid* at 628.

203 Johnsen, 'When Truth and Accuracy Diverge: The Fair Report of a Dated Proceeding' (1982) 34 *Stanford Law Review* 1041 at 1053.

204 Defamation Act 1996 s 14.

205 See also the similar approach to reports of dated public meetings taken in *Tsikata v Newspaper Publishing plc* [1997] 1 All ER 655.

2. PARLIAMENTARY REPORTS

The treatment of fair reports of Parliamentary proceedings was initially dominated by two analytical concepts peculiar to Parliament: freedom of speech in Parliament and Parliamentary privilege. Freedom of speech in Parliament was enshrined in Article 9 of the Bill of Rights 1688, which stated that 'the freedom of speech and debates or proceedings in Parliament ought not to be impeached or questioned in any Court or place out of Parliament'.

In early cases dealing with reports of Parliamentary speeches published by Members, defendants argued, unsuccessfully, that publication of a Parliamentary speech was a Parliamentary proceeding involving freedom of speech[206]. The courts took the view that 'Parliamentary proceedings' were limited to speeches made in the chamber of each House of Parliament. There has not yet been any decision on the application of Article 9 where a Member's speech is reported by a third party so that the Member and reporter can be regarded as joint publishers[207]. It seems that the reporter could not take advantage of Article 9, but the position of the Member has divided academic opinion. The narrower view is that Article 9 protects only activities in Parliament; the report takes place outside Parliament and is therefore not protected[208]. The broader, more persuasive view, is that the Member could invoke Article 9[209]. It is submitted that the latter view must be the correct one: the threat of liability against a Member for a third party's report of his speech would contradict the express purpose of Article 9 by inhibiting the Member's freedom of speech in Parliament.

Questions of Parliamentary privilege arose when the House of Commons authorised the publication and sale of reports and other Parliamentary proceedings. In *Stockdale v Hansard*[210] the defendant, the Government's printer, claimed that the House of Commons had a Parliamentary privilege to order the publication of whatever proceedings it chose; and that documents published under such privilege could not be actionable in defamation. The Court of King's Bench rejected this argument, saying that the inherent Parliamentary privilege to publish material

206 *R v Lord Abingdon* (1794) 1 Esp 226; *R v Creevy* (1813) 1 M & S 273.

207 A person is jointly liable for the repetition of his defamatory words by a third person if he knew of or ought to have anticipated the repetition (*Slipper v BBC* [1991] 1 QB 283).

208 Davis, 'Parliamentary Broadcasting and the Law of Defamation' [1948] *University of Toronto Law Journal* 385.

209 Leopold, 'The Broadcasting of Parliament—The Legal Implications of Recent Developments' [1987] *PL* 524 at 527; Leopold, 'Parliamentary Privilege and the Broadcasting of Parliament' (1989) 9 *LS* 53 at 60.

210 (1839) 9 Ad & E 1. For background to the case see Stockdale, 'The Unnecessary Crisis: The Background to the Parliamentary Papers Act 1840' [1990] *PL* 30.

only extended to publication to its own Members[211]. Any wider publication was subject to the ordinary rules of defamation.

Parliament responded with legislation. The Parliamentary Papers Act 1840 conferred absolute privilege on those publishing a 'report, paper, vote or proceeding' authorised by Parliament[212], or copies thereof[213]. Publishers of extracts from these documents were granted qualified privilege[214]. One difficult question arising from the Act is its application to broadcasting. The Defamation Act 1952 s 9 extended the qualified privilege for publishers of extracts to broadcasters, but made no similar extension in respect of s 2 of the 1840 Act. The Porter Committee, whose recommendations formed the substance of the 1952 Act, did not mention the point[215]. Perhaps the most sensible approach would be to say that if the entire contents of a report, paper, vote or proceedings were broadcast, the broadcaster could be said to be publishing a 'copy' of the original, even though the format of the 'copy' was different.

The main limitation on the scope of the Parliamentary Papers Act, however, was that it applied only to official reports, etc the publication of which had been authorised by Parliament. For unofficial, unauthorised reports protection had to be sought elsewhere. A statutory provision was unlikely as there was a long history of Parliamentary hostility towards unofficial reports of its proceedings. This took the form of resolutions and Standing Orders prohibiting unofficial reports[216]; as late as 1762 the Standing Orders were enforced by committing the printer of a newspaper in breach to the custody of the Serjeant at Arms[217]. It was only a remarkable chain of events that broke Parliament's stranglehold[218]. Unofficial reports had been appearing in newspapers with increasing frequency since 1768. In 1771 the House of Commons decided to prosecute eight printers for breach of the Standing Orders and the printers of the offending newspapers were ordered to appear before the House of Commons. Three printers took refuge in the City of London. When messengers from the House of Commons sought to remove them, officials of the City of London refused to allow it. Two City officials were sent to the Tower of London as a result. Meanwhile, the newspapers of the defiant printers continued to publish Parliamentary reports. The House of Commons realised that it had failed to stamp out unofficial reports and grudgingly

[211] *Lake v King* (1670) 1 Wms Saund (1845 edn) 131.
[212] Parliamentary Papers Act 1840 s 1.
[213] *Ibid*, s 2.
[214] *Ibid*, s 3.
[215] *Report of the Committee on the Law of Defamation* (Cmd 7536, 1948) at paras 92–93.
[216] For examples of such resolutions and Standing Orders see Leopold, 'The Broadcasting of Parliament—The Legal Implications of Recent Developments' [1987] *PL* 524, n 1.
[217] Thomas, 'The Beginning of Parliamentary Reporting in Newspapers, 1768–1774' (1959) 74 *English Historical Review* 623 at 624.
[218] Thomas, *ibid*; Black, *The English Press 1621–1861* (Stroud, 2001) 127–38.

accepted the situation. After 1771 there were no further attempts to enforce the Standing Orders against unofficial reports, although the Orders themselves were not revoked until 1971[219]. Reporters were not allowed to take notes until 1783. Even as late as 1839 the Court of King's Bench described unofficial Parliamentary reports as being allowed 'by sufferance'[220] and exposing the reporter to 'the danger of Newgate [prison] for breach of privilege'[221].

In *Wason v Walter*[222] the common law rose to the challenge by granting protection to unofficial fair reports of Parliamentary proceedings. The judgment of the Court of Queen's Bench, delayed in order to finalise in writing this decision on a point of 'importance and novelty'[223], was remarkable for its scope and depth of analysis. The crucial step in the Court's reasoning was that reports of Parliamentary proceedings should be treated like reports of judicial proceedings for two reasons. First, the circumstances of publication negatived malice[224]. Second, there was 'a preponderance of general good over partial and occasional evil' in protecting publication[225]. Great emphasis was placed on the 'preponderance of general good': the Court went on to say that it was of 'paramount public and national importance that the proceedings of the houses of parliament shall be communicated to the public, who have the deepest interest in knowing what passes within their walls'[226]. 'The public' here meant 'every member of the educated portion of the community'[227].

The analogy with reports of court proceedings continued when the Court considered what limitations should apply: it held that the conditions safeguarding the privilege for reports of judicial proceedings against abuse should also safeguard reports of parliamentary proceedings[228]. So, for instance, there was no protection for partial or garbled reports[229]; nor, presumably, for reports published maliciously[230].

[219] Leopold, 'The Broadcasting of Parliament—The Legal Implications of Recent Developments' [1987] *PL* 524, n 1.

[220] *Stockdale v Hansard* (1839) 9 Ad & E 1 at 212 (per Patteson J).

[221] *Ibid* at 153 (per Lord Denman CJ).

[222] (1868) LR 4 QB 73.

[223] *Ibid* at 82.

[224] *Ibid* at 87.

[225] *Ibid* at 88.

[226] *Ibid* at 89.

[227] *Ibid* at 90.

[228] *Ibid* at 95.

[229] *Ibid* at 94; *Cook v Alexander* [1974] QB 279.

[230] Cf Loveland, *Political Libels: A Comparative Study* (Oxford, 2000) at 29, where it is argued that it is not 'entirely clear' whether the privilege conferred is absolute or qualified. However, the Court's statement that 'whatever would deprive a report of the proceedings in a court of justice of immunity will equally apply to a report of proceedings in parliament' (p 95) seems to make it clear that qualified privilege was conferred.

Whilst its analytical side was important, the decision in *Wason v Walter*[231] also had a broader significance. The public's relationship with politics had evolved to the extent that by the later eighteenth century it was possible to identify 'public politics' and the influence of public opinion[232]. The relationship had developed further just before the decision in *Wason v Walter*, when the 1867 Reform Act had given the vote to a larger number of people than ever before[233]. The judges of the Court of Queen's Bench could scarcely have been ignorant of this, especially given the interest of Cockburn CJ in electoral law: in the 1830s he had had an extensive practice in electoral petitions[234], and had published a work on electoral law[235]. So the decision in 1868 to grant protection to unofficial reports of Parliamentary proceedings could be seen as more than simply an application of the existing principles governing reports of judicial proceedings. With its emphasis on the public's participation and involvement in parliamentary matters, *Wason v Walter* could also be seen as an attempt to develop the law of defamation in line with the major political changes of its time.

3. REPORTS OF PUBLIC MEETINGS

Qualified privilege for reports of public meetings was first acknowledged as a possibility in 1876; by 1881 it had become enshrined in statute. Before 1876 the courts had rejected the idea. In *Davison v Duncan*[236], for instance, Lord Campbell CJ observed that granting qualified privilege to a report of a public meeting 'would extend the privilege to an alarming extent'[237]. Even where statute required a medical officer's report made at a public meeting to be printed and made available for sale to the public, the Court of Exchequer refused to grant protection to a newspaper publishing an account of the meeting including a defamatory allegation in the medical officer's report[238].

In 1876 the judges' attitude softened at least to the extent of recognising the possibility of protection for reports of public meetings. In *Purcell v Sowler*[239] the defendant had published a report of a public meeting of the board of guardians of the Altrincham poor union, at which defamatory allegations had been made against the claimant. In particular it was

[231] (1868) LR 4 QB 73.
[232] Black, *The English Press 1621–1861* (Stroud, 2001) at 132.
[233] Loveland, *Political Libels: A Comparative Study* (Oxford, 2000) at 28.
[234] Stephen and Lee (eds) *Dictionary of National Biography* (Oxford, 1917) vol IV at 634.
[235] Cockburn, *Questions on Election Law, arising on the Reform Act* (London, 1834).
[236] (1857) 7 El & Bl 229.
[237] *Ibid* at 231.
[238] *Popham v Pickburn* (1862) 7 H & N 891.
[239] (1876) 1 CPD 781; (1877) 2 CPD 215.

alleged that the claimant had neglected his duties as the medical officer of the local workhouse. The defendant argued that the publication was privileged as being a report of a matter of public interest. The judgment of the Divisional Court, delivered by Brett J, began in a slightly confusing way, by stating that the question was whether the matter was 'a fair comment on a matter of public interest'[240]. This was difficult to understand, since the report was not a comment, and counsel had never sought to argue that it was. The focus of the judgment, however, was on whether the matter was of 'general public interest'. The Court concluded that it was not, and laid down a strict test, requiring 'either that the person of whom the defamatory matter is written was a person whose position and character are of general interest to the whole country, or that the subject-matter dealt with is one of interest to the whole country'[241]. On the facts, neither limb of the test was satisfied: the claimant only had 'a public character of a limited kind and in a limited district'[242], and his duties were confined to a limited area.

The Court of Appeal[243] upheld the Divisional Court's decision but could not agree with its reasons. The Court of Appeal took the view that the conduct of a medical officer in a poor-law union was a matter of public concern: it was not essential for the matter to relate to the conduct of national government. Cockburn CJ tentatively said that 'he was by no means saying that the proceedings of different bodies to whom part of the administration of the public business of the country is committed would not be matter of general discussion and publication'[244]. However, on the facts the report was not protected because it related to an *ex parte* charge; such charges should be subjected to a preliminary inquiry behind closed doors before being made public.

Despite the disagreement between the Divisional Court and the Court of Appeal over the details, both courts shared the same sense of purpose: each saw its task as being to define what information belonged in the public sphere. Also, neither court regarded the question as a simple factual one: as Mellish LJ pointed out, the fact that the public had been admitted to the meeting did not bind the court[245]. Instead, each court formulated evaluative criteria to identify what information was truly public. The essential difference between them was that whilst the Divisional Court's test depended purely on subject-matter, the Court of Appeal introduced an additional filter relating to the quality of the information.

[240] (1876) 1 CPD 781 at 787.
[241] *Ibid* at 788.
[242] *Ibid*.
[243] (1877) 2 CPD 215.
[244] *Ibid* at 219.
[245] *Ibid* at 221. See the similar approaches to reports of judicial proceedings in *Duncan v Thwaites* (1824) 3 B & C 556, *Ryalls v Leader* (1866) LR 1 Exch 296.

Parliament's interest in the subject prevented further judicial elaboration of the criteria set out in *Purcell v Sowler*[246]. A Select Committee of the House of Commons was appointed in 1879 to inquire into the law of newspaper libel. The Committee gathered materials and heard evidence, but ran out of time before it could report[247]. A second Committee, appointed in 1880, decided to make use of those materials and evidence. The first draft of its Report was proposed by Hutchinson, a Radical MP and one of the proprietors of the *Halifax Courier* newspaper[248]. The draft began its treatment of the protection for reports of public meetings with a comparison:

> In Scotland, for example, newspapers are more exempt from liability with respect to reports of public meetings than are the English and Irish journals, and one of the most important parts of the subject is the degree in which there should be reasonable immunity as regards such reports.[249]

It went on to recommend that fair and accurate reports of public meetings published without malice should be privileged 'when the publication of the matter complained of is for the public benefit'[250]. However, such protection should be conditional on the newspaper having inserted any reasonable letter or statement of explanation or contradiction at the claimant's request. These proposals formed the basis of what was to become the Newspaper Libel and Registration Act 1881 s 2.

An amendment to the draft report removed the comparison between the law in Scotland and the law in England and Ireland[251]. Hutchinson, however, had not forgotten it. In his speech introducing the Second Reading of the Newspaper Libel and Registration Bill (which embodied the Select Committee's recommendations), he said that the 'strongest argument'[252] for the Bill was that it brought English law into line with the position in Scotland. Another member of the Select Committee, Cameron, was also struck by the comparison with Scotland: seven years later he referred to evidence before the 1880 Select Committee that Scots law gave generous protection to reports of public meetings[253].

It appeared, therefore, that one powerful reason supporting the 1881 legislation was that it followed the successful Scottish model which had been outlined to the 1879 Select Committee. However, it is a great pity that the evidence given to the 1879 Committee was not preserved, because the

[246] (1877) 2 CPD 215.

[247] *Report from the Select Committee on the Law of Libel, House of Commons Parliamentary Papers 1880*, vol IX, p 301 (Paper 284) at iii.

[248] Stenton (ed), *Who's Who of British Members of Parliament, Volume I, 1832–1885* (1976) at 206.

[249] *Report from the Select Committee on the Law of Libel, House of Commons Parliamentary Papers 1880*, vol IX, p 301 (Paper 284) at v.

[250] *Ibid.*

[251] *Ibid* at vi.

[252] *Hansard's Parliamentary Debates*, 3rd Series, vol 261, col 220 (11 May 1881).

[253] *Hansard's Parliamentary Debates*, 3rd Series, vol 326, col 1261 (6 June 1888).

presentation of the law of Scotland made there did not correspond with the textbooks. Borthwick, writing in 1826, gave no indication of protection for reports of public meetings; indeed he suggested that the English law relating to reports of judicial and parliamentary proceedings only applied in Scotland 'with considerable abatement'[254]. A Scottish textbook published several years after the 1881 Act argued that it was 'reasonable'[255] to protect reports of public meetings, but the state of the common law in Scotland was 'not clear'[256]; the only dicta seemed to be against protection. It is difficult to escape the conclusion that the evidence to the Select Committee exaggerated the differences between English and Scots law.

Apart from the removal of the allusion to Scots law, Hutchinson's draft report was effectively adopted by the Select Committee. Hutchinson then brought forward the Committee's recommendations on reports of public meetings and other matters in the Newspaper Libel and Registration Bill[257].

When he introduced the Bill for its Second Reading Hutchinson articulated the fundamental role of the press, from which the protection for reports of public meetings flowed:

> A newspaper was the record and expression of what took place in public, of all political life, and of all municipal and social activity—in short, it was the record of everything outside the domain of strictly domestic intercourse[258].

The debate of clause 2 on the Second Reading focussed on the meaning of 'public meeting'. Some criticism was levelled at the phrase because of its alleged vagueness[259]. The slightly defensive response was that these words 'had been hit upon as the best that could be chosen'[260]; the Attorney General, who had chaired the Select Committee, invited those who made the criticism to 'be good enough to define what was a public meeting'[261].

Other contributors to the debate, however, went beyond questions of linguistic precision, and identified fundamental difficulties surrounding the concept of a public meeting. One difficulty was where admission was by ticket to, say, a political meeting[262]. More fundamental questions arose where a meeting of public importance was accessible only to a defined class: for instance, the Bill seemed not to apply to reports of shareholders'

[254] Borthwick, *A Treatise on the Law of Libel and Slander* (Edinburgh, 1826) at 205.
[255] Dykes, *Cooper on Defamation and Verbal Injury* (Edinburgh, 1906) at 182.
[256] *Ibid* at 183.
[257] *House of Commons Parliamentary Papers 1881*, vol IV p 223. The Bill was ordered to be prepared and brought in on 8 January 1881 and read the same day for the first time. (See *Journals of the House of Commons*, vol 136, pp 12 and 14 respectively.)
[258] *Hansard's Parliamentary Debates*, 3rd Series, vol 261, col 218–19 (11 May 1881).
[259] *Ibid* at col 220 (Inderwick) and col 228 (Labouchere).
[260] *Ibid* at col 223 (Cowen).
[261] *Ibid* at col 229.
[262] *Ibid* at col 226 (Ashton Dilke).

meetings[263], but that was 'the very class to which it was most necessary often, for the sake of the public, that attention should be called'[264]. Perhaps the most striking critique disregarded the question of general admission altogether and proposed that reports of proceedings of 'public bodies through which public money was expended'[265] should be privileged.

When clause 2 was considered by the House of Commons in Committee, the disputes over what constituted a 'public meeting' continued. One suggestion was that, to qualify as a public meeting more than twenty people had to be present[266]. Hutchinson objected to this, as it would tend to exclude meetings of churchwardens, vestries and other local authorities[267]. The main amendment proposed was that a meeting was public if reporters were admitted[268], but this was defeated[269].

The variety of ideas and approaches that the House of Commons brought to bear on the issue of 'public meeting' went far beyond a quibble about the meaning of words. Hutchinson's claim that a newspaper should record everything public provided a starting point, but deciding what belonged in the public sphere provoked profound theoretical disagreement. As with reports of judicial proceedings the idea that the report was merely extending the area of publicity enjoyed some support, but powerful arguments supported the more evaluative approach.

Clause 2 progressed through a Third Reading in the Commons without further debate[270]. In the House of Lords the focus of attention moved to the 'fair and accurate' requirement. In Lord Denman's view accuracy was too difficult a test, and clause 2 was therefore 'too hard'[271] on newspapers. He would have preferred a test of substantial truth, but the amendment was rejected[272]. In the end s 2 of the Act contained exactly the same wording as clause 2 of the original Bill.

The first case under s 2[273] concerned a report of a public election meeting, which the claimant admitted was fair and accurate. So there was no need to consider either of the matters that had troubled Parliament. Instead the dispute was over the requirement that 'publication of the matter complained of is for the public benefit'. In directing the jury Grantham J had asked them to decide, 'Is it on the whole for the public benefit that people should know what is publicly said at a public meeting?'[274] The

263 *Ibid* at col 222 (Gregory, a member of the 1880 Select Committee).
264 *Ibid* at col 227 (M'Carthy).
265 *Ibid* at col 225 (Macliver).
266 *Ibid* at col 504 (Makins) (13 May 1881).
267 *Ibid*.
268 *Ibid* at col 503 (Inderwick).
269 *Ibid* at col 505.
270 *Hansard's Parliamentary Debates*, 3rd Series, vol 265, col 603 (22 August 1881).
271 *Ibid* at col 718 (23 August 1881).
272 *Ibid* at col 813 (24 August 1881).
273 *Pankhurst v Sowler* (1886) 3 TLR 193.
274 *Ibid* at 195.

Divisional Court held that this was not a correct direction on the public benefit requirement: the Act required the jury to decide whether reporting the particular accusation was for the public benefit.

Although the public benefit requirement had not been subject to analysis in the Parliamentary debates, it had received attention in the Select Committee. The first draft of the report by Hutchinson had recommended granting privilege where 'publication of the matter complained of is for the public benefit'. Another member of the Committee, Courtney, proposed an amendment granting privilege instead where the publication of 'such Report' was for the public benefit[275]. Hutchinson, Courtney and Cameron favoured the amendment, but the other five members of the Committee present were against it. Perhaps Hutchinson did not think the point of much importance, for he made no attempt to introduce this form of words as the Bill went through Parliament. Indeed, it may be that he saw Courtney's failed amendment as simply putting his own view more clearly: when a claimant sued it was not distorting language to say that he was complaining about 'the report'. Whatever Hutchinson's view, the interpretation of the section given in *Pankhurst v Sowler*[276] highlighted the frustrations of legislation. But for two votes in the Select Committee, the Divisional Court's hands would have been tied.

Pankhurst v Sowler was the first reported case on s 2. It was also the last: in 1888 the Law of Libel Amendment Act repealed s 2 of the 1881 Act and replaced it with a new defence[277]. The first obvious difference between the 1881 provision and its 1888 counterpart was length: the 1888 provision was twice as long. The main reason for the difference was that the 1888 Act, consistently from its first appearance to enactment, listed those meetings and documents a fair report of which, in a newspaper, would be privileged. In the Bill as first presented[278] the privilege was given to fair reports of public meetings and meetings of vestries, town councils, school boards, boards of guardians, committees of any of these, select committees of either House of Parliament and others. There was also, originally, a more general category of reports 'of any other duly and legally constituted body or persons acting in a public capacity and for public purposes'[279]. As with the 1881 Act, the privilege was lost by proof

[275] *Report from the Select Committee on the Law of Libel, House of Commons Parliamentary Papers 1880*, vol IX, p 301 (Paper 284) at vi.

[276] (1886) 3 TLR 193.

[277] Law of Libel Amendment Act 1888 ss 2 and 4.

[278] *House of Commons Parliamentary Papers 1887*, vol III p 141 (Bill 340). The Bill received its First Reading on 27 July 1887, but the Second Reading was deferred (*Journals of the House of Commons* vol 142, p 404). It was reintroduced in the 1888 session, receiving its First and Second Readings on 10 February and 30 April without debate (*Journals of the House of Commons* vol 143, pp 18 and 189 respectively).

[279] This part of the clause was deleted under one of several amendments specified by the Attorney General as the price of government support: *Hansard's Parliamentary Debates*, 3rd Series, vol 326, col 1293 (6 June 1888).

of malice against the defendant and conditional on printing a reasonable statement of explanation if the claimant requested it. Unlike the 1881 Act, however, the 1888 provision in its original form did not require the publication to be for the public benefit.

The proposal to revisit a point so recently addressed by Parliament provoked hostility in the House of Commons. This was partly due to the interest of some of those promoting the Bill. Sir Algernon Borthwick was the proprietor of the *Morning Post* and President of the Press Newspaper Fund[280]. Wilfrid Lawson was later to become managing proprietor of the *Daily Telegraph* and Chairman of the Newspaper Proprietors Association[281]. Cameron was the son of a newspaper proprietor and was a former editor of the *North British Daily Mail*[282]. As one Member put it, the fact that the Bill was being brought forward by Members connected with the Press 'created a suspicion at once that it was to avert inconvenient actions which they thought ought not to be brought against them'[283]. Even when the Bill was on the verge of becoming law one Member tried to stop its progress, emphasising that 'it was promoted by a little knot of interested newspaper proprietors who took a vehement interest in it'[284].

There was also concern that the case for repealing the 1881 provision had not been made[285]. The earlier provision was thought to work 'tolerably well'[286], had not been complained about by the public[287] and offered sufficient protection for newspapers[288]. As one Member put it:

> The law was placed on a satisfactory basis by the Act of 1881, and if they were to go further in the way of privileged legislation for the Press, they would find the Press were like the Irish tenants—always coming forward with a request for more.[289]

The arguments advanced in favour of the Bill were both practical and theoretical. On the practical side it was claimed that the law was in effect unfair to newspapers in several respects. First, newspapers were vulnerable to persons who were 'perpetually on the watch for errors, and then went to a class of attorneys who were always on the look out for such matters'[290]. These claimants could make the newspaper's mistake 'worth more to them than a government annuity'[291]. Secondly, judges and lawyers

[280] Stenton and Lees (eds), *Who's Who of British Members of Parliament; Volume II 1886–1918* (1978) at 39.
[281] *Ibid* at 210.
[282] *Ibid* at 54.
[283] *Hansard's Parliamentary Debates,* 3rd Series, vol 326, col 1245 (Anderson) (6 June 1888).
[284] *Hansard's Parliamentary Debates,* 3rd Series, vol 329, col 1552 (Healy) (3 August 1888).
[285] *Hansard's Parliamentary Debates,* 3rd Series, vol 326, col 1244 (Anderson) (6 June 1888).
[286] *Ibid* at col 1267 (Howell).
[287] *Ibid* at col 1245 (Anderson).
[288] *Ibid* at col 1239 (Kelly).
[289] *Ibid* at col 1269 (Coghill).
[290] *Ibid* at col 1249 (Sir Algernon Borthwick).
[291] *Ibid* at col 1254 (Jennings).

were generally hostile to the press: 'the notion had appeared to have come into the minds of many of the learned Judges and of his learned Friends that newspaper proprietors were a part of the community who had no rights and duties whatever'[292]. This view of the judicial attitude to the press explained why the Bill enumerated those bodies reports of whose proceedings were privileged, rather than leaving judges to interpret the phrase 'public meeting'. Third, the rule that costs followed the event caused hardship to newspaper proprietors when a verdict of a trivial sum of damages was made against them[293].

The broader arguments advanced in support of the Bill made general claims about the benefits of the Press: Sir Algernon Borthwick, for instance, described the press as 'one of the greatest features of the public life in the country'[294]. But there were also more specific arguments about the theoretical benefits of the measure as compared with the 1881 Act. The first was that events since 1881 had made the Act outdated:

> The franchise had been had enlarged and there were more public meetings. New bodies had been created, and more were about to be created, and it was necessary that these should be protected.[295]

The second argument amounted to a direct attack on the 1881 provision. That provision, it was said, went no further than the common law: 'it really conferred no benefit on newspapers . . . somehow or other, the Parliament of 1881 failed to carry out the intention it had before it'[296]. If this criticism was right, the 1888 Act could be seen as correcting earlier legislative ineptness.

However the criticism did not really do justice to the 1881 Act. Certainly Parliament had not got itself into a muddle—the Act reproduced virtually word for word the recommendations of the Select Committee. The Select Committee believed that its recommendations accomplished a reform; and the 1881 Bill's main promoter described s 2 as a 'concession'[297] to the press. They were not mistaken. It was true that *Purcell v Sowler*[298] had tentatively allowed that reports of public meetings containing defamatory matter might be privileged if publication was for the public benefit, but these were dicta. There was no authority protecting fair reports of public meetings at common law. Of course, if the 1881 Act had not occurred, the courts might have gone on to grant protection for reports of public meetings in the way suggested by *Purcell v Sowler*. This development might even have been likely. On the other hand, it should be remembered

292 *Hansard's Parliamentary Debates,* 3rd Series, vol 326, at col 1242 (Addison).
293 *Ibid.*
294 *Ibid* at col 1248.
295 *Ibid* at 1257 (Darling).
296 *Ibid* at 1256 (Darling).
297 *Hansard's Parliamentary Debates,* 3rd Series, vol 261, col 219 (11 May 1881).
298 (1877) 2 CPD 215.

that Cockburn CJ seemed most strongly in favour of a privilege for reports of local government proceedings, and he had died in 1880. At the very least the Act of 1881 converted the common law chance of protection into a statutory certainty: after its enactment newspapers could have new-found confidence of a defence when publishing certain types of reports.

The attack on the 1881 Act might also have been taken as an implicit criticism of its promoters. One of those promoters, Cameron, was still a Member of Parliament, and was also a promoter of the 1888 Bill. He claimed that the problem with the 1881 Act was not the statute itself, but the courts' interpretation of it, which had been too narrow. The new Bill was proposed 'to amend the interpretation'[299]. Although he did not go into which part of the 1881 Act had been too narrowly interpreted, there was only one reported case: *Pankhurst v Sowler*[300]. There it had been held that the requirement that publication 'of the matter complained of' was for the public benefit required the defendant to show that the defamatory language was reported for the benefit of the public. This particular phrase had troubled Cameron earlier, when he was a member of the 1880 Select Committee: he had voted to amend it so that it said 'publication of such Report' was for the benefit of the public, but the proposal had been defeated by two votes[301].

If the 1888 Bill was designed to correct the decision in *Pankhurst v Sowler*[302] its approach was radical: the requirement of public benefit had been dropped altogether, and replaced with a list of bodies whose proceedings could be reported under the protection of the privilege. In essence Cameron seemed to be saying that the decision in *Pankhurst v Sowler* had placed a heavier burden on defendants than the authors of s 2 had intended. The public benefit test in the 1881 had been intended to allow the courts to privilege reports of proceedings of local government bodies, etc, but it had taken on a life of its own that the 1888 Bill intended to cut short.

Unfortunately for Cameron, his Parliamentary colleagues were enthusiastic about the independent requirement of 'public benefit'. One of them, for instance, described it as 'one of the great safeguards . . . against licentious practices'[303]. As a condition of Government support the Attorney General had insisted that the clause should not protect matter not published in the public interest[304]. This, however, was not considered by the House to be adequate: it was argued that 'public benefit' and 'public interest' might be 'divergent'[305]. In particular, there was concern that

299 *Hansard's Parliamentary Debates,* 3rd Series, vol 326, col 1261 (6 June 1888).
300 (1886) 3 TLR 193.
301 See above, p 264.
302 (1886) 3 TLR 193.
303 *Hansard's Parliamentary Debates,* 3rd Series, vol 326, col 1247 (Anderson) (6 June 1888).
304 *Ibid* at col 1265.
305 *Ibid* at col 1266 (Howell).

'public interest' might be taken to mean what the public was interested in. When the House of Commons considered the Bill in Committee an amendment adding the requirement of 'public benefit' was added[306]. A later attempt to substitute 'public importance' for both public interest and public benefit failed[307].

However, the story did not end there. In the House of Lords several amendments suggested by the National Association of Journalists were considered at the Committee stage[308]. One of these was that the privilege should not apply to 'matter not published in the interest of the public', and that the public benefit test be removed. The amendment was agreed[309]. An unsuccessful attempt was then made to reinstate the test of public benefit during the Third Reading of the Bill in House of Lords[310]. The Bill's promoter based his opposition to the public benefit test unashamedly on journalists' interests: 'What the journalists wanted was that the law should be clear, and that they should know what they could publish'[311]. In his view 'public concern' was the test that the journalists were happy with, so it should be law. The Commons, however, held firm, reintroducing the public benefit requirement when the Bill came back to them.

The basic structure of the 1888 Act remains in place today, but it has undergone some minor modifications. For instance, there is no longer a requirement of publication in a newspaper[312]. Perhaps the most interesting development was the addition of a category of reports where there was no requirement on the publisher to publish a statement of explanation or contradiction[313]. This was the idea of the Porter Committee, and found its way into law in the Defamation Act 1952. The reason behind the new category could perhaps be best described as editorial: there was a risk that so many people might want to respond to reports of some proceedings (such as those in international tribunals) that a newspaper would be swamped with tedious material that it was legally obliged to publish[314].

Retaining the structure from the 1888 Act has had two important consequences. The first is that the requirement of publishing statements of contradiction or explanation applies to books, films, and other media where it seems to have less coherence than it does in relation to newspapers with their core of regular readers. The second is that the courts continue to grapple with the two key controversial concepts used in the 1888 Act: 'public meeting' and 'public benefit'. Recently the House of Lords made it

306 *Ibid* at col 1307.
307 *Hansard's Parliamentary Debates,* 3rd Series, vol 327, col 760 (20 June 1888).
308 *Hansard's Parliamentary Debates,* 3rd Series, vol 329, col 308 (24 July 1888).
309 *Ibid* at col 310.
310 *Ibid* at col 1387 (3 August 1888).
311 *Ibid* at col 1388.
312 Defamation Act 1996 s 15.
313 See now Defamation Act 1996 s 15 and Schedule 1, Part 1.
314 *Report of the Committee on the Law of Defamation* (Cmd 7536, 1948) at para 107.

clear that 'public meeting' needed to be interpreted in the context of contemporary society, and was not limited to the meaning that it had in 1888[315]. This was rather ironic given that Members of Parliament in the 1880s could not agree among themselves what 'public meeting' meant.

In particular the courts still have to solve the problem (that Parliament avoided) as to when restrictions on admission prevent a meeting from being public. A press conference seems to be a special case, because there the intention of the organisers is to maximise the amount of publicity that the proceedings receive[316]. Limiting those attending to holders of freely available tickets, or to those paying an admission fee also seems acceptable: both situations seem to be covered by the statutory language 'whether admission is restricted or not'. The more difficult cases are where admission is limited to a predetermined class. For instance, in the 1880s Parliament was concerned that shareholders' meetings fell outside the definition, but, rather surprisingly, in *Ponsford v The 'Financial Times' (Limited)*[317] they were included. A fair report of a meeting of shareholders is now specifically protected by statute[318]. Restriction on the basis of the membership of a society remains controversial. In *Khan v Ahmed*[319] Lynskey J held that a meeting of the Pakistani Students' Society was a 'public meeting'. The Court of Appeal of Northern Ireland has said that this was wrong[320], but the House of Lords in the same case expressed no view[321].

'Public benefit' has also required judicial exposition. It seems that one key factor is the quality of the information reported: it is not for the public benefit to report unsubstantiated charges[322], and a report of proceedings omitting later relevant developments might also be difficult to justify. On the other hand, the importance of the subject-matter might justify reporting information of indifferent quality[323].

Ultimately the question that the courts face now is the same as the one they faced previously in relation to reports of judicial and Parliamentary proceedings: what belongs in the public sphere? Parliamentary intervention definitively placed certain reports in the public sphere, but, as the debates revealed, the Members themselves soon began to disagree about what was truly public: no general principle could be found. It was, and still is, a

315 *McCartan Turkington Breen (a firm) v Times Newspapers Ltd* [2001] 2 AC 277 particularly at 296 (per Lord Steyn).

316 *Ibid* at 292 (per Lord Bingham).

317 (1900) 16 TLR 248.

318 Defamation Act 1996 s 15, Schedule 1, Part 2, para 13.

319 [1957] 2 QB 149.

320 *McCartan Turkington Breen (a firm) v Times Newspapers Ltd* [1998] NI 358 at 373.

321 *McCartan Turkington Breen (a firm) v Times Newspapers Ltd* [2001] 2 AC 277.

322 *Ponsford v The 'Financial Times' (Limited)* (1900) 16 TLR 248.

323 *Tsikata v Newspaper Publishing plc* [1997] 1 All ER 655.

complex philosophical/political question ill-suited to traditional legal analysis. All that the courts really have to guide them is (now) the constitutional protection for freedom of expression[324] and their own philosophical/political convictions. The certainty that the National Association of Journalists asked Parliament for in 1888 remains unobtainable.

4. REPORTS OF PUBLIC DOCUMENTS

As well as protecting reports of proceedings the common law also shielded reports of certain documents. The origin of this category of qualified privilege was the House of Lords' decision in *Fleming v Newton*[325], an appeal from Scotland. The defendants were the directors of the Scottish Mercantile Society, a trade protection organisation that supplied its members with information about individuals' creditworthiness. Such information might be obtained from a variety of sources, but the information about the claimant had been obtained from a register of protests made against those who had dishonoured promissory notes. The register had been set up by a statute which required that it must be 'patent to all the lieges'.

Counsel for the defendant advanced two distinct grounds on which the publication was privileged. First they argued that registration of a protest was 'nearly equivalent to a judgment in the Scotch Courts'[326]. An extract from the register could, therefore, be seen as an abbreviated report of legal proceedings. Second, the register was 'a public document . . . open for the inspection of every body; it [was] therefore essentially public and the printing it . . . could not divest it of its public character'[327].

The House of Lords found for the defendant, delivering a judgment that interwove the two grounds counsel had advanced. Thus, Lord Cottenham LC asserted that registration had the effect of a judgment, and it was certainly lawful to publish a judgment[328]. On the other hand, greater weight seemed to be given to the 'public document' argument:

> I found my opinion upon this, that the publication of the fact proposed to be inserted in the [defendant]'s lists, has been made by the act of Parliament in certain Registers, the contents of which are public property, and the publication of them authorised.[329]

324 *McCartan Turkington Breen (a firm) v Times Newspapers Ltd* [2001] 2 AC 277 at 296–97 (per Lord Steyn).
325 (1848) 1 HLC 363.
326 *Ibid* at 366.
327 *Ibid* at 369.
328 *Ibid* at 378.
329 *Ibid* at 377.

He also emphasised the statutory language 'patent to all the lieges'. In his view this showed that any individual could search the Register and tell others what he found; here, in effect, the members of the Mercantile Society had appointed a common agent to do the search for them[330].

The first attempt to apply *Fleming v Newton*[331] suggested that it was viewed with ambivalence. In *Williams v Smith*[332] the proprietors of the *Hatters' Gazette* were sued for publishing the claimant's name in a list of those against whom county court judgments had been obtained. The information had been taken correctly from the register of county court judgments, but the claimant objected that the publication suggested that he had not satisfied the judgment. The question for the Divisional Court was whether the words were capable of bearing the innuendo that the judgment was not satisfied. However the Court also went on to consider *Fleming v Newton*. Pollock B expressed his agreement with Lord Cottenham's speech, saying that the earlier decision placed 'the publication of a mere extract from a record of judgments kept pursuant to statute on the same footing as a fair report of a judicial inquiry'[333]. On the facts of the case before him, however, there had not been publication of a 'mere extract' because the *Hatters' Gazette* was supplying information about creditworthiness. Furthermore, there was another distinction from *Fleming v Newton*: in the earlier case the statement was true at the time of publication, here it was false. Manisty J agreed, repeating some of the analysis.

Later courts found the analysis of *Fleming v Newton*[334] in *Williams v Smith*[335] very unconvincing. As Lord Esher MR put it, the reasoning in *Williams*' case was 'virtually in opposition to that of Lord Cottenham'[336]. It is submitted that Lord Esher MR was right, and that both grounds of distinction put forward in *Williams v Smith* were illusory. First, the context of publication in *Williams* and *Fleming* was identical: both cases concerned mercantile circulation of information about individuals' creditworthiness. Second, there was no finding about truth in *Fleming's* case, and certainly no mention of it in Lord Cottenham's judgment[337]. The Court of Appeal subsequently distinguished and disapproved *Williams v Smith*, but did not formally overrule it[338]. This disapproval seems to have been enough to prevent any further use of the case.

330 *Ibid* at 379.
331 *Ibid.*
332 (1888) 22 QBD 134.
333 *Ibid* at 139.
334 (1848) 1 HLC 363.
335 (1888) 22 QBD 134.
336 *Searles v Scarlett* [1892] 2 QB 56 at 62.
337 *Annaly v The Trade Auxiliary Co (Limited)* (1890) 26 LR Ir 11 at 27.
338 *Searles v Scarlett* [1892] 2 QB 56.

The privilege was limited to accurate extracts from the register or document in question, a limitation that could favour or hinder defendants. A reporter did not need to inquire behind the register or document; in one Irish case it was said that inaccuracies on the register were 'very unfortunate . . . but, whoever is to blame, [the reporters] . . . are not'[339]. Fault, however, was not decisive. In *Reis v Perry*[340] the reporter had applied for a copy of a deed using the statutory procedure; the copy supplied to him was incorrect, and the reporter had no privilege when he published it. As Day J put it, the publisher was responsible 'if he has not correctly extracted it, or if it has not been correctly copied'[341].

Parliament has also taken a hand in the development of this category. In the 1888 Law of Libel Amendment Act clause 4 it was originally proposed to protect fair reports of police and government notices issued for the information of the public[342]. The Attorney General initially objected to this protection, and since Government support was conditional on his approval, the promoters of the Bill moved an amendment to delete it with great regret[343]. However, after private negotiations of some kind an amendment re-introducing the protection was agreed without protest from the Attorney General[344]. A similar list of notices and documents which may be reported under privilege is still in force today[345].

This statutory privilege has not made the common law irrelevant[346]. Indeed, since the statutory position is tied to lists of specific documents and notices, the development and refinement of general principle can only come through common law. Two areas for refinement deserve attention. The first is where the extract published was supplied to the publisher by the authorities under a statutory procedure. In this situation it is submitted that the insistence that only a report of an accurate extract is privileged[347] looks too inflexible. As a matter of fairness it seems better to widen the privilege to where the report accurately relates what the publisher received from the authorities. An analogy is provided by the privilege for reports of government notices issued to the public, which simply requires a correct account of what the authorities told citizens. Furthermore, the current rule undermines the policy of having statutory procedures for supplying information. Such procedures are supposed to facilitate and regulate the availability of information, but if the information obtained must be an accurate copy for its repetition to be protected,

339 *Annaly v The Trade Auxiliary Co (Limited)* (1890) 26 LR Ir 11, 394 at 397.
340 (1895) 64 LJQB 566.
341 *Ibid* at 567.
342 *House of Commons Parliamentary Papers 1887*, vol III p 141 (Bill 340).
343 *Hansard's Parliamentary Debates*, 3rd Series, vol 326, col 1289 (6 June 1888).
344 *Hansard's Parliamentary Debates*, 3rd Series, vol 327, col 759 (20 June 1888).
345 Defamation Act 1996 s 15 Sch 1 Part 1.
346 Defamation Act 1996 s 15(4)(b) expressly preserves the common law privilege.
347 *Reis v Perry* (1895) 64 LJQB 566.

no citizen knowing the law would use the statutory procedure rather than inspecting the documents himself. At present the apparent helpfulness of any statutory scheme for supplying information is belied by the publisher's liability for the mistakes of others.

The second area for development relates to what constitutes a 'public document'. A Massachusetts court went perhaps too far when it held that a fire marshal's note on the back of an envelope was a public document[348], but the decision illustrates the potential for expansion. The obvious difficult case is a report of a pleading in a civil action before the case is heard. As explained above, the English Parliament decided that such a report should not be protected and the issue divided American state courts[349]. It might be objected that Parliament settled the matter in 1888, but the trouble with this objection is that the policy issues were never addressed. In particular there is a complex question about publicity: a pleading is a public document in the sense that it may be read by any member of the public, but is something else needed to make it a 'public document' in the sense required by the law of defamation? If so, what is that extra factor? Ultimately it comes down to the same question that has shaped every other category of privileged reports: what should the public sphere contain?

5. OTHER PRIVILEGED REPORTS

Nineteenth century English courts were very cautious about conferring qualified privilege on reports outside the four categories already discussed[350]. Courts in the United States, by contrast, were more flexible; and towards the end of the century their broader approach gained some, limited acceptance in England.

In New York the impetus for development came in the form of an 1854 statute conferring qualified privilege on reports of 'public official proceedings'[351]. The New York courts claimed that this did no more than codify the common law, but they went on to recognise protection in situations outside the traditional (English) common law categories. In *Edsall v Brooks*[352], for instance, protection was given to a report of proceedings before the commissioners of police into alleged disciplinary offences by a police officer.

The most influential development, however, was pure common law. In *Barrows v Bell*[353] the Supreme Judicial Court of Massachusetts held that a

348 *Conner v Standard Pub Co* 67 NE 596 (Supreme Judicial Court of Massachusetts, 1903).
349 See pp 244–245 above.
350 Eg, *Charlton v Watton* (1834) 6 Car & P 385.
351 Laws of 1854, p 314.
352 26 How Pr 426 (Supreme Court, New York County, 1864).
353 7 Gray 301 (Supreme Judicial Court of Massachusetts, 1856).

report of proceedings to expel the claimant from the Massachusetts Medical Society was privileged. Shaw CJ asserted that the American rule was wider than the English 'both for the proceedings before all public bodies, and for publication of those proceedings for the necessary information of the people'[354]. The reason for the difference was the 'necessary condition of society'[355] in America, where there were many public bodies whose meetings were reported. This called for a corresponding difference in legal rules. The Massachusetts Medical Society was a public body because it was a public corporation created to regulate an important public matter[356]. Shaw CJ also drew on the analogy with reports of judicial proceedings. He described the Society's proceedings as 'quasi judicial'[357], and borrowed one limitation on reports of court proceedings when he emphasised that the proceedings before the Society had terminated and could not therefore prejudice a later trial[358].

The decision in *Barrows v Bell*[359] was a classic example of common law development: it borrowed from existing rules and pushed the law forward in response to social change. Several American courts followed its example. In Missouri, for instance, the Supreme Court relied on *Barrows v Bell* when holding that a report of quasi-judicial extradition proceedings before the Governor of New York could be privileged[360]. In Alabama the use made of *Barrows v Bell* was more sophisticated. The Supreme Court had to decide whether a report of a grand jury's report to a court was privileged[361]. If the grand jury's report formed part of judicial proceedings there was no difficulty. However, on the facts the grand jury reported that no impeachable offence had been committed by the claimant, before them going on to make defamatory allegations against him. The Court applied *Barrows v Bell*, saying that the grand jury was 'essentially a public body'[362] whose actions were of public interest. However, only when the grand jury dealt with matters of public interest were reports of its proceedings protected. Criticisms of private citizens, for example, were not protected by the privilege[363]. In essence the privilege turned not only on the nature of the body, but on the nature of the content as well: both had to be public.

The brief influence of *Barrows v Bell*[364] in England came in *Allbutt v The General Council of Medical Education and Registration*[365]. The facts were very

354 7 Gray at 313.
355 *Ibid*.
356 *Ibid* at 314.
357 *Ibid* at 315.
358 *Ibid*.
359 7 Gray 301 (Supreme Judicial Court of Massachusetts, 1856).
360 *Brown v Globe Printing Co* 112 SW 462 (Supreme Court of Missouri, 1908).
361 *Parsons v Age-Herald Pub Co* 61 So 345 (Supreme Court of Alabama, 1913).
362 *Ibid* at 349.
363 *Ibid*.
364 7 Gray 301 (Supreme Judicial Court of Massachusetts, 1856).
365 (1889) 23 QBD 400.

similar to those in the American case, and concerned the Council's publication of its minutes and resolution to erase the claimant from the register of medical practitioners. The outcome was the same too, with the Court of Appeal acknowledging that it found *Barrows v Bell* 'instructive'[366]. As in *Barrows*, the Court examined the position and powers of the defendant, but the analysis was distinctive. The Court identified two separate reasons why publicity of the minutes and resolution were important. First, the Council's decisions were not subject to appeal; 'public opinion' was a safeguard against any abuse of power[367]. Second, the public were interested in knowing who had been disqualified and why: it was important to know whether a practitioner was qualified and also the reason for any disqualification (since a practitioner was not banned from practice by disqualification).

The decision in *Allbutt*'s case was remarkable not only for what it did, but how it did it. Recognising a new category of privileged reports was significant in itself, but the Court also advanced a concept of what was 'public' that was purely evaluative and purposive. Its only precursor in this regard was *Ryalls v Leader*[368], but that case was not cited to the Court. The potential applications of this concept were huge[369], but did not materialise. Instead, *Allbutt* seems to have been regarded as a dangerous precedent, and a later Court of Appeal virtually confined it to its facts[370].

After *Allbutt*'s case no further new types of report were recognised as being entitled to qualified privilege. In *Chapman v Lord Ellesmere*[371], for instance, a newspaper report of a decision by the stewards of the Jockey Club was held not to be protected. The Court of Appeal felt that the matter was not of sufficient public interest[372]. In New Zealand there seems to have been greater interest in racing: the Parliament promptly passed a statute to prevent *Chapman v Lord Ellesmere* being applied there[373].

The Court of Appeal's decision illustrated and exemplified the key theme that ran through all the cases surrounding reports: what was truly 'public'? The concept of the 'public' was both central and ambiguous. It could be taken literally, as when courts said that reports of judicial proceedings were privileged because anyone could attend. Another,

[366] *Ibid* at 413.

[367] *Ibid* at 409.

[368] (1866) LR 1 Exch 296.

[369] See *Sweet v Post Pub Co* 102 NE 660 (Supreme Judicial Court of Massachusetts) at 662, where *Allbutt's case* was cited in support of the assertion that 'especially in England . . . an increasing disposition is manifested to enlarge the protection afforded by privilege by broadening the field as to matters that may be properly published for the public information'.

[370] *Chapman v Lord Ellesmere* [1932] 2 KB 431 at 467 (per Slesser LJ).

[371] [1932] 2 KB 431.

[372] *Ibid* at 469.

[373] Williams, 'Dominion Legislation Relating to Libel and Slander' (1939) 21 *Journal of Comparative Legislation* 161 at 166.

different, literal interpretation was used in *Chapman v Lord Ellesmere*[374]: there was no privilege because not enough people followed racing. On the other hand, the 'public' could be taken evaluatively—as when the courts excluded reports of irrelevant defamatory statements or ruled that a particular matter ought to be in the public sphere. The story of qualified privilege for reports was the story of the conflicts and tensions between these competing ideas of 'the public'.

374 [1932] 2 KB 431.

11

Conclusion

THE MAKING OF the modern law of defamation was a lengthy and complex process. No single factor can be highlighted to explain what happened; rather, a host of different influences were at work, sometimes in combination, more often independently.

Some of those influences were to be expected. For instance, Parliament's intervention in relation to reports of legal proceedings and public meetings created profound changes, in the former case unintentionally[1]. We tend to think of statutory texts as the start of a story that then continues with their judicial interpretation, but the debates surrounding 'public meetings' touched on profoundly difficult and central issues in an enlightening way.

There was also an important academic influence at work. This was most obvious in the case law, where academic work was used as a basis for developing the law. Prominent examples included the use of Starkie's analysis of the libel/slander distinction[2] and qualified privilege[3], Fraser's category of absolute privilege for acts of state[4], and Salmond's exposition of exemplary damages[5]. The latter, with its use of Roman law, also served to highlight how borrowing from other legal systems might be accomplished via scholarly treatises. English law even imported its entire classification of evidence admissible in mitigation of damages through an American textbook[6]. On the other hand, academic authors could find themselves having to work against the case law, as they did when fair comment was coerced into partnership with the defence of truth[7].

The most powerful and profound influences, however, were judicial. Whether the law should adapt to social conditions, such as the prevalence of duelling[8] or the rise of the popular press[9], obviously involved questions

[1] Chapter 10.
[2] Chapter 1.
[3] Chapter 7.
[4] Chapter 9.
[5] Chapter 3.
[6] Chapter 3.
[7] Chapter 8.
[8] Chapter 2.
[9] Chapter 5.

of subjective, individual judgment. But even when it came to analysis, certain personalities inevitably stood out. For instance, the *Dictionary of National Biography*'s entry for Cockburn CJ claimed that he was the architect of the modern law of defamation[10]. Certainly he had a good claim, having contributed crucial judgments in *Campbell v Spottiswoode*[11] and *Wason v Walter*[12], for example. On the other hand, the failure of his objections to absolute privilege[13] illustrated that he did not get everything his own way. One of his main opponents on absolute privilege, Lord Esher MR, also deserves a special mention. He settled the form of the defence of qualified privilege[14], created the category of absolute privilege for acts of state[15], and formulated the test for reviewing damages awards[16]. He should also be remembered for his brilliantly perceptive analysis of the relation between malice and innuendo[17], even though that analysis was ultimately rejected. Finally, one should highlight the distinctive contribution of Jessel MR: but for his precipitate methods there might be no injunction for defamation today[18].

But it is always unfair to single out individuals in a team effort. What really made the law of defamation take its current form was the continuous judicial elaboration of rules and principles. It may be an impression created misleadingly by the changing nature of law reporting, but as the nineteenth century progressed, the judicial concern to make sense of all the historical materials seemed to increase. There is an increasing sense that to deliver a judgment might also be to make a contribution to the literature. In *Wason v Walter*[19], for instance, the Court delayed giving judgment in order to get the wording exactly right. Of course, it is impossible to quantify what effect this emphasis on writing had, but it was bound to encourage exposition, synthesis and discussion. It also facilitated the conscious development of principles, as the significance of precise choices of words in earlier cases could be explored. This judicial selection, shaping and polishing of ideas was ultimately what made, and continues to make, the law of defamation.

[10] *The Dictionary of National Biography* (Oxford, 1917) vol IV, 633–37 at 637.
[11] (1863) 3 B & S 769.
[12] (1868) LR 4 QB 73.
[13] See further, ch 9.
[14] *Hebditch v MacIlwaine* [1894] 2 QB 54.
[15] *Chatterton v Secretary of State for India in Council* [1895] 2 QB 189.
[16] *Praed v Graham* (1889) 24 QBD 53.
[17] *The Capital and Counties Bank v Henty & Sons* (1880) 5 CPD 514.
[18] Chapter 4.
[19] (1868) LR 4 QB 73.

Index

www.ingramcontent.com/pod-product-compliance
Ingram Content Group UK Ltd.
Pitfield, Milton Keynes, MK11 3LW, UK
UKHW020831290926
15470UKWH00009B/1850/J

9 781841 133041